The Rules of Sailing Races

THE RULES OF SAILING RACES

BRUNO BIANCHI+GABRIO DE SZOMBATHELY
Introduced and translated by Mary Blewitt

DODD, MEAD & COMPANY
New York

First published in the United States 1979

1 2 3 4 5 6 7 8 9 10

ISBN: 0-396-07765-X
Library of Congress Catalog Card Number: 79-88661
Printed in the United States of America
by The Haddon Craftsmen, Inc., Scranton, Penna.

Contents

Contents 7

The Rules of Sailing Races

Foreword to the English language edition
by Doctor Beppe Croce, President International Yacht Racing Union

It may be just one of those stories which begin under the Naples sun, in the sweep of the entrancing bay, but it is said that the deep friendship between Bruno Bianchi and Gabrio de Szombathely began during the Olympic Games in Naples in 1960 because of some none too fresh mussels.

They say that Gabrio, in bed after enjoying these and Bruno at his bedside, discussed the racing rules endlessly in the intense heat and, finding that they had much in common and were in complete agreement about what was, and has continued to be, their common hobby, they decided to set to work together on the subject so close to both their hearts.

This is not my story, but I do know that the Olympics led to collaboration between our authors for many long years, first sitting together on juries and then later writing this book of comments on and intepretation of the yacht racing rules.

Bruno Bianchi, from Genoa, has a helmsman's viewpoint of the rules after forty-five years of competitive racing at the highest level; his career includes an Olympic gold medal and vast experience in a number of Olympic classes.

Gabrio de Szombathely, born in Trieste of distant Hungarian origin, lawyer and judge, has also been sailing for forty years or more but has not been so involved in racing. His profound love of the sea grows from the opportunities offered by that splendid cruising ground, the northern Adriatic. He has sailed for sport and pleasure in widely different boats and has raced locally, particularly offshore.

The man of the sea and the man of law, both great admirers of Gerald Sambrooke Sturgess, and his illustrious predecessors, have brought to this attractive and often amusing book the weight of their experience. They view the scene from different angles, but are inspired by the same spirit and ideas based on the principle that the racing rules are not a weapon for attacking an adversary but a method of defence to be used within a framework of fair play which constitutes, or ought to, the ideal for every competitive sport.

From the first, the book has been welcomed by critics and public in Italy and the Mediterranean; it has been suitably revised and improved as necessary as the rules are changed.

Now the book ventures into all those waters where the sailors speak English in this up-dated translation by Mary Blewitt. It is said that Latins have law in their blood, thanks no doubt to their Greek and Roman descent that has perhaps unconsciously conditioned their culture and studies, even though it is also said that Mediterranean countries are too fond of splitting hairs in their interpretations of the law. This may or may not be true and experienced Anglo-Saxon readers will be able to compare the book with their own exemplary texts in the light of that coherent and simple interpretation of the law that is in their blood together with the salt water that forms an essential part of it.

It is the first time that in our small, but increasingly important, world of sailing a technical Italian text has been translated into English, a difficult test for the authors doubtless, but a clear example of the collaboration which spreads, with the growing diffusion of yachting, over national boundaries to become an international fact and a subject for discussion for an ever larger and better prepared public.

The authors' passion for the sea, their exceptional practical experience and their irony in my opinion mix most agreeably in a work which contributes to a greater knowledge of the rules and their correct interpretation. It enlarges the understanding of one of essential fundamentals on which the rules are based; I allude to fair sailing, which with superior speed and skill and with individual effort must underlie the conduct of all racing yachtsmen.

At the launching of this English language edition, I wish a well-deserved success to the authors, whom I thank for their generous contribution to the sport of yacht racing.

Introduction and Translator's Note
by Mary Blewitt

The extensive and interesting task of translating this book from Italian into English began, in a sense, at an intractable protest meeting during a Half Ton Cup World Championship at Trieste. I was fortunate enough to sit there on the international jury with Bruno and Gabrio. Their knowledge of the racing rules, their experience of racing and their sympathetic and tolerant manner towards all the owners and crews who came before them made me feel sure that what they had written must be of value to all who race.

Nor was I wrong, and in addition I discovered that it was invaluable for organizers. For instance, I found I had been perpetrating a number of errors from year to year in the RORC programme! Translating it, I have learned more about the scope and purpose of the rules than I ever expected to know, and I believe it to be a *vade mecum* not only for any serious racing person, but for any race officer, organizing club, protest committee, international jury and – dare I say it? – for at least one member of the RYA Racing Rules Committee – myself.

It is not intended as a 'good read'; it is a reference book where each rule is discussed, illustrated, even criticized, and most necessary, related to the other rules which touch on the same subject. It is a great joy to need a minimum of cross referencing; there is rarely any necessity to look at an earlier or later page to check, the text is repeated when required so that each comment is virtually complete in itself.

Let us take a general look for a moment at lawmaking and government with its division into the three arms – legislative, executive and judicial. This may be taking an over-serious view of rules which merely control a sport, but it is a logical exercise.

Legislature. Laws are made by the Racing Rules Committee of the International Yacht Racing Union (equivalent to a parliament), a group of people from various countries whose names are published yearly in the IYRU year book. They alter the rules once every four years in the November after the Olympic Games. The last changes were in November 1977 and there will be more in autumn 1981 after the Games at Talin. The intervening periods are used to study existing ambiguities or anomalies which have been exposed either by cases arising from various appeals around the world or by the changing nature of the boats or type of competition in fashion. Very often the alterations are minimal, and the principles and many of the basic rules have remained unchanged since the beginning in 1875, but there is a steady drift so that the rules of the 'thirties would seem very different from those of today, even though, as I have said, this is more apparent than real. In addition, the rule makers select and publish the most interesting and pertinent cases which are brought to their notice in IYRU Interpretations of the Yacht Racing Rules. Since the rules change every four years, each four-year group of cases is heard under different rules and this can be confusing. Yet thanks to the indefatigable Gerald Sambrooke Sturgess, the IYRU committee's chairman, all the old cases have been updated to conform to the 1977 rules and may well in the future be brought forward again. The majority of the cases in the IYRU case book are from the Royal Yachting Association (once the Yacht Racing Association) and the United States Yacht Racing Union (once the North American Yacht Racing Union), but there are others from a wide variety of countries including Finland and the Soviet Union.

The Executive Branch. It would be carrying our metaphor too far to develop this theme, but the reader might let his thoughts run along the lines of considering the organizing club as the civil service, the race committee as the police and the competitors as a self-policing citizen band.

The Judiciary. Although the protested yacht is often thought of as the "accused" and she may indeed be found "guilty" or "not guilty" of some infringement of the rules it makes more sense to compare the procedure which has evolved with that of the civil courts.

When someone feels aggrieved the protesting yacht (the plaintiff) lodges a protest (issues a writ) against the protested yacht (the defendant) or seeks redress against the race committee (suing the government used to take a particular form too). These procedures lead to a hearing where the case is examined by the protest committee (judge and jury) who decide for one party or the other resulting in disqualification or penalization (judgement) or dismissal of the case. The loser may then appeal – against a point of law not of fact – to the national appeals committee (Court of Appeal). In the U.S. there are also district appeals committees from which a case may go on to the USYRU Appeals Committee (Supreme Court or House of Lords).

The similarities must not be exaggerated, but they are there and the principles of fairness and natural justice are upheld within a necessarily rigorous framework. As in Anglo-Saxon law, case law also plays an important part, and protest committees as well as being bound by the rules themselves must also take this into consideration. Case law is represented not only by the cases just mentioned, selected and published by the IYRU, but also by those collected and published by various national authorities (to be had on application) such as the RYA, USYRU and others – although those in a foreign language will probably not be translated into English.

What influence should a competitor or a protest committee allow a case to have? First of all they are interpretations of the rules and all of them are interpretations by experienced appeal committees. The IYRU publishes only the most unusual or interesting and does not publish mere repetitions: this does not mean that those not published are wrong, they are probably just as right and just as reliable. On the other hand Homer nods, and even an appeal committee can interpret a complicated case in a manner which others are loth to accept and which it may be inadvisable to follow in the future. But normally a protest committee will be most unwise to go against an appeal ruling, for, most particularly if it is published by the IYRU, their decision will almost certainly be reversed if appealed. I say "almost" because the fact is that no two cases are alike and competitors and committees must study a case with great care to make sure that it is relevant and really fits their own; cases have a nasty habit, if looked at superficially, of turning round and biting the hand that sought to use them, proving damaging instead of advantageous.

In this book cases are used for illustration not only because they must be followed, for some of them are old and their point has been included in the rules themselves in subsequent changes, but because they give a more realistic and lively picture of the law as it stands and often raise a pleasing picture of contrast between the sombre protest room and the judges with their rotund oratorical language and the small bounding dinghies with their young spray-soaked helmsmen and crew who are the actors in the scene.

As the rules are altered every four years it is necessary to know the date of the case and whether it has been updated and to when. The IYRU case book is updated and conformed to the 1977 rules, so this book is updated in the same way. Thus some care needs to be taken both with the numbering of the rules which has been changed and with their wording when quoting cases; for instance NAYRU No. 93 of May 1963 has been updated to 1977 in the IYRU book. In 1977 rule 34 became rule 35 and so appears by that number here; the contents of the renumbered rule have remained virtually unchanged. Old cases not expertly updated will therefore have to be used with care unless a copy of the rules of the correct date are at hand.

I have made an effort to be consistent in the translation but this has not always been possible where there is a variety of words used to convey similar, or indeed different, concepts such as race committee, protest committee, jury, international jury. In Italian *giuria* is used throughout for what we normally call a protest committee; on the other hand the rules use *race committee* exclusively except in 77.6 where *international jury* and *protest committee* appear for the only time, while *jury* appears in rule 1.2. In the text I have tried to use *race committee* for the group running the day's races and *protest committee* for those hearing protests, even though they may be the same people. There are as yet unresolved problems in this area and the distinction is not always clear.

Throughout I have used *he* of persons and *she* of boats; I hope this will not be construed as an insult to my sex.

My particular thanks are due to Gerald Sambrooke Sturgess who has kindly read the English translation to smoke out glaring errors. It does not follow that he necessarily agrees with every point made and readers must understand that whilst the book expresses the views of two experts in the field this will not, nor should it, prevent protest and appeal committees from basing their decisions purely on the rules and case law. They are free to differ from the authors.

The drawings for this edition, although the same in content as the original Italian version have all been redrawn by Bill Streets. The International Yacht Racing Union has kindly allowed its rules to be reproduced intermittently throughout the book and its secretary general, Nigel Hacking, has also agreed to the use of extracts from the official interpretation for the rules. Since the originals of these are in English it has obviated double translation. The Royal Yachting Association kindly supplied printed material for the rules themselves which has small revisions to March 1978.

Thanks are also due to Janet Grosvenor in preparing the typescript and to the original authors for allowing additional and up-to-date material to be added under the supervision of the translator.

The fundamental rule of fair sailing

The rules of sailing races, built up by principles and case law for nearly a hundred years, are but the laws of a sport – a game played upon the water. For this reason the International Yacht Racing Union rule book has a fundamental rule, before ever it begins to enumerate the seventy-eight clauses and twelve detailed appendices under which all sailing races are run.

"A yacht shall participate in a race or series of races in an event only by fair sailing, superior speed and skill, and, except in team races, by individual effort. However, a yacht may be disqualified under this rule only in the case of a clear-cut violation of the above principles and only when no other rule applies."

Despite the initial discouragement, before even entering the rule book proper, of this rather tortuous English, it is possible to see what the seventeen members of the International Racing Rules Committee are trying to say. They tell us that unsporting practices are banned, even if they might not be listed in the rules. They tell us that speed, skill and individual effort (except in team races) are the components of success and of participation. It is not hard to imagine some sort of unpleasant trick by which an opponent might be prevented from sailing well, but clearly such a practice has no place when sailing under the rules of the IYRU.

A more specific purpose of this rule is to use it for protesting in a case where no other rule in the book applies. Over the years this has been found very difficult to use. When it very rarely does occur, the next revision of the rules takes care that the particular case is written thereafter into a specific new rule.

There was a case dealt with by the Dutch national authority (KNWV 1970/1 *Troffel* v. Race Committee; IYRU No. 57).

Two yachts which collided hoisted protest flags and kept them hoisted. *Troffel* saw this and did not protest herself. After the race the two agreed to go no further. They did not lodge protests against each other. *Troffel* then protested against them under the fair sailing rule, on the ground that this agreement was unfair. The protest committee decided that the protest was not valid for want of *Troffel*'s protest flag and that the fair-sailing rule was not applicable. The committee said, "It deals with racing only and not with subsequent events" and threw the protest out.

Troffel appealed, underlining that she was appealing not against the observed rule infringements of the two yachts involved, but against the agreement between them, which was discovered after the time limit for lodging

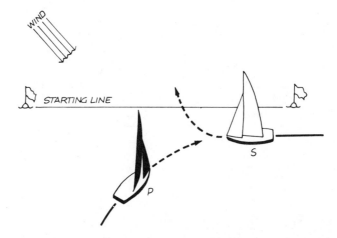

a protest had expired. The Dutch appeals committee upheld her appeal, noting that the fair-sailing rule can be invoked at any time. This case later led to the introduction of rule 33.2 (Contact between yachts racing). So now there is no need for recourse to the fair-sailing rule in similar cases, if yachts touch.

However, since the fundamental rule may be used only when no other applies, let us look at some cases when it was not accepted. In *Aldebaran* v. *Thalassa* (IYRU No. 23 *above*) P, on port tack, heard S shout "starboard" immediately after the starting signal and bore away to keep clear. But S, instead of sailing on, suddenly tacked, forcing P to bear away yet further to miss her stern. P protested under rule 41 but the committee decided that a port-tack yacht must keep clear and disqualified P under the fair sailing rule. P appealed and it was recognized that there had been a clear breach of rules 35 and 41. Attention was called to the second sentence of the fair sailing rule: S was disqualified and the decision against P reversed.

More difficult (as doubts could really arise on which rule to invoke) is the case of two Flying Juniors (FIV 1967/5). The first yacht protested the other because she was followed by a launch giving her advice in a foreign language which the others could not understand. Reversing a decision of the jury, which had disqualified her under the fair sailing rule, the appeals committee decided that it was a clear case of an infringement of rule 59 (outside assistance).

A third example (RYA 1967/13, Ullswater YC) shows B coming to the last of four races in a series with such good points that she could easily win it only to find herself relentlessly hindered by A for long enough to ensure that she could no longer win. It was clear that A had acted deliberately just to harm P with no regard for her own placing, and the club asked whether B could have protested under the rule. The Council's answer was as follows: "The application of the fair sailing rule should be considered in the light of the fact that this was a competition consisting of four races of which three were to count; none of the races was an individual event. Legitimately delaying an opponent is accepted in team racing provided no rule is broken, and similar tactics in an event of this nature do not infringe the fair sailing rule."

It does seem that the fundamental rule is destined to continue as an affirmation rather than a statute.

Part I
Definitions

ABBREVIATIONS AND DEFINITIONS

The following letters indicate the international and national authorities for the rules of sailing races.

FIV   Federazione Italiana Vela
IYRU   International Yacht Racing Union
KNWV   Koninklijk Nederlands Watersport Verbond
NAYRU   North American Yacht Racing Union
RYA   Royal Yachting Association (formerly YRA)
USSRYRF   USSR Yacht Racing Federation
USYRU   United States Yacht Racing Union (formerly part of NAYRU)
YRA   Yacht Racing Association

Generally the following letters are used to indicate yachts in the drawings.

I   Inside yacht   P   Port tack yacht
L   Leeward yacht   S   Starboard tack yacht
O   Outside yacht   W   Windward yacht
        M   Middle or intervening yacht

Definitions: Throughout the text, when a definition is used specifically in its defined sense, it is set in italics. By reason of rule 3.1, the definitions which are introduced in Part I cannot be altered by any other instructions.

Figure numbers: These are not numerically complete as changes in rules have meant deletion of some diagrams since the original edition.

Racing

Racing – A yacht is *racing* from her preparatory signal until she has either *finished* and cleared the finishing line and finishing *marks* or retired, or until the race has been *postponed, abandoned* or *cancelled*, except that in match or team races, the sailing instructions may prescribe that a yacht is *racing* from any specified time before the preparatory signal.

1. The initial moment of the definition

This first definition begins by identifying the moment when a yacht becomes subject to the racing rules – the moment when, five minutes before the start, the preparatory signal is hoisted or displayed (international code flag "P" or a blue shape as proposed in rule 4.4 or any other signal prescribed by the national authority or the sailing instructions). It is obvious (and the preamble to Part IV confirms it) that before the preparatory signal all competitors must, like other folk, obey the International Rules for Prevention of Collision at Sea. It is also obvious that yachts while racing must nevertheless observe these international rules in relation to all other vessels which are not racing, but may be met with in the course of the race itself.

2. Anticipation of the initial moment

The definition of *racing* envisages the possibility of advancing this initial moment even earlier than the five-minute signal; however, it must be stressed that this can only happen in two well-defined cases: "in match or team racing". The tactical duel between two helmsmen (or two teams) almost always begins before the five-minute signal, and it is therefore right for all these typically competitive manoeuvres to be controlled by specially written rules.

Think of a sail-off after two boats have tied (see rule 11) or one of the long duels in the America's Cup when both contenders try to keep the other in her wake before the start so as to cover her and hinder her every move and so they each try to work into the best position by sailing in wide circles long before the preparatory signal. Again in team racing the declared intent is to control and obstruct certain boats of the opposing team and the tactics must be begun much sooner than is normal in individual racing. Anyway when yachts are to be *racing* before the preparatory signal it must be written into the sailing instructions.

There is another virtual exception to the general rule that *racing* begins at the five-minute gun and continues until the finish and that is "when the race is to

3. Rules of the road during hours of darkness

continue after sunset" in which case the period of time or the place at which the international collision rules . . . shall replace the corresponding rules of Part IV (see rule 3.2(b)ii) must be published in the sailing instructions. In practice this concerns only offshore and coastal racing which lasts through whole or part of the night – and indeed may finish (though never start) in the dark. At night it is difficult, if not impossible, to identify another boat under sail from her navigation lights or make out whether she is racing or not, so all must obey the collision rules.

Remember that not all the racing rules cease to take effect at night however; only some of Part IV (Right-of-way rules when yachts meet) is replaced, that is rules 38, 39 (in so far as they permit alterations of course), 40, 42 and 43 do not apply. You could object that rules 42 and 43 are really necessary and that they should continue after dark because the collision rules lack any corresponding prescriptions about marks and obstructions. However, these are two rules of exception, applicable only in particular cases (see Part IV, section C) when they override any conflicting rule in section B and therefore to use them on their own would be difficult, bringing added complications and risks while the intention of the present arrangement is to simplify and unify the regulations to avoid accidents.

4. General rules in force before the preparatory signal

Naturally not all the rules begin to apply only five minutes before the start and there are many prescriptions which a yacht intending to race (see the preamble to Part III) must obey both before her preparatory signal and whilst racing or be disqualified. These cover entries, rating certificates, ownership, club member on board; shifting ballast, anchors, life-saving equipment, sail numbers, forestays and flags and cabbages and kings. All these are commented on elsewhere; just remember that in order to be able to start many rules must be complied with long before the five-minute gun.

5. Right of way rules in force before the preparatory signal

Still on the definition of *racing* and the right-of-way rules look at the preamble to Part IV – Rights and obligations when yachts meet – and you will notice that, as we have already said, it only applies between yachts "racing in the same race" or "racing in different races" (when different classes are racing in the same area at the same time).

It is important to realise that the obligation to obey these rules of Part IV may exist even before the five-minute signal; that is "from the time a yacht intending to *race* begins to sail about in the vicinity of the starting line". There is no contradiction here with the definition of *racing*, it refers merely to applying the rule of the road and admits the possibility that in particular situations (it is impossible to state a general rule and facts must be examined case by case) the rules of Part IV must be obeyed even before the preparatory signal.

For example, when different classes, starting at five-minute intervals, are manoeuvring near the starting line after a five-minute gun of one class but before that of the others, it is obvious that they must all be sailing under and governed by the same rules. Remember too that yachts hanging around, "intending to *race*" but not yet *racing* may yet be disqualified under rule 31.2, perhaps for "seriously hindering a yacht *racing*" or for "infringing the sailing instructions" if these for instance expressly forbid later starters getting mixed up with the classes starting.

6. Rules in force only after the preparatory signal

A quick look is needed here at the preamble to Part V – Obligations of helmsman and crew in handling a yacht – this clearly states that, unlike Part IV, "a yacht is subject to the rules of Part V only when she is *racing*". Part V deals with ranking as a starter, sailing the course, touching a mark, fog signals, setting and sheeting of sails, owner steering another yacht, leaving etc. and these can all be ignored until *racing* has started, that is after the preparatory signal.

7. The end of the definition

It now only remains to see when a yacht is no longer *racing*. The definition says clearly and precisely that this is when she has "finished and cleared the finishing line and finishing *marks*". It is not enough to cut, or even cross the line, it must be cleared completely, marks included (and the mark may well be a committee boat, much larger than the normal buoy). This is not as strange as it may seem at first sight: a boat may *finish* – in the sense of the definition – by just crossing the line with her bow and then drift on to a mark of the finishing line, she is still indubitably governed by the rules and has infringed rule 52 (Touching a mark). This no longer applies if she suffers the same misfortune after clearing the finishing line with all her hull, crew and equipment well away from the line and all its marks.

But what happens when she cuts the finishing line and then, instead of carrying on to cross and clear, turns back and then gets into the same sort of trouble? The rule does not change; she is no longer *racing* and this is confirmed by rule 51.5 – "it is not necessary for a yacht to cross the finishing line completely; after *finishing* she may clear it in either direction." However even though she is no longer *racing* a boat will be ill-advised to hang around as she is still liable to the rules of Part IV, which as we have seen above are applicable until she has left the vicinity of the course, and can be caught by rule 31.2 if she gets in the way of another boat which has not yet finished.

To sum up, a yacht ceases to *race* not only when she finishes and clears the line but also when she retires, and, as far as the rules of the road are concerned, has left the vicinity of the course. Finally the rules are no longer binding from the moment any race has been postponed, abandoned or cancelled (see comment to rule 5).

Starting

Starting – A yacht *starts* when, after fulfilling her penalty obligations, if any, under rule 51.1(c), (Sailing the Course), and after her starting signal, any part of her hull, crew or equipment first crosses the starting line in the direction of the course to the first *mark*.

. When to start

The interpretation of this definition presents no problems but needs to be clearly understood and analysed with care. First of all when can you begin to start? Clearly only after the starting signal made in the way and with the means provided for by rule 4.4. If by chance a yacht sets off before her proper signal she cannot *start*, in the sense of the definition, until she returns as required by rule 51.1(c) if it is in force (that is across the extensions of the line after a general recall) or at any rate as laid down in rule 8 (Recalls).

2. How to start   How can you carry out a start correctly? The rule defines that "a yacht starts when any part of her hull, crew or equipment first crosses the starting line . . ." (for "starting line" see rule 6). You will notice that to start it is enough to cut the line and there is no need to cross it and clear it, that is go beyond the line completely and that it is enough to cross it (it is always referred to as crossing) with any part of the hull, crew or equipment: the top of the mast, the trailing edge of the rudder, the boom, some part of the man on the trapeze or theoretically the end of a loose sheet dangling overboard.

G. Sambrooke Sturgess cites a possible case (YRA 1950/11 Royal Northern Yacht Club) of a yacht which, in order to keep up against the tide, anchored before the start with the anchor on the course side of the line and he explains that as far as starting is concerned even the anchor below must be considered part of her.

Unlike the requirement for finishing the definition does not say that this "any part" must be in its normal position, obviously because no one wants to cross the starting line early while everyone is trying to reach the finishing line just as soon as possible.

3. The direction in which to start   Nowhere except in rule 51.1(c) does the rule expressly require a yacht to stay waiting for the starting signal on the pre-start side of the line.*

But can we say that a start is valid when a yacht tries to start correctly by crossing the line from the wrong, or course, side of the line? Absolutely not, because the definition requires the line to be crossed "in the direction of the course for the first *mark*" (that is the buoy to be rounded after the start); and logically, in order to be able to do so, a yacht must first be wholly on the right, or pre-start, side of the line itself.

If you have any doubts about this read rule 51.1(b) which obliges "a yacht which either crosses prematurely or is on the course side of the starting line or its extensions at the starting signal to return and *start* in accordance with the definition", and rule 8 (Recalls) which prescribes that "when at her starting signal any part is on the course side of the starting line or its extensions" a yacht to be able to re-start "shall wholly return to the pre-start side of the line or its extensions . . .". Further confirmation can be found in rule 44 (Returning to start), which requires a yacht to return "wholly to the correct side."

4. Sailing the course   Starting is considered completed, with all that follows, when a yacht first touches the line. In other words the fact that she has crossed the line even by one centimetre confers on her all the rights and lays on her all the obligations

---

* This can, however, be prescribed in sailing instructions, generally when races are overcrowded and an excessive number of competitors with the consequent enormous length of the line makes the race committee's job of controlling the start more difficult. If the line is crossed before the starting signal the penalty is automatic disqualification and the risk is run for a given period before the start, usually the last five minutes (or minute) so that this rigorous prescription is called the five-minute rule or the minute rule. Often the ban refers to space as well as time, it may be forbidden to sail beyond the starting line or its extensions, or into the triangle formed by the ends of the starting line and the first mark of the course. Certainly the summary disqualification laid down by the minute rule is not really very fair. Think of the poor innocent chap who finds himself forced to cross the fatal line. It would be better, right from the beginning, to limit the number of entries and starters thus avoiding regattas which are run with great difficulty and sometimes as a result, badly.

deriving from her newly-acquired status of a starter; and it does not matter, for example, that a moment later the tide or other competitors force her to sail back across to the other side of the line, so that to get to the first mark she crosses it a second time. FIV 1966/5 (fig. 1) shows A, before the starting signal manoeuvring on the wrong (course) side of the line where she nevertheless has right of way under rule 36 in respect of B on port tack on the pre-start side, but at the starting signal A, still on the wrong side of the line, loses her rights in that instant (until she returns "wholly") and therefore must keep clear (rule 44.1) of all yachts that are starting or have started correctly, and here this includes one that has already crossed the line after the gun but has been then forced to go back again to the pre-course side.

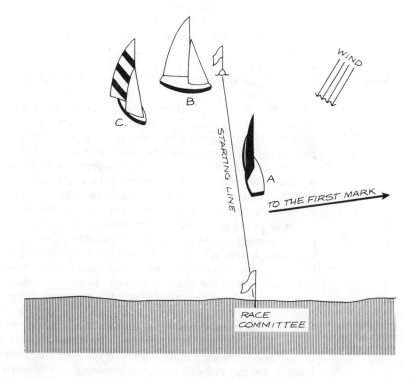

Fig. 1

5. The consequences of having started

Crossing the line correctly and therefore *starting*, in the sense of the definition, leads to various consequences; one of the most important is that of having right of way over all the yachts that were premature starters and are still on the wrong, or course side of the line, trying to get back, but we shall be talking more about this when we look at rules 44 and 51.

Another consequence (see rule 38.1) is the acquisition of the right by one yacht to luff another "as she pleases" and no longer merely "slowly". On the other hand having started she can no longer bear away below a proper course but when off the wind must obey rule 39. For same-tack yachts even that very important rule 42 (Rounding or passing marks or obstructions) comes into force only after starting, and still on this subject it must not be forgotten that a mark of the starting line begins to have a required side for a yacht only "when she starts" (rule 51.3), thus explaining for example why the yacht that finds herself over the line at the moment of the starting signal can, just because she has not yet started, come back to the pre-start side of the line without having to pass the marks on the outside except in the case of rule 51.1(c).

An analogous case is that envisaged by rule 50 on the strength of which, under certain aspects and for certain effects, a yacht is considered to have started because she has been manoeuvring near the starting line between the preparatory signal and the start even though afterwards she does not cross the line and *start* in the sense of the definition; but as we shall see this fiction affects the final results in the classification more than, anything else. To look at the matter in more depth the comment on the various rules involved should be consulted.

6. Starting late

The rule just mentioned, rule 50 (Ranking as a starter), brings to mind the very similar case of a yacht that comes to the start late. Can she start late and if so how late? There is no doubt that since there is no explicit ban some delay is permitted. The difficulties only arise about how much, since the rule gives no guidance; the answer must be found in the general principles that should govern sailing races; principles to be looked for in the rule as a whole and in any of its regulations which may help. With this premise it seems above all logical that the delay must not be unreasonably long (you cannot expect a race committee to wait for ever for a late-comer, especially when the possibilities of her being placed become more and more improbable with the passing of time). The criterion to bear in mind could be that of being near the starting line in the last five minutes and the race committee should establish, case by case, if the late-comer is near enough in this period to justify starting in spite of her lateness, especially as there may be circumstances beyond her control. Anyone can be held up at the last minute by an easily-repaired gear failure or a technical hitch or by an unexpected calm perhaps with a contrary current to stop them from being able to sail the last important hundred or two hundred metres. In conclusion the question must be decided in each case as a question of fact but to make an analogy with rule 50 the late-comer should at least be in the vicinity of the line at the moment of the starting signal. There are of course particular exceptions in long races, for example in a six-hundred-mile race which is going to last four or five days it would be absurd to stop a yacht competing because one of her crew members had not been able to arrive in time due to difficulties with the train or a car breakdown or some such. In this case the race committee should be sensible and let her start a good number of hours after the rest of her class.

Finishing

Finishing — A yacht *finishes* when any part of her hull, or of her crew or equipment in normal position, crosses the finishing line from the direction of the course from the last *mark,* after fulfilling her penalty obligations, if any, under rule 52.2, (Touching a Mark).

1. In normal position

In conformity with the definition of starting the definition of finishing is realized by the act of cutting (there is no need to cross but it is always called crossing) the finishing line with any part of the hull, crew or equipment – see point 2 of the comment to the definition of starting. The only difference between the two definitions consists in the fact that when finishing the "any part" of the crew and equipment must be in a normal position at the moment in which it cuts the finishing line. Otherwise competitors would obviously try to finish earlier by sticking out an arm or the spinnaker boom.

2. Finishing direction

It is necessary to highlight the fact that a yacht must cross the finishing line "from the direction of the course from the last *mark*" (meaning by this the last mark to be rounded before the finishing line). This is similar to the start which requires the starting line to be crossed "in the direction of the course for the first *mark*". It helps to stop a wild competitor who has happened on the starting line

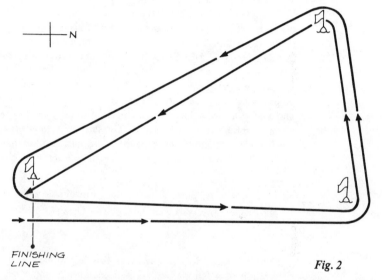

FINISHING
LINE   *Fig. 2*

from some quite different direction creating confusion and danger when meeting others on opposite courses, but its main aim is to stop race committees setting their finishing lines, and describing them in the relevant sailing instructions, in such a way that competitors have to round a limit mark in order to finish and cross the line. Rule 51.1(a) is symptomatic in that it lays down uncompromisingly that "a yacht shall start and finish only as prescribed in the starting and finishing definitions" and this means that a race committee cannot, either deliberately or by mistake, prescribe finishing in a direction other than that from the last mark. For further clarification look at the comment to rule 51.

In the decisions of FIV 1966/3 (*Malia* v. Giuria C. N. Livorno) it was held that a yacht had to be considered to have finished correctly when she crossed the finishing line coming from the direction of the last mark even if in doing so she left the limit mark of the finishing line to starboard when according to the race instructions it should have been left to port (see fig. 2); when sailing instructions require a yacht to cross the line coming, not from the direction of the last mark, but from the opposite direction they modify the definition of starting contained in Part 1 of the rule which is not within their power (rule 3.1). The Italian Appeals Committee added that in a situation of this sort the race committee should either have laid an additional mark that would have thus become the last mark of the course or should have made it clear in sailing instructions that the finishing line mark had to be left to starboard. IYRU No. 22 mentioned in the comment to rule 51 also applies. Mistakes of the same sort can easily happen where a course is shortened, especially if it is decided on and signalled after the start while the racing is going on (see rules 5.1(b) and 4.1 "S") and if the sailing instructions are lacking in detail or imprecise. In any case remember that instructions containing dispositions different from or contrary to those in the definitions of Part I must be considered null and void; sailing instructions can modify some of the rules but not all of them and not Parts I and IV – see rule 3.1.

Finally let us remember that even after having *finished* the race in the sense of the definition, that is after having cut the finishing line, a yacht is still subject to the rules until she has cleared the finishing line and the marks "in either direction" (rule 51.5) and "left the vicinity of the course" (preamble to Part IV). Therefore until she has got herself clear of the line and the mark she has finished yes, but may, for example, foul a mark onto which she has drifted, or if on port tack not given water to someone finishing on starboard tack and so on and will still be liable to disqualification under rule 52.1(a)(iii) in the first example and rule 36 in the second. The same story holds for yachts that have finished the race and then use means of propulsion other than those permitted by rule 60 to clear the finishing line. See point 7 of the definition of *racing*.

Luffing

Luffing – Altering course towards the wind until head to wind.

The text of this definition is short, simple and clear and only a very brief description of a few particulars is necessary. A yacht begins to luff when, independently of minor variations due to wind and sea, she changes from a steady course to one which curves up towards the wind. We need to look a little more closely, however, at what is the extreme limit of the luffing manoeuvre because if she passes beyond this limit she tacks and immediately loses the rights (or is freed from the obligations) that derived from the fact that she was luffing or was on a certain tack. According to the definition a luff lasts "until head to wind". The significance of this sentence is unequivocal and means that a yacht continues to be luffing even if, having really finished head to wind, she succeeds nevertheless in remaining where she is bow on to the wind; and what counts in this limit position is not the sails (which may even be aback) but only the direction of the hull with respect to the wind (fig. 3).

This is precisely why any right to luff that a yacht may have under, say, rule 38 includes a right to remain head to wind and any other yacht clear astern (or overlapped to windward) is obliged to respond to the luff; and she must be considered as "luffing" with all its effects as long as she succeeds in remaining in this position, that is to say until she is not forced either (a) to go beyond the direction of the wind, that is to tack, or (b) to curtail her luff, bearing away on the same original tack. RYA 1967/1 (Royal Engineers Sailing Association) deals with this and is discussed under rule 41.

Finally we should add that the definition we are looking at mostly applies in rules 38 (Same tack – luffing and sailing above a proper course after starting), 40 (Same tack – luffing before starting), 41 (Changing tacks – tacking and gybing) and 42 (Rounding or passing marks and obstructions) and most particularly, because of its bearing on the right to take an inside yacht upwind on the wrong side of a mark, (42.1(d)) as well as the so-called anti-barging rule, 42.4.

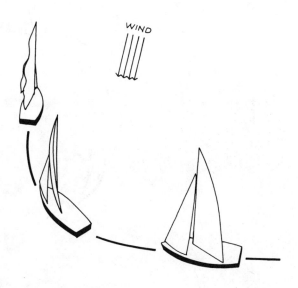

Fig. 3

Tacking

Tacking – A yacht is *tacking* from the moment she is beyond head to wind until she has *borne away*, when beating to windward, to a *close-hauled* course; when not beating to windward, to the course on which her mainsail has filled.

1. The beginning

In the last definition we saw that the uttermost limit of luffing is reached with the head-to-wind position. Relating that to this definition it is reasonable to understand why tacking begins from the moment a yacht is beyond head to wind as it is then that she begins to bear away to take the wind on the other side of her sails, that is, on the other tack.

2. The end

Let us see now how long this manoeuvre lasts; on this subject the rule establishes that the phase of movement and passage from one tack to another lasts until the yacht (starting from the position which is, even by only a little, beyond the head to wind position) bears away;

(a) to a close-hauled position when beating to windward

or

(b) onto the course on which her mainsail has filled if she is not beating to windward (fig. 4).

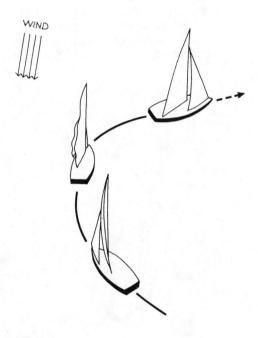

Fig. 4

(a) The first case deals with a situation where a yacht tacks while beating to windward and in this case the tack is considered completed (and therefore she is no longer *tacking* but *on a tack*) when she is sailing on a close-hauled course. To clarify this concept better we should look at the judgement expressed by the RYA in IYRU No. 32 (RYA 1967/8 Cyprus Services Sailing Association) which establishes that "when beating to windward, a yacht has completed her tack when she is heading on a close-hauled course regardless of her movement through the water or the sheeting of her sails".

The RYA was absolutely right because without getting mixed up in complicated interpretations it limited itself to following the literal sense of the definition responding to the evident practical necessities. In fact a tack (which is a displacement of the bow from one tack to another, that is a short and transitory phase between one course and the next) is perfected and terminated when a yacht no longer needs to continue such a manoeuvre for the simple fact that her hull is on a close-hauled course, that is to say on that course which allows her to sail and work to windward. The fact that at this point the yacht still has no way on is irrelevant to the effects of the definition of tacking (because this is now over) just as the fact that her sails are flapping and are not carrying is irrelevant too.

(b) The same conclusion is reached in the second case when a yacht changes tacks to a course that is not close hauled; the definition here specifies that the tack is finished when she is on a course on which her mainsail has filled, that is when this sail (and not any other sail) is set in such a way that it will carry. And we can repeat that the fact that her hull is not moving through the water has no bearing on the matter, it is enough for her to be on the course on which her mainsail is full.

These distinctions may seem Byzantine but with thought appear logical and show in their right light when the two main applications of the definition of tacking are considered: those envisaged by rules 41 (Changing tacks, tacking or gybing), and 42 (Rounding or passing marks and obstructions). In particular rule 41 deals specifically with those reversals of the rights and obligations between two yachts that happen with a tack (or a gybe) and must therefore be as precise as possible about the moment, so common when racing, when situations are completely reversed.

Bearing Away   *Bearing Away* — Altering course away from the wind until a yacht begins to gybe.

This definition is quite straightforward and no comment is needed. The manoeuvre is the exact opposite of luffing and turns the bow further away from the direction of the wind (fig. 5). The only important point to notice is the final limit, this is reached at the moment in which a yacht begins to gybe and so we will look at this point with the next definition.

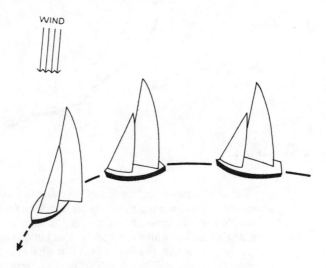

WIND

Fig. 5

Gybing
Gybing — A yacht begins to *gybe* at the moment when, with the wind aft, the foot of her mainsail crosses her centre line, and completes the *gybe* when the mainsail has filled on the other *tack*.

The definition of gybing logically follows that of bearing away because by continuing to bear away a yacht finishes by finding herself with the wind astern until at a certain moment she gybes and her whole sail comes over to the other side (fig. 6). As usual the rule has to specify when the gybe begins and ends because such moments mark the borderline between one situation within the rule to another quite the opposite. Think of the various rules governing a yacht on port tack and at the complete reversal of rights and duties which follows when by gybing she passes onto starboard (rule 36); or think of a yacht "on a tack" in respect of another which is "tacking" or "gybing" (rule 41).

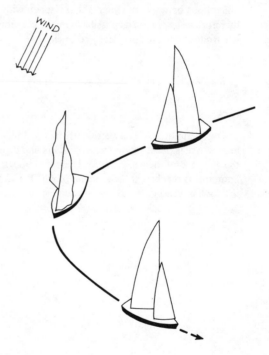

Fig. 6

The gybe begins when "the foot of her mainsail crosses her centre line". It is clear therefore that, contrary to what is laid down for other situations (see for example the definitions of "luffing" or "tacking"), what counts is not the position of the hull with respect to the wind but that of the sail with respect to the centre of the hull. In addition note that what counts here is the position of the foot of the mainsail (which in practice is the same as the boom to which it is attached); and the reason is clear because it would be extremely difficult to rely on the position of any other part of the sail given how often a mainsail is twisted by the wind while gybing.

The gybe ends "when the mainsail has filled on the other *tack*". Here the final moment is expressed in more elastic terms for a sail can begin to fill at various different angles; however because a gybe is quick, even in light winds, it is unlikely that any problems could arise on this point. Remember that a gybe (as well as a tack) is completed at this moment even if the boat is not yet moving ahead on her new course.

On a tack

On a Tack — A yacht is *on a tack* except when she is *tacking* or *gybing*. A yacht is on the *tack (starboard* or *port)* corresponding to her *windward* side.

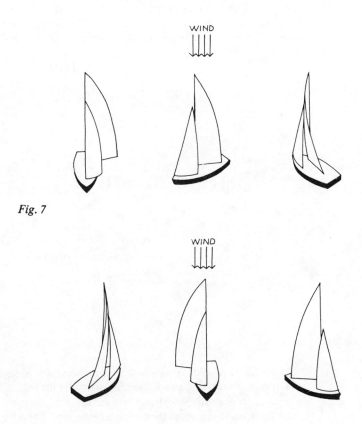

Fig. 7

Fig. 8

The definition is simple: a yacht begins to be "on a tack" when she has finished "tacking" (see definition) or when she has finished "gybing" (see definition). From another point of view we could say that a yacht is no longer "on a tack" from the moment in which she begins to tack or from the moment in which she begins to gybe and these two actions are described under their respective headings. The definition then goes on to distinguish tacks according to the side from which the wind blows; and specifies that "a yacht is on a *tack*, *starboard* (fig. 7) or *port* (fig. 8), corresponding to her *windward* side".

Close-hauled   *Close-hauled* – A yacht is *close-hauled* when sailing by the wind as close as she can lie with advantage in working to windward.

The definition has lost a certain part of its importance since the law was changed (both the racing rules and the International Rules for the Prevention of Collision at Sea) which required a sailing ship reaching or running to give way to one working to windward (a measure dictated by the very limited ability of a square-rigged ship when close-hauled). This does not mean that sailing close-hauled does not still have its own importance in certain situations (rules 42.1(c), 42.4, 43).

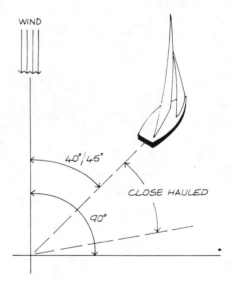

Fig. 9

To sail "close-hauled" is to sail close to the wind and further to sail "with advantage when working to windward;" and this is the reason why, as far as the rule is concerned, you have to consider the direction of the hull's longitudinal axis in respect to the direction of the wind. The position of the sails does not decide if a yacht is close-hauled; on a reach the sails may be pinned hard in but this is not "close hauled".

Finally you cannot make arbitrary distinctions between pinching and sailing full-and-by because close-hauled must be understood, not in a restrictive sense, but bearing in mind that every course which permits a yacht to work to windward comes within the definition even if in some boats the angle between the direction of the wind and the longitudinal axis of the hull is little less than 90° (fig. 9).

Clear astern
Clear ahead
Overlap

Clear Astern and *Clear Ahead; Overlap*—A yacht is *clear astern* of another when her hull and equipment in normal position are abaft an imaginary line projected abeam from the aftermost point of the other's hull and equipment in normal position. The other yacht is *clear ahead*. The yachts *overlap* when neither is *clear astern;* or when, although one is *clear astern,* an intervening yacht *overlaps* both of them. The terms *clear astern, clear ahead* and *overlap* apply to yachts on opposite *tacks* only when they are subject to rule 42, (Rounding or Passing Marks and Obstructions).

Generally speaking the definition applies only to yachts on the same tack because different-tack yachts are controlled by rule 36 with the exception of rule 42 (Rounding or passing marks and obstructions) in Part IV C when it is applied only in particular cases; indeed it is the definition itself which reminds us that in these cases the words clear astern, ahead and overlap can exceptionally be applied even to yachts on opposite tacks.

WIND

Fig. 10

These words, so typical of racing jargon, are found in rules 37 (Same tack – basic rules), 38 (Same tack – luffing and sailing above a proper course after starting), 39 (Same tack – sailing below a proper course after starting) and 42 (Rounding or passing marks and obstructions). That is to say particularly in those rules dealing with cases of yachts about to hit each other or so near as to run the risk of collision. Two yachts are considered "overlapped" when any part of the hull or equipment (point 1 of the comment to the definition of *finishing*) of one of them is "abaft an imaginary line projected abeam from the aftermost point of the other's hull and equipment" (fig. 10). Note that the definition takes an imaginary line from the stern and not from the bow.

It is important to stress that an overlap is not conditional on the yachts being on or almost on the same course, it is enough for one to be totally or in part within this famous line. Or if this has not happened it is enough for the two yachts not yet overlapped to be linked by a third yacht which overlaps both and creates a chain. It is, however, absolutely essential that the intervening yacht – the link – is between the other two. In fig. 11 A and C are overlapped, B acting as the link; in fig. 12 A and C are not overlapped.

In addition to the imaginary stern line in certain cases the establishment of an overlap depends on distance. Rule 38, for example, provides that an overlap does not exist as long as the two yachts are not clearly within two overall lengths of the longer yachts; and rule 42.3 lays down that an overlap is valid

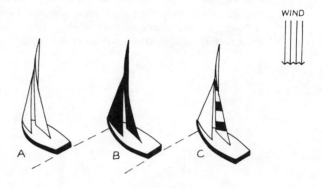

Fig. 11

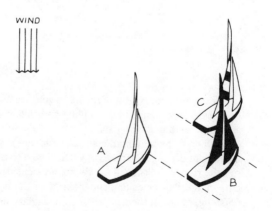

Fig. 12

only if established while the yacht clear ahead is still more than two lengths from the mark.

Where the rule does not prescribe any other obligation (see for example rule 37.3 which does not set any limit of distance for a yacht overtaking to leeward) the overlap only becomes real when the distance between the yachts is such that the possibility of an accident or incident cannot be excluded, bearing in mind naturally in each case the actual conditions of wind and sea at the moment in relation to the type of boat racing.

Leeward and Windward   *Leeward* and *Windward* — The *leeward* side of a yacht is that on which she is, or, when *luffing* head to wind, was, carrying her mainsail. The opposite side is the *windward* side.
When neither of two yachts on the same *tack* is *clear astern,* the one on the *leeward* side of the other is the *leeward yacht.* The other is the *windward yacht.*

As defined by the rules the limit between the two zones "windward" and "leeward" is the longitudinal axis of the hull and it follows that everything on the side from which the wind is blowing is to windward and everything on the opposite side is to leeward (fig. 13). Indeed to indicate the leeward side the rule talks of that side on which the yacht is "carrying her mainsail," meaning by this, in the case of a boat with more than one mast, the sail of the principal mast. "The opposite side is the *windward* side". As we have seen (definition of luffing) a yacht is still *luffing* (that is she has not yet begun to *tack*) even when she is stationary head-to-wind; the rule specifies that in this position the leeward side is that in which the mainsail was carried before she luffed head to

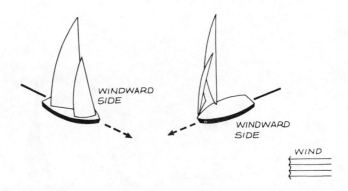

Fig. 13

wind. Or, to look at it another way, until she goes beyond this position she has not changed tacks and continues to be considered (fig. 14) still on the same tack (definition On a tack).

Finally the rule looks at the case of two yachts on the same *tack* when neither is *clear astern* (that is to say that they are overlapped) and indicates which of the two should be considered the leeward yacht and which the windward (figs. 15 and 16). A series of applications of this particular will be found above all under rules 37, 38, 39 and 40.

Proper Course *Proper Course* – A *proper course* is any course which a yacht might sail after the starting signal, in the absence of the other yacht or yachts affected, to *finish* as quickly as possible. The course sailed before *luffing* or *bearing away* is presumably, but not necessarily, that yacht's *proper course*. There is no *proper course* before the starting signal.

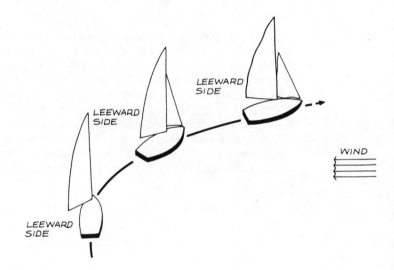

Fig. 14

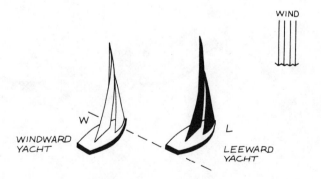

Fig. 15

Scattered through the rule there are certain prescriptions (see rules 38.1, 39 and 42.1(b)) which are rigidly linked to the definition of *proper course*. From this we can accept that, apart from the cases considered in these particular rules, a yacht racing may sail whatever course she chooses (provided of course that she is not obliged to keep clear), even if her course is not really that which she should sail "to *finish* as quickly as possible", that is to say the shortest and straightest course from the start right through to the finish, rounding the prescribed marks in between. Naturally the proper course must be judged in the light of the particular meteorological and tidal conditions of the moment and in relation to the type of boat. For example look at NAYRU 6 (fig. 17) where it was held that L was not sailing above her "proper course", even though she was heading to windward of the mark, because her windwardness was justified by the big sea running which gave her a lot of leeway.

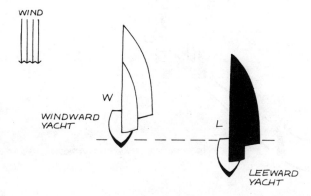

Fig. 16

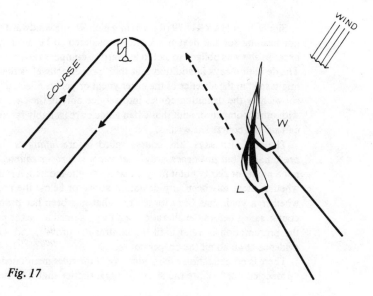

Fig. 17

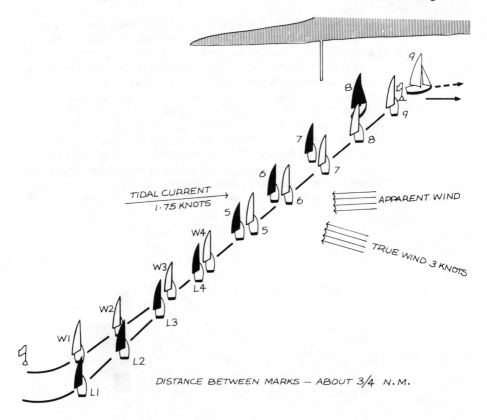

Fig. 18

Similarly in NAYRU 79 (fig. 18) in which W, the windward yacht, although not heading for the next mark was considered to be on a "proper course" because she was obliged to sail to leeward to compensate for the cross current. The definition says in addition that this "proper course" is that which a yacht might sail "in the absence of the other yacht or yachts affected": a detail which shows how the definition comes into service only in the case of an encounter with other competitors but that when alone or reasonably far away each yacht can sail the course she wishes.

The rule also says "the course sailed before *luffing* or *bearing away* is presumably, but not necessarily, that yacht's "*proper course*." The phrase is not a model of clarity but it means that if at some moment it is necessary to see whether there has been any deviation above or below the proper course (or whether a yacht has been forced off what has been her proper course), the course sailed before the alteration can be presumed to be the proper one. And the presumption is valid until the contrary is proven, and when there is no evidence at all about the proper course.

There is no obligation even under any of the rules mentioned above, to sail a "proper course" before the starting signal (notice that it is the signal and not when the yacht crosses the starting line that is the changing point). The reason is obvious, it is seldom practicable to sail a course "to finish as quickly as possible" until the starting signal. After it, on the other hand, it is logical for everyone to sail a course that gets them across the starting line so avoiding pointless changes in direction just when the crowding is at its worst.

The subject of "proper course" (a question of fact – see rule 71) must be considered case by case and each protest committee has to study the actual situation at the moment and place where the incident occurred, taking into account conditions of wind, sea, current or tide, etc., with respect to the type of boat and deciding what would have been or could have been her proper course if the yacht had been on her own. Clearly the further the distance to the next mark the greater will be the difficulty of determining the proper course; in an offshore race for example where the next mark may be dozens of miles away it is not always easy to reach a conclusion. Here the presumption of a proper course already mentioned will hold good.

Mark

Mark – A *mark* is any object specified in the sailing instructions which a yacht must round or pass on a required side.
Every ordinary part of a *mark* ranks as part of it, including a flag, flagpole, boom or hoisted boat, but excluding ground tackle and any object either accidentally or temporarily attached to the *mark*.

The great majority of races throughout the world are run round buoys, but since this is not always true the rules use the word *mark* instead, and this covers any "body" which may be used instead of a buoy, it may be a boat or a ship or the Fastnet Rock or indeed an island.

To qualify as a "mark" it is necessary for this "body" first of all to be easily identifiable and then clearly defined in the sailing instructions together with the determination of the side on which it must be left (see rule 3.2(a)ii): the sailing instructions must describe "all the *marks* and state the order in which and the side on which each is to be rounded or passed"). Whenever the sailing instructions set a course through a buoyed channel, if there are no other details, it will be wise to treat all buoys as *marks* in the strict sense.

A mark has a required side for a yacht "as long as she is on a leg which it begins, bounds or ends" (rule 51.3). Except in these circumstances a "mark" does not fall within this definition and becomes a simple obstruction. To clarify this distinction it is enough to say that if you touch a *mark*, while it is a *mark*, you will be penalized (rule 52) but once it has been down-graded to an *obstruction* you can run into it with no other consequences than perhaps a scratch on your paintwork. For other information on *marks* look at rules 6, 7, 9 and 51.

Parts of a mark

As we have seen a mark can take any number of forms and so the details in the definition ensure that in so far as rule 52 is concerned not every part of the object indicated in the sailing instructions as a mark need count as if it were the mark itself because sometimes this could be unfair.

First of all "every ordinary part of a mark ranks as part of it", whether above or under the water. Among those under water are the foundations of a breakwater acting as a mark and the hull of a mark boat. Where a mark consists of a rock, island or other natural object we believe it is too wide an interpretation to include as part of the submerged mark (therefore untouchable) the area of the surrounding sea bed on which a yacht may go aground (here the case envisaged in rule 64 is preferable).

On the other hand you could not, in our opinion, say the same for the underwater part immediately touching the out-of-water bit; (think of a rock going vertically into the sea) because the continuity and nearness of the parts in and out of the water makes it fairer to consider them as one, which if touched will actualise the infringement envisaged by rule 52.1. Anyway these are pretty rare events which must be examined and decided case by case as to whether it is really possible to find a substantial distinction between what is truly running aground and what may be considered touching a mark so that the incident can be firmly set in one or other category.

Likewise it can only be decided case by case whether in reality you are dealing with an "ordinary" part of a mark or not. To this end it is necessary to look and see whether the part is an ordinary permanent (even if not fixed) part of the buoy, vessel, construction or natural feature that is the mark; or whether on the contrary there is something out of the ordinary, an unusual occurrence, or an object accidentally or temporarily attached to the mark (as might be a rope hanging over the side which is not part of the normal rigging of a ship or fishing gear sticking over the edge of a breakwater or jetsam caught up on a buoy or on moored ships, etc.).

In particular "the flag, flag pole, boom or hoisted boat" count as parts of the mark while ground tackle is excluded both above and below water. On this last point NAYRU 3 stated "a floating log or buoy that supports a mooring chain or rope to which a mark is attached is part of the ground tackle of a mark and is not part of the mark. Consequently there is no penalty for touching such log, buoy, or any line or chain leading from it to the mark or to the submerged mooring."

Obstruction

Obstruction — An *obstruction* is any object, including a vessel under way, large enough to require a yacht, when not less than one overall length away from it, to make a substantial alteration of course to pass on one side or the other, or any object which can be passed on one side only, including a buoy when the yacht in question cannot safely pass between it and the shoal or object which it marks.

The words "obstruction" and "mark" are often linked in the rules governing the movements of yachts near such "objects", but while a *mark*, in the strict sense of the definition, delimits the starting and finishing lines and the course (has a required side – rule 51.3, and must not be touched – rule 52) an *obstruction* has nothing to do with racing or the course except in so far as it gives rise to a duty to pay attention to the particular rules mentioned above.

An obstruction may be anything you can imagine from a buoy to a vessel (whether it is a little boat or a transatlantic liner under way or at anchor), from a mole or breakwater to land in general from jetties and hards sticking out along the course, to islands, from floating logs to swimmers and so on. Note particularly that another yacht racing can be an obstruction (see IYRU No. 67 discussed on page 189). It need only be something large enough to require a yacht "when not less than one overall length away from it to make a substantial alteration of course to pass on one side or the other".

Note that this change of course has to be "substantial" and therefore a small correction of the helm to avoid some little thing in the way will not be enough. Note also that the yacht must have to alter her course not less than one length from the obstruction (that is when she is still a certain distance off) and not when she is right on top of it. This does not imply however that she can pretend to avoid it at the last moment with a substantial alteration of course when she had already seen it some way off and could therefore have avoided it earlier more easily.

Finally among those obstructions which can be passed only on one side (as for example the end of a breakwater) the definition particularly mentions a buoy marking shallows or, for example a wreck, "when the yacht in question cannot safely pass between it and the shoal or object which it marks": the shoal or wreck is considered to have a theoretical extension out to whatever marks and limits it, on condition that this is so near that there is no safe passage between the two, then mark and shoal or wreck will make a single continuing obstruction with all the effects of the rule. A typical application is found in rule 42.3(f) which envisages the case of a yacht wishing to establish an overlap between "another yacht clear ahead and a continuing obstruction such as a shoal or the shore".

Postponement
Postponement — A *postponed* race is one which is not started at its scheduled time and which can be sailed at any time the race committee may decide.

A postponement may be for 15 minutes or a month and is signalled as described in rules 4.1 "AP" and 5.

Abandonment
Abandonment — An *abandoned* race is one which the race committee declares void at any time after the starting signal, and which can be re-sailed at its discretion.

A race can only be abandoned after the start and only for reasons of safety and fairness (rule 5.1(b)) and it can then be re-sailed or not. If it is re-sailed the competitors must be informed of the date and time (rules 5.3 and 13) otherwise it can be declared void, that is to say cancelled definitely from the programme. For the relative signals see rule 4.1 "N", "N over X", and "N over first substitute".

Cancellation
Cancellation — A *cancelled* race is one which the race committee decides will not be sailed thereafter.

A cancelled race will not be re-sailed. Cancellation can be decided on for any reason before the starting signal (rule 5.1(a)) but for limited reasons only after the starting signal: because of dangerously bad weather, insufficient wind or because a mark has disappeared or shifted or for other reasons which prejudice "the safety and fairness of the competition" (rule 5.1(b)). For the signals see rule 4.1 "N over first substitute".

Part II
Management
of races

Authority and Duties of Race Committee

The rules of Part II deal with the duties and responsibilities of the race committee in conducting a race, the meaning of signals made by it and of other actions taken by it.

Race organizers are advised to consult IYRU Racing Rules Appendix 12 – Organization of principal events – as well as what follows here. Much of Appendix 12 is complementary to the rules of Part II themselves but there is also a wealth of experience condensed into a few pages of excellent advice on such subjects as rescue launches, boat parks, publicity and life-saving equipment.

Rule 1. General authority of race committee and jury

1.1 All races shall be arranged, conducted and judged by a race committee under the direction of the organising authority, except as may be provided under rule 1.2. The race committee may delegate the conduct of a race, the hearing and deciding of protests or any other of its responsibilities to one or more sub-committees which, when appointed, will hereinafter be included in the term "race committee" wherever it is used.

1.2 For a special regatta or series, the organising authority may provide for a jury to hear and decide protests and to have supervision over the conduct of the races, in which case the race committee shall be subject to the direction of the jury to the extent provided by the organising authority.

1.3 All yachts entered or *racing* shall be subject to the direction and control of the race committee, but it shall be the sole responsibility of each yacht to decide whether or not to *start* or to continue to *race*.

1.4 Unless otherwise prescribed by the national authority, the race committee may reject or rescind any entry without stating the reason.
However, at all world and continental championships, no entry within

established quotas shall be rejected or rescinded without first obtaining the approval of the I.Y.R.U. or the duly authorised international class association.

1.5   The race committee shall be governed by these rules, by the prescriptions of its national authority when they apply, by the sailing instructions, by approved class rules (but it may refuse to recognise any class rule which conflicts with these rules) and, when applicable, by the international team racing rules, and shall decide all questions in accordance therewith.

1. The race committee

The body which runs a race is always known as "the race committee". This race committee, composed of several people can, up to a point, especially for choosing the course, starts and finishes, come down to one person: the "officer of the day". He is the poor chap who has to run the whole operation and must be armoured against ingratitude and loss of holidays, must work like a beast and be at the receiving end of all the complaints, if not the curses, of the competitors, especially those who finish badly and feel they have to justify their lack of success in someway or another.

2. The protest committee (or jury)

The race committee acting under the direction of the organizing club has the job of hearing and deciding protests but this duty can be delegated in the case of particular regattas or a series to a special jury which will hear and decide protests and will supervise the overall conduct of the races rather than the organizing club as is usual. Some clubs set up a permanent jury of their own or, as we have said, for special occasions a jury can be nominated by the organizers and indeed in certain major championships by national or international authorities.

The importance of such a jury is underlined by the decision in FIV 1962/2 (*Marina* v. C.V.I.) This clarified the point that even though the sailing instructions contained a warning that "the organizing club" reserved to itself the right to alter the sailing instructions it was perfectly valid to shorten course under orders from "the jury, that is from the body which has the supervision over the conduct of the race (rule 1.2)".

The power to decide protests normally belongs to the race committee but is delegated to a jury when the organizers so think fit. The relationship between the two bodies is clearly explained by the classic example of a competitor who seeks redress (rule 68.5(a)) from the race committee, and his "protest" is judged and decided by the protest committee. Note that while the action under rule 68.5(a) is universally called a protest it is not so in theory.

In this book the term protest committee is generally used rather than jury or race committee.

Some clarification of the powers of a jury can be drawn from Appendix 8 of IYRU Racing Rules on this specific subject (see para 7 of the Terms of Reference of an International Jury under Racing Rule 77.6) Here we see that the jury "shall perform the following functions:

1. make final decisions on all matters relating to entries and to the measurement of yachts;
2. authorize any variations from or additions to (a) the racing rules, such as national letters, distinguishing numbers, recall procedures, etc., and (b) the sailing instructions or other special instructions issued to the competitors;

3. authorize the substitution of reserve crew and yachts;
4. hear and decide all protests;
5. offer advice to the organizing authority of the race committee on such subjects as have a direct bearing on the fairness of the competition;
6. direct the race committee to the extent provided by the organizing authority in rule 1.2 (General authority of race committee and jury)".

The decisions of international juries are final and since there is no right of appeal, it follows that their cases do not get discussed and printed by appeal committees and so we deal only with cases which started life before a protest committee (or perhaps a jury under rule 1.2) which have then gone on appeal to the national authority in their respective country.

There is also a system whereby clubs can refer cases to national authorities for rulings on difficult problems.

3. A competitor's responsibility

It follows from what we have been saying that the race and the competitors are "subject to the direction and control of the race committee" (and, if there is one, of the jury), and this needs no explanation. "But it shall be the sole responsibility", continues the rule "of each yacht to decide whether or not to start or to continue to race"; this means that although your entry has been accepted and you are under the control of the race committee the latter are not responsible for everything that may happen to you. The race committee for example cannot know or control the ability of your crew or the real soundness of your equipment. This warning in the rule is directed particularly to offshore racing where only the competitor with his detailed knowledge of his boat and his conscience as a seaman can really judge the state of preparation of boat and crew and where, more than in other races, serious or even fatal accidents can happen in circumstances and for reasons quite outside the control of the race committee:

4. Refusing entries

If there are no special prescriptions by the competent national authority the race committee may refuse or rescind an entry without giving a reason for so doing. This means that an entry already accepted can at a later date be thrown out. It is unnecessary to say that such a step must only be taken in exceptional cases; unless of course entries are refused because there are already too many competitors or because the terms of race entry have not been fulfilled, etc., when it will not be difficult to explain the reasons to the competitors excluded.

The fact that there is no need to give a reason for such refusals must not be taken as a licence for arbitrary decisions. As an example such a facility might fairly be used to keep away some competitor who had given clear and repeated evidence of indiscipline and bad behaviour.

Bear in mind the recommendation by the IYRU itself (see the comment to rule 26) when it reminds race committees "Rule 1.4 empowers them to reject an entry if they are satisfied that one of its purposes is to promote a commercial enterprise". However, this power to reject or rescind entries is not unlimited and cannot be exercised in world or continental championships – except as far as members are concerned – without IYRU or a class association permission.

5. Rules in force while racing

The last paragraph of rule 1 indicates the rules that alone can and must govern while racing (see also rule 2(a) and rule 3.2(a)i) naming first of all as is right the IYRU Racing Rules; in fact class rules cannot override these just as some sections of the racing rules cannot be overridden by instructions (see rule 3.1)

The race committee must also respect any prescriptions of the national authority; these are special regulations laid down by each single racing authority on those subjects and in those sectors where the rule itself has omitted to do so (usually using the phrase 'unless otherwise prescribed by the national authority") and these prescriptions are printed in italics at the end of the relevant rule. They are enforced in the country of each national authority and hold good for foreign competitors racing in those waters; and this is why it is important (as rules 2(a) and 3.2(a)(i) prescribe) that in international races the notice of race and the sailing instructions mention them and possibly copy them out or make a résumé of the most important.

Rule 2. Notice of race

The notice of a race or regatta shall contain the following information: —

(a) That the race or races will be sailed under the rules of the I.Y.R.U., the prescriptions of the national authority when they apply and the rules of each class concerned.

(b) The date and place of the regatta and the time of the start of the first race and, if possible, succeeding races.

(c) The class or classes for which races will be given.

The notice shall also cover such of the following matters as may be appropriate: —

(d) Any special instructions, subject to rule 3.1, (The Sailing Instructions), which may vary or add to these rules or class rules.

(e) Any restrictions or conditions regarding entries and numbers of starters or competitors.

(f) The address to which entries shall be sent, the date on which they close, the amount of entrance fees, if any, and any other entry requirements.

(g) Particulars and number of prizes.

(h) Time and place for receiving sailing instructions.

(i) Scoring system.

(j) When it is essential to determine the result of a race or a series of races which will qualify a yacht to compete in a later stage of the event, that decisions of protests shall not be subject to appeal. A national authority may prescribe that its approval be required for such a procedure.

There is an obligation to publish certain information in the notice of race and the mandatory points are listed in sub-paras (a), (b), and (c) of rule 2. It is enough to read them to understand that they are essential and that without them no notice would really be given at all. Sub-paras (d) to (j) cover points which have to be included but only when they are appropriate.

The rules do not state (as they do in the case of sailing instructions (3.1)) that the contents of the notice of race rank equally with the rules themselves but certainly what is published binds the organizers and the competitors (unless the organizers reserve the right to modify the notice of race in case of need.

It should be said here that special instructions (rule 2(d)) "which may vary or add to these rules" are extremely important in the case of offshore racing. Here details of special safety regulations as well as rating cannot be left until just before the race since they may affect design and therefore these notices of race are of the utmost importance in order to inform the competitors in good time of the various regulations they will have to keep.

Rule 3. The sailing instructions 3.1 Status

(a) These rules shall be supplemented by written sailing instructions which shall rank as rules and may alter a rule by specific reference to it, but except in accordance with rule 3.2(b)(ii), Continuing after Sunset, they shall not alter Parts I and IV of these rules, The Fundamental Rule, Fair Sailing, or rules, 1, 2, 3, 22.3, 26, 51, 52.1, or 58, or the provision of rule 68.3(a), (Protests), that International Code flag "B" is always acceptable as a protest flag,
provided however, that when so prescribed by the national authority, this restriction shall not preclude the right of developing and testing proposed rule changes in local regattas.

(b) No condition of entry or deed of gift shall waive the right of appeal, except as otherwise prescribed by the national authority or in accordance with rule 77.6, (Appeals), and on receipt by the race committee of the prior written approval of the national authority concerned.

In contrast to the notice of race the sailing instructions are explicitly declared to rank as the rules themselves and precisely for this reason they must obviously be available to competitors on the day and at the time and place indicated in the notice of race (rules 2(h) and 3.3), because they contain prescriptions which are integrated with the rule and which no competitor can ignore. But their importance increases when they not only complete but even modify the rule as permitted by rule 3.1 *with exceptions*.

The exceptions that sailing instructions cannot alter are:

the Fundamental Rule
Part I: Definitions
Part IV: Right-of-way rules (except as allowed by rule 3.2(b)(ii) at night)
Rules 1. General authority of race committee and jury
2. Notice of race
3. Sailing instructions
22.3 Clothing and equipment
26. Advertisements
51. Sailing the course
52.1 Touching a mark
58. Receiving assistance
68.3(a) The provision that international code flag B is always acceptable as a protest flag.

An example of how far these modifications can go is given by FIV 1969/13. A yacht, disqualified without a hearing for having sculled, appealed against the decision criticizing, among other things, the summary procedure followed by the race committee. However the appeals committee confirmed the decision observing that the appellant "would have been right to criticize the procedure adopted to disqualify him if there had not existed a prescription in the sailing instructions, strange and little to be recommended though it was, which went as follows 'the jury will disqualify on the spot and without a hearing any crew seen by the jury on the water infringing the rules and above all moving the tiller more than normal'.

"This prescription was pretty drastic," added the appeals committee, "and maybe justly criticized. However, it does not modify any rule of Parts I or IV or any other rule listed in 3.1 and therefore it has the force of a rule (rule 3.1). It follows that it must be respected by whoever has freely agreed to race when such a rule has been published. If a competitor does not wish to sail under such conditions he need only refuse invitations of this sort; if he accepts, however, he must abide by them."

When altering any racing rule "specific reference" must be made to it; IYRU No. 74 (USYRU 177) gives an example where neither sailing instructions, nor notice of race, specifically referred to a change and were held to be deficient so that the race was ordered to be re-sailed.

Sailing instructions must always be in writing because they must be available to everyone and in precise terms; nevertheless rule 3.5 permits oral instructions on the understanding that they "shall not be given except in accordance with the procedure specifically set out in the sailing instructions". They must be used with the maximum discretion and only in cases of real necessity, for reasons of time or place which allow no other solution.

The facility given by rule 3.4 to modify sailing instructions already issued should also be used with discretion. In this case, however, there exists an obligation to inform all the interested boats in writing if practicable. (This means that here too oral communication should be a rare exception and used only when there is no other way, for example when the boats are already out in the sailing area.) In addition you will notice that alteration may not be made or communicated after the warning signal, commonly called the ten-minute gun (rule 4.4).

As for the notice of race, so for the sailing instructions there are mandatory items listed in part (a) i–ix of rule 3.2 and others in part (b) i–xxii, which are only required when certain particulars of the race in question make them appropriate. The rule naturally cannot cover the great variety of procedures convenient and suitable in different circumstances which depend on the sort of race, the type of boats, the weather, etc. Let us look briefly at these points one by one, beginning with part (a) which lays down the information which is mandatory in each case. To avoid repetition, the IYRU rule is only given before each comment.

3.2 Contents

(a) The sailing instructions shall contain the following information: —

(i) That the race or races will be sailed under the rules of the I.Y.R.U., the prescriptions of the national authority when they apply, the sailing instructions and the rules of each class concerned.

This practically repeats the details of rules 1.5 and 2(a) requiring specification in advance of the various regulations which competitors must obey while racing.

(ii) The course or courses to be sailed or a list of *marks* or courses from which the course or courses will be selected, describing all *marks* and stating the order in which and the side on which each is to be rounded or passed.

Describing the courses gives rise to more uncertainties and comment than any other point because the terms used are so often vague and insufficient. We can never stress strongly enough the importance of being clear and exact (indeed we urge organizers to keep strictly to what is prescribed here).

In one case an offshore course up and down the coast was written into sailing instructions as follows: "Starting mark, mark 1, mark 2, mark 3 and return to starting mark."

The intention had been to have the boats sail back round marks 1 and 2 again in reverse order but a yacht that missed them out was held to have sailed the course correctly as they had not been specifically mentioned.

Sometimes the opposite occurs; that is the sailing instructions are very clear, but the competitors do not read them carefully enough. We remember for example one race with a course which was more or less an equilateral triangle. A few leaders shortly after the start could not see the first buoy and losing their sense of direction ended by sailing directly for the second, down-wind mark followed soon after by most of the competitors like a flock of sheep. Having realized their mistake when they had almost reached the second mark they then protested in mass against the race committee saying that the direction of the first mark was badly indicated. It was easy to refute their protests, however, particularly as the sailing instructions had a diagram of the course which showed unmistakably that the starting line was laid exactly at right angles to the first leg of the course and so the direction to the weather mark was adequately exact and easily understandable even without its being visible.

Finally in all these cases bear in mind the opinion expressed by the NAYRU Appeals Committee (No. 66) dealing with an imprecise and therefore ambiguous description of the line: "when a reasonable doubt exists as to an interpretation of a sailing instruction, it must be resolved in favour of a contestant even though as in this case he was the only one to take advantage of it". This is a very valuable observation because it is not fair for anyone who is not at fault to suffer for the mistakes of others.

    (iii) The course signals.

    (iv) The classes to race and class signals, if any.

    (v) Time of start for each class.

These are quite clear and there is no need to comment on them.

    (vi) Starting line and starting area when used.

Rules 6 and 7.1 deal with different methods of laying down starting lines and we will deal with those when we get there. As far as the contents of the sailing instructions are concerned no difficulties arise when using a normal system starting on a line between two buoys or between a buoy and a mast (on this subject it is interesting to note that rule 6(a) requires the mast or staff be "clearly identified in the sailing instructions") but the same cannot be said for a transit (rule 6(c)) that is the extension of a line through two stationary posts. A transit line can and usually does have "a *mark* at or near its outer limit, inside which the yachts shall pass".

In these cases sailing instructions must be clearer than ever and give complete details as follows:

(a) describe the characteristics of the buoys and the flags which may be on top of them;

(b) specify, when necessary, if certain buoys serve only to indicate, especially in the case of very long lines, the approximate bearing of the line (simple obstructions only) or whether you are talking of real and proper starting *marks* (rule 52.1);

(c) indicate on which side the limit marks are to be left;

(d) specify if this last obligation persists afterwards, that is to say whether these starting marks become marks of the course in later rounds;

(e) specify if certain mark boats are to count as *marks* or not and whether this is so only at the start or also afterwards;

(f) specify finally (especially when there is no diagram of the finishing line and if an indication is lacking of the prescribed side of the starting marks) in which direction the finishing line is to be crossed.

Finally let us look at NAYRU 86. In the 1961 Atlantic Coast Penguin Championship the race committee adopted the special starting system called "open gate" or "gate start", which is used when the number of starters is very high to avoid piling up on the starting line with a lot of recalls.

A competitor protested because none of the methods specified by rule 6 was used; but he was held to be wrong in both first and second instance. The Appeals Commmittee laid down that according to rule 3.1 the rules can be integrated with and (except Part I and IV, etc.) modified by the sailing instructions, with the object of allowing case by case and place by place any adjustment necessary in the particular circumstances, and they decided that the race committee had the power to use any method of starting that they considered most convenient, given that rule 6 (Starting and finishing lines) is not among those rules which cannot be altered.

> (vii) Finishing line and any special instructions for shortening the course or for *finishing* a shortened course. (Where possible it is good practice for the sailing instructions for *finishing* a shortened course not to differ from those laid down for *finishing* the full course.)

The various ways in which a finishing line can be arranged are discussed under rule 6.

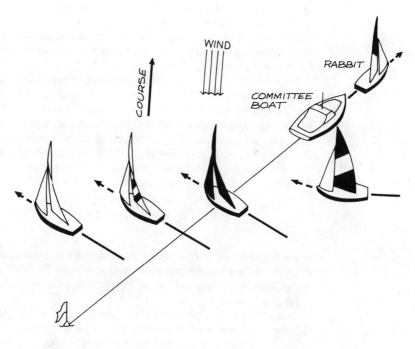

Fig. 20

As regards sailing instructions, remember what was said in para 6 about the starting line: it is essential to be extremely precise and clear in describing the marks which limit the line.

As with a starting line, things can be complicated because of the definition of *finishing*, which specifies that the finishing line must be crossed from the direction of the last *mark*. On this subject have another look at para 2 of the comment to the definition (and particularly at FIV 1966/3 quoted there), and remember that sailing instructions (rule 3.1) cannot modify the definition itself, and that therefore a yacht which follows the definition and not the contrary sailing instructions will be in the right.

A typical case of inadequate obscure sailing instructions is reported in YRA 1938/19. This deals with a starting line (fig. 21) laid between a buoy and a point on the shore, the buoy to be left to starboard as were all the other marks of the course. This line became the finishing line at the end of the race but in the opposite direction, that is with the obligation to pass as before between the shore and the buoy leaving the latter to port. During the last leg of the first round the race committee signalled a shortening of the course and some yachts, because the sailing instructions were not specific, took care to "finish the round which was still to be completed by the leading yacht", that is to say they first rounded the outer limit mark leaving it to starboard and only afterwards crossed the line in the same direction as the start. On the strength of rule 4.1S(b) they were right (this obliging them to complete the round before finishing) because the sailing instructions did not contain any particular details for shortening course.

Note though that this case could not happen now, because with the present rule it would have had a different solution (in the modern definition of *finishing* the finishing line must be crossed from the direction of the last mark whatever the instructions say) but we wanted to bring it to the attention of organizers and underline the necessity of not forgetting "any special instructions for shortening the course or for *finishing* a shortened course" and to make it easier to understand why rule 3.2(a) recommends that a shortened course should finish in the same way as the full course.

(viii) Time limit, if any, for *finishing*.

Except where rule 10 lays down that if there are no other instructions "one yacht *finishing* within the prescribed limit shall make the race valid for all the yachts in that race", any method can be used to fix a time in which a yacht must finish to be classified.

One way is to establish (and simple things are the best) that only yachts finishing within a set time will be classified (for example 4 hours from the start).

Another way (which is almost the same thing) is to decree a mean minimum speed to be maintained; in this case the true length of the course through the water must be calculated (not as theoretically laid down in the instructions when it would then be enough to give a fixed time).

Again the instructions may establish a fixed time limit independent of the start time which is simple, clear and reasonably acceptable when you want to finish before dark.

Sometimes the instructions copy rule 10 (or say nothing about it at all which is the same thing) so that the finish of the first yacht within the time limit saves the race for all, even for those who finish after the given time. Sometimes one

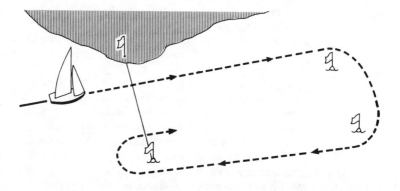

Fig. 21

finds a disposition which fixes a time limit by referring to the finishing time of the first yacht, e.g. only those yachts will be classified which finish within 30 minutes of the finishing time of the first yacht.

In some instructions you find that if the first yacht has not finished all the rounds of the programmed course within a certain time the classification will be worked out on the basis of the order of arrival of the last round completed. Here however the time limit really enters only up to a certain point, because it could be said that results by means of an automatic reduction of the course. (But where is the shortening signal prescribed by rule 4.1 "S"? Someone will certainly ask.) The truth is that when the instructions are too complex, trying to provide for every eventuality, they end by becoming a source of doubt, giving rise to quibbling discussions and controversies and this goes for all instructions when they lose simplicity and clarity.

Finally look at FIV 1965/3 where the appeals committee observed that shortening course was not incompatible with the fact that the instructions had fixed a time limit "it being clear that the first provision (shortening course) which is in force throughout the race has no connection, but can co-exist with the second (the time limit) which affects the period of time the race lasts; for example think of a race in which a shortened course is planned and signalled but which is never finished because it is overtaken by the time limit.

(ix) Scoring system, when not previously announced in writing, including the method, if any, for breaking ties.

A large number of different ways of calculating results are in use. Among the most common points systems are that of the Star class (one point for having finished and one point for every boat behind you), and that of the Flying Dutchman the same except that the first gains an extra quarter of a point, that of the Snipes points equal to the square of the number of entries for the first and equal to the same number minus one for the second and so on), and the old Olympic scoring now used by the RORC (calculated on the formula $p = 101 + 1000 \log A - 1000 \log n$ where p is the number of points, A the number of entries and n the place, and the 1977 Olympic method (zero points for first, then 3, 5, 8, 10, 11·7 successively; seventh and further boats receive their finishing place plus 6).

It is not the place here to discuss the virtues of the various methods but we have shown one or two to underline the importance of explaining in the sailing instructions precisely what system is being used. Sometimes entries are muddled with starters or there is no proper definition of the term "number of starters" which refer to the race of the series in which most boats started or to each race separately or those accepted by measurers at the event.

Imprecise and insufficient sailing instructions are the source of considerable trouble, as to the minimum number of valid races required in a series and the races which each competitor can (or cannot) discard. Let us see what can happen. In one championship the intention was to sail six races "one of which will not be counted in the final results"; in fact only five races were completed and the race committee produced a final classification based on the points for all five races without discarding any of them. A competitor protested sustaining that a discard had to be made just the same; and his appeal (FIV 1964/1) was accepted because it was held (for reasons of interpretation which need not be discussed here) that the main object of the rule was to eliminate from the points a yacht's worst race so that a race in which she had been placed badly (or not at all) would not weigh unfairly against her because of bad luck (no yacht could discard a race in which she had been disqualified). It was consequently decided that this criterion was to be applied even when fewer races were completed than those intended just as long as the number did not fall below the minimum prescribed (which in this particular case was four).

Finally note that the points system may already have been published in writing in the notice of race (rule 2.1).

As far as ties are concerned remember that if it is not possible to use the general criterion laid down in rule 11 (Ties) the sailing instructions must state what is to be done. And if even these fail to solve the problem as a last resort the final method envisaged by rule 11 must be used (equal prizes for both or a division of the prizes). The methods employed to resolve ties are varied (for example giving the prize to the yacht which has beaten the other more often, or to that which has had more first places and if that still gives a tie, more seconds and more thirds and so on, or to that which has been placed better in a given trial chosen beforehand, or to the winner of the last race etc, etc) but there is no need to go into this argument as it is not within the scope of this book.

We go on therefore to part (b) of rule 3.2 which groups together those matters "the sailing instructions shall also cover as may be appropriate".

(b) The sailing instructions shall also cover such of the following matters as may be appropriate: —

(i) The date and place of the race or races.

(ii) When the race is to continue after sunset, the time or place, if any, at which the International Regulations for Preventing Collisions at Sea, or Government Right of Way Rules, shall replace the corresponding rules of Part IV, and the night signals the committee boat will display.

Instructions of this sort are almost exclusively for offshore racing; we need therefore only repeat that in order to avoid arguments afterwards it is advisable in the sailing instructions to establish a set time when the change of rule occurs at sunset and at dawn. If the sailing instructions have not established a time almanac times should be referred to the yacht's position.

Rule 3.2(b)(ii) talks also of a "place" at which the international rules will substitute the racing rules. Frankly dealing with a change which the rule itself ties to sunset — that is based on visibility — we are unable to give an example of such a "place".

(iii) Any special instructions, subject to rule 3.1, which may vary or add to these rules, or class rules, and any special signals.

It is impossible to comment on all potential variations in rules and we should only remind readers that some cannot be altered (see page 49) and that when sailing instructions try to over-ride these the sailing instructions themselves must be considered null and void. In addition remember that IYRU rules can only be varied by *specific* reference to them in sailing instructions unless the particular rule includes the words "unless otherwise prescribed in the sailing instructions".

(iv) Eligibility; entry; measurement or rating certificate; declaration.

Eligibility refers to the conditions required before a yacht is accepted for any particular race (as for example being a member of a class association or of a recognized sailing club, having succeeded in certain eliminating trials, or respecting certain age limits). Entries will be discussed under rule 18, measurement certificates under rule 19 and declarations under rule 14.

(v) Any special instruction or signal, if any, regarding the carrying on board and wearing of personal buoyancy. .

This paragraph speaks for itself, see also rule 4.1 "Y".

(vi) Names, letters and distinguishing numbers and ratings, if any, of
the yachts entered.

The distinguishing marks of the different competitors are essential, unless a
race is between two or at most three yachts and they must be spelled out clearly
to everyone. For sail numbers, letters and class signs see rule 25.

Rating, in handicap classes, serves to provide a theoretical length for yachts
from which a time factor may be used to provide corrected time. FIV 1963/1
shows us the case of a yacht which was allowed to start *sub judice* because her
provisional rating certificate did not print her rating. By the end of the race the
rating was available and published but to no avail because the appeals
committee affirmed the principle that in handicap racing the rating to be used
must be available so that it may be put up before the start, and it then remains
unchanged for that race. The sole possibility of modification is the discovery of
a technical error by the rating authority for it is only fair that the competitors
know their opponents' ratings when racing.

On the same subject take a look at the case quoted by Gerald Sambrooke
Sturgess (RYA 1934/4) about a handicap printed as a certain figure in the
programme, then corrected by hand on those copies of the programme given to
the other competitors. Faced with the question as to which handicap should be
applied the RYA decided that the valid handicap was that corrected by hand
and distributed to the competitors.

(vii) Any special instructions governing the methods of starting and
recall.

(viii) Recall numbers or letters, when used, of the yachts entered.

For starting systems see rules 4.4, 6 and 7. For recalls see rules 8 and
51.1(c).

(ix) Time allowances.

These allowances must be published before the start both for time on time
and time on distance systems – or indeed any other system so that during the
race competitors can see how they are progressing.

(x) Length of course or courses.

This may be necessary when the time limit before the start depends on mean
speed (see rule 3.2(a)viii) or when handicaps are worked out with a time-on-
distance system (see rule 3.2(b)ix).

(xi) Method by which competitors will be notified of any change of course.

Instructions describing the courses are dealt with in rule 3.2(a)(iii). The methods to be used to alter programmed courses before the start are given in rule 4.3. This part of rule 3.2(b) concerns those changes of course which are decided on and signalled (notably on lakes because of the variable wind conditions) after the start, that is while the race is in progress, usually at the end of a round or at a given mark. It is unnecessary to add that instructions of this sort must be as precise as possible otherwise they will fall foul of rules 3.4 (Changes) or 3.5 (Oral instructions).

(xii) Information on tides and currents.

(xiii) Prizes.

See rules 14 (Award of prizes) and 11 (Ties); the same subject appears in rule 2(g) (Notice of race).

(xiv) Whether rule 72.4 (Alternative Penalties), will apply.

(xv) Any special time limit within which, and address at which, a written protest shall be lodged, and the prescribed fee, if any, which shall accompany it.

(xvi) Time and place at which protests will be heard.

(xvii) When it is essential to determine the result of a race or a series of races which will qualify a yacht to compete in a later stage of the event, that decisions of protests shall not be subject to appeal. A national authority may prescribe that its approval be required for such a procedure.

It is extremely awkward when the organizers of an important series cannot present the trophy at the end because a competitor wishes to appeal. However, it is logical that before any competitor loses his right of appeal the ability and experience of the protest committee must be considerable; that is why any "national authority may prescribe that its approval may be required for such a procedure". In fact the RYA prescribes that: "in these circumstances written approval shall be obtained from the RYA and prominently displayed at the time and place of the competition". This written approval is requested in writing giving the composition of the proposed jury.

This rule does not cover international racing such as Olympic or World Championships, because, unlike some classes which have their own appeals jury (see for example the case quoted in para. i of rule 3.2(a)) in the IYRU organization no super-national jury of second instance exists. This is explained by the fact that the juries for these special regattas are always composed of experienced men of well-known ability whose decisions are difficult to criticize. The same argument is dealt with in rule 2(j) (Notice of race).

(xviii) Whether races *postponed* or *abandoned* for the day will be sailed later and, if so, when and where.

A re-sail may or may not happen, but if it does competitors must know about it beforehand. After racing, however, the communication of this information is covered by rule 5.3.

(xix) Disposition to be made of a yacht appearing at the start alone in her class.

This paragraph can also cover cases when more than one yacht comes to the start but less than the minimum laid down in the sailing instructions (for example "the race will not take place if at least three competitors do not appear at the start"). Similar dispositions may be laid down for example concerning the minimum number of yachts which must be entered or which must effectively *start* in order to make a race valid. Remember that this may already have been dealt with in the notice of race (rule 2(e)) where "any restrictions or conditions regarding entries or number of starters or competitors" may be laid down.

(xx) Time and place at which results of races will be posted.

(xxi) Location of official notice board and signal stations ashore.

It is generally advisable to state where and when a notice board will be displayed with the official results and other instructions, such as alterations to sailing instructions etc. Better still if competitors are made responsible for going and checking every day what has been put up there.

(xxii) Whether rule 60.3, (Means of Propulsion), is in effect and the signals to be used.

3.3   DISTRIBUTION
The sailing instructions shall be available to each yacht entitled to *race*.

3.4   CHANGES
The race committee may change the sailing instructions by notice, in writing if practicable, given to each yacht affected not later than the warning signal of her class.

3.5   ORAL INSTRUCTIONS
Oral instructions shall not be given except in accordance with procedure specifically set out in the sailing instructions.

Rule 4. Signals

INTERNATIONAL CODE AND OTHER FLAG SIGNALS

Unless otherwise prescribed by the national authority or in the sailing instructions, the following International Code flags shall be used as indicated and when displayed alone shall apply to all classes, and when displayed over a class signal they shall apply to the designated class only:

4.2 SIGNALLING THE COURSE

Unless otherwise prescribed by the national authority, the race committee shall either make the appropriate signal or otherwise designate the course before or with the warning signal.

4.3 CHANGING THE COURSE

The course for a class which has not *started* may be changed: —

(a) when the only change is that a starting *mark* is to be shifted, by shifting the *mark* before the preparatory signal is made; or

(b) by displaying the appropriate *postponement* signal and indicating the new course before or with the warning signal to be displayed after the lowering of the *postponement* signal; or

(c) by displaying a course signal or by removing and substituting a course signal before or with the warning signal.

4.4 SIGNALS FOR STARTING A RACE

(a) Unless otherwise prescribed by the national authority or in the sailing instructions, the signals for starting a race shall be made at five-minute intervals exactly, and shall be
either: —

System 1	Warning Signal	— Class flag broken out or distinctive signal displayed.
	Preparatory Signal	— International Code flag "P" broken out or distinctive signal displayed.
	Starting Signal	— Both warning and preparatory signals lowered.

In System 1 when classes are started: —

(i) at ten-minute intervals —
the warning signal for each succeeding class shall be broken out or displayed at the starting signal of the preceding class, and

(ii) at five-minute intervals —
the preparatory signal for the first class to start shall be left displayed until the last class *starts*. The warning signal for each succeeding class shall be broken out or displayed at the preparatory signal of the preceding class,
or: —

System 2	Warning Signal	— White shape.
	Preparatory Signal	— Blue shape.
	Starting Signal for first class to start	— Red shape.

In System 2 each signal shall be lowered one minute before the next is hoisted.
Class flags when used shall be broken out not later than the preparatory signal for each class.
In starting a series of classes:
(i) at ten-minute intervals —
the starting signal for each class shall be the warning signal for the next, and

(ii) at five-minute intervals —
the preparatory signal for each class shall be the warning signal for the next.

(b) Although rules 4.1 "P" and 4.4(a) specify five-minute intervals between signals, this shall not interfere with the power of a race committee to start a series of races at any intervals which it considers desirable.

(c) A warning signal shall not be made before its scheduled time, except with the consent of all yachts entitled to *race*.

(d) When a significant error is made in the timing of the interval between any of the signals for starting a race, the recommended procedure is to have a general recall, *postponement* or *abandonment* of the race whose start is directly affected by the error and a corresponding *postponement* of succeeding races. Unless otherwise prescribed in the sailing instructions a new warning signal shall be made. When the race is not recalled, *postponed* or *abandoned* after an error in the timing of the interval, each succeeding signal shall be made at the correct interval from the preceding signal.

4.5   FINISHING SIGNAL
Blue flag or shape. When displayed at the finish.
Means: —
"The committee boat is on station at the finishing line."

4.6   OTHER SIGNALS
The sailing instructions shall designate any other special signals and shall explain their meaning.

4.7   CALLING ATTENTION TO SIGNALS
Whenever the race committee makes a signal, except "S" before the warning signal, it shall call attention to its action as follows: —
Three guns or other sound signals when displaying "N", or "N over X", or "N over First Substitute".
Two guns or other sound signals when displaying the "First Substitute", "AP", or "S".
One gun or other sound signal when making any other signal, including the lowering of "AP" when the length of the postponement is not signalled or of "N" over "X" or of "First Substitute".

4.8   VISUAL STARTING SIGNALS TO GOVERN
Times shall be taken from the visual starting signals, and a failure or mistiming of a gun or other sound signal calling attention to starting signals shall be disregarded.

1. Flag signals

The signals listed in rule 4 are not exclusive, others may be prescribed in the sailing instructions, by the national authority or by class associations. In fact, however, nowadays other signals are increasingly rare and the IYRU systems are in worldwide use. Naturally the rule does not go into detail about their use but logically to make them official, sailing instructions must specify where, when and how they are to be displayed; and this will normally be where ever the race committee, whether ashore or afloat, settles down to run the start and the finish. Up to a certain time before the start, signals may also be displayed at the organizing yacht club or elsewhere; (there for example signals for a few hours' postponement or for defining the whereabouts of the course chosen for that day (see rule 3.2(b)xxxi). Other signals (such as abandonment, cancellation, shortening course) may be displayed by a special committee boat circulating in the starting area but to avoid mistakes she should fly some distinctive flag already specified in the sailing instructions.

Before looking at the signals one by one note that when a signal is displayed above a class signal it normally applies for that class only. When there is no class flag the signal applies to all the classes in the programme.

"AP", Answering Pendant — Postponement Signal
　　Means: —
　　(a) "All races not started are *postponed*.
　　The warning signal will be made one minute after this signal is lowered."
　　(One sound signal shall be made with the lowering of the "AP".)
　　(b) Over one ball or shape.
　　"The scheduled starting times of all races not started are *postponed* fifteen minutes."
　　(This postponement can be extended indefinitely by the addition of one ball or shape for every fifteen minutes.).
　　(c) Over one of the numeral pendants 1 to 9.
　　"All races not started are *postponed* one hour, two hours, etc."
　　(d) Over code flag "A".
　　"All races not started are *postponed* to a later date."

(a) *Postponement for an indefinite period.* The well-known pendant, an inevitable companion of long waits in flat calms, invokes the postponement of the race to some later time (rule 5.1(a)) on the same day. It can be hoisted at any moment before the starting signal and means that the starting signal instead of being at the printed time will be postponed for an undetermined time, that is to say postponed until the series of starting signals required by rule 4.4(a) is begun or begins again.

To tell competitors that the end of this indeterminate period is at hand and to call their attention to the beginning of the starting period the answering pendant has to be lowered exactly one minute before the new warning signal; that is 11 minutes before the new start. It must be accompanied by a gun (or whatever sound signal is being used) so as to wake up all those half asleep waiting for the wind.

Hoisting the answering pendant, because it is a signal which causes a change in the programme, is always accompanied not by one but by two guns or other sound signals (rule 4.7) as are the signals for shortening course and general recall.

(b) *A postponement for exactly 15, 30 or 45 minutes.* When you are not waiting for wind and it is possible to foresee by how much the start will have to be postponed, precise periods can be signalled by means of units of a quarter of an hour.

Postponing the start by fifteen minutes is signalled by hoisting the answering pendant over a ball or shape; by thirty minutes over two balls or shapes; forty five minutes over three and so on. Every ball or shape counts for fifteen minutes, they only have to be added up and there you are.

If the forecast turns out to have been too optimistic so that at the end of the postponement period (for example forty five minutes represented by an answering pendant over three balls) a further fifteen minutes is needed it is enough to "add another ball or shape".

(c) *Postponement for one or more hours.* The system of the answering pendant and balls and shapes in (b) above could be used but for simplification the rule lays down that for a postponement of an hour or more the code number pendant corresponding to the number of hours of postponement is hoisted under the answering pendant. The postponement of an hour and a fraction of an hour can be signalled by coupling numeral pendants and balls; for example a postponement for an hour and a half can be signalled by displaying the answering pendant over two balls in their turn placed over numeral pendant one (rule 4.1(c)).

(d) *Postponement to a later day.* To get this message across the answering pendant is flown over international code flag A and the date, time and place for the resail must be notified to those concerned by signal or otherwise (rule 5.3). This signal may only be a conventional signal as specified in the sailing instructions (for example International Code flag Q may mean that all starts are postponed to the same hour on the next day).

"B" — Protest signal.
  When displayed by a yacht.
  Means: —
  "I intend to lodge a protest."

"I" — Round the Ends Starting Rule
  Broken out one minute before the starting signal is made, accompanied
  by one long sound signal. (This signal is used only when it is prescribed
  in the Sailing Instructions.)
  Means: —
  "The one-minute period relating to the Round the Ends Starting Rule
  51.1(c) has commenced."

When displayed by a yacht means that she is acknowledging an infringement of a rule of Part IV according to Appendix 3.2 as prescribed by sailing instructions.

"L" — Means:
  (a) When displayed ashore:
  "A notice to competitors has been posted on the notice board."
  (b) When displayed afloat:
  "Come within hail," or "Follow me."

No comment is required.

"M" — Mark Signal.
  When displayed on a buoy, vessel, or other object.
  Means: —
  "Round or pass the object displaying this signal instead of the *mark*
  which it replaces."

This flag is used in an emergency when a substitute mark has had to be placed (see rule 9). The new mark with flag M atop, replaces the old with all the effects of rules 6 (Starting and finishing lines), 51 (Sailing the course) and 52 (Touching a mark). Substitution is only allowed when the new mark is in the identical spot of the old. Only in this way can competitors realize that the replacement has taken place unless they are supplied with further information, extremely improbable in an emergency.

"N" — Abandonment Signal.
    Means: —
    "All races are *abandoned.*"

"N over X" — Abandonment and Re-sail Signal.
    Means: —
    "All races are *abandoned* and will shortly be re-sailed.
    The warning signal will be made one minute after this signal is lowered."
    (One sound signal shall be made with the lowering of "N over X").

"N over First Substitute" — Cancellation Signal.
    Means: —
    "All races are *cancelled*".

No comment on the last three is needed except that rule 4.7 requires all of them to be accompanied by three guns (or other sound signals)

"P" — Preparatory Signal.
    Means: —
    "The class designated by the warning signal will *start* in five minutes exactly."

·The Blue Peter signals 5 minutes to the start and must be accompanied by a gun or sound signal (see 4.4(a) system 1).

"S" — Shorten Course Signal.
    Means: —
    (a) at or near the starting line
    "Sail the shortened course prescribed in the sailing instructions."
    (b) at or near the finishing line
    "*Finish* the race either:
        (i) at the prescribed finishing line at the end of the round still to be completed by the leading yacht or
        (ii) in any other manner prescribed in the sailing instructions under rule 3.2(a) (vii)."
    (c) at or near a rounding *mark*.
    "*Finish* between the nearby *mark* and the committee boat."

A course may be shortened before the start for any reason but afterwards only for bad weather, for insufficient wind or a mark missing or shifted or for "other reasons directly affecting safety or the fairness of the competition" (rule 5.1).

Flag "S" serves in both cases and can be displayed as required: (a) on the starting line or near it; (b) on the finishing line or near it; (c) in any other place (always naturally on the course). Let us look at the three cases one by one.

(a) When displayed on the starting line (before the start) flag "S" brings into force the prescriptions that have been laid down in the sailing instructions for shortening course (but if none exist flag "S" before the start is meaningless).

(b) When displayed on the finishing line (practically speaking this can only happen after a race has started) it means that the race will *finish* at the prescribed finishing line at the end of the round still to be completed by the leading yacht. This is only so, however, when the sailing instructions do not give other directions for *finishing* under rule 3.2(a)(vii), that is when there are no special prescriptions for shortening course generally or for the finishing line in the case of a shortened course.

In FIV 1965/3 which we have already mentioned when dealing with rule 3.2(a)(viii) it was observed that "when the sailing instructions do not expressly forbid shortening course the race committee can always do so by applying rule 5.1(b); and in this case the course will be shortened in the way prescribed by rule 4.1S(b)(i) on the understanding that for that race no "other manner prescribed in the sailing instructions under rule 3.2(a)(vii) exists".

Let us also remember the recommendation in rule 3.2(a)(vii) that as far as possible sailing instructions for *finishing* a shortened course should not differ from those laid down for *finishing* the full course; it is always preferable to shorten course by cutting down the number of rounds and finishing at the ordinary finishing line. In this context YRA 1938/19 (which we have already mentioned in the comment to rule 3.2(a)(vii) is worth looking at again stressing as it does that to finish the round the finishing line must be crossed in the direction of the course from the last mark.

(c) The third case in rule 4.1S(c) requires the shortened course signal to be displayed "at or near a rounding *mark*".

This can happen when for one of the reasons listed in rule 5.1(b) the committee want to finish the race as soon as possible.

In such urgent cases the committee boat must move to meet the competitors and place itself near them setting a finishing line between the boat itself and a *mark* of the course. The boat displaying flag "S" must be the committee boat itself or some other official boat and to avoid mistakes it is a good thing for it to fly a blue flag or shape which, displayed at the finish, means "the committee boat is on station at the finishing line" (rule 4.5).

Dealing as we are with a signal which, as those of postponement and general recall, has a great effect on the normal running of the race it is accompanied by two guns or other sound signals (rule 4.7)

"X" – Individual Recall
  Broken out immediately after the starting signal is made, accompanied by one long sound signal.
  Means: –
  "One or more yachts have started prematurely or have infringed the Round the Ends Starting Rule 51.1(c)."

Flag "X" is the recall signal for premature starters (rule 8) or for yachts which have infringed the rule requiring them to come back across the extensions of the line (rule 51.1(c)). It must be displayed immediately after the starting signal and must be accompanied by a long sound signal to call the attention of the culprits.

"Y" – Life Jacket Signal
    Means: –
    "Life jackets or other adequate personal buoyancy shall be worn while *racing* by all helmsmen and crews, unless specifically excepted in the sailing instructions."
    When this signal is displayed after the warning signal is made, failure to comply shall not be cause for disqualification.
    Notwithstanding anything in this rule, it shall be the individual responsibility of each competitor to wear a life jacket or other adequate personal buoyancy when conditions warrant. A wet suit is not adequate personal buoyancy.

No comment.

"First Substitute" – General Recall Signal.
    Means: –
    "The class is recalled for a new start as provided in the sailing instructions."
    Unless the sailing instructions prescribe some other signal, the warning signal will be made one minute after this signal is lowered.

This means a general recall and a new start (see rule 8.3(a)) and guns are required but even more noise is often needed to ensure that the yachts return and do not disappear over the horizon.

Red Flag – Displayed by committee boat.
    Means: –
    "Leave all marks to port."
Green Flag – Displayed by committee boat.
    Means: –
    "Leave all marks to starboard."
Blue Flag or Shape – Finishing Signal.

No comment.

2. Signalling the course

Courses are extremely varied both in length and type, they can be long offshore races, transoceanic races, short seven-mile races for Snipes and such like or even shorter for sailboards. They may be classical triangles, they may be windward and leeward legs between two marks or they can be rectangular, based on four marks particularly adapted for planing centreboard boats; then there are courses with a great number of legs especially in areas where navigational buoys are already laid. In every instance the course must be competently and precisely described in the instructions (rule 3.2(a)ii) and frequently there will be more than one course because, unless you are dealing with Olympic-type races starting out at sea which the race committee can orientate according to the wind, the organizers will have provided more than one course (especially near the coast with a shore line) so as to have some choice according to the wind. Even when races start offshore good instructions usually lay down shorter or reserve courses for particular weather conditions (too much or too little wind). All these variations can be distinguished by letters or numbers and the competitors thus informed of the course chosen before the race. The course signal must always be displayed before or contemporaneously with the warning signal, never afterwards (rule 4.2).

3. Changing the course

After the start the course can be shortened but it cannot be changed in the sense that you cannot choose another. However, particular systems (rule 5.1(c)) altering the course during a race are permitted (see also the comment rule 3.4(b)xi). As we have already seen in rule 4.2 (Course signals) everything to do with the courses must be decided on and signalled at least ten minutes before the start and not after the warning signal. Included in the course signals are those prescribing the required side for marks (a red flag to port and a green flag to starboard). There are two ways a change of course can be communicated:

(a) by displaying the postponement signal and signalling the new course before or at the same time as the warning signal that precedes the postponed start. Before displaying the warning signal you must always remove the postponement signal (it cannot logically co-exist with a signal activating a start as discussed in paragraph 4);

(b) displaying a new course signal or taking away that already displayed and substituting another (in both cases before or at least with the ten minute signal). Naturally system (a) which is linked to a postponement allows probably at least fifteen minutes but while in reality (given that the postponement is given some time before the start and that the new course is signalled simultaneously) can be very much more. Whereas with system (b) tied to the ordinary timetable, much less time is available before the start (unless the change is signalled well before the ten-minute gun). Precisely for these reasons the rule recommends the use of system (a) when the fact of changing course brings with it other lengthy operations (moving the committee boat, moving line marks and for the competitors the possible alteration of sails aboard which can only be done before the five-minute gun).

Olympic regattas and courses have their own change of course built into them whereby during the race itself the leg to the weather mark remains a windward leg but may change bearing.

4. Starting signals

Everyone knows that starting consists of a warning signal (the class flag) followed at exactly five minutes by the preparatory signal (International Code flag "P") followed in its turn also at five minutes exactly by the lowering of both flags at the moment of the start. This means that using intervals of five minutes between signals the warning signal must be displayed ten minutes and the preparatory signal five minutes before the time fixed for the start. The rule, however, permits the use of larger or smaller intervals when prescribed by the national authority or by the sailing instructions (rule 4.4(b)).

Another system common in America is also described in the rule: at ten minutes a white shape is hoisted, at five minutes a blue shape and at the start a red shape. The three shapes may have the advantage of being more visible because flags are invisible when the wind is directly to or from them and in a calm. In addition rule 4.4(a) system 2, prescribes that each shape must be lowered one minute before the next is hoisted and these intervals of one minute during which no shapes can be seen undoubtedly draw the attention of the competitors to the next signal and help to mark the time.

Rule 4.4(c) lays down that "a warning signal shall not be made before its scheduled time except with the consent of all yachts entitled to *race*", and it is obviously logical that a race start cannot be made earlier than published because a competitor, once he knows the starting time, will prepare as seems best to him and must not be subject to surprises.

Rule 4.4(d) admits that there may be an error in the timing of the interval between one or other of the signals for starting a race and recommends that when this happens there should be a general recall or that the race should be abandoned or postponed. Since this is only a recommendation if the mistake does not affect the start seriously (for example if there is a difference of at most one or two seconds, or if the error is in the first interval between the ten and the five minute gun) it may be ignored. Otherwise a new start is needed paying attention to rule 8.2(b) or the sailing instructions when a general recall has been given, and to rules 5.2 and 5.3 in cases of postponement or abandonment.

If the race committee decides against a general recall, postponing or abandoning and lets the race go on because they believe that the mistake in the timing of the intervals is not important and has not damaged anyone, "each succeeding signal shall be made at the correct interval from the proceeding signal", so that the intervals which follow between signals are correct. Thus if the warning signal is a minute late on the scheduled time the preparatory and starting signals must be one minute late so that there remains exactly five minutes between each signal and the competitors can check equally well once they have got the first signal. See also rule 4.8 (Visual starting signals to govern).

5. Finishing signals

"Blue flag or shape" which when displayed at the finish means the committee boat is on station at the finishing line. No comment is required here but remember the definition of *finishing* which requires a yacht to cross "the finishing line from the direction of the course from the last *mark*".

6. Other signals

This may cover a great variety of signals meaning for example: "put on life jackets", "permission to remove lifejackets", "the five-minute rule applies", "protest received", etc. For such signals which must be written into the instructions, there are no particular rules; included are those which indicate required sides of *marks*, the magnetic course for the first mark, courses written on blackboards, etc., and since these form part of signalling the course they are subject to rules 4.2 and 4.3.

7. Calling attention to signals

We have already seen how many guns (or other acoustic signals) must accompany each signal. Rule 4.7 divides signals into three categories according to their importance and assigns three guns to "N" (abandonment), to "N over X" (abandonment and re-sail) and to "N over first substitute" (cancellation), because of their decisive and definitive effect on the race; it requires two guns for the answering pendant (postponement), for "first substitute" (general recall) and for "S" (shortened course) because of their considerable effect in modifying the normal running of the race. Finally it requires only one gun for all other signals (with the exception of "S" when it is displayed before the warning signal because since there is still time before the start it is superfluous to call attention to it).

But what are all the other signals which must be accompanied by a sound signal? Does the rule mean only those signals made with flags (including the other signals in paragraph 6) or does it include those for example made with a shape, by letters on a board, by loud hailer or other similar means?

In RYA 1967/2 (St. Mawes Sailing Club) the RYA specified that the term "any other signals" in rule 4.7 refers only to the signals listed in rule 4.1 (with the already mentioned exceptions of "S" before the ten-minute gun, and in rule 4.4. This is authoritative and unexceptionable but nevertheless we think it advisable (especially for the signals in 4.2 and 4.3, Courses and changes of courses) to be generous with sound signals whether guns, hooters, klaxons or bells.

8. Visual starting signals to govern

Finally rule 4.8 specifies that the start time must be based on the visual signals ignoring misfires, or mistakes in the sound signals. This perfectly accords with the letter and spirit of the various parts of the rule, because the signal real and proper is that given by the flag or the shape (in rule 4.4) and the guns or other acoustic signals serve only to draw the attention of the competitor to the signals displayed. IYRU No. 70 (RYA 1974/7 *Rebel* and *Ubibug* v. Race Committee) stresses that "rule 4.8, while under the heading 'visual signals to govern' refers only to starting signals and the taking of time. In the circumstances covered by rules 4.7 and 8.2(b), it is of less importance that the visual and sound signals should be made contemporaneously. They are, however, mandatory unless the sailing instructions provide otherwise."

This decision has been corroborated by more recent case (RYA 1977/1 *Windhover 20* v. Race Committee) where it was held that "there is no onus upon a premature starter to respond to a recall when the visual signal is not accompanied by the prescribed sound signal".

**Rule 5.
Postponing,
abandoning or
cancelling a
race and
changing or
shortening
course**

5.1   The race committee: —

(a) before the starting signal may shorten the course or *postpone* or *cancel* a race for any reason, and

(b) after the starting signal may shorten the course by finishing a race at any rounding *mark* or *abandon* or *cancel* a race because of foul weather endangering the yachts, or because of insufficient wind, or because a *mark* is missing or has shifted or for other reasons directly affecting safety or the fairness of the competition.

(c) after the starting signal may change the course at any rounding *mark* subject to proper notice being given to each yacht as prescribed in the sailing instructions.

5.2   After a *postponement* the ordinary starting signals prescribed in rule 4.4(a), (Signals), shall be used, and the postponement signal, when a general one, shall be hauled down one minute before the first warning or course signal is made.

5.3   The race committee shall notify all yachts concerned by signal or otherwise
        when and where a race *postponed* or *abandoned* will be sailed.

To re-capitulate from Part I, to *cancel* a race means to erase it from the
programme; it will never be sailed, and this cancellation may be decided upon
both before and after the start; *postponement* means putting the start off until
later, a decision taken naturally before the start; *abandonment* means stopping
a race which has already been started which can then either be re-sailed or
cancelled.

Before the start the race committee has absolute powers to cancel, postpone
or shorten course, as rule 5.1 says they can take such a decision "for any
reason".

After the starting signal, however, the powers of the race committee are
limited and well defined; they can shorten course ("by finishing the race at any
rounding mark"), or they can abandon or cancel a race, but only for the
particular reasons which the rule first specifies (foul weather endangering the
yachts, insufficient wind or the disappearance or shifting of a mark) or
generically "for other reasons directly affecting fairness or the safety of the
competition". This definition is abstract and ample but in practice the three
examples given in the rule are those which generally in fact happen although we
could add a fourth to them, a common occurrence affecting both the safety and
fairness of the race; that is sunset, with the inevitable invisibility and
uncontrollability of the competitors; except of course when rule 3.2(b)(ii) is
used in the race instructions.

What happens after one of the decisions considered in rule 5 has been taken?

In the case of *cancellation* it is clear that nothing more can happen.

In the case of *shortening course* (see rule 4.1S) the race will go on to the
finish (if it is not in due course subjected to later cancellation or abandonment
which can naturally happen even with a shortened course).

In the case of a *postponement* rule 5.2 itself lays down that the starting
procedure must be begun again including changes of course when needed. Rule
5.2 also prescribes that the postponement signal (see rule 4.1AP) must be
"hauled down one minute before the first warning or course signal is made".
This is logical because the answering pendant implies a postponement of the
start and is therefore obviously incompatible with the various starting signals
and displaying both would be contradictory.

In the case of *abandonment* (and a postponement to another day) the race
committee must by means of the proper signal (see rule 3.2(b)xviii) or in some
other way inform all interested yachts of the date, time and place of the re-sail.

What, however, should be done when the abandonment is signalled after one
or more boats have already crossed the *finishing* line? Should the race be
considered *abandoned* and therefore null and void for everyone or should the
yachts which have arrived be considered as having *finished* in the sense of
definition and have they therefore acquired the right to a classification and any
prize?

Fairness demands, we believe, that the second solution be adopted even
though the rule does not expressly offer advice on this sort of case. The race is
over for those who have already finished and have thus a right to be classified,
and abandoned for reasons prejudicial to the safety or fairness of the

competition for all the others, which will be classified as yachts which have not finished. Obviously the race committee since it is a facility and not an obligation (see the definition of *abandonment*) will avail themselves of the discretion not to re-sail the race.

The race committee must be careful not to exceed its powers as IYRU No. 85 (USYRU 200) illustrates. Here about 120 yachts in numerous classes sailed the same course. The last classes to arrive at a mark which had shifted by 7/8th of a mile were the Tartan 27's and Cal 25's. Various protests about the position of the mark were lodged after the finish but none from any Tartan 27 or Cal 25. The protest committee cancelled all the races, a decision which was in turn appealed by a number of Tartans and Cals. The US Appeals Committee in its decision declared: "the contention of the protest committee fails to distinguish between different procedures under which a race may be cancelled.

"Had the race committee, while the races were under way, concluded that the shifting of the racing mark adversely affected the fairness of the competition, it could have made the appropriate cancellation signal under rule 4.1. That timing and method of cancelling the races would have been a proper exercise of their discretion under rule 9.1. If" – they went on – "the protest committee had . . . cancelled only those races for the classes in which protests had been filed, the matter would in all probability have ended there. However, they went further and cancelled races in which no protests were filed, no hearing held and 'no evidence of any adverse effect on the competition' appears in the record." The races for the two classes were reinstated.

This opinion is confirmed by an Italian appeal case (FIV 1970/7) as follows: "a yacht which has *finished*", in the sense of the relevant definition, has acquired the right to be classified as has any yacht that has satisfied the conditions prescribed in the notice of race and the sailing instructions, that is of competing and finishing a given course while respecting the predetermined rules of racing. For this reason any abandonment or cancellation of the race decided on after one yacht has correctly *finished* cannot destroy her right to a result because otherwise it would do away with the object of every competition: to give prizes to the best, understanding by this such yachts that, thanks to their greater capacity, have succeeded in finishing the race before the others and in a reasonable time. And in fact there is no doubt that an abandonment or cancellation which affects all the competitors indiscriminately, damages those already *finished* and unfairly helps the others which have showed themselves to be less able than the first (and you might even encourage a competitor to wait behind on purpose with the only object of getting the race cancelled).

"According to rule 5.1(b)" – continued the appeals committee – "abandonment and cancellation can exceptionally be adopted after the start only for reasons of safety or because of circumstances which could prejudice the fairness of the race and distort the results. We remember for example the case of a committee boat in a storm, which cut short the race and left the finishing line to go to help a large number of competitors in danger disregarding the arrival of a few boats just at the finishing line.

"However, even in exceptional cases foreseen by rule 5.1(b) the opinion of this appeals committee is that a yacht which succeeds in finishing acquires the right to be classified in the order of arrival. Even here cancellation should be avoided as far as possible. It is often fairer to abandon the race without a re-sail and classify as equal all those not finished with points under rule 11 or as if they had retired.

"Race committees should remember that this may be fair when there is no handicap but it may well be that in a handicap race in such circumstances as we have been discussing the race must be cancelled or abandoned, including those who have already finished, for they have not won by arriving first, they have only achieved a certain elapsed time which will then be liable to correction."

The rule also provides (rule 5.1(c)) for a change of course adopted after the start, that is during a race. Changes of this sort are normally justified by a late change in wind direction which if marked, could prejudice the fairness of the competition.

Two conditions are laid down for changing the course:

1. the sailing instructions must provide for it and describe it and the accompanying signals in detail;
2. the change must be made at a rounding *mark* where yachts can see the signals. For example the windward leg is commonly changed after the first round whenever the wind changes more than, say, 25° while the boats are completing the first round; to show that the weather mark has been moved a signal is displayed on the committee boat near the chosen mark (normally number one) which warns of the change and gives the new direction for marks numbers two and three. With this abundant and repeated sound signals are made when any competitor passes to call his attention to what is going on.

Rule 6. Starting and finishing lines

The starting and finishing lines shall be either: —

(a) a line between a *mark* and a mast or staff on the committee boat or station clearly identified in the sailing instructions;

(b) a line between two *marks;* or

(c) the extension of a line through two stationary posts, with or without a *mark* at or near its outer limit, inside which the yachts shall pass.

For types (a) and (c) of starting or finishing lines the sailing instructions may also prescribe that a *mark* will be laid at or near the inner end of the line, in which case yachts shall pass between it and the outer *mark.*

The rule itself instructs us how finishing and starting lines must be constituted and lists three fundamental types.

(a) The first of these is represented by a "line between a *mark* and a mast or staff" (see for example fig. 1a); the mark will necessarily be at sea while the mast can be either on the committee boat or ashore, probably where the race committee is standing. What matters is that the sailing instructions (rule 3.2(a)vi) describe both ends exactly and completely and indicate their characteristics (for example, a buoy with a checked white and blue flag, a red buoy with a spherical orange top mark, a black and white light buoy flashing green, a buoy bearing the figure "one", a black buoy marked with the letter A; a white and red horizontally striped mast, a mast with black and white longitudinal stripes surmounted by a white flag, a white mast surmounted by a red triangle with the point downwards, etc.).

In order to avoid competitors crowding round the committee boat (or if the committee is ashore to avoid them coming too close in if there are rocks or other dangers inshore) another mark can be laid to show the inner limit of the line. In this case, for starting and finishing (see the definitions in Part I) the line to cross continues to be that joining the outside buoy with the mast and competitors need only leave the inner limit mark on the prescribed side (see definition of *marks* and rule 51.3). However, when the starting line is very long a half-way mark is often laid with different characteristics from the limit mark. This must not be considered a *mark* in the sense of the definition but merely an *obstruction*.

(b) The second type of line described by the rule consists of "a line between two *marks*"; this differs little from the preceding line and is valuable for its simplicity and for the little likelihood of problems developing in unusual situations unlike the third system which can give rise to considerable problems.

(c) The third type of line suggested by rule 6 consists not of a line between two marks but of "the extension of a line through two stationary posts", that is in a straight line to infinity passing through two given points (or other objects which must be conspicuous and clearly visible, generally consisting of boards or of high poles variously coloured surmounted by flags or other distinctive signals).

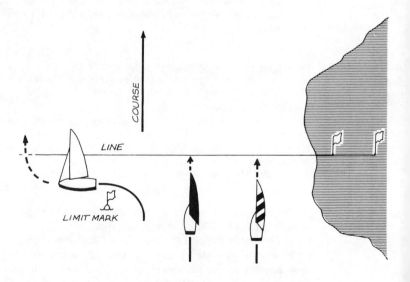

Fig. 22

This limitless transit line leads to difficulties particularly at the finish if competitors are not channelled in some way to an area where the committee aligning the two posts can see them easily, which is why such a line may have "a mark at or near its outer limit, inside which the yachts shall pass".

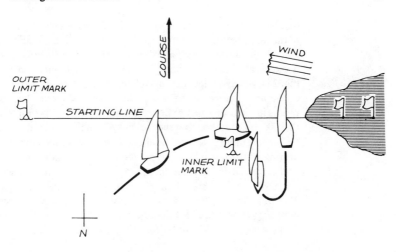

Fig. 23

Problems arise with transit lines when the outer limit mark is badly laid. Sambrooke Sturgess gives an example of this quoting RYA 1933/9 Royal Corinthian Yacht Club, where the sailing instructions showed the starting line between the buoy and two posts ashore. Because of the tide the buoy dragged ten metres to the precourse side of the line (fig. 22). Between the five-minute gun and the start two yachts passed the mark on the required side and then, keeping themselves always on the pre-course side of the line sailed a longish way out to sea parallel to the line; at the starting gun they crossed the line regularly and started. This manoeuvre gave them an advantage and the other competitors, who had kept on the right side of the line without going beyond the limit mark, protested; however, the RYA Council upheld the first two and decided they had acted as required by the racing rules since they had left the limit mark on the required side and had not crossed the line before the starting signal. They observed (and this recommendation is reprinted in the *Guide on arrangements of principal events*, published by the IYRU itself) that this would not have happened if the race committee had re-laid the limit mark if not exactly on the transit line at least on the course side of it.

This not unusual difficulty was the subject of an important decision, once IYRU No. 49 but no longer published, in which it was established that the course of the yacht in fig. 23 breached rule 6(c) because she could not be considered to have started between the inner limit mark and the outer buoy. On this occasion the jury recognized that "it is physically impossible to lay a mark exactly on the starting line".

The new rule 51.3 of the 1973 edition of the rules cleared this matter up for while the old rule laid down that "a starting *mark* has a required side for a yacht when she *starts*" (that is when she crosses the line) the new addition reads "a starting limit *mark* has a required side for a yacht from the time she is approaching the starting line to *start* until she has left the *mark* astern on the first leg". It is clear, looking again at fig. 23, that the yacht is on the wrong side of the mark before she starts, that is on the side other than that prescribed.

(d) From a transit with a limit mark it is a short step to the sort of line which is often called the three-buoy line. Here the determination to keep buoy "A" (fig. 24), which competitors must leave on a prescribed side, on the course side of the line, has led to the mark being laid 100 metres beyond the line. This results in the transit being effectively infinite and competitors can cross it where they like on condition that they leave "A" on the required side. A second buoy, "B", is laid more or less on the line so as to give competitors an indication of the bearing of the line which has no required side. After the start in each round yachts must leave all three marks, A, B, and C, on the same side. Thus at the start "B" and "C" are not *marks* in the sense of the definition and under rule 51.3 but simply obstructions; the most obvious consequence of their lower rank consisting of the fact that the competitors can hit them without incurring the penalties provided for by rule 52 (Touching a mark).

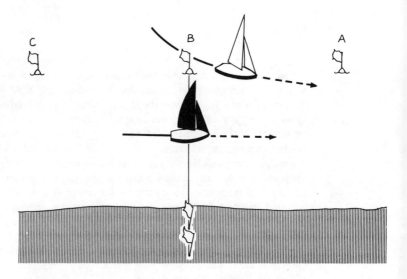

Fig. 24

The three-buoy system is thus a refinement of the transit line outlined in rule 6(c) and is mainly used when the race committee has to be ashore and cannot move the line to the direction of the wind and the first leg of the course, nor angle the finishing line at a right angle to the last leg according to normal procedure. In addition this system has the advantage of eliminating incidents subject to the starting rules because anything that happens at buoy "A" comes under the ordinary rules of the course making the job much easier for both competitors and protest committees.

(e) Other systems. In any case it must be underlined that the starting and finishing lines indicated in rule 6 are not exclusive because on the strength of rule 3.2(a)(vi) sailing instructions can prescribe or modify rules (for the exceptions see p. 49) and can therefore permit the use of other types of line. On this subject the US Appeals Committee (NAYRU 86) dismissed an appeal from a competitor who maintained that the gate start was illegal and explained the reason for its decision: "The rule cannot be expected to describe all possible procedures and programmes which race committees may decide upon to meet a variety of circumstances. The establishment of the starting line is not covered by Parts I or IV so that it is within the authority of the race committee to establish a special starting line and procedure such as a gate start."

Bear in mind anyway that to avoid excessively long lines, or methods of starting very different from the traditional ones (or as we shall see with rule 8 so as not to have to use some sudden-death system such as the one-minute rule) Appendix 12 recommends that the number of starters in important races should be limited to between forty and sixty yachts. And if that is not possible it recommends making the competitors race in series with a final between the best-placed boats in the preliminary heats.

Rule 7. Start of a race   7.1
STARTING AREA
The sailing instructions may define a starting area which may be bounded by buoys; if so, they shall not rank as *marks*.

7.2   TIMING THE START
The *start* of a yacht shall be timed from her starting signal.

A "starting area" consists of a zone defined by buoys within which all yachts intending to start in a given race must remain. The system is used in the United States and arises from localities where a number of clubs whose contingent race areas create considerable confusion because of the general movement of a lot of boats and because – from the point of view of rule 50 – it can be established without doubt who is a starter.

Any doubts the race committee may have about late starters are pretty well eliminated when a starting area is established by laying down in the sailing instructions that yachts not in the starting area at the starting signal will not be considered as starters and cannot thereafter sail the race.

It follows from the above that the buoys are not *marks* in the sense of the definition, that is to say they have no required side and they may be touched with impunity being mere *obstructions* without activating rule 52 (Touching a mark).

Timing the Start   Rule 7.2 lays down that a yacht's start shall be timed not from the moment when she crosses the starting line but when the starting signal is given for everyone.

The effect of this rule is most apparent in handicap racing particularly when the handicap consists of a correction to each yacht's elapsed time (the time taken from the start to the finish) for the time starts to run for everyone from the starting signal and not from the moment when each competitor crosses the starting line. However, in pursuit races the sailing instructions cancel this rule and arrange for each boat (or type) to start at a given time hoping that everyone will cross the finishing line together. Rule 7.2 also affects the working out of the time limit when this is determined by a given period of time from the start (not when it is fixed at a given hour of the day).

Rule 8. Recalls

8.1   Unless otherwise prescribed by the national authority or in the sailing instructions, the race committee may allot a recall number or letter to each yacht, in accordance with rule 3.2(b) (viii), (The Sailing Instructions), using yachts' national letters or distinguishing numbers when practicable.

8.2   When, at her starting signal, any part of a yacht's hull, crew or equipment is on the course side of the starting line or its extensions, or she is subject to rule 51.1(c), (Sailing the Course), the race committee shall:

(a) When each yacht has been allotted a recall number or letter —
display her recall number or letter as soon as possible and make a suitable sound signal. As soon as the recalled yacht has wholly returned to the pre-start side of the line or its extensions, the race committee shall so inform her by removing her recall number or letter. This is the preferred procedure.

(b) When no recall number or letter has been allotted —
make a sound signal and leave the class warning signal at "the dip" or display International Code Flag "X" until she has wholly returned to the pre-start side of the line or its extensions, or for such shorter period as the race committee considers reasonable.
The responsibility for returning shall rest with the yacht concerned.

(c) Follow such other procedure as may be prescribed by the national authority or in the sailing instructions.

8.3   (a) When there is either a number of unidentified premature starters, or an error in starting procedure, the race committee may make a general recall signal in accordance with rules 4.1, ("First Substitute"), and 4.7, (Calling Attention to Signals). Unless otherwise prescribed by the national authority or in the sailing instructions, new warning and preparatory signals shall be made.

(b) Except as provided in rule 31.2, (Disqualification), rule infringements before the preparatory signal for the new start shall be disregarded for the purpose of *starting* in the race to be re-started.

While rule 6 studied starting lines from a purely anatomical point of view, rule 8 deals with the problems that arise when things start to go wrong.

1. The concept of premature starters

Let us now try to clarify which yachts can, indeed must, be recalled. The rule clearly repeating the concepts already laid down in the fundamental definition of *starting* (see Part I) says that a recall must be made for a yacht that, when her starting signal is given, is found to be on the course side of the line or its extensions with any part of her hull, crew or equipment.

Sometimes there is an obligation to return even before the starting signal, particularly in the case laid down by rule 51.1(c) for those yachts which have crossed the line during the minute preceding the starting signal (obviously only when the sailing instructions do not lay down something different); in this case the return can be made only outside the starting line *marks*, that is only across the extensions of the line: and this is called "the round-the-ends-rule".

To be in the wrong it is enough for anything to be over the line, the belly of the spinnaker when starting to leeward, the head of a man on a trapeze and, theoretically, a sheet that slipped overboard its end crossing the line. In the first note to the comments of the definition of *starting* we referred to an old case (RYA 1950/11 Royal Northern Yacht Club) of a yacht which in order to hold up against the strong current had anchored before the start with her anchor on the course side of the line, the anchor and chain or cable underwater were parts of the yacht too and therefore at the start she was a premature starter.*

Remember that rule 8.2 talks of yachts which are over "the starting line or its extensions". The phrase is not clear, however, unless considered together with rule 8.2(a) and (b) which require the recall signal to be removed when the recalled yacht returns to the pre-start side of the line or its extensions and means that a yacht need not return by passing back across the real line (that is between the starting line marks) but can do so simply by turning outside the marks and returning across the extensions of the line itself (see fig. 136)

2. Individual recalls

The race committee must be able to recall any premature starter immediately. To this end the rule lays down that each yacht may be assigned a recall number or letter, listed in the sailing instructions (rule 3.2(b)viii) and recommends wherever possible the use of the sail numbers themselves (which is today usually impracticable because of the high numbers involved).

In the case of recalls these numbers or letters must (rule 8.2(a)) be displayed as soon as possible accompanied by a suitable sound signal. Putting this into practice produces two problems. First the tardy display of the signal brings with it the question "can an excessive delay in the display of the signal exonerate the recalled competitor from his obligation to re-start?". It is undoubtedly a delicate question particularly when the competitor has not realized that he was over the line (because if he knew he should return anyway, and by not doing so would lose, at least as far as his sporting conscience is concerned, the right to sign his declaration that he has fully observed all the rules while racing).

In our view a competitor must obey even a delayed recall signal although he may perhaps "protest" the race committee under rule 68.5(a) and seek redress; one thing is certain, there is no general rule which can be established beforehand, every case must be examined individually under all its aspects. For example, a yacht might be recalled but not obey the recall and continue (enjoying the rights under Part IV accorded to her by rule 44.2) to the finish or a yacht might succeed in demonstrating that she did in fact return correctly so that the race committee absolves her. This latter happened more or less to Elvstrom (Finn gold medallist) in one of the races at the Naples Olympics in 1960.

The second problem arises not from any delay in displaying the recall signal

---

* It will be up to the race officer to decide whether the premature start requires a recall or whether it is such a small offence that it gives no advantage to the competitor who has committed it and therefore has no effect on the fairness of the race.

In a start what counts is to make sure that all the competitors have an equal chance; if all start very slightly early (or if a competitor's advantage is really negligible) we believe that the boats may be left to race on without qualms of conscience because in such conditions any recall would end by becoming a punishment disproportionate to the fault and a general recall might even harm those who should not be penalized.

but from not flying it at all. The question was resolved in RYA 1954/5 (Royal Gourock Yacht Club) a yacht that realized she was a premature starter and did not correct her mistake was held to be unjustified in going on racing without re-starting. The decision is certainly very hard but it is correct because if there has been some infringement she must be punished under the rules.

But does the same answer hold good if the premature starter does not know and if the committee does not make any signal? In our opinion if nobody (including the culprit) realizes what has happened there is nothing to be done about it but if some other competitor is aware of it and protests the absence of a recall signal will not protect her from being duly penalized by a protest committee. This opinion was expressed in NAYRU 73: "the absence of a recall signal for a premature starter does not exonerate a yacht from her obligation to start correctly", but this case is no longer published because the rule itself in 8.2(b) now states that "the responsibility for returning shall rest with the yacht concerned.".

3. Sound signals

We must also consider what the term "suitable sound signal" means. The terms used by the rule is unspecific and covers gun-shot, siren, whistle, foghorn, bell, verbal recall with or without a megaphone, etc. What is certain is that this sound signal has nothing to do with the sounds required by rule 7 (Calling attention to signals) and the noise can therefore be produced by different means provided it is loud and long enough to be heard through the chaos of a start.

RYA 1965/2 (St. Mawes Sailing Club) holds that the sailing instructions must prescribe what sound signal will be used on each different occasion in a race; and adds that whenever it is intended to make recalls not by displaying numbers or letters but with a loud-hailer or megaphone it is, nevertheless, always desirable to make a distinctive noise immediately after the start to warn competitors of the fact that there is at least one premature starter and that there will therefore be one or more recalls.

IYRU No. 70 (RYA 1974/7 *Rebel* and *Ubibug* v. Race Committee) states: "the requirements of IYRU racing rule 8.2(b) regarding the making of a sound signal is mandatory, as it is essential to call the attention of all yachts starting to the fact that one or more of them was subject to recall. There is no onus upon a yacht to respond when a sound signal is not made." This has been corroborated by RYA 77/1 *Windhover No. 20* v. Race Committee.

4. Other methods

The commonest method of recall is not that of showing a specific number or letter for each premature starter but of firing a shot (or making some other sound signal) and at the same time lowering the class signal to the dip or hoisting International Code flag "X" as laid down in rule 8.2(b). In this case each competitor must check his position and the responsibility for returning "shall rest with the yacht concerned".

In a race with a lot of starters the "minute rule" may be used (or 2, 3, 4 or 5 minutes to choice) under which any yacht on or over the line in the minute (or 2, 3, 4 and 5 minutes) before the start is disqualified. However this ferocious prescription is usually modified by rule 51.1(c) which combines the one-minute and the round-the-ends rules (fig. 136) allowing a yacht which is over the line in the minute before the start to re-start by returning not across the line itself but across one of its two extensions.

The beginning of this particularly critical period is signalled with Code flag "I" and sound signal different from the starting signals laid down in the sailing instructions. These must also establish if the one-minute rule applies immediately, for the first and every other start, or only after one or more general recalls following a normal start. Unadapted rule 51.1(c) requires the round-the-ends rule to be applied automatically after a general recall. A variant of the minute rule disqualifies any yacht which enters a triangle formed by the start line and the first mark, but this method does not make anything simpler.

All in all these systems help to stop competitors crossing the line before the start and therefore avoid problems of returning boats which have been pushed across the line by their competitors or have been trying brilliant but risky starts from the course side of the line. Gerald Sambrooke Sturgess (*Yachting World*, 1962, page 406) has said that he is in favour of the strict one-minute rule for the above reasons and because he believes that the application of the rule right from the very beginning shows competitors the race committee's powers and quietens the more exuberant competitors in later races. Furthermore he observes "judging from the very audible expressions of disgust and exasperation from helmsmen who in the unencumbered starts of other days had by means of perfectly calculated times and distances always been just on the line near the committee boat and were now subject to a general recall because a number of unidentified premature starters in the middle of the line had rendered all their efforts useless.

"There is much to say in favour of imposing the five-minute rule right from the very beginning".

These observations are fair but a yacht is often forced across the line by another's fault, without being able to prove it and may thus be irremediably disqualified. In conclusion then this rule resolves many otherwise difficult situations, but it remains punitive. The truth is that one is forced to use it only when there are too many starters and it therefore underlines yet again that the fairest and best racing means avoiding huge fleets through opportune limitation of the number of starters. Appendix 12 of the IYRU rules suggest wording for the use of these special starting systems by race committees.

5. Recrossing the starting line   It is enough for the recalled yacht to return to the pre-start side of the line or its extensions "wholly" (that is when no part of the yacht remains on the course side). In particular case of rule 51.1(c) she must return, not across the line, but only across its extensions as shown in fig. 136. Returning puts her in a legitimate position as far as the effects of rule 44 (Returning to start) are concerned but does not exonerate her from having to *start* by crossing the line between the two limit marks (or the transit line) in the direction of the first mark of the course.

In order to inform the yacht when she has wholly crossed, more exactly than can be judged from aboard, the race committee "shall so inform her by removing her recall number or letter" or by informing her by voice if possible or by some other way laid down by the sailing instructions. This clearly means that a recall number must be kept up until the yacht has returned, so much so that when dealing with a race with several laps the recall number can be left up to be seen at the end of each round, to remind any yacht that she started incorrectly or rather to remind her that she has not yet *started* at all.

When rule 8.2(b) is in force, without individual recall numbers or letters, the appropriate signal is displayed until a yacht has "wholly returned to the pre-start side of the line . . . or for such shorter period as the race committee considers reasonable". For instance in a regatta with a large number of classes when there is a new start every ten minutes and the starting gun of one class is the ten minute gun of the later class it is unlikely that a recall signal will be left up for longer than five minutes and certainly any boat which has not turned back in that time would probably not still be able to see the signal.

It can also happen that a recalled yacht comes back correctly across the line but the committee does not immediately acknowledge it as it should and is late with the signal authorizing her to re-start. We believe that once she has effectively completed her obligations a yacht which has put herself in the right need not be further prejudiced by the inefficiency of others and has the right to re-start without waiting. Naturally in the case of contestation there may be problems of fact needing suitable proof; but certainly a competitor who when starting goes through a period of extreme tension cannot be expected to wait patiently while some unaware and distracted race official fails to carry out his side of the bargain.

6. General recall (rule 8.3(a))

Experience shows that when there are too many starters (a common source of trouble) and when therefore the line is too long, competitors at the centre hidden by sails, or those too far from the limit marks to see them clearly, begin unconsciously to push forward and vacillate on the line; then those nearby not to be left behind and not realizing that the others are already over, sail over too so that the whole central section of the long line of yachts begins curving out more and more until the premature starters are too many to be identified or recalled and a general recall is inevitable.

In this case, as when there is a mistake in the starting procedure, a general recall avoids injustices by beginning the whole thing over again, starting with the warning signal unless the national authority or the sailing instructions prescribe otherwise. Most important, a general recall cancels all breaches of the rules committed at the annulled start together with any committed before the preparatory signal of the new start (and this is obvious since a yacht is *racing* from the first preparatory signal and continues to be so, notwithstanding the general recall, until she has *finished*).

Even those making a good start lose out so a general recall is marginally the best way to put matters right when the only alternative is to let everyone go, thus rewarding indiscipline; and from this point of view the inexorable selection brought about by the various minute rules is understandable and may be preferable. It should be remembered that rule 8.3(a) can be applied only when there is a number of unidentified premature starters. When these can be identified there is no need for a general recall and all yachts over the line can be penalized. In one case a race officer, after three or four starts, finally allowed the race to go on when all but ten yachts were across the line; the ten "goodies" were identifiable and all the others were disqualified and the race officer was considered to have been right to disqualify known premature starters which did not return even though there had been so many.

Remember that the expunging of all faults committed before the preparatory signal of the new start is complete except as provided in rule 31.2 – Disqualification. Under this rule a yacht can be disqualified before or after racing that is before the preparatory signal and after having arrived, finished or retired, whenever she has seriously hindered a yacht or has infringed the sailing instructions.

Rule 9. Marks   MARK MISSING

9.1   (a) When any *mark* either is missing or has shifted, the race committee shall, when possible, replace it in its stated position, or substitute a new one with similar characteristics or a buoy or vessel displaying International Code flag "M" – the *mark* signal.

(b) When it is impossible either to replace the *mark* or to substitute a new one in time for the yachts to round or pass it, the race committee may, at its discretion, act in accordance with rule 5.1, (Postponing, Abandoning or Cancelling a Race and Changing or Shortening Course).

9.2   MARK UNSEEN

When races are sailed in fog or at night, dead reckoning alone need not necessarily be accepted as evidence that a *mark* has been rounded or passed.

In spite of the generality of its title this rule is limited to the procedure to be followed when a mark of the course is missing or has moved. More about marks is to be found under the definition of *mark* and in rules 51 (Sailing the course) and 52 (Touching a mark).

1. A mark which has shifted   By the expression "shifted" the rule alludes to some movement of the mark, generally due to wind or currents, and almost always arising from its being badly laid so that the characteristics of the course indicated in the sailing instructions are modified.

These cases must be looked at one by one to see on each occasion whether the shift has been such as to make the race unfair; either because some yachts have been able to reach the mark in its new position more easily than others (and bear in mind that a few metres of difference may mean you can lay it – or not – on one tack) or in the sense that yachts may have deliberately sailed a special course to arrive at the point where the buoy should be but is not, or again in the sense that they will have tacked too early and so on.

Facts alone can tell whether a small shift has really altered the course or whether a hundred metres has made no difference at all to anyone.

An unusual case was looked at by the USSR YRF and is now IYRU No. 56. Yachts P and S, close hauled on different tacks, were nearing the end of the starting line on converging courses (see fig. 25). P (on port) did not bother about altering course to give way, and in addition, after the starting signal, ended up with her port side against the buoy, dragging it along for a short distance; as soon as it was free the buoy sprang back and touched S on her starboard side and S protested P for breach of rules 36 and 52.1 as was logical and, relying on rule 9.1, asked the jury to order a re-sail. Her first protest was accepted and P was disqualified, her second request however which would have led to the race being abandoned under rule 12 (Yacht materially damaged) was refused because the jury held that "rule 9.1 applies only to a mark which is nowhere near its designated position and does not apply to a mark which shifts as a result of another yacht touching it".

2. Mark missing   A missing mark infers that the buoy has sunk or disappeared as for example when a committee has optimistically allowed a manned vessel to act as a mark and that vessel, deciding that its duty is to go and rescue someone, suddenly leaves its appointed place. In this case it is evident that, if the mark of the course is missing, the course is faulty and cannot be completed in accordance with rule 51 and so the race is null and void. The only question could arise when some competitors find the buoy still in place and visible and therefore are able to finish the race while others arriving later find it gone. Would the first boats because they finished the race, have therefore acquired a right not to have it annulled? According to us no, because as we have already said every race presupposes that all competitors are placed on a par so that the best can win, but when this parity is lacking the race is indubitably no longer valid.

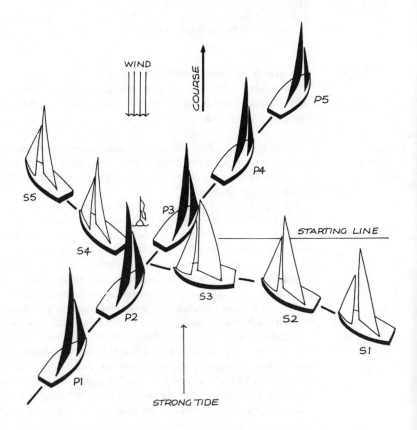

Fig. 25

Think for example how in a series of races even the last finishers have a right to some points towards their final classification. Why then should they be deprived of these by circumstances which are not "an act of God" and which are in no way their own fault? Indeed we maintain that it would be unfair in such cases to give (as cyclists do) an equal number of points to all those who did not find the buoy because we really have no right to do so.*

Gerald Sambrooke Sturgess reports a curious case (YRA 1936/1 Royal Yacht Club of Tasmania) about an up-and-down course round a buoy with a flag on it. This buoy was submerged and not found by the first three competitors but was seen under the water by the fourth and successive yachts which rounded it and then expected to be classified and awarded the prizes. The RYA on a question and answer from the race committee dismissed this request and decided that in this case the mark must be considered accidentally missing, and, since it was not visible to the first three competitors, concluded that it was not fair that the others who had been able to catch a glimpse of it should thereby derive an advantage.

3. Action by the race committee

When a mark is no longer there because it has moved or disappeared the committee must:

(a) put it back in its proper place (that is to say if it has only shifted and if they get there in time to do so);

(b) or substitute it, still in exactly the same place, with another mark which must have similar characteristics to that which has disappeared so competitors remain unaware of the change;

(c) if neither of these is possible the committee must replace the mark with a buoy or a boat displaying international code flag "M" which is the signal distinguishing the substitute from the missing buoy (rule 4.1);

(d) if none of these remedies is possible within the time available then and only then can the committee at its discretion act in accordance with rule 5.1 and choose one of three solutions; shortening course by finishing the race at or before the missing mark, cancelling or abandoning the race.

4. Mark unseen

This rule deals with problems arising in those races which take place at night or in fog when visibility is reduced and therefore a yacht cannot see the mark of the course but, knowing from the sailing instructions exactly where it is, she must be sure that she has rounded it by keeping an accurate DR.

However, this dead reckoning need not necessarily be accepted as sufficient proof of rounding. The race committee must be sure from the evidence that the method of dead reckoning is acceptable and results in confirmation that the mark has been left on the prescribed side with an ample margin. If, however,

---

* We should underline here that this idea about the facility conceded by rules 9.1 and 5.1 is a personal opinion only and refers strictly to marks missing or shifted, that is to say to something which is almost always the fault of the organizers. On the other hand (see for example the end of the comment to rule 5) when you are dealing with events arising from *force majeur* (bad weather, lack of wind or other reasons of a meteorological character which prejudice the safety of the race) we believe that the yacht with the greater speed which succeeds in arriving should be awarded the prize since overcoming typical manifestations of the sea is indivisible from racing. When, however, one is dealing with events which are due to the inefficiency of the organization this is not so especially as they may give rise to action under rule 68.5 – seeking redress against the race committee.

the margin is too small or if the dead reckoning appears inexact or slapdash it need not and should not be accepted as adequate proof on its own of the rounding of a mark which no one in the yacht concerned had been able to see.

Rule 10.
Finishing within
a time limit

Unless otherwise prescribed by the national authority or in the sailing instructions, in races where there is a time limit, one yacht *finishing* within the prescribed limit shall make the race valid for all other yachts in that race.

We have already looked at different time limits when commenting on rule 3.2(a)(viii) which refers to the various prescriptions to be found in the sailing instructions.

When nothing is laid down in the sailing instructions or by the national authority rule 10 will be automatically in force and this saves the race for all starters when at least one yacht suceeds in finishing within the established time limit. Do not forget, however, that to use rule 10 the sailing instructions must set a time for the limit because otherwise the rule is meaningless.

What happens if the only yacht to finish within the time limit is later disqualified and removed from the classification there being no others finishing before the set time? In our opinion the subsequent disqualification of the first and only yacht to arrive within the time limit cannot nullify the race because rule 10 requires only that she *finishes* (that is that she crosses the finishing line from the direction of the last mark) and does not require her to be classified as well. Given that a time limit is necessary to avoid too long a race it is clear that rule 10 tries to temper its strictness timing in all boats when one finishes, indifferently whether she has committed some breach of the rules during the race or not.

However, we cannot come to the same conclusion if the disqualification of the first boat arose from not completing the course or not finishing properly and that is logical because this would be a non-arrival rather than a disqualification (see also rule 73.1) and so she could not be said to fulfil the condition required by rule 10.

Rule 11. Ties

When there is a tie at the finish of a race, either actual or on corrected times, the points for the place for which the yachts have tied and for the place immediately below shall be added together and divided equally. When two or more yachts tie for a trophy or prize in either a single race or a series, the yachts so tied shall, when practicable, sail a deciding race; if not, either the tie shall be broken by a method established under rule 3.2(a)(ix), (The Sailing Instructions), or the yachts so tied shall either receive equal prizes or share the prize.

This rule covers two possibilities. The first deals with a tie (either crossing the line together or the same corrected time) which affects the points. In the first case the points the two tied boats would have received if they had not been tied are added together and divided by two: if one boat would have got two points and the other three then each boat will get two and a half points. The second deals with a tie for a trophy or prize in a single race, or more probably a series. Here rule 11 says that the yachts shall sail a deciding race but this is prudently watered down by the words "when practicable" because in fact a sail-off is often extremely difficult to organize. And rule 11 hastens to suggest other ideas such as solving the tie by whatever method is laid down in the sailing instructions (see rule 3.2(a)ix); and there are a number of ways: e.g. drawing lots, giving the preference to the yacht which arrived in front of the other more often, or to the yacht that is better placed, or to the yacht which has been better placed in a given race – say the longest, etc., or to the yacht which has got more firsts, and in case of another tie more seconds, more thirds, etc., or to the yacht which will be better placed in a future race of the series, etc., or by dividing the prize (presumably without the use of a saw) or by giving of equal prizes to all.

Rule 12. Yachts materially prejudiced

When:
(a) the race committee, upon its own initiative, decides; or
(b) a yacht seeks redress from the race committee within the time limit prescribed by rule 68.3(e) (Protests);
on the grounds that through no fault of the yacht concerned, her finishing position has been materially prejudiced by:
(i) an action or omission of the race committee; or
(ii) rendering assistance in accordance with rule 58, (Rendering Assistance); or
(iii) being disabled by another vessel which was required to keep clear;
the race committee shall make such arrangement as it deems equitable, which may be to let the results of the race stand; to adjust the points score or the finishing time of the prejudiced yacht; or to *abandon* or *cancel* the race, provided that the race committee shall not act under this rule before satisfying itself by taking appropriate evidence that its action is as equitable as possible to all yachts concerned, for that particular race and for the series, if any, as a whole

1. Rendering assistance

Rule 58 requires all competitors who can do so to help any ship, vessel or person in danger. It usually happens that while doing so the rescuer sees herself overtaken by all the rest who have not stopped to help because they were too far away from the incident or because when they arrive the rescue is already over. It is obviously unfair that virtue not only goes unrewarded but is penalized. The rule in these cases permits the committee to make any arrangements it deems equitable to put the competitors on a level again (and also to stop any tendency on the part of competitors to pretend not to have seen a dangerous incident). The race committee may cancel or abandon a race and re-sail it, it may present the rescuing yacht with a special prize if the race cannot be repeated and it may in some cases award points to the rescuing yacht although this last is difficult because the choice is large. A yacht's average points in the series may be given to her, points may be awarded to her according to her position at the last mark before the incident, time may be subtracted from her elapsed time to arrive at a new corrected time and so on. What is important is that the protest committee hears all the evidence and does the best that it can for all the yachts.

Making some arrangement is, however, discretionary and not mandatory, for instance if the rescuer is the last yacht in a single race, so that in fact it makes no difference to any results, then the race committee can leave things as they stand without feeling that it has been unfair or unjust.

2. Damaged when not at fault

Rule 12 gives the race committee powers to take similar steps to look after a yacht damaged by another which should have kept clear but has caused a collision instead. It is logical that in this case the damaged yacht, a competitor like the others, must (if the damage can be easily repaired) be put on a par with those equally innocent, but more fortunate.

3. A mistake by the committee

The third case provided for by rule 12 is that of an injustice arising from an action or omission of the race committee (a typical example is a mistaken individual recall which removes every possibility from the incorrectly recalled boat of getting a good place). In this as in the other cases the committee itself can put things right – or as right as possible on its own initiative or on information and a simple request from the damaged boat. When this does not happen however the competitor may formally ask for redress under rule 68.5.

IYRU No. 38 (RYA 1968/14 *Francessa II* v. Race Committee) lays down: depending upon the circumstances, "such other arrangements" could, in appropriate conditions, include the following:

(a) to arrange a sail-off between the prejudiced yacht and those which at that time were ahead of or close to her, if they could be identified;

(b) to award the prejudiced yacht break-down points;

(c) if the incident occurred close enough to the finishing line for the race committee to determine with some certainty her probable finishing position, to award her the points she would have obtained had she finished in that position;

(d) to award her points for the race equal to the average points, to the nearest tenth of a point, of her best five races.

Rule 13. Races to be re-sailed

When a race is to be re-sailed: –

13.1   All yachts entered in the original race shall be eligible to *start* in the race to be re-sailed.

13.2   Subject to the entry requirements of the original race, and at the discretion of the race committee, new entries may be accepted.

13.3   Rule infringements in the original race shall be disregarded for the purpose of *starting* in the race to be re-sailed.

13.4   The race committee shall notify the yachts concerned when and where the race will be re-sailed.

The repetition of a race arises from the *abandonment* (see definition and rule 5.1(b) of a previous race followed by the decision to re-sail it (rule 3.2(b)xviii) a decision accompanied by an indication of the date, place and time of the re-sail (rules 5.3 and 13.4).

Logically in this new race everyone who was already entered, whether they started or not, can take part. But additionally the rule allows the committee a discretionary faculty to accept new entries as well "as long as they are subject to the entry requirements of the original race".

How far reaching is this phrase? It really only means that the new entries must conform to the restrictions or conditions of entry and the numbers of entries or starters (rule 2(e)) and, obviously pay the correct dues (rule 2(f)) and be eligible with valid measurement certificates rule 3.2(b)iv).

Remember that in such cases all previous rule infringements of whatever sort are null and void.

Rule 14. Award of prizes, places, points and declaration requirements

14.1 Before awarding the prizes, the race committee shall be satisfied that all yachts whose finishing positions affect the awards have observed the racing rules, the prescriptions of the national authority when they apply, the sailing instructions and the class rules.

14.2 The sailing instructions may prescribe that in a particular instance the race committee may require the member in charge of a yacht to submit within a stated time limit a signed declaration to the effect that "all the racing rules, the prescriptions of the national authority when they apply, the sailing instructions and the class rules were observed in the race (or races) on (date or dates of race or races)." A yacht which fails to observe the above requirement may, at the discretion of the race committee, be disqualified, or regarded as having retired.

Naturally before giving a prize to a competitor the race committee or jury must be sure that he has not committed any breach of the rules or sailing instructions. Normally a jury will have dealt with any cases and, if necessary, have penalized any culprit even before the classification for prizewinners has been compiled. Therefore this prescription in the first part of rule 14, which is expressed in mandatory terms, is pushing at an open door and would be so obvious as to appear superfluous if it was not necessary to remind those concerned not to be in too much of a hurry to present the prizes before going home.

Paragraph 2 of the same rule, however, is less peremptory and suggests that the sailing instructions require a declaration and that when a yacht fails to sign this within the prescribed time she will be penalized or regarded as having retired.

The first part of the rule imposes a check before presentation of the prizes while the second recommends declarations not so much to be followed blindly, washing one's hands of responsibility with regard to the prizegiving (because, declarations or not, what count are the protests and decisions), but to draw certain conclusions from their absence. This explains why declarations must be presented within a determined time (say 2 hours) often running from the arrival of the competitor himself or from the last arrival of the class; when the time is over the absence of a declaration is taken to mean that the competitor, realizing that he had infringed a rule, has retired; however this does not allow him to escape any protest which may eventually be lodged against him.

In a series with a large number of competitors, the yachts are commonly listed on a sheet of paper and each competitor signs against his yacht's name.

This list which is headed by a collective declaration is made available at the Regatta office and must be signed within a given time limit.

Declarations simplify things very much and even avoid some protests because a competitor seeing a protest flag hoisted against him during a race may go to discuss matters with his adversary as soon as he comes ashore and then, perhaps because he has heard other witnesses and realizes that he has been in the wrong, does not sign the declaration and thereby retires.

In offshore racing declarations are used widely and these may sometimes be sent by post as the competitors may go straight to their home ports without coming ashore. Here declarations serve two additional purposes – firstly they give the time each yacht believes she has crossed the finishing line and when possible the yacht ahead and astern of her. This gives the organizers a chance to reconstruct the finishing order if some sail numbers have been missed in the dark. Secondly they serve to record permitted breaches of the rule – for example if an engine is used to rescue a man overboard or to avoid a tanker in fog in breach of rule 60 (Means of propulsion). The facts must be given on the declaration although the committee will, when they consider the use of the engine, probably take no further action.

Part III
General
requirements

Owner's Responsibilities for Qualifying his Yacht

A yacht intending to *race* shall, to avoid subsequent disqualification, comply with the rules of Part III before her preparatory signal and, when applicable, while *racing*.

While Part II groups together the rules governing race organization, Part III lays down the duties of a competitor before the start of a race. This explains why the preamble is mainly directed at those "intending to race" requiring compliance with Part III even in the period before the preparatory signal (rule 4.4) when *racing* begins.

The preamble goes on to add that these rules must also be observed when applicable while *racing* and this is logical because a yacht must, for example, have her rating, ballast, lifejackets, sail numbers, etc., in order at the finish as well as at the start of the race.

Rule 18. Entries Unless otherwise prescribed by the national authority or by the race committee in either the notice of the race or the sailing instructions, entries shall be made in the following form: —

FORM OF ENTRY

To the Secretary. . . . . Club

Please enter the yacht. . . . . for

the . . . . race, on the . . . .

her national letters and distinguishing number are . . . .

her rig is . . . .

the colour of her hull is . . . .

and her rating or class is . . . .

> *I agree to be bound by the racing rules of the I.Y.R.U., by the prescriptions of the national authority under which this race is sailed, by the sailing instructions and by the class rules.*
> Name. . . . .
> Address . . . .
> Telephone No. . . . .
> Club. . . . .
> Address during event. . . . .
> Telephone No. . . . .
> Signed. . . . . Date. . . . .
> *(Owner or owner's representative)*
> *Entrance fee enclosed*

Each national authority, usually requires a very different form to the one given above. Entry by telephone may be permitted, or entries without any formalities not subject to any closing date, etc. There are certain requisites, however, for any entry: a valid rating certificate (see rule 19), the name of the owner and the sail number for instance, and these must be supplied at any rate in time for the yacht to appear on the list of entries for distribution to other competitors (see rule 3.2(b)vi).

However, if there are no special instructions the entry form can be run off as above and sent by the organizers to those wanting to enter. We must urge competitors who scorn to use forms and send in incomplete and laconic snippets of information on odd pieces of paper at least to supply all the data listed above.

1. Late entries

There is no reason why late entries should not be allowed after the closing date, they will probably be at the discretion of the organizers (in fact rule 1.4 gives organizers discretion as to whom they let in anyway) and the acceptance of a late entry is often reasonably accompanied by a demand for what is in effect a fine — an extra entry fee. However, competitors arriving breathless at the race office at the last moment should not be surprised if they are not allowed to enter.

2. Limitations on entries

We have seen elsewhere (rules 6 and 8) that too many starters cause difficulties. To avoid these and keep the competition fair it is sensible to plan for a limitation of entries giving early warning of this intention in the notice of race. Appendix 12 recommends limiting the number of starters in important races to between 40 and 60.

If there is no such limit it is advisable to divide the competitors and run eliminating heats, if possible using some system which mixes them up so that the maximum possible number of yachts meet each other. Then a proportion of the yachts best placed in these heats (not less than four) take part in the final, re-starting the points from zero. This system has been tried out and has given excellent results.

Rule 19.   19.1   Every yacht entering a race shall hold such valid measurement or rating cer-
Certificates   tificate as may be required by the national authority or other duly authorised body, by her class rules, by the notice of the race, or by the sailing instructions.

19.2   It shall be the owner's responsibility to maintain his yacht in the condition upon which her certificate was based.

19.3   (a) The owner of a yacht who cannot produce such a certificate when required, may be permitted to sign and lodge with the race committee, before she *starts,* a statement in the following form:

To the Secretary. . . . . Club
UNDERTAKING TO PRODUCE CERTIFICATE
The yacht . . . . competes in the . . . .
race on condition that a valid certificate previously issued by the authorised
administrative body, or a true copy of it, is submitted to the race committee
before the end of the series, and that she competes in the race(s) on the
measurement or rating of that certificate.

        Signed . . . .
        (Owner or his representative)
        Date . . . .

(b) In this event the sailing instructions may require that the owner shall lodge such a deposit as may be required by the national authority, which may be forfeited when such certificate or true copy is not submitted to the race committee within the prescribed period.

From the earliest times sailing races have been between boats with different characteristics and sizes, and with the passing of the years the importance of putting competitors as far as possible on equal terms where the boats are concerned has been recognized. If the boats are equal the best crew should win. This aim has been arrived at little by little, controlling and handicapping more and more precisely until each race is reserved for yachts of the same "class".

To be admitted to any competition a yacht must be able to prove that she "measures" and this is achieved by means of a measurement certificate certifying that she has passed inspection necessary to be considered in class. Very refined and intricate systems of measurement have grown up and the rule therefore requires an owner to have a valid certificate and not to invalidate it while racing by changing his boat in any way.

1. Issue of certificates

Certificates may print the measurements of some or many parts of the boat and give a 'rating', that is a figure arrived at from the conglomerations of factors.

Certificates are issued by various administrative bodies, usually the national authority or their delegates. In some countries governmental regulations on material used and strength of construction exist and any such must be looked at in each individual country.

Rule 19.3 allows a yacht to race even without producing her certificate to the organizers provided the owner gives a declaration undertaking to submit before the end of the series a valid certificate dated before the start of the series. The certificate must exist before the start of the series because the yacht's conformity to the measurement rules must be a question not only of fact but of certification also. Organizers should, and usually do, take particular care to state clearly what they want in this regard in sailing instructions.

2. Validity of certificates

When entering a yacht must have a certificate issued by the competent authority which must be valid, that is complete and not out of date. In FIV 1963/1 (*Cigno Nero* v. *Mila II*) *Mila II*, in a race using RORC ratings, presented a provisional rating certificate with no indication of the rating or the second-per-mile allowance. The jury had accepted her entry with reservations, allowing her to start *sub judice*. *Cigno Nero* protested and on the appeal which followed the Italian national authority held that the provisional certificate was incomplete and could not be valid; they went on to hold that the yacht in question was not capable of presenting a valid certificate before the start she must, for this reason, be precluded from admittance to that kind of race, even *sub judice*.

3. Controlling the rating

The various general powers reserved for a race committee or jury certainly include that of carrying out partial measurement checks before the race to make sure that at least some of the yacht's measurements still correspond to those on the certificate. Rule 19 itself not only requires a yacht to hold a valid certificate but states that it is the "owner's responsibility to maintain his yacht in the condition upon which her certificate was based".

The reason for inspections is well expressed in the Italian measurement rule: "boats, with the passage of time, can undergo changes in shape and weight; sails can stretch so as to be larger than the permitted sizes; the fact that a boat possesses a valid rating certificate cannot therefore offer an absolute guarantee that she measures at any moment. For this reason, and in so far as is possible, partial checks will be carried out in major races, checks to be based on and controlled by the data on the certificate. This document must accompany the boat to the race just as do the mast, boom and rudder." These inspections must naturally be carried out by qualified experts such as official measurers, nominated either by the national authority or by the class association. They may also be done by members of the jury, not listed as measurers, if they concern parts of a yacht which are easy to inspect, for example, prescribed equipment, sail stowage and movable ballast. This does not mean that in case of necessity the jury cannot directly inspect the rest of the boat too – her sail measurements or her weight – but they would certainly be well advised to ask for official confirmation from a measurer whenever they meet something wrong. In practice, if the competitor does not agree immediately that his boat does not measure, this sort of case always gives rise to a controversy (following a protest or under rule 73.2) over measurement and, as a result, the intervention of an official measurer becomes mandatory under rule 68.4(a).

A curious measurement case was considered in FIV 1967/3 (*Mistral* v. YC Adriaco). In a previous race *Mistral* had been the subject of a protest about measurement but had not allowed the measurer, nominated by the jury under rule 68.4(a), to carry out the necessary inspection. Because of this the same jury allowed her to start in a later race but only on condition that a check was then carried out. However *Mistral* persisted in refusing any inspection and was disqualified and removed from the results list of the second race.

Mistral appealed saying that the decision was unfair because there had been no protest against her in the second race and because as she had presented the required certificate and her entry had been accepted she was absolutely in order. The Italian appeals committee dismissed the appeal observing "the acceptance of an entry which allowed a start *sub judice* should always be avoided since a yacht must have a valid certificate to enter a race and she must keep to it. In this particular case doubt had already been cast on the validity of *Mistral*'s certificate by the previous protest and by the impossibility of checking the alleged infringement of the measurement rule."

The appeals committee added "an entry and start *sub judice* may occasionally be acceptable in those few cases when a measurement protest has been lodged so short a time before the race as not to allow proper inspection". This had not arisen in the case of *Mistral*; she had had all the time necessary to allow an inspection to take place had she so wished, and the certificate could then have been accepted or refused as foreseen by the procedure in Part VI. The appeals committee concluded that *Mistral* should not even have been disqualified – as her entry could not have been accepted her entry fee should have been repaid to her.

Another odd case arose in FIV 1969/9 (*Grande Zot* v. Race Committee) about a competitor suspended after a measurement check in the middle of a series when he refused to open up the double bottom of his boat to show that the 10 kilos of ballast on his certificate were still there. The Italian Appeals Committee, confirming the decision of the race committee, stated: "it must be remembered that every yacht racing is subject to inspection by the race committee (rule 1.3) and must keep to the terms on the basis of which her racing certificate was issued (rule 19). If therefore the measurer asks for verification that ballast declared is in fact there, he is simply carrying out a duty which the rule lays on him. The fact that unusual ballast was stored in a place accessible only by forcing open part of the structure does not justify a refusal to allow such an action for the builder of the hull should have taken care to arrange easy access for inspection. The possibility of verifying the boat's conformity with any part of the certificate whenever the measurer considers it necessary is paramount."

4. Conformity of yacht to certificate – mistakes

Rule 19.2 requires an owner to keep his yacht in the same condition as that on which her certificate was based. National measurement rules often lay down that it is his duty to do what he can to keep his boat in conformity with class rules and this means that, without waiting for inspection at races, the owner must continuously keep his boat within the rule as it was at the moment of measurement when his certificate was issued.

This is a reasonable demand and the only difficulty arises when data are written down or measured incorrectly and it seems only fair that an owner should not be expected to stay with (and pay for) an error made by an official and confirmed by an official document especially when he is ignorant of the very existence of the mistake and naturally believes in the validity of the certificate. The problem was touched on but not resolved in *Cigno Nero* v. *Mila II*, quoted before, where measurements and certificate differed. The appeals committee found that certain maximum measurements had been exceeded and held that this was sufficient to disqualify *Mila II* observing that "such maximum measurements came to light because they are those normally inspected before a race as they control these elements of a yacht (genoa foot, spinnaker size, black bands) that can be changed or modified more easily than others; such changes can modify the rating and time correction factor, which have to be publicly posted before a race and which must be definite and final for that race, as rule 4 of the RORC general conditions require.

In the course of the rating change which was then ordered by the national authority in the above case it was realized that other details of the yacht did not correspond to the data on the certificate and as a result of these later checks the final new rating came out less than that on the certificate, thus helping the yacht. This last problem was not fully discussed for the yacht was disqualified for other reasons, but the appeals committee hinted that the fact that the new rating was lower than the first could not have justified the existence of differences and said "to allow such justification would open the road to arbitrary changes of rating, uncontrolled and very probably illegal, and favour the growth of doubt and uncertainty not to mention suspicion in a delicate and complex sector which must be controlled with constant rigour.

"In addition" – they continued – "if such infringements of ratings as did not augment the rating were legalized this would nullify the general rule whereby each handicap must be available to all competitors before the start. For obvious administrative reasons it is impossible to recalculate ratings in haste when similar infringements are met with before a race, and if a violation were discovered after the race one could not expect the results to be upset."

Finally the committee stated "when a boat is inspected after a normal protest, if the resulting data does not agree with that on her certificate, she must be disqualified because she is not in possession of a valid measurement or rating certificate at the time of the race".

Bearing in mind what has been said we may conclude that if an initial measurement mistake exists, written into the official measurement certificate, it cannot be ignored even when the owner knows nothing of it and believes his certificate. In truth if the basic principle is to accept entries only from yachts correctly rated there is no valid reason to ignore the principle to the detriment of all the other competitors notwithstanding the good faith of the owner because in all fairness the conformity of the yachts racing must prevail.

Remember what rule 68.4(b) states about small deviations in excess tolerances due to normal wear or damage which will not affect the performance of a yacht.

Rule 20. 20.1 Unless otherwise prescribed in the conditions of entry, a yacht shall be
Ownership of eligible to compete only when she is either owned by or on charter to and has
yachts been entered by a yacht or sailing club recognised by a national authority or a
member or members thereof.

20.2 Two or more yachts owned or chartered wholly or in part by the same body
or person shall not compete in the same race without the previous consent of
the race committee.

Competitors must be brought within the reach of the IYRU Racing Rules and so rule 20 makes it mandatory for yachts to be owned by clubs or their members, and these clubs must be recognized by the national authorities which in their turn form part of the IYRU itself. Only thus can competitors be made to respect the rule under threat of being suspended or expelled from their respective organizations leading in practice to a ban on taking part in competitive sailing worthy of that name anywhere in the world.

Para. 2 of rule 20 forbids two or more yachts owned or chartered by the same person to take part in the same race. This is to avoid the possibility (or even the merest suspicion) of any form of favouritism or team racing which would give one man an advantage over another. Note that the ban deals with the fact of competing, that is of *racing* in the sense of the definition, not with, for example, entering the yacht. However, the race committee at its discretion may allow such double participation after having considered and weighed the seriousness and sportingness of those concerned.

You will also notice that here it is the owner (or charterer) in question who counts and not the helmsman. A second fairly similar case appears in rule 55 which forbids a yacht owner to helm another yacht in a race in this way without having the specific permission of the race committee. Why, you may ask, are the two bans not merged into one rule? Because one concerns the obligation of an owner and so forms part of Part III and the other deals with the duty of a helmsman and is therefore to be found in Part V.

**Rule 21.
Member on
board**

Every yacht shall have on board a member of a yacht or sailing club recognised by a national authority to be in charge of the yacht as owner or owner's representative.

It follows logically from the preceding rule on ownership that every competing yacht shall have aboard at least one member of a recognized sailing club; that is to say recognized by the appropriate national authority affiliated to the IYRU.

This means that there must be someone on board (the owner or his representative) who can answer for everything to do with observance of the IYRU Rules and the sailing instructions. He will be responsible then for entering the yacht, her conformity to her rating certificate, her presentation for inspection, her conduct during the race, the declaration and the collection of prizes, protests etc. For all this you can see that the term "on board" used in the rule is really much wider than its strict literal significance because in effect this responsible person will have to do as much before and after as during *racing* in the strict sense.

The reason for rule 21 is quite obvious when large yachts have professional crews. Although this is not as common as it once was when the professional was the rule and the owner limited himself to being the chap who paid the captain and crew for the pleasure of meeting other yacht owners. Today the paid hand appears occasionally in big boats in offshore racing, but in the main crew and skippers are amateurs, even if only in the very wide sense explained in Appendix 1 of the rules.

Rule 21 does not talk of an amateur but a "member" aboard, who could indeed not be an amateur Theoretically it is one thing to have an amateur on board (usually laid down in the notice of race) or indeed for the whole crew to be amateurs and quite another to obey rule 21 by having on board a club member who, through his club and national authority forms part of the structure which the IYRU controls. In practice, however, the two conditions merge and in almost all races admission is reserved to amateurs who are also members of recognized clubs.

Many national authorities (including the British and Italian) prescribe that for compliance with rules 20 and 21 personal membership of the national authority is enough.

Rule 22. 22.1 GENERAL RESTRICTIONS
Shifting ballast Floorboards shall be kept down; bulkheads and doors left standing; ladders, stairways and water tanks left in place; all cabin, galley and forecastle fixtures and fittings kept on board; all movable ballast shall be properly stowed under the floorboards or in lockers and no dead weight shall be shifted.

22.2 SHIPPING, UNSHIPPING OR SHIFTING BALLAST; WATER.
No ballast, whether movable or fixed, shall be shipped, unshipped or shifted, nor shall any water be taken in or discharged except for ordinary ship's use, from 21.00 hours on the day before the race until the yacht is no longer *racing*, except that bilge water may be removed at any time.

22.3 CLOTHING AND EQUIPMENT
(a) A competitor shall not wear or carry any clothing or equipment for the purpose of increasing his weight.
(b) A class which desires to make exception to rule 22.3(a) may so prescribe in its class rules. However, unless a lesser weight is prescribed in the class rules, the total weight of clothing and equipment worn or carried by a competitor shall not be capable of exceeding 20 kilograms when saturated with water.
For the purposes of 22.3(b), water pockets or compartments in the clothing and equipment of a competitor shall be permitted unless otherwise prescribed in the class rules. The weight of the water in pockets or compartments shall be included in the total weight.

We have seen that apart from the size of the sails one of the most easily alterable characteristics of a boat is that of the weight of its hull and it is to this that rule 22.1 refers. It prohibits the removal or taking aboard of all those bits which can be moved but are fundamentally part of her such as floorboards, bulkheads, doors, steps, water-tanks and the whole agglomeration which, together with much else, is taken into consideration at measurement.

It equally prohibits the landing of cabin equipment, bunks, mattresses, cushions, etc., and of the fo'c'sle gear such as ropes and tools, excluding the anchor and chain dealt with separately in rule 23. All this constitutes the ordinary necessary equipment for living on board without reducing the boat to an empty hull and without skimping on gear indispensable for navigation and safety to try and lighten the boat. We can say that everything that was not on board and was not taken into consideration at measurement can be taken ashore without fear of violating the rule, but this principle is subject to many abuses and therefore needs to be carefully and strictly controlled. For the same reason movable ballast must be stowed in such a way that it cannot be moved around too easily and it must be firmly fixed for safety.

While the first part of rule 22 prevents lightening the boat the second paragraph stops any modifications to the weight, up or down, designed to suit weather conditions immediately before the race, the object being to avoid extra ballasting in heavy weather as much as lightening in calms. For this reason in addition to laying down a general ban on any alteration affecting the data on the rating certificate, the rule particularly prohibits, from 9 p.m. on the evening before the start (that is when the forecasts may well be still unreliable) *any* movement of ballast, whether shipped, landed or shifted, nor may any water be taken in or discharged except for the ship's use. Movable ballast means almost any heavy material (lead, stones, abnormal quantities of fuel, food or other stores) which can be embarked or disembarked or moved around with a certain amount of ease. First among these is water which, when taken out of or put into the tanks, or carried in containers, represents by far the most easily managed and elusive of ballasts; this prohibition is over-ruled only in so far as it concerns water necessary for 'ordinary ship's use' (an adjective indicating moderation) and naturally bilge water that collects by accident from outside is an exception.

These prohibitions last logically from the evening before the race until the yacht is no longer *racing*. However, you will notice that there is no particular restriction on the number of crew (unless in the sailing instructions or the class rules) although men too are heavy, but under rules 56 and 57 they cannot embark or disembark between the preparatory signal and the end of the race.

The deliberate immersion of crews for their clothes to absorb water and therefore weight gave rise to a number of cases in the past both in the U.S. and in Great Britain though the decisions were different in each country. Sometimes it could be justified as an involuntary dip or because the garments worn were not such as to sop up large quantities of water, but by and large it was a method of illegally shipping ballast and using it as trim. The argument against control was that if the habit were stopped it would favour heavy helmsmen and crew. Finally it was decided that such weight would be dangerous if someone went overboard because even if it did not lessen buoyancy it hindered swimming and made rescue more difficult. Faced with this the IYRU, after experiments at the Kiel Olympics finally decided to adopt what is now rule 22.3. Permission to carry water pockets has been added since. First comments on this rule criticized it for the phrase "for the purpose of increasing his weight" observing that this would mean investigating the competitor's "intent". We believe, however, that this sortie into criminal law is unnecessary; there is no need to consider intent when all that is wanted is a check on whether the crew member is wearing padded clothes and whether their weight exceeds 20 kilos.

**Rule 23.
Anchor**

Unless otherwise prescribed by the national authority or by her class rules, every yacht shall carry on board an anchor and chain or rope of suitable size.

**Rule 24. Life
saving
equipment**

Unless otherwise prescribed by the national authority or her class rules, every yacht, except one which has sufficient buoyancy to support the crew in case of accident, shall carry adequate life-saving equipment for all persons on board, one item of which shall be ready for immediate use.

Little need be said about these rules which are clearly there to guarantee minimum safety equipment for boat and crew to be aboard while racing. As far as anchor and chain is concerned this is not considered movable ballast under rule 22 and can be shipped after the 9 p.m. time limit. None of this of course can over-rule any class rule such as is found in the IOR forbidding the re-stowage of anchors once their stowage place has been recorded on the rating certificate.

Infringement of rules 23 and 24 is mandatorily penalized both by procedure under rule 68 as a result of a protest and under rule 73, that is without a protest (but with a hearing). The same would apply to an order to wear lifejackets when prescribed by sailing instructions (3.2.(b)(v) and signalled correctly (4.1"Y") by the race committee. See the comment to rule 63 (Anchoring and making fast) for more on anchors.

Rule 25. Class emblems, national letters and distinguishing numbers

Every yacht of an international class recognised by the I.Y.R.U. shall carry on her mainsail, and as provided in (d)(iii) on her spinnaker: —

(a) An emblem, letter or number denoting the class to which she belongs.

(b) A letter or letters showing her nationality, thus: —

25.1

Code	Country	Code	Country	Code	Country
A	Argentine	IL	Iceland	NK	Democratic People's Republic of Korea
AL	Algeria	IND	India		
AR	Egypt	IR	Ireland		
B	Belgium	IS	Israel	OE	Austria
BA	Bahamas	J	Japan	P	Portugal
BL	Brazil	K	United Kingdom	PH	Philippines
BR	Burma			PR	Puerto Rico
BU	Bulgaria	KA	Australia	PU	Peru
CB	Colombia	KB	Bermuda	PZ	Poland
CI	Grand Cayman	KBA	Barbados	RC	Cuba
CP	Cyprus	KC	Canada	RI	Indonesia
CR	Costa Rica	KH	Hong Kong	RM	Roumania
CY	Sri Lanka	KJ	Jamaica	S	Sweden
CZ	Czechoslovakia	KP	Papua New Guinea	SA	South Africa
D	Denmark			SL	El Salvador
DR	Dominican Republic	KR	Rhodesia	SR	Union of Soviet Socialist Republics
		KS	Singapore		
E	Spain	KT	Trinidad and Tobago		
EC	Ecuador			TA	Republic of China (Taiwan)
F	France	KZ	New Zealand		
G	Federal Republic of Germany	L	Finland	TH	Thailand
		LX	Luxembourg	TK	Turkey
GO	German Democratic Republic	M	Hungary	U	Uruguay
		MA	Morocco	US	United States of America
		MO	Monaco		
GR	Greece	MS	Mauritius	V	Venezuela
GU	Guatemala	MT	Malta	VI	U.S. Virgin Is.
H	Holland	MX	Mexico	X	Chile
I	Italy	MY	Malaysia	Y	Yugoslavia
		N	Norway	Z	Switzerland

(c) A distinguishing number allotted to her by her national authority. In the case of a self-administered international class, the number may be allotted by the class owners' association.

On sails made on or after 1st April 1977, a yacht's national letter(s) shall either be separated from her distinguishing number by a horizontal line approximately five centimetres in length or be placed above the number.

When there is insufficient space to place the letter or letters showing the yacht's nationality in front of her allotted number, it shall be placed above the number.

Assuming a Flying Dutchman yacht belonging to the Argentine Republic to be allotted number 3 by the Argentine national authority, her sail shall be marked:

$$\begin{matrix} FD \\ A-3 \end{matrix} \text{ or } \begin{matrix} FD \\ A \\ 3 \end{matrix}$$

(d) (i) Unless otherwise prescribed in the class rules, the class emblems, letters or number, national letter(s) and distinguishing numbers shall be above an imaginary line projecting at right angles to the luff from a point one-third of the distance measured from the tack to the head of the sail; shall be clearly visible; and shall be placed at different heights on the two sides of the sail, those on the starboard side being uppermost, to avoid confusion owing to translucency of the sail.

(ii) Where the class emblem, letter or number is of such a design that when placed back to back on the two sides of the sail they coincide, they may be so placed.

(iii) The national letters and distinguishing numbers only shall be similarly placed on both sides of the spinnaker, but at approximately half-height.

(e) National letters need not be carried in home waters except in an international championship.

(f) The following minimum sizes for national letters and distinguishing numbers are prescribed:

Height: one-tenth of the measurement of the foot of the mainsail rounded up to the nearest 50 mm.

Width: (excluding number 1 and letter I) 66% of the height.

Thickness: 15% of the height.

Space between adjoining letters and numbers: 20% of the height.

Classes which have a variable sail plan shall specify in their class rules the sizes of letters and numbers, which shall, when practicable, conform to the above requirements.

25.2 Other yachts shall comply with the rules of their national authority or class in regard to the allotment, carrying and size of emblems, letters and numbers, which rules shall, when practicable, conform to the above requirements.

25.3 A yacht shall not be disqualified for infringing the provisions of rule 25 without prior warning and adequate opportunity to make correction.

In the earliest sailing races flags of various sorts and fashions were used to distinguish one boat from another. Later when flags were not adequate because of the increase of competitors, sail numbers started to appear. More competitors still, grouped by now in classes, led to the necessity of distinguishing the classes — by a letter or a number — and then by means of various fantastic emblems also on the sails. Then, within each class every yacht was assigned a progressive number for personal identification and today in international races one or more letters of the alphabet inform everyone of the yacht's nationality without having to look at any flags.

Racing classes have become more and more complicated and it is necessary to distinguish international classes recognized by the IYRU from those which have not been so recognized. Para. 1 of rule 25 lays down the requirements for these IYRU classes. Such a yacht must carry an emblem, letter or number for her class, letter or letters for her nationality and a distinguishing number for herself and there are further rules for the positions of all these and their sizes.

Para. 2 merely states that other yachts, not having international status, must comply with the rules of their national authority and class and adds that these rules shall, when practicable, conform to the requirements of rule 25.1.

Finally para. 3 establishes that no yacht shall be disqualified for infringing the provisions of rule 25 "without prior warning and adequate opportunity to make correction". This is intended to avoid situations where a yacht might be penalized for infringing some detail and thus formally committing a violation of rule 25, an infringement which has in fact neither damaged others nor benefited herself. Sailing instructions themselves may give the prior warning required as in RYA 1977/3 (*All at Sixes and Sevens* v. RC).

Sailing instructions, as empowered by rule 3.1, can make the prescription more rigorous than it appears in rule 25. For example in FIV (1965/7 *Vira* v. *Aldebaran IV*) the sailing instructions forbade all changes in sail numbers, and a competitor, protested and disqualified for using a sail number other than his own, appealed on the grounds that the race committee had authorized this change when he entered and that the protest committee had not even allowed him to state this circumstance at the hearing. However the appeals committee dismissed the appeal and confirmed the disqualification observing that such a prescription in the sailing instructions could not be over-ruled and that in the case in question not even the race committee could authorize a similar change. They concluded that the appellant was to be considered as a non-starter because his sail number did not agree with that on his rating certificate.

Another decision of the Italian Appeals Committee (1964/2 *Marlin* v. *Nauta*) has established that, in a race which had no special prescriptions a yacht can even very exceptionally race without a sail number as long as she has been authorized by the race committee or jury and the fact has been publicized to all competitors who could thus identify their adversary without the usual distinctive signs. It is unnecessary to add that this sort of concession should be made rarely with good reasons and all competitors must be informed of it as far as possible before the start of the race.

Rule 26.
Advertisements

26.1   The hull, crew or equipment of a yacht shall not display any form of advertisement except that: —

(a) One sailmaker's mark (which may include the name or mark of the manufacturer of the sail cloth) may be displayed on each side of any sail. The whole of such mark shall be placed not more than 15% of the length of the foot of the sail or 300 mm from its tack whichever is the greater. This latter limitation shall not apply to the position of marks on spinnakers.

(b) One builder's mark (which may include the name or mark of the designer) may be placed on the hull, and one maker's mark may be displayed on spars and equipment.

26.2   Marks (or plates) shall fit within a square not exceeding 150 mm × 150 mm.

26.3   A yacht shall not be disqualified for infringing the provisions of this rule without prior warning and adequate opportunity to make correction.

In the 1977 rules rule 3.1 now lays down that rule 26 cannot be altered or omitted as has been done in the past. It is a rule which does not require particular explanation, but it may be useful to look at IYRU 43 which clarifies what is meant by advertising:

Interpretation   The hull, crew or equipment of a yacht owned or sponsored, wholly or in part, by a group or organization, shall not display any wording or emblem that specifically relates to such owner or sponsor.

Comment   Entries may be sponsored and/or financed by another person, body or organization. The IYRU is not averse to the sponsoring of entries and is indeed glad of the help that has been given to the competitors in various races, which undoubtedly added to the interest in them. Nevertheless, it is concerned that yacht racing should remain a sport and reminds race committees that IYRU rule 3.4 empowers them to reject an entry if they are satisfied that one of its purposes is to promote a commercial enterprise.

Rule 27.
Forestays and
jib tacks   Unless otherwise prescribed in the class rules, forestays and jib tacks (not including spinnaker staysails when not *close-hauled*) shall be fixed approximately in the centre-line of the yacht.

Rule 27 (frequently altered by class rules) aims to standardize the point of attachment of the forestay in such a way as to stop unorthodox foresails creeping in by means of moving this particular point. (The prohibition was introduced after 1930 so as to stop any repetition of events in the KSSS centenary race in Stockholm when a six metre arrived with double headstays and with the jibs tacked to a curved track on deck.) The rule says nothing about backstays which can be attached anywhere including off centre. The prohibition does not affect spinnakers (controlled by rule 54.3) or other foresails when on a free leg of the course (see rule 39).

You might well think that the two rules 27 and 54 should be together, however, the first refers to the correct positioning of standing rigging and is therefore the business of the owner before the race while rule 54 deals with running rigging during the race and therefore concerns the helmsman and crew and is correctly placed in Part V.

Rule 28. Flags   A national authority may prescribe the flag usage which shall be observed by yachts under its jurisdiction.

As national usage varies enormously, the IYRU leaves each national authority complete liberty to prescribe for yachts under its jurisdiction. One of the main problems of race officers is to know whether a yacht is racing or not and in many countries it is the rule or custom that an ensign shall not be worn while racing but the national ensign is rehoisted on the stern, the moment after a yacht finishes or retires from a race.

Part IV
Right~of~way

Rights and Obligations when Yachts Meet

The rules of Part IV do not apply in any way to a vessel which is neither intending to *race* nor *racing;* such vessel shall be treated in accordance with the International Regulations for Preventing Collisions at Sea or Government Right of Way Rules applicable in the area concerned.

The rules of Part IV apply only between yachts which either are intending to *race* or are *racing* in the same or different races, and, except when rule 3.2(b)(ii), (Race Continues After Sunset), applies, replace the International Regulations for Preventing Collisions at Sea or Government Right of Way Rules applicable to the area concerned, from the time a yacht intending to *race* begins to sail about in the vicinity of the starting line until she has either *finished* or retired and has left the vicinity of the course.

The first paragraph of the preamble to Part IV puts the racing man in his place. Cruising yachts may still in fact extend traditional courtesy and keep out of the way of boats racing, but at close quarters, if there is any possible risk of collision, the rules of Part IV will not apply and the ordinary everyday international regulations will. It applies to encounters between any two vessels one of which is racing and the other not. In crowded shallow waters such as the Solent, sail gives way to steam since the oil tankers and other big ships cannot keep clear and the yachts racing must follow the international rules for prevention of collision at sea and also the port authority regulations.

The title and the second paragraph of the preamble state that Part IV lays down the rights and obligations of helmsmen when two or more yachts meet racing. This is the kernel of the rules, for Part IV governs the infinitely various situations that arise between yachts: the race real and proper. It starts "from the time a yacht intending to *race* begins to sail about in the vicinity of the starting line", from which we can deduce that the rules of Part IV can be enforced even before the preparatory signal (rule 4.4(a)) mentioned in the definition of *racing*.

Similarly the preamble tells us that the right-of-way rules are aimed not only at yachts which are *racing* in the same or different races, as can happen when more than one class is competing in the same area, but also at a yacht about to *race*. They apply not only to yachts whose preparatory signal has already been made but also to those about to start shortly afterwards that find themselves near the starting line waiting for their warning signal. All yachts sailing in one area should sail to the same rules thus those which are not yet, or are no longer, *racing* may be disqualified if they have seriously hindered a yacht which is *racing* (31.2). A breach of the sailing instructions (for example these may say expressly that yachts must not get in the way of the class starting ahead) will also lay a yacht open to disqualification under the right-of-way rules.

Until when do the rules of Part IV hold good? Until a yacht has *finished* the race (or has retired). But this is not all because a yacht continues to be under these rules until she "has left the vicinity of the course", that is to say until she has sailed far enough away from the start or finish and from the race area itself not to be able to hinder other competitors still *racing*. A yacht which finishes or retires and then stays close to the others cannot expect to observe the International Rules for Prevention of Collision at Sea but must continue to obey the same rules as the others until she has got far enough away to have lost all contact with them.

Part IV is valid for the whole of every race except at night as stated in the preamble. This is provided for by rule 3.2(b)(ii) and, at the time indicated in the sailing instructions, the IYRU Rules are substituted by the international rules for the prevention of collision at sea. IYRU No. 87 deals with an interesting case of luffing after dark under these rules. They again give place to the racing rules in the morning, see also rule 6 (Starting and finishing lines), rule 7 (Start of a race) and rule 50 (Ranking as a starter).

SECTION A — **Obligations and Penalties**

Rule 31. 31.1 A yacht may be disqualified or otherwise penalized for infringing a rule of
Disqualifi-   Part IV only when the infringement occurs while she is *racing,* whether or not
cation   a collision results.

         31.2 A yacht may be disqualified before or after she is *racing* for seriously hindering a yacht which is *racing,* or for infringing the sailing instructions.

While Part II of the Rules lays down the duties of the organizers and Part III the obligations of the owners, Part IV deals exclusively with encounters between yachts. The first rule of Part IV therefore tells us naturally that no infringement committed while *racing* can go unpunished whether or not it results in a collision. We have already looked in detail at the meaning of "while she is *racing*" in Part I and we need only remember here that the time when a yacht is subject to penalization begins at the preparatory signal (4.4(a)) and continues until she has cleared the finishing line (or until she retires or until the abandonment, postponement or cancellation of the race).

Rule 31 itself, however, extends this period in two well-defined cases:
(a) when a yacht which is not yet or is no longer *racing* "seriously hinders another yacht which is *racing*". Such is the case of a yacht which, before her class preparatory signal, sails about near the starting line (or near the course) with other classes starting earlier from the same or nearby lines and

seriously hinders, that is to say injures the chances of, another competitor already *racing*. Similarly, a yacht which has *finished* but does not clear the line or leave the area of the race and seriously hinders other competitors still *racing* may be disqualified.

(b) for a breach of any special sailing instruction that lays down penalties for the infringement of particular prescriptions in the period before or after that normally meant by *racing*.

Rule 31 is limited in its effects to infringements of Part IV. This does not mean that the other rules do not carry any penalty if they are broken but only that these right-of-way rules are not enforced except during the race real and proper. Finally we should make clear that the penalties in rule 31 refer to disqualification and to those less drastic: re-rounding the mark (rule 52.2) and the 720° turn and the percentage penalty (Appendix 3).

Rule 32.
Avoiding
collisions

A right-of-way yacht which fails to make a reasonable attempt to avoid a collision resulting in serious damage may be disqualified as well as the other yacht.

Rule 31 just touches on collisions when it lays down the principle that a yacht can be penalized for an infringement of Part IV even without a collision. However, rule 32, still on the subject of collisions, states a general principle in which one of the main objects of the rules, that of avoiding serious damage, finds its strictest application. There is a fundamental legal principle that you may not avail yourself of your rights to such an extent that you inflict avoidable damage, not even damage to someone who is in the wrong. For example when driving, the car on the main road has the right-of-way over the car from the minor road, but this does not mean that the former can run into the latter without braking and without trying to avoid an accident. At sea (and especially so in competitive sailing, organized, never let us forget, for enjoyment) it would be absurd to allow the right-of-way yacht, on the strength of her right, seriously to damage a competitor who did not give way to her. Rule 32 therefore arises only because the investor has the right-of-way. In racing it is quite common to touch your adversary slightly just so as to give a concrete demonstration of your right and to underline the consequences of his error. These slight collisions (followed of course by a protest) are tolerated and rule 32 comes into force only when serious damage has been caused. It is not possible to lay down a hard and fast rule for judging the seriousness of the damage and whether disqualification of the right-of-way yacht is proper and necessary. Each case must be considered individually and the result will depend on the judgement and good sense of the protest committee.

IYRU 36 (RYA: Salcombe Yacht Club 1968/2) is interesting on this point.

1. Question: What constitutes "*serious* damage"; expressed in terms of percentage, cost of repairs to total value of the yacht, or in any other terms?

   Answer: It is not possible generally to define the term "serious damage" as used in rule 32. In determining whether or not the damage resulting from a collision is serious, consideration must be given to its extent and cost relative to the size and value of the yacht concerned – whether it was feasible or prudent for her to continue racing; and, if so, whether the damage markedly affected her speed and materially prejudiced her finishing position.

2. Question: The sentence in the 1960 rules: "these right-of-way rules are framed particularly to avoid collision", does not appear in the 1969 rules. From this omission is it correct to assume that a right-of-way yacht is entitled to ram any non-right-of-way yacht, provided no *serious* damage results?

Answer: The revised wording of rule 32 is designed so as not to penalize a right-of-way yacht merely for touching a yacht which should have kept clear.

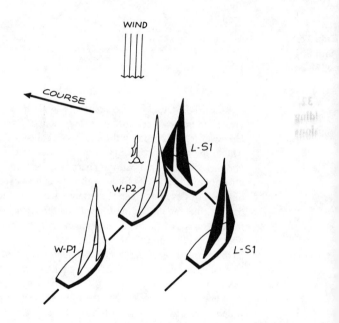

Fig. 26

Anyway it must not be forgotten that to apply rule 32 it is not enough to know that serious damage has been caused by the right-of-way yacht; it must also be clear that her effort to avoid a collision was "reasonable" (and of course possible). Only if she appears to have tried seriously can it be considered that there was no infringement. The wording of the rule does not perhaps underline this requirement adequately, although we consider it extremely important because it is hard to believe that a mere gesture is enough. One principle has been confirmed in IYRU No. 53 (NAYRU 140). In fig. 26 yachts WP and LS were rounding a mark of the course, LS, outside and ahead, tacked as soon as she could and finished in contact with WP's bow. On appeal LS was disqualified for infringing rule 41.2 by tacking too close. As for WP she seemed to have made no attempt to avoid LS which was seriously damaged. It was held, however, that she had no time to avoid an unexpected "illegal" tack by LS. The decision stated "disqualification under rule 32 is permissible, not automatic". However, the right-of-way yacht cannot always invoke the unexpectedness of the event. Another case, IYRU No. 51, speaks clearly on this subject (RYA 1971/4 *Hellhound* v. *Hare*). The organizers began well by setting two courses round the same buoy in opposite directions (fig. 27) and as a consequence yacht P (505) inevitably arrived one way at the mark to leave it to port and yacht S (Soling) from the other to leave it to starboard; rounding in opposite ways S hit P. It was discussed at length whether rule 36 (the two boats were on different tacks) should apply or rule 35 (S sustained that had she changed course she would have been held to have infringed this rule) or rule 32 (P suffered serious damage).

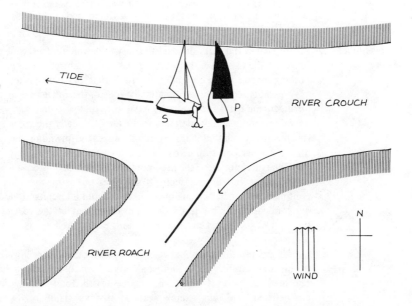

Fig. 27

The RYA, not without criticizing the race committee for their course setting, disqualified P under rule 36 for having failed to keep a good look-out and they also disqualified S for infringing rule 32, maintaining that she should have realized that P was not responding (S had hailed her) and appeared to be out of control, for this reason S could and should have taken avoiding action earlier.

Another similar case referring to rule 32 is reported in the comment to rule 42 (fig. 69) IYRU No. 37 (RYA 1968/6 *Howdee Doodee* v. *Sooky*).

Rule 33. Rule   ACCEPTING PENALTY
infringement   A yacht which realises she has infringed a racing rule or a sailing instruction is
                           under an obligation either to retire promptly or to exonerate herself by ac-
33.1   cepting an alternative penalty when so prescribed in the sailing instructions,
                           but when she does not retire or exonerate herself and persists in *racing*, other
                           yachts shall continue to accord her such rights as she may have under the
                           rules of Part IV.

33.2   CONTACT BETWEEN YACHTS RACING
                           When there is contact between the hulls, equipment or crew of two yachts,
                           both shall be disqualified or otherwise penalized unless:
                           either

                           (a) one of the yachts retires in acknowledgement of the infringement, or
                           exonerates herself by accepting an alternative penalty when so prescribed in
                           the sailing instructions,
                           or

                           (b) one or both of these yachts acts in accordance with rule 68.3, (Protests).

33.3   When an incident is the subject of action by the race committee under rule
                           33.2 but under no other rule of Part IV, it may waive the requirements of rule
                           33.2 when it is satisfied that the contact was minor and unavoidable.

1. Accepting a   Until 1973 the rules decreed that a yacht which infringed a rule "should"
penalty   retire. By then however this wording was widely interpreted as good advice and
                           nothing more and the compulsory form "shall" was substituted.

                                A penalty does not automatically follow the infringement of a rule; an
                           infringement may, for example, have been unavoidable because of another
                           yacht's mistake and in such a case the latter is really the culprit. It cannot be
                           repeated too often that in these circumstances the unwilling rule-breaker would
                           do well to ward off trouble by flying a protest flag immediately (rule 68.3(a));
                           but if she does not do so she need not therefore retire (indeed she may be unable
                           to fly her protest flag at once). If she does not retire the other yachts must
                           continue to treat her as one of themselves from all points of view, both rights
                           and obligations. No-one can be considered out of the race until a formal
                           decision has been taken by a competent body, such as race committee or a
                           jury.

                                The greatest difference between sailing and other sports has for years been
                           the disqualification rule. In almost all other forms of sport breaches of rules are
                           punished in various ways, but rarely with total elimination from the
                           competition: only in sailing was a mistake paid for by irredeemable
                           disqualification. This was not always fair because often only minor mistakes
                           were involved and so it was decided to introduce lesser penalties. Thus the
                           penalties in Appendix III were born and can be used instead of disqualification;
                           they come into force only if they are expressly adopted for a given race and are
                           provided for in the sailing instructions. An alternative penalty always in force,
                           however, unless excluded by sailing instructions is that of exoneration by re-
                           rounding the mark (rule 52.2) and another that of returning to the pre-start side
                           of the line after a premature start (rule 8). IYRU No. 2 (RYA 62/25) examined
                           the following question: Yachts A, B and C are racing with others. A protests B
                           and B is disqualified. B did not retire from the race and subsequently protested
                           C over an incident. Is this protest from a disqualified yacht valid?

                                The reply, once one has read rule 32, can only be in the affirmative. C does not acquire the right to steal from B and go unscathed just because B is a thief who has robbed A. Similarly if the protest committee holds on the evidence that C in relation to B has infringed any of the rules then C must be disqualified even if A's protest against B is accepted and B is disqualified. Retirements are few because competitors rarely realize that they have infringed the rules. The great majority, 90 per cent or even more, react to an incident on impulse, without thought, and only after a minute or two when they calm down recognize that they have acted wrongly. The true sportsman who knows the rules well enough to understand that he is in the wrong will retire. On the other hand someone who relies on his rights not only will not retire but will press on, aware that he is in the wrong, but thinking that in the end he will be able to fix it with the person whom he has injured, "me today, you tomorrow". The rules however do and must ignore such people and assume that competitors are in good faith.

2. Contact between yachts racing

This rule first appeared in 1973 (as rule 67) but it had been used experimentally for some years before that and was often included in sailing instructions. Its object was to put an end to any shady deal between competitors which allowed a collision to be tacitly, or indeed explicitly, ignored, with the result that the guilty party did not retire as rule 33 required, and the right-of-way yacht did not protest.

That such collusion is undoubtedly wrong and has always been considered a violation of the Fundamental Rule – Fair Sailing – was confirmed in IYRU No. 57 (*Troffel* v. the Bergumermeer YC Race Committee) (discussed on page 18).

When an incident is the subject of action by the race committee under rule 33.2 the penalization (which is obligatory) stems from the rule itself and from the simple fact of a collision not followed up by a protest or retirement (or acknowledgement).

The race committee can act under rule 33.2, even if it has not seen the incident directly; it is enough to know about the collision from a trustworthy source, whether from another protest or from the report of a race officer who witnessed the incident himself but if such clear evidence is not forthcoming the committee would be wise to follow the procedure laid down in rule 73. Once there is evidence of a collision both (or more) yachts must be penalized. Nor must it be thought that this summary justice is excessive. One of the two boats is certainly to blame and the other has shown that she is not really interested in the race. It must also be remembered that the application of this rule is not always compulsory: paragraph 3 gives a race committee a let out, it need not proceed if it is satisfied that contact was minor and unavoidable. Take for example certain crowded starts on too short lines with the lightest of airs and perhaps a strong tide; some slight contact then may well be inevitable even for the most expert and self-disciplined of helmsmen unless a helicopter can lift him out of the hurly-burly.

The RYA (1977/4 *Bottoms Up* v. *Adios*) described minor contact as envisaging "collisions such as might occur in drifting conditions at the start . . . certainly not in winds gusting force 3 to 4 when yachts should be under full control. Such an interpretation would lead to the conclusion that any contact which did not result in serious damage was minor".

Rule 33.2 must be rigorously applied against both yachts, even if they have been protested against by a third; and since both the yachts in the collision have to be penalized there is no need to discover which is guilty. This is confirmed by IYRU No. 65 (Finland's Seglerförbund) where it was said "the fact that a third yacht, C, witnesses an incident and protests against A and B for infringing rule 33.2 does not relieve them of their obligation for one of them to retire", in acknowledgement of full responsibility for the collision, or that one or both of them should have shown a protest flag and subsequently lodged a written protest.

IYRU No. 65 has now been omitted because it has been superseded by No. 89 which deals with 33.2 and 33.3 in some detail.

Rule 34. Hailing

34.1 Except when *luffing* under rule 38.1, (Luffing and Sailing above a Proper Course after Starting), a right-of-way yacht which does not hail before or when making an alteration of course which may not be foreseen by the other yacht may be disqualified as well as the yacht required to keep clear when a collision resulting in serious damage occurs.

34.2 A yacht which hails when claiming the establishment or termination of an *overlap* or insufficiency of room at a *mark* or *obstruction* thereby helps to support her claim for the purposes of rule 42, (Rounding or Passing Marks and Obstructions).

Just as golfers cry "fore" sailors announce their intentions by hailing. Rule 34 encourages and recommends this but does not make it obligatory. It is useful, but whether it is necessary depends on particular circumstances in each case and therefore it is up to the protest committee to decide whether the lack of a hail is in fact such a violation of any rule as to require a penalty. However in addition to the general principle of rule 34, certain specific rules (38.4, 42.1, 43) make hailing obligatory in certain circumstances. Generally speaking the rule recommends hailing "before making any alteration of course which may not be foreseen by another yacht"; that is to say as a warning signal, but clearly rule 34 also recommends hailing during the period of time in which a yacht is actually carrying out an alteration of course. A car can make its presence known by hooting: this may not be popular, but it gives good warning, and a yacht which has loudly made its presence known to the others and made clear what its intentions are can be accused of exaggeration but certainly cannot be penalized for an infringement of rule 34. Our recommendation is to be generous, even spendthrift with your hailing!

The rule, however, does not ask for a hail every time you change course otherwise racing would be chaotic. Rule 34 specifies a hail only when dealing with a change "which may not be foreseen by the other yacht" and this must not be overlooked by the protest committee.

Rule 34.2 also clearly recommends that a yacht should hail when "claiming the establishment or termination of an *overlap* at a *mark* or *obstruction*". There comes a moment in the race when everyone converges, where every situation becomes more complicated, and where even the most obvious and ordinary happenings may not impinge on the minds of those who are already deeply immersed in their own affairs and have not noticed what others are up to. Only luffing is expressly excluded from rule 34 and can be begun and ended without hailing. This is because, as we shall see, it is considered a defensive manoeuvre, it is predictable and in addition it very rarely leads to serious damage. This does not mean that a good loud hail will not be very useful to warn your neighbour and is not therefore equally commendable (rule 42.1 which deals with a question of luffing before a mark insists on a hail). Not only should the right-of-way yacht hail but it can do no harm if the yacht that is in the wrong and is getting herself into trouble hails too. The old saying states "a man warned is a man half saved" and even if a penalty is forthcoming at least serious damage may be avoided. Hailing normally, but not necessarily means shouting; but a siren, a fog-horn, beating your hands on deck any sound will do that calls attention to what is happening.

SECTION B — **Principal Right-of-Way Rules and their Limitations**

These rules apply except when over-ridden by a rule in Section C.

Rule 35. Limitations on altering course

When one yacht is required to keep clear of another, the right-of-way yacht shall not so alter course as to prevent the other yacht from keeping clear; or so as to obstruct her while she is keeping clear, except:
(a) to the extent permitted by rule 38.1, (Same Tack — Luffing and Sailing above a Proper Course after Starting), and
(b) when assuming a *proper course:*
either

      (i) to *start,* unless subject to rule 40, (Same Tack — Luffing before Starting), or to the second part of rule 44.1(b), (Returning to Start),
or

      (ii) when rounding a *mark.*

It is universally accepted at sea that, when ships are on converging courses, any change of course shall be definite and above all else predictable. This is because each skipper must be able to be sure of understanding the other's intentions, so that he can rapidly and correctly adjust his own course to avoid collision. The same rule holds good in racing. For this reason in addition to the various rules which give right-of-way to certain yachts, the rule lays down that they shall "not so alter course as to prevent the other yacht from keeping clear; or so as to obstruct her while she is keeping clear".

RYA 1968/3 (*Solna* v. *Westra*) lays down: "a right-of-way yacht must not trick or obstruct another yacht which is giving way". In other words competitive sailing, unlike fencing, boxing and football, does not allow feints for reasons of safety, and the right-of-way yacht is not expected, once she has chosen her proper course, to change it close to another which must keep clear. A point to be underlined is that rule 35 applies only to the right-of-way yacht. This can be seen clearly in NAYRU 63 (*Gypsy* v. *Fantome*). We can see (fig. 29) that before the start F forced G slightly up to windward (pos. 2) and then dropped astern of her (pos. 3). "When clear ahead G luffed, preparatory to tacking, and as her sails started to shake, she observed that F had rounded up inside her in a position to windward so that had she tacked she would have been

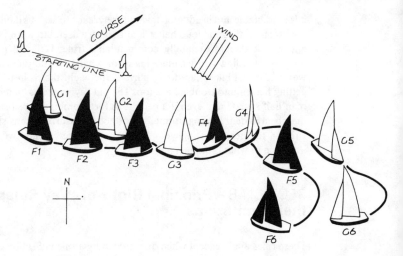

Fig. 29

struck by F, approximately amidships, while in the act of tacking (pos. 4). Thereupon G ceased luffing and bore away with the intention of gybing and returning to the starting line only to discover that F (at pos. 5) had also altered course to leeward so that if G had gybed she would have collided with F while doing so. Subsequently F gybed and headed for the starting line followed by G." Had there been a collision at position 4 G would have infringed rule 41, for

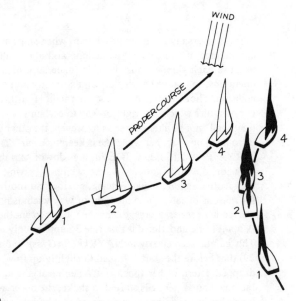

Fig. 30

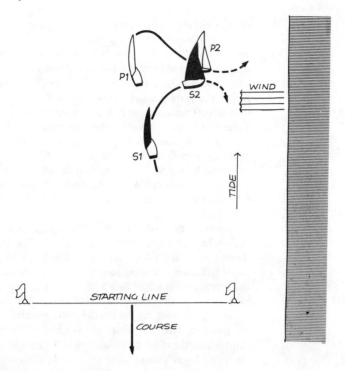

Fig. 31

F was on a tack and had there been a collision at position 5 G would have infringed rule 37.1 F being leeward yacht.

These were the facts stuffed with complications. G protested, accusing F of a breach of rule 35 for obstructing her while in the act of keeping clear (and also for a breach of rule 40) but the appeals committee decided that rule 35 was not applicable to F in positions 3 and 4 because she was no longer the right-of-way yacht (also notice that in position 5 she was already within the ambit of rules 37.1 and 41.1 and therefore could no longer raise any question of being hindered). They concluded "the facts as presented give no indication that either yacht infringed any rule . . .".

IYRU No. 10, *Vixen* v. *Proteus* (NAYRU 93) is similar. In fig. 30 the port-tack yacht P bore away to pass astern of the right-of-way yacht S on starboard. Immediately S tacked too passing on to port tack; seeing this P luffed up again on to her original course and protested S for breach of rule 35. P's alteration of course "did not of itself require the starboard-tack yacht to maintain her course. To rule that the right-of-way yacht must do so for this reason alone would seriously and unnecessarily limit her rights under basic opposite-tack rule 36." This statement lays down an important principle and with good reason modifies the implication that the right-of-way yacht, once she has chosen her course may not change it. Here too, when S begins to tack and passes beyond the head-to-wind position she ceases to be subject to rule 35 because she is no longer the right-of-way yacht: instead she is subject to rule 41 (without however violating it because she has carried out the manoeuvre far enough away from P, for the latter not to have to change her course yet again to avoid her). The principle that the right-of-way yacht can alter course without infringing rule 35 is repeated in RYA 1967/5, *Nausicaa* v. *Sylmer* (fig. 31). Before the start the two yachts S and P manoeuvring near the line sailed themselves into position 2, S on starboard and P on port tack. S protested under rule 36, and accused P of not keeping clear. P counter-protested S under rule 35 for having luffed up more and more instead of holding her original course. The decision went in favour of S, recognizing her right to luff until she was close-hauled on the starboard tack (when P was naturally obliged to keep clear of her under rule 36). In this particular situation there was no question of hindrance as it was held that the distances were such that there was never any risk of collision.

However, the right-of-way yacht cannot profit to the point where she deliberately harms her adversary. In IYRU No. 36 (RYA 1968/2, Salcombe Yacht Club) the RYA Council was asked if rule 36 (opposite tacks) over-rode rule 35 in such a way as to entitle a starboard-tack yacht to steer a course deliberately to hit a port-tack yacht by luffing or bearing away. The reply was in the negative since rule 35 is part of section B of Part IV and always applies.

Still on the same subject the following question was then put "if in fact rule 35 qualifies rule 36, how many independent witnesses are needed to substantiate the claim of a non-right-of-way yacht that rule 35 was broken by the right-of-way yacht?" And this was the reply worthy of the question: "The race committee must be satisfied from the weight of the evidence that a right-of-way yacht infringed rule 35."

In conclusion it may be said that it is not that the right-of-way yacht is strictly obliged to maintain her course; she may alter it but will sometimes in fact, sail into a position in which she loses that right. What matters is that in changing course she should not prevent the other yacht from keeping clear of her; that is to say she must not make it impossible, or extremely difficult, for the other yacht to carry out her obligation. Nor may she trick the other yacht; she cannot deliberately force her to manoeuvre to keep clear and then not profit by this concession even though she could do so. Nor may she reach the point where she obstructs the other yacht; and for this let us look at the definition from RYA 1972/2 (Barnt Green Sailing Club): "Obstruct, in the context of rule 35, means putting the non-right-of-way yacht at a disadvantage greater than that which she would have suffered in complying with her obligations if the right-of-way yacht had held her course." We should add to this that "to obstruct" means to manoeuvre in such a way as to prevent the other yacht, completely or in part, from correctly carrying out her obligation to give way.

Rule 35 also covers the case of the right-of-way yacht which so manoeuvres that she forces the other, in order to keep clear, to modify her course more than necessary. (It is understood here that "more than necessary" means more than that which would have been necessary if the right-of-way yacht had kept to the rule.)

You must remember, however, that the application of rule 35 is always subject to a number of conditions: – competitors must be on converging courses and in imminent danger of collision, one with right-of-way and the other with the corresponding obligation to keep clear. If these elements are lacking rule 35 is irrelevant. Such common ploys as the false tack which induces an opponent to copy an expected manoeuvre and thus lose ground, or pretending to hoist a spinnaker so than an opponent really hoists one, infringe no rule and are only examples of accepted racing expertise.

1. The exceptions to rule 35

Rule 35 makes it clear that luffing (by the leeward yacht or by that clear ahead) as defined by rule 38.1 is an alteration of course quite within this rule. Strictly speaking, after the start the luff (if all the various requirements of rule 38 are present) is not a true "exception" simply because in such a manoeuvre the leeward yacht in no way prevents the other from keeping clear; her luff is purely defensive, an action on its own freely permitted. The 1973 edition of the rules introduced another qualification about the start into rule 35 that permits the right-of-way yacht to assume a *proper course* to *start*, even if, by doing so, she obstructs the yacht which is about to keep clear of her or is keeping clear of her. It is considered unfair to make the right-of-way yacht keep her course (and therefore make a late start) just when she is about to cross the starting line; and it is clear that if this were not so she would lose out precisely because she had right of way. This right ceases to exist in the case of a premature starter returning to start again (44.1(b)).

In fact NAYRU 42 excludes rule 35 where one yacht without warning begins constantly and steadily to luff another that is overtaking her to windward. Again NAYRU 20 (fig. 32) shows that the windward yacht can not invoke rule 35 even when, after a legitimate luff, the leeward yacht bears away so sharply that she causes a slight collision. It is her own fault for not keeping a reasonable distance.

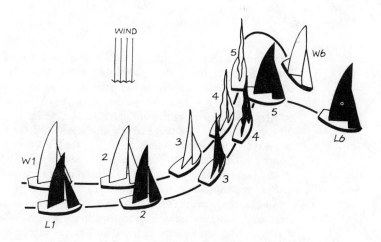

Fig. 32

IYRU No. 52 (RYA 1971/5 *Flamingo* v. *Gadfly*, Bassenthwaite SC), shows us in fig. 33 the usual story of an encounter between two yachts complicated by an unexpected wind shift. In position 1 yacht P, port tack, was calmly and effortlessly passing ahead of S when the wind veered 45° in favour of S; both yachts then changed course to starboard for the new wind direction with the result that S had to bear away sharply to avoid a collision with P, after which she protested P for an alleged infringement of rule 36 and P protested

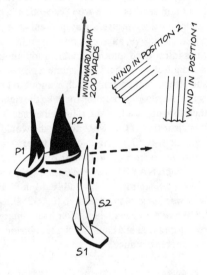

Fig. 33

S for an infringement of rule 35. Neither of the two yachts was held guilty. Not S because, being the right-of-way yacht "she was entitled to take advantage of the wind shift, but she was bound by rule 35 not to alter course so as to prevent P from keeping clear. As S altered course again to avoid a collision with P she did not infringe rule 35." As far as P was concerned the decision recognized that had the wind not shifted she was keeping clear and was crossing ahead of S. In conclusion the RYA commented as follows: "Since 1969 it is not, as it was previously, a defence under rule 35 that a right-of-way yacht alters course by luffing or bearing away to conform to a change in the strength or direction of the wind."

For the same reason (see also NAYRU 71) changes of course caused by involuntary mistakes during a manoeuvre do not fall within the scope of rule 35 if they appear maliciously intended to damage others; the real difficulty consists therefore in weighing up carefully whether such intent can be excluded in each individual case and with it rule 35.

The last part of rule 35 states that when rounding a mark the right-of-way yacht has the right to assume a proper course for just the same reasons as she is allowed to assume a proper course to start. The yacht which must keep clear is presumed to be able to foresee that the right-of-way yacht is going to round the mark and to have enough foresight to keep well clear of her and let her do what she wants.

Rule 36.
Opposite tacks
— basic rule

A *port-tack* yacht shall keep clear of a *starboard-tack* yacht.

We have already seen in Part I (Definitions) that "a yacht is *on the tack* (*starboard* or *port*) corresponding to her *windward* side." It is then easy to understand the meaning of rule 36, described as basic for yachts on opposite tacks (just as 37 is basic for yachts on the same tack). The principle of rule 36 is simple and unequivocable and has the great advantage of controlling very nearly every situation that can arise between yachts on different tacks. There are only a few exceptions, rules 42.1(a) and (b), 42.2, 44.1 and 45.1 which will be discussed later. Nothing needs to be said about the text of the rule which is quite clear, but it is interesting to look at a decision of the U.S. national authority containing an essential principle when applying this rule, this is NAYRU 32 (and a later similar decision in NAYRU 90).

The facts were as follows:

8-metre S (starboard-tack) protested 8-metre P (port-tack) because she had had to bear away and pass astern of her to avoid a collision. The race committee deduced from the available evidence that nothing would have happened if S had held her course without bearing away and dismissed the protest. The case went to appeal and the appeals committee decided differently: "Had S held her course and had P crossed her, an incontrovertible fact would have been established and a protest by S would have been disallowed. But S actually bore away, and the prognostication that P would have crossed her was based (1) on an estimate of clearance by inches, and (2) on the constancy of the speed and course of each yacht, two factors which, owing to the vagaries of the wind, are subject to rapid changes. Reasonable doubt exists as to whether P would have cleared S had the latter held her course.

"When there is reasonable doubt as to the ability of the port-tack yacht to cross ahead of a starboard-tack yacht, the starboard-tack yacht is entitled to bear away and protest, and the burden of proof rests on the port-tack yacht to prove that she would have cleared the starboard-tack yacht. On the facts submitted P has failed to prove that she would have cleared S." Thus the race committee's decision was reversed and S's protest was sustained.

This decision may seem draconian but try and imagine the infinite number of protests that would arise had the decision gone the other way. If rule 36 allowed all the infinite variations of "if," and "but," on the part of the port-tack yacht it would have been exposed over the years to a series of most subtle exceptions and would have been considerably weakened; racing would be chaotic and the number of collisions enormously increased by the uncertainty engendered when opposite-tack yachts met. A similar case was decided by the Italian Appeals Committee (FIV 1968/7, *Flash* v. *Siguela*.) Here the starboard-tack yacht, S, protested port-tack yacht, P, maintaining that there had been a collision. The race committee faced with conflicting evidence decided that the proof of collision was not sufficient and dismissed the protest. The appeals committee reversed this decision and disqualified P for violation of rule 36 saying: "while accepting the facts found by the race committee according to rule 71 we are, however, of the opinion that the appeal must be upheld because the race committee had not looked at the facts in the particular light of rule 36, a basic rule which gives absolute precedence to the starboard-tack yacht (with those exceptions in rules 42, 44 and 45 which are not in question here). It was found as fact that the two yachts were on opposite tacks, that the two courses were convergent and that the two yachts had found themselves nearly colliding, we must conclude that the lack of further evidence must be to the disadvantage of the port-tack yacht, that is the yacht which was in these circumstances undoubtedly obliged to keep clear and which has not been able to provide sufficient evidence or to show that she was able to complete her obligations. And we must add that the fact that there was no collision makes no difference to the rightly strict application of rule 36, because a collision is not in any way a necessary element of an infringement of this rule."

So don't – when talking about yachts on different tacks – mention leeward or windward, bearing away or luffing, overtaking or overlapping, on the wind or off the wind, safety of navigation, sailing along the coast or what you will, all these arguments will be perfectly useless when confronted with the universal statement of rule 36; a port-tack yacht must always give way to a starboard-tack yacht and if the latter has to alter course to avoid her there can be no doubt about the former's guilt (unless she succeeds in proving the contrary, an almost impossible undertaking). From this elementary conclusion there follows an equally clear recommendation: anyone sailing on port tack should do all he can to keep well away from anyone on starboard because he is unlikely to be able to prove that he is right, even if he is.

When opposite-tack yachts meet and the encounter is complicated by one of them tacking or gybing the limit between one tack and the other needs to be borne in mind; check carefully when such manoeuvres begin and end in the sense of the respective definitions because rule 36 can only be applied to yachts *on a tack* and not when either is *tacking* or *gybing*.

Let us look at an example, RYA 1967/1 (Royal Engineers Sailing Association – fig. 34). Here we can see that immediately after the starting signal (position 2) White was unable to fetch the outer distance mark on starboard tack, and on the other hand was too close ahead of Black to be able to tack without infringing rule 41; accordingly White could only luff up head to wind and stay in that position until Black tacked and crossed the starting line (pos. 3). However, Black not content with having thus gained several lengths on her adversary (see pos. 4), protested that White, on the strength of rule 36 should have given way rather than putting herself head-to-wind and making Black tack.

White defended herself saying she had only headed up as was her right without going beyond a head-to-wind position; and the RYA Appeals Committee accepted her argument observing that "by definition a yacht is luffing until she is head to wind and starts tacking from the moment she is beyond head to wind. Therefore as White had started, she was entitled to luff head to wind; suddenly if she had cleared the starting line, slowly if she had not.

Fig. 34

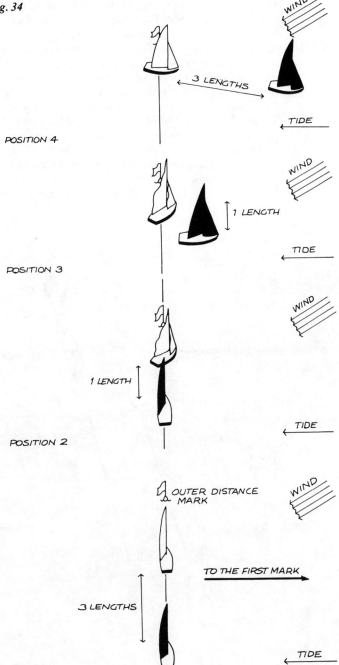

WIND

3 LENGTHS

TIDE

POSITION 4

WIND

1 LENGTH

TIDE

POSITION 3

WIND

1 LENGTH

TIDE

POSITION 2

OUTER DISTANCE
MARK

WIND

TO THE FIRST MARK

3 LENGTHS

TIDE

POSITION 1

If the race committee is satisfied that White did not pass beyond the head-to-wind position until after Black had tacked White did not infringe either rule 36 (because she had always been on starboard tack) or rule 41.1 (because in tacking she had not obstructed Black)." Thus a starboard-tack yacht has rights under rule 36 until, when tacking, she goes beyond a head-to-wind position (thus beginning to sail on the port tack), or when gybing until the foot of her mainsail has gone across the centre line of the hull.

Conversely a port-tack yacht, when tacking, only acquires the rights of a starboard-tack yacht when she has finished her tack (that is to say when she had borne away when beating to windward to a close-hauled course or to the course on which her mainsail has filled if she is not beating to windward) or her gybe (that is to say when her mainsail has filled on the new tack).

As an example we can look at IYRU No. 35 reporting a decision of the USSR YRF. Fig. 35 shows two overlapped yachts running on port tack. In

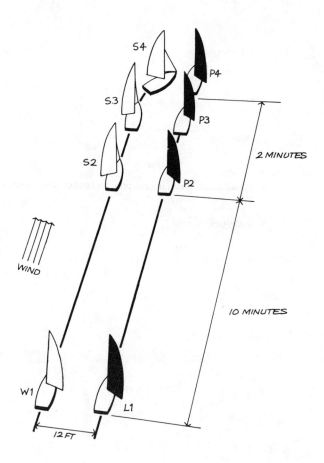

Fig. 35

position 2 the windward yacht, S, gybed and became starboard-tack yacht. About two minutes after the gybe S hailed P and began to luff till the yachts touched. The question was whether S had the right-of-way under rule 36 or did rule 35 apply. The Soviet national authority answered that "S, having completed her gybe in accordance with rule 41.1 was the starboard-tack right-of-way yacht under rule 36, and P as the port-tack yacht was bound to keep clear. On opposite tacks rule 38.1 did not apply so S had not the right to luff 'as she pleased'. Nevertheless, she was not bound to hold her course and could alter it by luffing in such a way that she did not infringe rule 35." A question was also asked in the same case as to what would happen if the starboard-tack yacht S while running, established either a windward or a leeward overlap from clear astern on a running port-tack yacht, P, and the answer was that even in this case rule 36 must apply and whatever happened P must give way to S. A similar application of rule 36 appears in IYRU No. 45 (RYA 1970/1, *Falcon* v. *Tracy*) which is discussed on the comment to rule 42.3(a) in fig. 71.

There is nothing more to say about rule 36. Like a "No Smoking" sign it has the great advantage that everyone can understand it, it is unequivocal and is not susceptible to quibbling distortions.

Rule 37. Same Tack — Basic rules	WHEN OVERLAPPED A *windward yacht* shall keep clear of a *leeward yacht.*
37.2	WHEN NOT OVERLAPPED A yacht *clear astern* shall keep clear of a yacht *clear ahead.*
37.3	TRANSITIONAL A yacht which establishes an *overlap* to *leeward* from *clear astern* shall allow the *windward yacht* ample room and opportunity to keep clear.

Just as rule 36 contains the rules governing encounters between opposite-tack yachts, rule 37 lays down the basic principles governing encounters of yachts on the same tack. It describes itself as a basic rule, as is rule 36, but while the latter is terse and brief, rule 37 is divided into three paragraphs each referring to a different case: (1) yachts on converging courses, (2) yachts on the same course but not overlapped and (3) yachts overlapped on parallel courses.

1. Yachts overlapped on converging courses

Converging courses sooner or later create the danger of collision. On this point rule 37.1, like rule 36, establishes precisely, simply and peremptorily that "a windward yacht shall keep clear of a leeward yacht": there can be no intermediate answers. A classic example of the application of rule 37.1 appears in RYA 1967/6 (*Get Weaving* v. *Very Dodgy*). In fig. 36 we see L, shortly before the start sailing towards the line converging on yacht W (on the same tack) keeping herself carefully on the pre-start side of the line. L hailed W to keep clear but W did not respond and L's bow hit W's port side. W protested under rule 40 (Same tack, luffing before the start). The race committee upheld by the appeals committee not only dismissed W's protest but disqualified her because "a leeward yacht sailing a steady converging course towards the windward yacht is not luffing as, by definition, luffing involves an alteration of course". So W was disqualified for infringing rule 37.1.

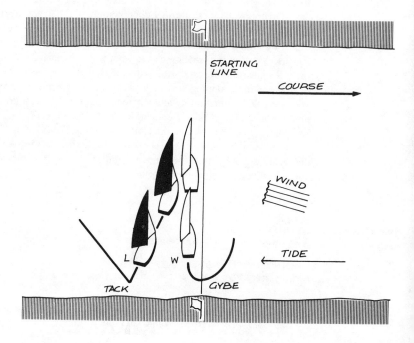

Fig. 36

A second similar example IYRU No. 24 (RYA 1965/10, *Eucalyptus* v. *Little Buddha*) makes the matter clearer. Fig. 37 shows that before the start yacht L passed astern of W (position 3), overtook her to leeward and sailed a steady course converging with that of W. W protested, invoking rule 40, (luffing before the start) but this went against her because she was disqualified on the strength of rule 37.1, the race committee accepting as a fact that, between positions 4 and 5, L the leeward yacht kept a steady convergent course without luffing, leaving W, the windward boat, ample room and opportunity to give way. It was also observed that in this case rules 37.2 and 37.3 did not apply because, dealing with converging and not parallel courses, there was no case of over-taking or of overlap.

What emerges from this is that in the case of the same-tack yachts on converging courses, rule 37.1 always applies and the windward yacht must give way without discussion provided that the course of the leeward yacht is a steady course, and that it is not subject to variations: the presence of these elements is enough to exclude rules 37.2 or 37.3 from applying.*

It is of no importance where and when the two courses converge. In the cases we have looked at we see that the windward yacht must give way to the leeward yacht even on the starting line, and without there being any distinction between the period before or after the starting signal.

To emphasize the paramount force of rule 37 look at a limit case where two same-tack yachts are sailing on two different legs of the course, as happened in RYA 1966/2 (*Athena* v. *Alitea*). In fig. 39 you can see that L tacked and put herself to leeward of W (position 2). W wished to gybe round the mark which was to be left to port and go off on her course for the next mark but L, by

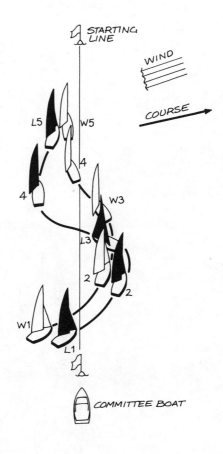

Fig. 37

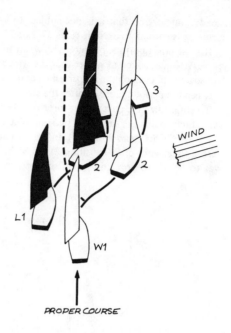

Fig. 38

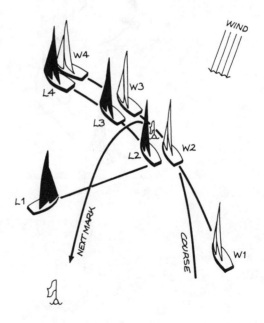

Fig. 39

putting herself to leeward, now acquired the right to hold her course under rule 37.1 and W as windward yacht had to keep clear of her. (Notice how the fact that L has passed the buoy on the wrong side is irrelevant or only relevant in that it precludes 42.1(b) from coming into force). To satisfy your curiosity W later bore away causing a collision and gybed and was disqualified under rule 37.1 (and under rule 41.1 for having gybed in front of a yacht *on a tack*).

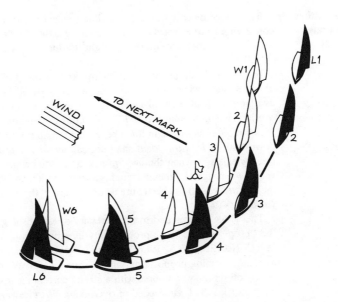

Fig. 40

In the case of *Athena* v. *Alitea* rule 37.1 could be applied precisely because L found herself on the wrong side of the mark, and so no question of rounding the mark arose between the two yachts, and no question of room for the inside yacht (rule 42). We shall see that only when two same-tack yachts "are about to round or pass a mark or obstruction on the same required side" (even if they have not yet *started* in the sense of the definition) does rule 42, which provides exceptions to rule 37, come into force, and, starting two lengths from the mark or the obstruction, supplants rule 37 for the whole time necessary to complete the rounding or passing of the mark (see points 4 and 5 of the comment to rule 42).

When rounding the mark is completed rule 37 returns in full force and the leeward yacht again has the right-of-way. See for example NAYRU 12 (fig. 40). As the result of a collision at position 5 W was disqualified for infringing rule 37.1 because she failed to assume her proper course to the next mark quickly. "In this case" says the decision "rule 42 makes exception to rule 37.1, windward yacht keeps clear, only so far as to require the outside yacht although holding right of way, to give the inside yacht room to round the mark. The room to which W was entitled was only that sufficient in the circumstances to round safely and clear the mark."

L never at any moment had the right to luff under rule 38 but this does not matter because as the leeward yacht she had the right under rule 37.1, and "was entitled to sail up to her proper course".

2. The relationship between rules 37 and 38   The preceding case raises the inevitable question about rule 37: does a yacht converging from leeward, in addition to the right of way given to her by 37.1, at a certain moment have the right to luff the windward yacht under rule 38?

In the 1973 edition of the rules the key to the problem was in para. 3 of rule 37 itself where – in the case of yachts on parallel courses – the leeward overlapped yacht was forbidden to sail above her proper course while the overlap lasted. Now in the 1977 edition this prohibition disappears from rule 37.3 but continues to be in force because it remains in rule 38.2. Here it is laid down that "a *leeward yacht* shall not sail above her *proper course* while an *overlap* exists, if when the *overlap* began . . . the helmsman of the *windward yacht* (when sighting abeam from his normal station and sailing no higher than the *leeward yacht*) has been abreast or forward of the mainmast of the *leeward yacht*".

The whole thing is tied to the necessity of establishing, case by case, what this "proper course" is, a problem anything but simple. Look for example at IYRU No. 25 (RYA 1966/3, *Fundador* v. *Ariadne*) where the question assumes alarming proportions: fig. 41 shows L and W rounding a mark and sailing off on the new course with a strong current against them. At a certain moment (pos. 3) L succeeded in overtaking W to leeward and asked her for room to sail nearer the shore where the current was less; W refused and a collision resulted. The RYA Council disqualified W holding that "when, owing to a difference of opinion on the proper course to be sailed, two yachts on the same tack converge, the windward yacht, W, is bound by basic rule 37.1 to keep clear. From the evidence there seems no doubt that, in accordance with rule 37.3 L gave W ample room and opportunity to keep clear".

So far so good; but what is interesting is that the council observed that "there can be more than one proper course. If W had kept clear and protested, the basis for her protest would have been that L, without luffing rights, sailed above her proper course. L's defence and counter-protest would be that the course she was sailing was, for her, a proper course, and that therefore W infringed rules 37.1 and 39. Which of two different courses is the faster one to the next mark cannot be determined in advance and is not necessarily proven by one yacht or the other reaching the next mark ahead. The criterion for a proper course then seems to be whether the yacht sailing it has a logical reason for its being a proper course and whether she applies it with some consistency."

One cannot but agree with this; but it underlines the difficulty of defining exactly what is in fact a "proper course". And if readers have not already appreciated the uncertainty and subjectiveness of such decisions the U.S. Appeals Committee (NAYRU 6) states "when there is doubt that a yacht is

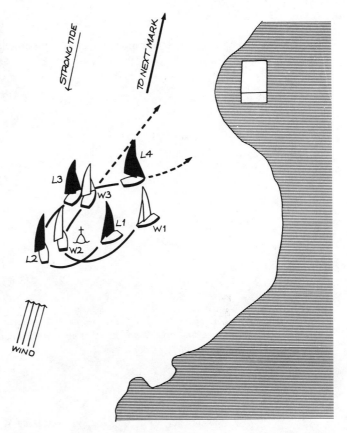

Fig. 41

sailing above her proper course, she should be given the benefit of the doubt" and there is no reason not to go along with this. But certainly it does not do much to simplify the matter or help a protest committee to determine the proper course with all the consequences that flow from it.

However do not lose heart with such pessimism; let us try to reach some conclusion. Personally we believe that for simplification every variation can be reduced to one of the following four cases without looking for intermediary solutions:

(a) Yachts sailing on steady converging courses: this is governed by rule 37.1 and the leeward yacht has the right of way (it making absolutely no difference whether her course is "proper" or not), as long as she maintains her course without alteration (see fig. 42). Indeed we can say that what counts is the course of the leeward yacht and it is quite unnecessary for the windward yacht's course to be steady.

(b) The ban on changing course refers above all to luffing. The right-of-way leeward yacht cannot, once she has established an overlap, within the two-

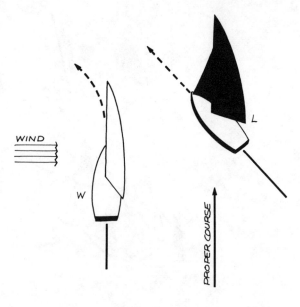

Fig. 42   The windward yacht, W, must keep clear of the leeward yacht, L, which is sailing on a steady converging course; it does not matter whether this course is "proper" or not.

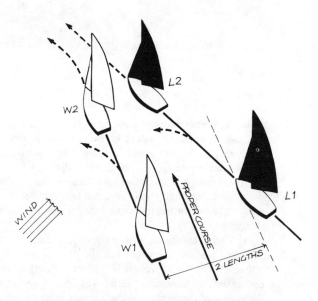

Fig. 43   Although L is overlapped within the 2 lateral lengths required by rule 38.3 she cannot luff W but must continue on her steady course if she does not want to lose her rights under rule 37.1.

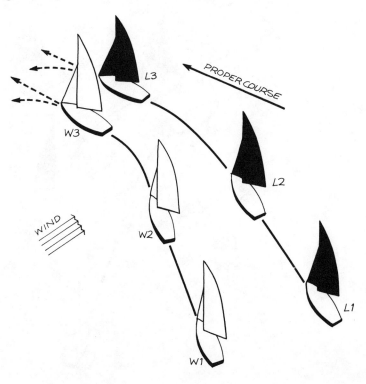

Fig. 44   W and L are on converging courses – A keeps clear as she is bound to do by rule 37.1 and puts herself on a parallel course to L; in pos. 3 L is overlapping and can luff further, but not "above her proper course" (rule 37.3).

length distance envisaged by rule 38.3, also luff the other yacht "as she pleases" (fig. 43); if she does so she loses her rights under rule 37.1.

(c) It may happen that this same right-of-way leeward yacht – once the windward one has kept clear by putting herself on a parallel course – wants to luff further; she may do so but only up to a certain point because whatever happens "she shall not sail above her proper course while an overlap exists" (fig. 44). Notice here the difference between "luff as she pleases" and sailing "not above a proper course".

(d) Finally it may happen that the leeward yacht does not insist on her steady converging course, and bears away on to a course parallel to the windward yacht's: at this point, if she has thus established an overlap under rule 37.3, she will naturally have the right to luff the windward yacht but not beyond "her proper course" (fig. 45).

How should things be governed in that transitory phase from the moment the leeward yacht begins to change her steady converging course until she is on a course parallel to the windward yacht? We believe that during this time the

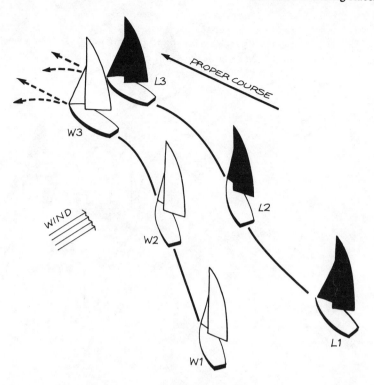

Fig. 45   W and L are on converging courses; in pos. 2 L does not take advantage of her right under rule 37.1 and alters course parallel to W but this is not her proper course and L has the right to luff up to (but not above) her proper course.

leeward yacht has no rights; not under rule 37.1 because she has changed her previously steady and convergent course, and not under rule 38.1 because rule 38.2 forbids her to luff above her proper course during the existence of the overlap.

To understand a rule thoroughly it is necessary to see why it arose in the first place. In order therefore to understand the relationship between the two rules discussed above it must not be forgotten that the luff envisaged by rule 38 began as a defensive manoeuvre against a yacht trying to pass to weather; it follows that it can never be used, just to make trouble, by a yacht establishing an overlap to leeward (whether on converging or parallel courses). To sail up to leeward and overtake with right-of-way and in addition to luff an adversary to the limit is the kind of behaviour found long ago in naval battles but it certainly has no place in racing, the fundamental principles of which aim to prevent questionable manoeuvres (rule 35) and accidents generally (rule 32).

3. Yachts on the same course when not overlapped (37.2)

The second paragraph of rule 37, which in a sense is an exception to the fundamental rule of 37.1 is also very precise and cannot be misinterpreted: if two yachts sailing on the same tack are not overlapped, the clear-astern yacht must keep clear of the yacht ahead of her, either by altering course if she is following in her wake, or by getting further away if she is catching up on a parallel course but is too close.

The definition in Part I talks of a "windward" or a "leeward" yacht only "when neither of two yachts on the same *tack* is *clear astern*"; this means that, thanks to the definition, rule 37.2 is limited to the case of a yacht that is sailing faster than the yacht ahead of her, obliging the overtaker – indifferently whether she is to windward or to leeward – to keep clear of the yacht being overtaken. This is logical because there is no justification at sea for one boat coming up behind another and running into her.

When the clear-astern phase changes into that of an overlap, rule 37.2 clearly ceases to have any force and if the overlap is established to leeward it is

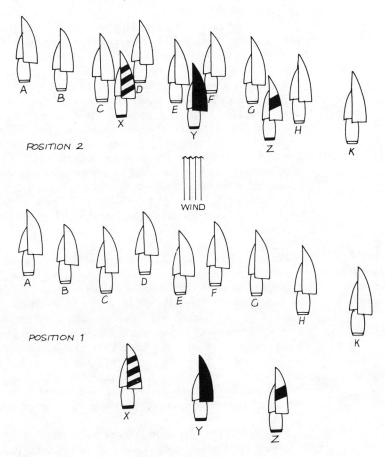

Fig. 46

superseded by 37.3 with all the consequences that flow from it. No further explanation of 37.2 is needed but it is as well to look at IYRU No. 27 (RYA 1966/9, St. Mawes Sailing Club). Replying to a series of questions the RYA clearly show the phases of a race and the developments of the various possibilities of rule 37. The competitors (fig. 46) have only just started and are sailing towards a rocky promontory half-a-mile distant which must be left to port; a group consisting of A to K sail into a zone of less wind so that yachts X, Y and Z, profiting from some lucky gusts, catch them up but find no room to pass between them unless one of those ahead pulls in her main sheet to make space. In this situation the following question was first asked: "As between A and B who has to keep clear if: (a) A was clear ahead at the start; (b) A was not clear ahead of B?" The RYA replied: "(a) If A was clear ahead of B, B, as the yacht clear astern under rule 37.2 must keep clear; (b) as soon as B established an overlap to leeward of A (pos. 1) A becomes bound by rule 37.1 and B by rule 37.3." (That is to say A must keep clear of the yacht to leeward, on the strength of the overriding obligation even on parallel courses), and B must obey 37.3 and 38.2 (that is she must leave A room to keep clear and must not luff above her proper course).

This is right at the beginning of the race, the following question was asked about the later situation: "Who makes room for X who makes the first overlap to leeward of the yacht ahead of her?" (i.e. to leeward of yacht C). The reply was that as there was no room for X, Y and Z to sail between the respective overlapping yachts "unless everyone pulls in his sheets", 42.2(a) (passing an obstruction, i.e. the nearby headland on the same side) applied. X, Y and Z were bound to keep clear "in anticipation of and during the passing manoeuvre" with regard to C and D, E and F and G and H respectively. We shall see later what happens in this case under rule 42 but we should add that the RYA concluded that in such circumstances if X had fouled C she would have infringed rule 37.3 (for having established an overlap to leeward without leaving the other necessary room to keep clear), and if X had fouled D he would have infringed rule 37.1 (because he had not kept clear of a leeward yacht.) Needless to add that the same holds for Y in relation to E and F and for Z in relation to G and H.

4. Yacht establishing an overlap to leeward (37.3)

We have seen that rule 37.1 governs cases of yachts on converging courses but this is true only up to a certain point for it is a general rule which establishes a basic right of way for the leeward yacht but with no precise details. Rule 37.2 and above all rule 37.3 make distinctions: the first excluding rule 37.1 when yachts are not overlapped, and the second dealing with the particular case of overtaking to leeward; dispositions requiring the overtaking leeward yacht to leave "ample room and opportunity." The 1977 edition removed from rule 37.3 what was virtually a repetition of the ban in 38.2 (then 38.1) on luffing above a proper course while an overlap existed; this change, as we have already seen on page 28, has made no difference. At any rate it is difficult to see what advantage a faster yacht, capable of overtaking to leeward, would derive from luffing.

IYRU No. 27 (fig. 46) clearly indicates that "ample room" for the overtaken windward yacht means enough room to allow her, in her turn, to keep clear, and indeed that if it is impossible to give so much room the leeward yacht must not even establish an overlap. It is a short step from this consideration to the realization that the prescriptions of rule 37.3 only apply to an overlap which is established by the overtaking yacht: (a) from a position clear astern (b) to leeward. You cannot therefore rely on rule 37.3 when these premises are lacking, that is to say when you have not started from a position clear astern or when the overlap has been established to windward (in this last case the leeward yacht can defend herself by luffing "as she pleases" under rule 38).

IYRU No. 11 (RYA 1963/10, *Holmes* v. *Hennig*) is interesting for the light it throws on various aspects of rule 37. In position 2 of fig. 47, L was clear

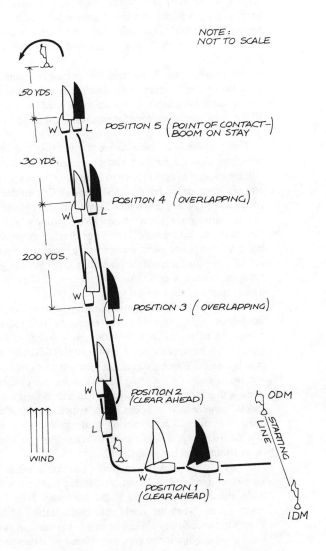

Fig. 47

astern of W. At that moment rule 37.2 required L to avoid W and so she had to alter course either to windward or leeward. Not wishing to risk a luffing match, permitted by rule 38, L preferred to establish an overlap to leeward and in doing so had, under rule 37.3, to be careful to leave W (the windward yacht) "ample room and opportunity to keep clear". Later, 50 yards from the buoy, L began to luff slightly so as to be able to round it but W refused to give way, hailing to her that she was the overtaking boat and therefore could not call for water, and a collision took place. L protested under rule 37.1, but was disqualified by the race committee. She then appealed and her appeal was upheld: the council holding that while W never sailed "below her proper course" to the mark (and therefore was not in breach of rule 39) the slight luff by L was a justified alteration of course because her aim was to arrive at the mark. Thus L had never sailed "above her proper course" (forbidden by rule 38.2) and as a result W was disqualified for breach of rule 37.1 for failing to keep clear.

It is another clear illustration that in cases of conflict between two courses both held to be "proper" that which must prevail is the course of the yacht which has established the overlap to leeward because it is *her* proper course which must be the evidence for establishing if there has been any infringement of rules 37.3 and 38.2.

This judgement is also note-worthy because it contains another important principle; that the leeward yacht's obligation to leave the windward yacht "ample room and opportunity to keep clear" is not a continuing one. This had already been stated by the U.S. Appeals Committee in a previous decision (NAYRU 36) where it was laid down that "this obligation cannot be construed as a continuing one"; that is to say an obligation which persists over a period of time. Just as the leeward yacht, her overlap established, must immediately leave the windward yacht the necessary room to keep clear, so the latter must at once take advantage of the possibility given her and get away. Otherwise any delay or hesitation on the part of the windward yacht might well turn to the disadvantage of the leeward yacht.

How strong is this obligation to keep clear which lies on every windward same-tack yacht and which is expressly referred to, even in rule 37.3, compared to the other obligations on a yacht establishing an overlap to leeward? We can see a good answer to this question in NAYRU 72 (fig. 48). Just before the starting signal, the leeward yacht (L) was sailing fast while the windward yacht (W), waiting for the starting gun preferred to jill along with her main well off; ten seconds after L had established an overlap to leeward L's shroud touched W's boom. The appeals committee disqualified W for infringing rule 37.3, observing that, immediately the overlap had been established, W "had ample room to keep clear either by luffing out of the way or by trimming in her mainsheet".

Analysing this situation carefully you will see that W was not required to keep clear under rule 37.3 until an overlap had been established. It was L who under rule 37.2 had to avoid W and her boom, even if it was let off more than normal. Later when the overlap had been established and the situation altered W was not specifically obliged to haul in her main so as to make it fill normally, but her new obligation to give way left her with two choices, one of which was to haul in her boom just enough to let L pass comfortably without having to alter course.

We have stressed this point so that it will not be said that the NAYRU decision contradicted IYRU No. 27 (fig. 46) which we looked at earlier. There are two different questions because the latter decision is about an overlap which could not develop as envisaged by rule 37.3 for lack of room while the former deals with failure to fulfil obligations as required by the rule after a perfectly reasonable and permissible overlap.

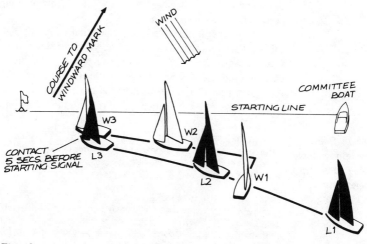

Fig. 48

Co-ordina- between s 37.1, 37.2 37.3

The three sub-paragraphs of rule 37 are obviously all of a family but it is interesting when we have seen how each of these related clauses works in its own sphere to consider the exact limits between their respective competence; and we can only repeat parrot-like IYRU No. 46 (RYA 1970/2, Grafham Water S.C.). This deals with the rights and obligations of a yacht clear astern, AN, which then establishes an overlap to leeward of a yacht ahead, AD. You should know that the two actors in this hypothetical case (pretty frequently met with while racing) are broad reaching on parallel and proper courses towards the next mark. AN as we have said is initially "clear astern of and directly behind AD but is travelling slightly faster and establishes an overlap of a few feet to leeward of AD's stern but inside the end of her boom". The RYA Council was then asked the following questions:

1. Is AN complying with rule 37.2 if: (a) in establishing an overlap she steers a course which will not take her clear to leeward of AD's boom end? (b) She maintains such a course after the overlap is established either until a collision occurs or until such time as it is impossible for AD (who has maintained her course) to take action to keep clear without causing a collision?

2. At what point are AN's obligations under rule 37.2 superseded by her rights as leeward yacht under rule 37.1? (b) In the circumstances described can AN be said, *prima facie*, to be complying with her obligations under rule 37.3 to allow AD ample room and opportunity to keep clear?

The council replied that the questions were based on a misunderstanding of the application of the relevant rules and went on:

"As soon as AN establishes an overlap to leeward from clear astern on AD, rule 37.2 ceases to apply; AD becomes bound by rule 37.1 and AN becomes bound by rule 37.3."

"The phrase 'ample room and opportunity to keep clear' in rule 37.3 means that in order to fulfil her obligations to keep clear under rule 37.1, AD is entitled to luff head to wind if she pleases and if, in so doing, any part of her hull, crew or equipment touches any part of AN's hull, crew or equipment, AN has not given AD 'ample room' to keep clear.

"It is a general principle in the rules that when the right of way suddenly shifts from one yacht to another, the yacht with the newly-acquired right of way must give the other yacht a fair opportunity to keep clear. In the present case, the right of way held by AD under rule 37.2 is suddenly transferred to AN under rule 37.1, consequently AN must give AD "ample . . . opportunity to keep clear. AN's obligation under rule 37.3 is not a continuing one".

Rule 38. Same tack-luffing and sailing above a proper course after starting

LUFFING RIGHTS
After she has *started* and cleared the starting line, a yacht *clear ahead* or a *leeward yacht* may *luff* as she pleases, subject to the *proper course* limitations of this rule.

38.2   PROPER COURSE LIMITATIONS
A *leeward yacht* shall not sail above her *proper course* while an *overlap* exists, if when the *overlap* began or, at any time during its existence, the helmsman of the *windward yacht* (when sighting abeam from his normal station and sailing no higher than the *leeward yacht*) has been abreast or forward of the mainmast of the *leeward yacht*.

38.3   OVERLAP LIMITATIONS
For the purpose of this rule: An *overlap* does not exist unless the yachts are clearly within two overall lengths of the longer yacht; and an *overlap* which exists between two yachts when the leading yacht *starts*, or when one or both of them completes a *tack* or *gybe*, shall be regarded as a new *overlap* beginning at that time.

38.4   HAILING TO STOP OR PREVENT A LUFF
When there is doubt, the *leeward yacht* may assume that she has the right to *luff* unless the helmsman of the *windward yacht* has hailed "Mast Abeam", or words to that effect. The *leeward yacht* shall be governed by such hail, and, when she deems it improper, her only remedy is to protest.

38.5   CURTAILING A LUFF
The *windward yacht* shall not cause a *luff* to be curtailed because of her proximity to the *leeward yacht* unless an *obstruction*, a third yacht or other object restricts her ability to respond.

38.6   LUFFING TWO OR MORE YACHTS
A yacht shall not *luff* unless she has the right to *luff* all yachts which would be affected by her *luff*, in which case they shall all respond even when an intervening yacht or yachts would not otherwise have the right to *luff*.

Earlier on we have said that rule 38 was designed to permit defensive manoeuvres by a leeward yacht in danger of being passed to windward by an overtaking yacht.

The 1961 rules explicitly said that "a yacht may luff as she pleases to stop another on the same tack from passing her to windward." The wording of the rule has since been partially modified but the intention has remained the same; that of preventing a tactic which, on any point of sailing, leads inevitably to the leeward yacht's sails being blanketed, and therefore to her being slowed down with easily imagined consequences. Because the act of overtaking harms the overtaken yacht it follows that the latter is allowed to take energetic defensive action, not only by luffing, that is altering course into the wind until she reaches a head-to-wind position, (definition Part I), but by luffing "as she pleases", that is to say almost without limits.

You may think this reaction, as permitted by the rule, is out of proportion to the offence since practically speaking, as we shall see shortly, such a luff is not blunted by any conditions except that of the *proper course* limitations of rule 38 itself. The reality is not so awful, however, because the yacht trying to pass to windward knows perfectly well what risks she runs and is, therefore, or should be, ready to react to the other's attack (she knows too that if she tried to pass to leeward rule 37 would smooth the way for her). Again the very small angle between the courses of the two yachts in such luffing duels is very unlikely to lead to serious damage in case of a collision (although rule 32 (Avoiding collisions) is always valid).

he right to

Who has the right to luff "as she pleases"? It is given to a yacht "clear ahead" and to a "leeward yacht". It is conceded not only to the yacht which has already been overlapped by the overtaking yacht (remember on the same tack it is impossible to be to leeward without an overlap) intending to pass to windward but also the yacht which at an earlier phase realizes that her opponent while still astern, is about to catch her up and establish an overlap: the yacht theatened with a windward overlap can logically defend herself in anticipation before the overlap becomes reality.

And what does "luff as she pleases" mean? It means that the yacht clear ahead or to leeward: (1) can luff to the extreme limit of the definition of luffing, that is to say "alter course towards the wind until head to wind" and remain in that position; (2) can, without infringing rule 35, by luffing obstruct the windward yacht and even prevent her from keeping clear; (3) can complete her luff rapidly and energetically without worrying whether the windward yacht has sufficient room to respond to it.

Here is an example of what a yacht with the right to luff can do. IYRU No. 58 (KNWV (Holland) 1970/2), shows us two yachts both hard on the wind on the same tack (fig. 49). L was ahead and to leeward of W and at a certain moment in spite of being so close wanted to tack and so started to luff. W suddenly seeing L ahead hailed her and began to luff too. L, hearing the hail, bore away but a collision was inevitable. W then protested L for infringing rule 41.1 (Changing tacks – tacking and gybing) and the race committee upheld the protest. L appealed saying that she had not tacked at all but had limited herself to luffing up to the position where she was head to wind and no more. The KNWV was of the same opinion holding that it was true and that she had therefore only made use of her right to "luff as she pleased" as permitted by rule 38.1. Result: W was disqualified for not having responded adequately to the luff.

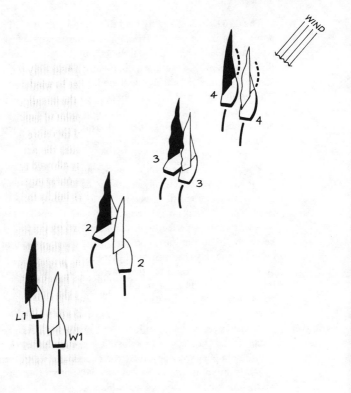

Fig. 49

Again we may look at a typical case in NAYRU 42 (fig. 50) Both yach
were sailing free on the starboard tack with jibs winged. While W w
establishing an overlap to windward of L the helmsman of the latter remov
the stick from his jib (position 2), shouted "I'm coming up" and imme
ately luffed W deliberately and constantly. Unfortunately W failed to ke
clear her boom touching L's deck. Five to ten seconds passed between t
hail and the contact. The U.S. Appeals Committee ruled that "a yacht whi
attempts to pass on the windward side of another yacht on the same ta
assumes an obligation to be prepared for the possibility that the leeward ya
will luff sharply, head to wind if she pleases, and therefore should establish a
maintain her overlap at a sufficient distance so as to be able to respond to a
and keep clear". L was absolutely within her rights to luff sharply and
was disqualified. Note that the windward yacht may not even cause a
curtailment of the leeward yacht's luff by her proximity unless an obstructic
a third yacht, or something else limits her ability to respond (rule 38.

This last case contains practically all the elements necessary to underst
the rule; it remains only to see where a yacht can luff as permitted by rule
She can luff "after she *started* and cleared the starting line". (That is not o

having cut the line in the sense of the definition but also when every part of the hull, crew or equipment have crossed the line.) Before the *start* and before clearing the starting line the right to luff is governed not by rule 38 but exclusively by rule 40.

How widely can rule 38 be applied? The defensive action provided for by rule 38 has a general application, in the sense that, after clearing the starting line a leeward yacht may avail herself of it everywhere and always. Only rule 42 (Rounding or passing marks and obstructions) replaces rule 38 when the leading yacht arrives two lengths from a mark or obstruction but becomes irrelevant when the rounding or passing is over.

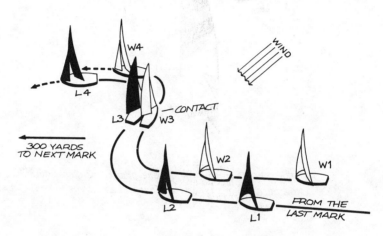

Fig. 50

verlap
in two
ths
)

"An overlap does not exist unless the yachts are within two overall lengths of the longer yacht," (see fig. 51). It follows that outside this distance rule 38 ceases to have effect and rule 37 is the correct one to apply.

In fig. 52 we see that in position 1, the leeward yacht, L, just because she is to leeward has the right to continue steadily on her course and W, the windward yacht, sailing faster on a converging course, must keep clear (rule 37.1). If, however, W, the faster boat, comes within two lengths she runs the risk of L availing herself of rule 38, altering her steady course, and starting to luff "as she pleases" in order not to be passed to windward.

This two-length limit does not mark a limit between the two rules – 37.1 and 38 – in the sense that a yacht overtaking another to leeward on a converging course (and therefore with right of way under rule 37.1) can, once she has an overlap within the two-lengths, start to luff "as she pleases" (see fig. 37). She must either sail steadily on her converging course when the windward yacht must keep clear unconditionally, or, once on a course parallel to that of the windward yacht, she can avail herself of rule 38.2 to head up but only up to, and not above, her "proper course". To repeat, this is because unrestrained luffing is only permitted as a method of defence against a yacht trying to pass to windward which must not degenerate into a means of attack to be freely used

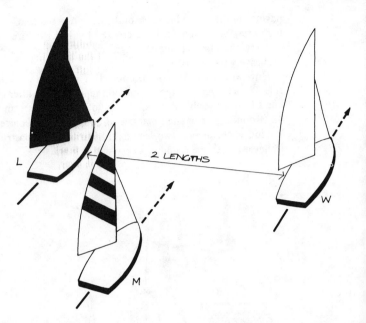

Fig. 51 L can luff W as she pleases. Under rule 38.2 M is not involv
because she has no overlap (but L, being clear ahead, can also luff M as s
pleases under rule 38.1).

by any yacht which starts an offensive by closing in from leeward.

We have seen that a windward overlap is governed by rule 38 whenever i
established within two overall lengths of the longer yacht, rule 38.3 adds t
"the overlap that exists between two yachts when the leading yacht *starts .*
shall be regarded as a new *overlap* beginning at that time". Nothing stra
here, indeed it is logical since the right to "luff as she pleases" is conceded o
"after the start and having cleared the starting line" (rule 38.1); therefore
obvious that nothing earlier, including an overlap can fall within rule 38.

Another case is envisaged in the second phase of rule 38.3 where it says
overlap which exists between two yachts, "when one or both of them compl
a *tack* or *gybe* shall be regarded as a new *overlap* beginning at that time". O
after having finished her change of tacks and being once again *on a t*
(definition Part I) will each yacht have assumed the position which will or
not allow her to avail herself of rule 38. There is an example of this in positi
of fig. 59 (NAYRU 65 discussed in section 3 of the comment to rule 38 on p
144).

Another example turns up in RYA 1968/7, *Coppersmith* v. *Fidelity* (fig.
where L and W were rounding a mark of the course, L simply bearing a
while W took a wider sweep which included a tack and thus overlapped
windward. L luffed up to defend herself and touched W. The race comm

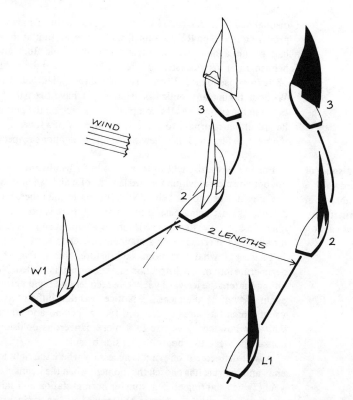

Fig. 52   In position 1 W must keep clear of L on a steady converging course. In position 2 W (being faster) enters the 2-length limit and establishes an overlap under rule 38. As a result L can alter course and luff W as she likes to prevent her passing to windward.

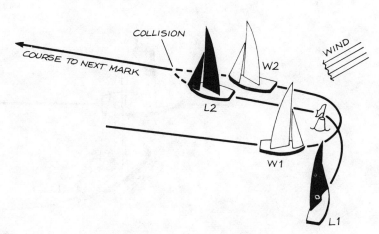

Fig. 54

disqualified L under rule 38.2 holding her guilty of having sailed above her proper course. The RYA Council said, however, that at the end of her tack W had begun a new overlap as understood in rule 38.3 and, given that the helmsman of W was astern of the mast of L, L had the right to luff under rule 38.1. In consequence W was disqualified for violation of rules 37.1 and 38.5. Without taking any notice of what might have been the previous situation between the two yachts the completion of a tack on the part of one of them and her resulting nearness to the other started a new overlap which, from that moment, determined their new rights and obligations respectively.

3. Helmsman of the windward yacht abreast or forward of the leeward yacht (38.2)

For the leeward yacht to be able to luff a windward yacht freely, she must not only be clearly within the two lengths of which we have already spoken but she may not be too far behind with respect to the other. Since such a luff is a defence against being passed to windward there is no reason for its existence once the overtaker has succeeded in his intention and has reached a position so far ahead as to render such a manoeuvre useless.

To repeat what has been said before, this defensive action must no degenerate into mere obstruction just because it has failed. Not even if, during a luffing match, the leeward yacht can recover and regain ground, is she allowed again to "luff as she pleases". Notice also that luffing "as she pleases" by a yacht which has already dropped too far behind and so rams her adversary with her bow can give rise to a more dangerous collision than any lateral contact between two boats almost side by side.

A well-defined cut-off point is necessary where the right to luff as you please ends and the rule has chosen the moment when the helmsman of the windward yacht (when sighting abeam from his normal station and sailing no higher than the *leeward yacht*) is abreast or forward of the main mast of the leeward yacht. Once this situation is reached the leeward yacht must not "sail above her *proper course*".

A good example appears in NAYRU 76 (fig. 55) where L luffs W and you

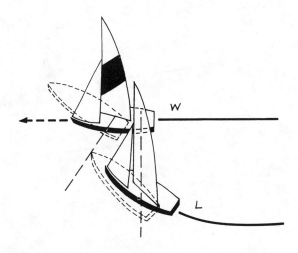

Fig. 55

can see how in the first position the helmsman of W has not yet reached mast-abeam position and therefore L still has the right to luff; while after the luff (dotted line) W has reached mast abeam and L must return to her "proper course" or to a course not "above her proper course".

This diagram also shows why rule 38.2 requires the bearing to be taken when the windward yacht is not sailing any higher than the leeward yacht: when the windward yacht luffs the bearing swings towards the bow of the leeward boat. For the same reason the helmsman of the windward yacht may not move forward to take his bearing, he must maintain his normal position. A point of view further forward than normal would falsify the bearing.

Whenever the bearing falls abeam, or forward, of the mast of the leeward yacht, the latter has no right to luff "as she pleases" (and if she has had the right she loses it and must put herself back to, at least, her proper course).

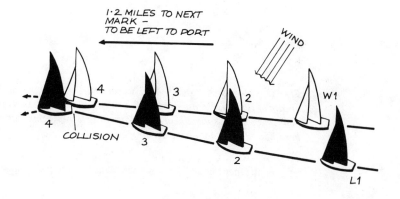

Fig. 56

NAYRU 74 provides another example. In fig. 56 L established an overlap to leeward within the two required lengths (pos. 1) and she kept this overlap until there was a collision (pos. 4). The U.S. Appeals Committee held that rule 38.2 was applicable and observed that when L established her overlap from astern to leeward of W within the two lengths required by rule 38 the helmsman of W was forward of the mast of L; and in consequence L had no right to sail above her proper course while this overlap continued. The decision explains and clarifies the point we have made before in the relationship between 37 and 38: a yacht establishing an overlap to leeward is sailing faster and eventually her mast comes abeam and then forward of the windward boat's helmsman but she cannot at this point avail herself of rule 38 and start to luff, but must continue to sail "not above her proper course" for the duration of the overlap; until, that is, having completely overtaken her adversary she finds herself clear ahead.

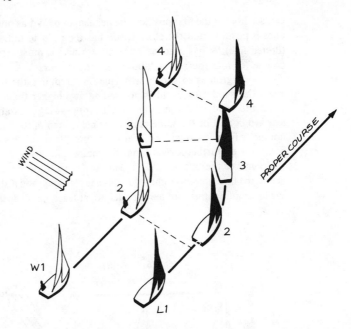

Fig. 57 Overlap established to windward: W's helmsman is not (pos. 2) abeam of L's mast so under rule 38 L may luff as she pleases (pos. 3) until W's helmsman has L's mast bearing abeam or astern. At this stage L·must curtail her luff and sail "not above her proper course".

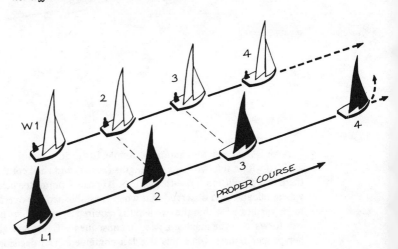

Fig. 58 Overlap established to leeward: L's mast right from the very beginning of the overlap (pos. 2) is astern of W's helmsman. For this reason L may not sail "above her proper course" during the overlap's existence (that is even when (pos. 3) W's helmsman drops astern of L's mast). Only when L is finally clear ahead (pos. 4) can she again "luff as she pleases".

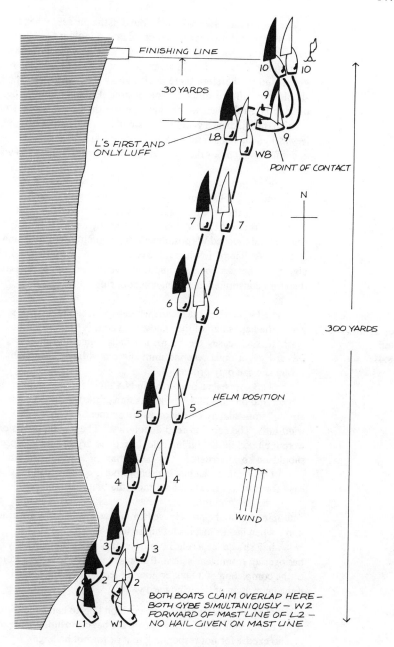

FINISHING LINE

30 YARDS

L'S FIRST AND
ONLY LUFF

L8

W8

POINT OF CONTACT

N

10   10

9

9

7   7

HELM POSITION

6   6

300 YARDS

5   5

4   4

WIND

3   3

2   2

BOTH BOATS CLAIM OVERLAP HERE—
BOTH GYBE SIMULTANIOUSLY—W2
FORWARD OF MAST LINE OF L2—
NO HAIL GIVEN ON MAST LINE

L1   W1

Fig. 59

The key to this essential rule is found in the phrase "when the overlap *began* or at any time during its existence". Have a look at fig. 57, an example of an overlap established to windward, and you will realize how, in such a case, the overlap begins with the helmsman of the windward yacht astern of the leeward yacht's mast; therefore there is absolutely no reason why the leeward yacht should not luff the other as she pleases. Looking now at fig. 58 where an overlap is established to leeward, we see that from the first moment of the overlap the windward yacht's helmsman is by the nature of things, ahead of the leeward yacht's mast; the case foreseen by rule 38.2 is realized at this moment and it follows that for the whole duration of the overlap the leeward yacht may not luff.

There is just one last case to look at, NAYRU 65 (fig. 59). After a simultaneous gybe, a new overlap began (position 2) and at that moment the helmsman of the weather yacht W was forward of the mast of yacht L. The overlap was never broken and finally, shortly before the finishing line, L luffed sharply and touched W (position 8). "Inasmuch as W's helmsman was forward of the mast line of L when the overlap began, the latter had no right to sail above her proper course while that overlap continued to exist and her luff therefore constituted an infringement of rule 38.2."

4. Hailing to stop or prevent a luff (38.4)

Rule 38.4 provides the means whereby you can prevent or stop an illegal luff where the helmsman of the windward yacht is forward of the leeward yacht's mast. In such cases the helmsman hails "mast abeam" or similar, and the leeward yacht must respond immediately without discussion. If she thinks it wrong she can only protest.

The U.S. Appeals Committee, in NAYRU 78, has commented aptly on this subject and on rule 38.5. The helmsman of the windward yacht shouted "mast abeam" immediately before or at the moment of contact in a violent head-to-wind luffs. The decision read as follows: "The hailing provisions in rule 38.4 were included in the 'luffing rule' to reduce arguments and protests and they should be so interpreted. The helmsman of a windward yacht who fails to protect his rights by hailing in proper time is entitled to little consideration. It is easy for him to see when he attains the 'mast abeam' position. On the other hand, the helmsman of the leeward yacht is, as a rule, in no position to determine 'mast abeam'. Hence he must rely on, and be governed by, a hail to know when he has lost his luffing rights.

"A hail should, as a rule, be unnecessary when the leeward yacht established her overlap from clear astern. But when an overlap results from convergence, or the completion of a tack or jibe, the leeward yacht should be held blameless if the helmsman of the windward yacht:

(a) that attains the 'mast abeam' position fails to hail either before the leeward yacht begins to luff or the instant she begins to luff. Failure to notice a luff is no excuse for not responding to it or for not hailing.

(b) that attains the 'mast abeam' position during a luff, fails to hail in time to enable the leeward yacht to bear away before contact.

"Since the helmsman of W, in the case before us, failed to hail in time to enable L to bear away before contact, the decision of the race committee is reversed, L is absolved from blame, and W is disqualified for infringing rule

38.5 in not keeping sufficiently clear of L to enable her to avoid contact by curtailing her luff as soon as she was obligated to begin doing so by the hail of 'mast abeam'."

The U.S. Appeals Committee have saved us an explanation and backed by all the weight of their authority we can only recommend a plea of "guilty" to all those helmsmen of windward yachts who fail to hail or who hail too late or have not bothered to leave their opponent enough water to bear away and curtail the luff.

5. Curtailing a luff (38.5)

In NAYRU 78 which we have just looked at, the weather yacht was considered to have infringed rule 38.5 and was disqualified for not having left the leeward yacht enough room to bear away when she was obliged to curtail her luff. We also saw that rule 38.5 required the windward yacht to keep herself far enough away to be able to avoid the leeward yacht's luff immediately, even when it was unexpected and sudden as well as long lasting.

This obligation is hardly surprising because, as we have said, the windward yacht trying to pass to windward knows perfectly well that she may be subject to a defensive luff from her opponent and must therefore always be ready and able to respond without running the risk of a collision. Swift and prolonged luffing is allowed and equally, when the luff finishes unexpectedly and suddenly, the leeward yacht is free to turn away as she likes.

Talking of rule 37 we saw (NAYRU 20 and IYRU No. 3 – figs. 32 and 38) that a "leeward yacht which has legally luffed a windward yacht may bear away suddenly and the windward yacht is obliged to keep far enough away . . . to give the leeward yacht room to bear away both suddenly and rapidly upon being hailed 'mast abeam' ".

We have also already seen in the decision of NAYRU 42 that the windward yacht "should establish and maintain her overlap at a sufficient distance so as to be able to respond to a luff and keep clear". In fact rule 38.5 justifies a curtailment of a luff only when the windward yacht cannot respond because an obstruction (definition Part I) a third yacht, or another object restricts her.

An amplification of this rule appears in NAYRU 44 (fig. 60). Yacht M, thanks to her spinnaker, came up between yachts W and L; all three were on the same tack, W, to windward and L to leeward.

In position 3 M overlapped both within the prescribed lateral distances. Up to this point all three yachts had been sailing on parallel courses but now W gybed (perfectly regularly and permitted by rule 41) on to starboard putting herself, equally correctly, on a direct course to the next mark. Almost immediately afterwards, (pos. 4) L luffed M violently and, since the latter did not respond, collided with her. In her turn W had to luff sharply to avoid M by passing astern of her.

After the incident W protested M for violation of rule 36 and L protested poor M invoking rule 38. The appeals committee held that "W, on the starboard tack was an obstruction to both M and L, and M, overlapped inside L, was entitled under rule 42.1(a) to room from L to pass the obstruction, which L failed to give her. It is to be noted also, in accordance with rule 38.5, that a windward yacht is not subject to disqualification when her ability to respond to an otherwise legitimate luff of a leeward yacht is restricted by an obstruction.

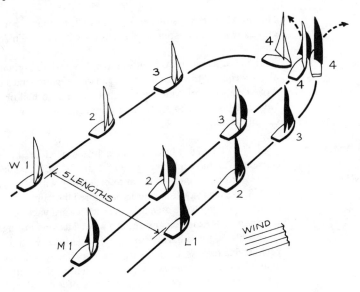

Fig. 60

"Since M was the victim of another yacht's neglect of the rules, namely L's improper luff, she was correctly exonerated from failing to keep clear of W."

6. Luffing by two or more yachts (38.6)

Up to now we have been dealing with the case of only two yachts overlapped under rule 38 but fairly often a number of boats are involved. When this happens the rule does not change and the yacht wishing to luff must be in such a position that she can, in fact and by right, luff all yachts which could be affected. That is to say all those yachts which, because they are affected, must respond to avoid a collision (fig. 61).

The only variant is that yachts which "would not otherwise have the right to luff" now must luff if luffed themselves. Rule 38.6 does not present any difficulties and may leave a doubt only about the lateral distance necessary between the first yacht to leeward and all the others, to comply with the two lengths required by rule 38.3 to make the overlap valid. In our opinion the rule allows no extension of this two-lengths limit in the sense that, for example, in fig. 62 L could luff W if there were more than two lengths between them (Note that the particular rule about the "intervening" yacht between two others – see definition "clear astern" – is quite different and has nothing to do with an overlap under rule 38.3.)

In conclusion it is necessary to respect the wording of rule 38.6 which means that "the right to luff all the yachts, etc.", is conditional also upon the existence of a valid overlap within the two lengths applying to "all the yachts which would be affected by her luff".

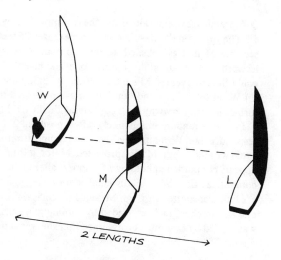

Fig. 61   L can luff M but not W. Thus L's luff is permitted only if W is not involved.

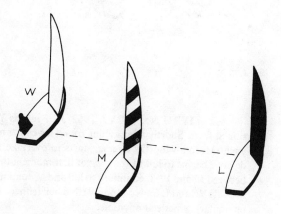

Fig. 62   L can luff both M and W. W, although she is beyond the mast-abeam position in respect of M must respond to M's luff (provided that M is responding to L's luff) since she is really responding to L's.

A practical example illustrates the rule more clearly. Let us look at NAYRU 18. The yachts in the class in question measured 25 feet overall and in fig. 63 we see that M had established an overlap with W to windward and with L to leeward both at lateral distances of one length. You will also notice that: (a) L could have prevented M's intervention by luffing and restricting her passage, (b) W on the other hand could not have narrowed the passage since rule 39 forbids her to bear away (c) L could individually luff M and W under rule 38.6.

In this situation immediately after position 2 L luffed slightly and M responded but W maintained her course and trimmed in her main boom to avoid contact with M. W protested M for infringement of rule 38.1. The appeals committee upholding M's appeal after her disqualification by the race committee said: "W is not disqualified for failing to respond in the usual way to L's luff, transmitted through M, since no collision resulted, W having avoided one and in effect had responded by trimming in her mainsheet. As no protest was lodged by L, it must be assumed that she was satisfied with the response to her luff."

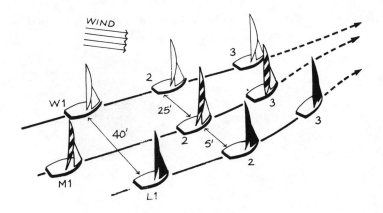

Fig. 63

Look at IYRU No. 4 (RYA 1962/31, Bensons Yacht Club – fig. 64) about similar facts. Shortly after gybing round a weather mark (in the order L, M, W) yacht M, following L's course, starts to overtake to windward (pos. 1). L in defence begins to luff M (pos. 2); at that moment there were some four lengths between M and W. L continues to luff and M continues to respond (pos. 3) until M fouls W, and L fouls M (pos. 4). No hail (either of "mast abeam" or "water" or similar) is made at any time.

The questions put to the RYA were as follows:

1. Is L entitled to luff?
2. Where L's vision is restricted by her proximity to M, and therefore she is in doubt as to the relative positions of M and W is L entitled under rule 38.4 to continue her luff until hailed to curtail or stop her luff?

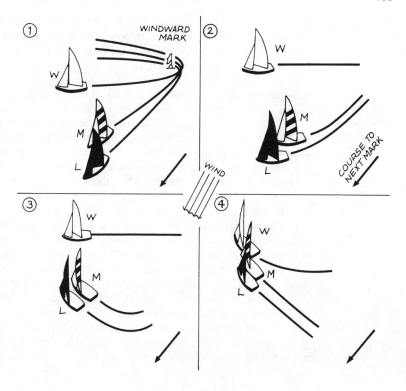

Fig. 64

3. If, after the foul, M retires, presumably because she has failed to respond or to curtail the luff in time, has W any recourse against L?
The answers were as follows:

1. The relative positions shown in figs. 1, 2, and 3 indicate that L was entitled to luff M in accordance with rule 38.1, until they reached position 4, where M's ability to respond further was restricted by the presence of W. At position 4 neither L nor M held luffing rights over W. L therefore became bound by rule 38.2 not to luff, and both were required by rule 38.2 not to sail above their proper courses during the existence of the overlap which, in accordance with rule 38.3, began when M was clearly within two overall lengths of W.

2. When, or shortly before, position 4 was reached, M should have called for water under rule 42.1(a) on L.

3. In accordance with rule 68.1, W could, if she thought fit, have protested against L.

In a final example IYRU No. 48 (NAYRU 130 *Keuka* v. *Benino* – fig. 65), we find the three yachts *Benino* (W) to windward, *Keuka* (M) in the middle, and *Kestral* (L) to leeward sailing towards the next buoy on slightly converging courses, all on the port tack and all sailing above their proper course. When they each came within two lateral lengths of the neighbouring boat they were already overlapped. M had the right to luff W and L had luffing rights over both M and W. W, sailing faster, moved ahead to a mast-abeam position and then bore away slightly making straight for the buoy, but fouled M. It must be remembered that L was always a little ahead of M (and the latter in fact had always kept clear of her), M hailed W to keep clear but W never hailed M or L.

The U.S. Appeals Committee settled the affair as follows: First of all they established that, at the moment of contact, M had lost her luffing rights over W as shown by the fact that M's bow hit W near her counter (which also implied that M was sailing above the proper course required by rule 38.2). But remember that L was near M with luffing rights over both M and W.

A doubt could arise as to whether, at a certain moment L, like M had also lost her luffing rights over W but the committee continued "since L retained luffing rights over M and there was doubt as to whether her luffing rights over W had terminated, she was, in the absence of a hail from W, within her rights in continuing to sail above a proper course". Thus L's right was held to include M – the intervening yacht – in relation to W. No blame therefore attached to M, which, keeping clear of L, had correctly observed rules 38.6 and 37.1.

So poor W came out of it badly, and was disqualified for infringing rule 37.1 "by bearing away upon and causing a collision with a leeward yacht close aboard", and rule 38.6 because "while M had not lost her luffing rights to W, W's helmsman either had not come abeam of L's mainmast or, if he had, he had not hailed her to that effect".

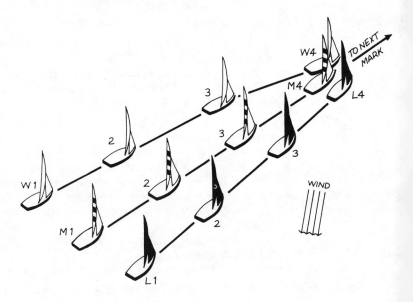

Fig. 65

Rule 39. Same tack sailing below a proper course after starting

A yacht which is on a free leg of the course shall not sail below her *proper course* when she is clearly within three of her overall lengths of either a *leeward yacht* or a yacht *clear astern* which is steering a course to pass to leeward.

Rule 39 has a limited scope both because the area concerned is already dominated by the basic rule 37.1 (a windward yacht shall keep clear of a leeward yacht) and because the 1965 modifications to this rule restricted it to "free legs" of the course.

"A free leg of the course" does not mean that rule 39 applies only on those limited legs planned for and described in the sailing instructions as "reaching" or "running" legs. On the contrary, given the inconsistency of the wind even a leg intended and announced as a windward leg can and does often become a "free leg". When this happens rule 39 applies because it is always valid on any leg where the proper course for the next buoy requires an off-wind point of sailing. (Off wind that is in relation to the wind at that moment and not in relation to the way the sails are set which may be wrong.)

Once this condition has been established rule 39 will apply provided that the yacht concerned is clearly within three of her overall lengths of the other yacht. The length that counts is that of the windward yacht (contrary to rule 38.3 where what counts is the length of the longer yacht).

In the new wording of the rule the superfluous phrase "after having started and after having cleared the starting line" has been eliminated. Superfluous because a yacht about to cross the starting line cannot be thought to be sailing on any leg of the course, nor can there be any 'proper course'. In practice, therefore, all cases involving bearing away are controlled before the start by rule 37.

Let us look in detail at what this rule forbids. As happens in practice we have spoken of a prohibition on bearing away. Reading the text the prohibition imposed on the clear-ahead windward yacht refers to her "sailing below her proper course" which is quite different. Look back at the definitions of "proper course" and again at NAYRU 79 (fig. 18) and you will see what this is about. The appeals committee said: "the diagram shows that after W had crossed L's bow at position 3, she sailed the shortest course to the mark and therefore did not sail below her proper course, the course she might sail, in the absence of the other yacht affected, to finish as quickly as possible, although she was at all times headed below the course made good in order to compensate for the transverse current. Therefore she could not be construed as having infringed rule 39." (In fact W, having been disqualified by the race committee for infringing rules 37.1 and 39, was cleared on appeal because it was held that L had overlapped (pos. 4) from astern and to leeward and could not therefore (rule 37.3) sail above her proper course, just as she could not (rule 38.1) force W to luff as long as the latter was not sailing below her proper course.)

We have identified the yacht that must respect the prohibition and the area in which it is valid and it only remains to see who can benefit from it. It protects (a) a yacht which establishes an overlap to leeward within the three-lengths distance and (b) a yacht clear astern (within the same distance) sailing a course to pass to leeward (this means that rule 39 is not relevant for a yacht following in another's wake).

In a certain sense the shadow of basic rule 37.1 falls across rule 39, but where is the exact line to be drawn between these two rules? In rule 37.1 the windward yacht must generally speaking keep clear of the leeward yacht, while rule 39 only forbids her to "sail below her proper course" and forbids it only in the particular situation. However, rule 39 does not apply to yachts on *converging* courses when rule 37.1 governs (in fact rule 39 refers almost always to parallel courses).

There should be no possibility of conflict with rule 37.2 because while the latter requires the yacht *clear astern* to keep clear, rule 39 concerns the yacht *clear ahead* and then only if the other is steering a course to pass to leeward. Similarly rule 37.3 governs the behaviour of a yacht overlapping to leeward from *clear astern* while rule 39 imposes a limitation on the windward yacht *clear ahead*. To finish let us remember that rule 39 (like rules 37, 38 and 40) applies to yachts on the same tack as is clear from the titles of the rules, and from the definitions of leeward and clear astern.

Rule 40. Same tack – luffing before start

Before a right-of-way yacht has *started* and cleared the starting line, any *luff* on her part which causes another yacht to have to alter course to avoid a collision shall be carried out slowly and in such a way as to give a *windward yacht* room and opportunity to keep clear, but the *leeward yacht* shall not so *luff* above a *close-hauled* course, unless the helmsman of the *windward yacht* (sighting abeam from his normal station) is abaft the mainmast of the *leeward yacht*. Rules 38.4, (Hailing to Stop or Prevent a Luff); 38.5, (Curtailing a Luff); and 38.6, (Luffing Two or more Yachts), also apply.

Rule 40 resembles rule 38 but refers to the period before the start (indeed to be precise refers to the period before a yacht clears the line itself). It is suitably adapted and moderated because of the obvious impossibility of permitting luffing matches among crowded yachts counting the seconds to throw themselves over the line when the starting signal goes. This last, however, does not mean that rule 40 ceases to apply when before the start yachts sail off a long way from the line. Look for example at fig. 29, NAYRU 63, and at the comment to rule 34 in which a series of duels are described which take the two yachts further and further away from the starting line. This distance makes no difference to the fact that G, clear ahead (pos. 3) may luff F only slowly (pos. 4) and a luff (including a head-to-wind luff which, in rule 38, is a defensive manoeuvre against the overtaking windward yacht) is allowed only if it is carried out in a way so as not to cause trouble: that is slowly.

Certainly here a luff is not so much a defensive action but a tactic which in the vicinity of other yachts allows a yacht to get set for the start or to head up to lose speed so as not to be forced to cross the line prematurely.

There is another relevant difference between the two rules; rule 40 speaks in general of luffing while rule 38 in the case of the overlapped yacht speaks of "sailing above her proper course" because a "proper course" (see definition Part I) exists only after the starting signal while rule 40 is concerned with what happens before starting and before having cleared the starting line.

Sailing above a close-hauled course means to head up without making headway, that is without gaining any advantage (see definition of *tacking*). Luffing on the other hand, as its definition explains, means altering course towards the wind until head-to-wind. But before the start these tactics, even if carried out slowly, may result in an over-enthusiastic attack against an opponent, so we again find a situation where the leeward yacht can act only if "the helmsman of the *windward yacht* (sighting abeam from his normal station) is abaft the mainmast of the *leeward yacht*". This has been discussed on page 144.

When the helmsman of the windward yacht is level with or forward of the leeward yacht's mast the latter is instantly limited to sailing not above a close-hauled course.

The fact that the rule talks not only of "luffing" but also of "sailing above a close-hauled course" reminds us that rule 37, (basic same-tack rule), is still valid before the start and before clearing the line. With a suitable mixture of rules 37 and 40 we can therefore (as far as the discipline to follow before clearing the line) draw two principal conclusions – that is to say:

(a) the leeward yacht (that is the overlapping yacht) has the right of way until she is sailing a close-hauled course (unless she has the helmsman of the windward boat abaft her mast when she can luff head-to-wind).

(b) that the yacht clear ahead (which not being a leeward yacht need not obey rule 40) can luff and sail as she likes with respect to the yacht which is clear astern of her.

Up to this point it is all reasonably clear but sometimes (always before the start) a yacht clear astern succeeds in overtaking another and overlaps her to leeward. Has she also the right to luff under rule 40? The RYA has given its opinion on this particular set of circumstances in RYA 1963/13 (*Complex III v. Yeoman*), fig. 66 shows what happened. Before the start L overlapped W to leeward and started a slow luff (pos. 4) while her mast was still astern of W's helmsman. Because W did not respond to the luff a collision took place (pos. 7) still before the starting signal. Both yachts protested and the protest committee disqualified L for infringing rule 40. The same protest committee nevertheless itself put a series of questions to the national authority (rule 77.2(a)) and the latter gave the following answers:

1. L had established her position as leeward yacht by bearing away to pass under W's stern. Therefore, L was not entitled to luff so as to affect W until L was abreast or forward of the "mast abeam" position. The race committee found as a fact that when L luffed, she was 15 feet to leeward of W, and decided that at this distance the luff did affect W. The council sees no reason to differ from this decision. L is disqualified under rule 40.

2. Had L converged from leeward on a steady course she would have had right of way throughout under rule 37.1

3. As soon as L had reached the "mast abeam" position and had the right to luff slowly under rule 40, W should have kept clear. W is disqualified under rule 37.1 for failing to do so.

This decision is given here, even though it is now out of date, to show up more clearly the modifications made to the old rule 40 which was applied in the

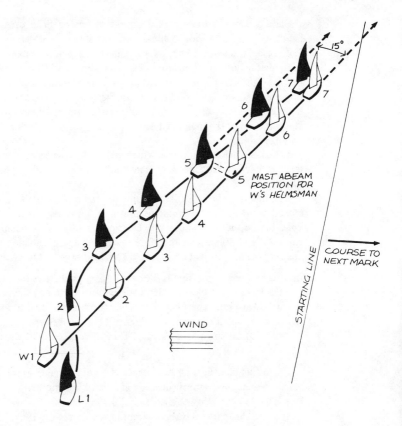

Fig. 66

above judgement. In truth the new rule 40 no longer allows luffing when the leeward yacht is beyond the mast-abeam position so that actually a yacht, which, before the start, establishes an overlap to leeward may luff immediately (be it understood slowly and leaving the other yachts the room necessary to reply) even if her mast is not yet abeam the windward yacht's helmsman. The only thing that matters is that the leeward yacht should "not luff beyond close-hauled course" while she is still abaft the mast-abeam position. All this is true before the start but after the starting signal announcing the beginning of a "proper course" (see the definition) the overlapping leeward yacht will have acquired the right (a) to luff without limit, that is above her proper course, if at the moment she started and crossed the starting line she was already beyond the abeam position (otherwise rule 38 would prevent her luffing: see the case of an overlap established by a leeward yacht – rule 38.2; and that of an overlap already existing between two yachts when that ahead *starts* – rule 38.3). (b) To luff, but only within the limits of rule 37.3 (that is not above a proper course) if at the starting signal she had not yet reached the mast-abeam position with respect to her opponent.

As far as the "room" and the "opportunity to keep clear" that the leeward yacht must allow to the other are concerned, it is evident here too that an analogy exists with the similar prescription in rule 37.3 and the reader should look there for an explanation of this point.

Note that rules 38.4 (Hailing to stop or prevent a luff); 38.5 (Curtailing a luff) and 38.6 (Luffing two or more yachts) apply to situations governed by rule 40 and explanations will be found in the comment to rule 38.

Up to the beginning of the Second World War when 95 percent of racing boats had fixed keels, the start was regulated by an undeviating unquestioned rule. They were heavy boats and needed a lot of room to sail in and time to get way on but once they had way on they were difficult to stop. Ideally therefore they started with full way close-hauled on the starboard tack; the yacht which succeeded in carrying out this tactic with the greatest skill had an overriding right-of-way to which there were no exceptions: there were no discussions about rule 36. After the war with the arrival of centreboard dinghies in great numbers, start lines were lengthened and restrictions put on the area for pre-start tactics. Yachts had perforce to adopt other methods of starting. It was one thing to write a beautiful perfect rule, it was another to expect it to be observed in a start of fifty or more boats. So it became necessary to modify (or indeed create) rules to allow them to stay as near as possible to the start line with their sails flapping, naturally on starboard tack with elbow touching elbow, until the starting signal gave the best, or the luckiest, the chance to haul in their sails and start. At the same time it became necessary to outlaw cunning or unsporting intentions, aimed at eliminating as many competitors as possible with short sharp unexpected luffs. And thus rule 40 was born, its text more or less the same today, at least in intention. However a general reappraisal of this whole situation has been going on for some years and the IYRU are now being urged with some force to limit the number of starters at least in the main international races.

Why should not a good helmsman, aware of his own tactical ability, begin his run-in far from the start line and considerably before the starting signal (in a small centreboard boat seconds seem like hours), close-hauled on starboard tack and, without ever altering his course, *start* with full way on? This concept is gaining ground and has been sustained by various national authorities and from a sporting point of view one can only agree. That is why in the 1973 editions a first timid amendment supporting these ideas was published which now appears in the 1977 edition as rule 35b.

Rule 41.   41.1   BASIC RULE
Changing tacks,   A yacht which is either *tacking* or *gybing* shall keep clear of a yacht *on a tack*.
tacking and
gybing   41.2   TRANSITIONAL
                A yacht shall neither *tack* nor *gybe* into a position which will give her right of way unless she does so far enough from a yacht *on a tack* to enable this yacht to keep clear without having to begin to alter her course until after the *tack* or *gybe* has been completed.

41.3   ONUS
        A yacht which *tacks* or *gybes* has the onus of satisfying the race committee
        that she completed her *tack* or *gybe* in accordance with rule 41.2.

41.4   WHEN SIMULTANEOUS
        When two yachts are both *tacking* or both *gybing* at the same time, the one
        on the other's *port* side shall keep clear.

During a race each competitor continually tries to improve her position
relative to her opponents. This leads inevitably to frequent changes of tack, by
tacking, or gybing, in close, indeed very close quarters, with other yachts. Such
activity has given rise to rule 41 which controls by a few simple prescriptions
and a mass of case law all changing of tacks.

**1. Yachts
tacking and
gybing and
yachts on tacks
(41.1)**

Rule 41.1 makes a general statement, laying on any yacht tacking or gybing
the duty to keep clear of any other yacht steady on a tack. Let us look at
NAYRU 63 shown in fig. 29 and discussed in the comment to rule 34.
"At position 4" – went the judgement – "G began a gradual luff as a
preliminary to tacking. As a result F became a windward yacht ... G,
however, could not pursue her intention to tack because doing so would have
infringed rule 41.1 in that she would not have been able to fulfil her obligation
to keep clear of F, a yacht on a tack."

F's favourable position can be maintained even if she changes course
because by definition, when a yacht is not *tacking* or *gybing* she is *on a tack*,
thus a yacht luffing up or bearing away still has the right of way over a yacht
which is changing tacks. Alternatively you may say that a yacht which is only
luffing or bearing away is not considered to be a yacht tacking or gybing. These
are absolutely different concepts clearly defined in Part I. The appropriate
definitions need to be studied carefully to understand when a tack or gybe
begins or ends.

The general principle contained in rule 41.1 holds good everywhere and at
all times. There are exceptions in the case of rounding a mark or clearing an
obstruction because then it will be the outside yacht to give the inside
overlapping yacht enough water to tack or gybe to achieve her end (rule
41.2(a)) and the yacht clear astern which must keep clear (rule 42.2(a)) of a
yacht clear ahead which gybes with the same object. Another exception
appears in rule 43 when, for reasons of safety, precedence is conceded to a
yacht forced to tack to avoid an obstruction. A third exception exists when the
yacht tacking or gybing has started correctly and finds herself near a
premature starter returning to start. In this case the premature starter must
keep clear of the tacking yacht (rule 44.1(a)). Finally there is a fourth exception
where a yacht is re-rounding a mark after having touched it (rule 52.1) because
she must keep clear of all the others (rule 45.1).

**2. Right of way
acquired
through a tack
or gybe
(41.2)**

Up to now we have considered the most simple case where in general a yacht
tacking or gybing is mixed up with another remaining on a tack. This situation,
governed by rule 41.1, is not subject to any variations and in its elementary
clarity is not susceptible to misreadings or misinterpretations.
The next paragraph, rule 41.2, deals on the other hand with a more

particular case, that of the yacht which by means of a tack or gybe wishes to get herself into a position which "will give her right of way" with regard to the other yacht on a tack; one for instance when changing tacks that will give her the advantage of starboard tack (rule 36) leeward or clear ahead (rules 37 and 38) or inside at the mark (rule 42).

In this case the whole thing becomes more complex because rule 41.2 lays down that such tacks and gybes must be carried out at a "distance" which does not hinder the yacht on a tack. And up to this point there would be no difficulty (indeed it could be still governed by rule 41.1), were it not for the complication that at a certain moment the initial situation is turned completely upside down and the tacking yacht which at first has to keep clear and at a correct distance suddenly acquires rights over her adversary who stayed on a tack. What therefore is this distance?

Rather than express it in terms of fixed measures the rule establishes an abstract criterion and lays down that this distance shall be such that a yacht on a tack "can keep clear without having to begin to alter her course until after the *tack* or *gybe* has been completed".

Now if we want to analyse rule 41.2 it is easy to see what "completed" means by looking at the respective definitions in Part I: a tack finishes "when she has borne away, when beating to windward, to a *close-hauled* course" (remembering that it is enough that she is pointed along the course even if she is not yet moving and her sails not yet full), or "if not beating to windward, to the course on which her mainsail has filled" and a gybe is complete when "the mainsail has filled on the other *tack*".

The real difficulty lies however in evaluating whether the distance chosen for this manoeuvre has been enough to "enable a yacht on a tack to keep clear, etc." On this point NAYRU 50 gives us useful guidelines when deciding a case where a yacht, A, close-hauled in 4 to 7 knots of wind tacked putting herself in front of B, on the same tack at a distance of 6 to 10 feet from her bow and on the same course. In the next three seconds B gained and narrowed the distance to two or three feet. B then tacked and protested claiming that A had infringed rule 41.2 by tacking too close. The race committee allowed the protest and A appealed.

The appeals committee reversed this decision saying: "The important consideration here is that the yacht which will have to take steps to keep clear after another yacht's tack has been completed, is not obligated to begin to alter her course prior to the completion of the tack, that is until the other yacht has borne away to a close-hauled course. The facts found by the race committee indicate clearly that B held her course for about three seconds after A's tack had been completed and then was able to tack without interfering with A. The information confirms by actual performance that the requirements of the rule were complied with and that A's tack was made properly and at sufficient distance from B. The decision of the race committee is therefore reversed and the disqualification of A nullified."

The carefully calculated explanation above is certainly a classical example of its kind although the appeals committee itself invites us not to rely always on similar arguments and it finishes thus: "but the conclusion must not be drawn from this decision that it is always right to keep 8 feet distance from a competitor. The minimum distance ahead to put between two yachts when changing tacks depends on the distance sailed by the overtaking yacht in the time which passes between the moment in which she has gone on to the new tack and the collision, it depends on the size and the manoeuvrability of the yachts in question, on the strength of the wind and that of the sea. The faster the overtaking yacht is sailing the further ahead the tacking yacht must put herself. Thus a relatively small and slow yacht must get much further ahead of a faster yacht than of a yacht of her own size."

3. Onus of proof in case of protest (41.3)

There can be no general rule for the determination of a fair distance and so each case must be studied separately and decided on its own, bearing in mind all the elements we have spoken of above, that is type of boat, speed and acceleration of the yachts, condition of the sea, wind, time, etc.

It is not an easy question, however, because it is difficult enough to reconstruct the actual facts but it is still more difficult to establish what did not happen but might have. In view of these often insurmountable difficulties, and in order to avoid decisions no better than throwing dice the rule has taken a short cut by laying down (rule 41.3) that the "onus of satisfying the race committee that she completed her *tack* or *gybe* in accordance with rule 41.2" must lie on the yacht which tacks or gybes. With this strict system of proof (which is similar to that in rule 42.3(d) and (e) and rule 43.2(b)iii) the desired result is reached: tacking and gybing too close are discouraged.

The onus of proof is absolute and integral. An example is given in RYA 1967/9, *Siris* v. *Petrel* (see fig. 67), which deals with an incident the facts of which were found to be as follows by the protest committee: W and L were both sailing close-hauled on the starboard tack between a half and three-quarters of a length from each other laterally. Finding herself more or less covered L tacked to pass astern of W and the latter protested asserting that she

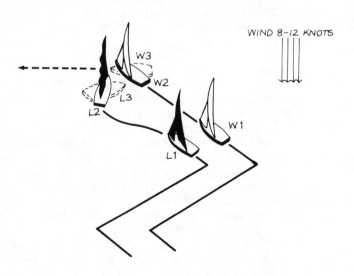

Fig. 67

had been forced to bear away to avoid a collision. The protest committee held that there was no collision and the doubt arose that W's bearing away had been unnecessary. But the appeals committee disagreed and judged as follows: "It is difficult to see how the protest committee could have been satisfied that L had discharged the onus placed upon her by rule 41.3; nor is this borne out by any of the diagrams submitted. Protest committees must be satisfied that a yacht in tacking complies with rule 41.3". This means that if the proof provided by the yacht which has tacked or gybed is not clear-cut but shadowed by even the smallest doubt it cannot be said that the requirements of rule 41.3 have been satisfied and her disqualification will be inevitable.

4. Simultaneous tacks or gybes by two yachts. (41.4)

When this situation arises the yacht "on the other's port side shall keep clear". But what does "on her port side" mean? Look at fig. 68 (NAYRU 28) where P tacks onto port tack at exactly the same moment at which S tacks on to a starboard tack. Given that P was not on a tack when S began to tack, only rule 41.4 could apply. On the basis of this P had to keep clear of S until both yachts were on their new tacks, after which rule 36 applied; and on the strength of this P being on port tack, had to continue to keep clear. In fact P was disqualified for violation of rule 36 which was held to be applicable by the time the collision took place.

Looking at fig. 68 you might have thought that each of the two yachts could legitimately believe that she had the other on her own port hand. But this illustrates perfectly that the situation must be viewed not as it is during or at the end of the manoeuvre but as it was at the beginning (that is to say when the head-to-wind position is passed when tacking – as in positions P.1 and S.1 in fig. 68 – and when the foot of the mainsail crosses the centre line of the yacht when gybing). If both yachts find themselves simultaneously in this situation, that is to say if both begin tacking simultaneously rule 41.4 applies. If on the

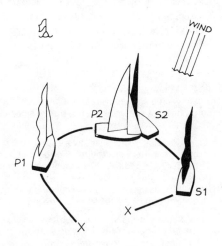

Fig. 68

other hand one of the yachts has, even by only a second or two, begun to tack or gybe before the other this latter, being still on a tack, immediately acquires rights under rule 41.1, but she must take care in her turn to complete her tack or gybe without tripping over rule 35 (Limitations on altering course).

SECTION C — Rules which Apply at Marks and Obstructions and other Exceptions to the Rules of Section B

When a rule of this section applies, to the extent to which it explicitly provides rights and obligations, it over-rides any conflicting rule of Section B—Principal Right-of-Way Rules and their Limitations, except rule 35, (Limitations on Altering Course).

Rules 42, 43, 44, and 45 form part of Section C which groups together the exceptions to the basic rules of Part IV. Thus rule 42 makes an exception to rules 36 and 37. Rule 43 makes an exception to rule 41.1 and rules 44 and 45 make exceptions to rules 36 and 37, 38 and we must examine them in turn. Only in the case of rule 35 is there no exception at all.

The exceptions in the rules of Section C prevail over the general rules only "to the extent to which it explicitly provides rights and obligations." This is to say that outside the cases considered here (rounding a mark or obstruction, tacking for reasons of safety, returning to the start, etc.), these rules cannot be applied analogously to similar cases not within the precise case laid down and foreseen by these rules of Section C.

Section C overrides any conflicting rule of Part IV Section B except rule 35, and there can be no exceptions to Section A: rules 31, (Disqualification), 32 (Avoiding collision), 33 (Rule infringement) 34 (Hailing) 35 (Altering course). This is logical because these rules contain prescriptions designed specifically to prevent any manoeuvre which can cause damage to other yachts.

Rule 42.   42.1   ROOM AT MARKS AND OBSTRUCTIONS WHEN OVERLAPPED
Rounding or   When yachts are about to round or pass a *mark,* other than a starting *mark*
passing marks   surrounded by navigable water, on the same required side or an *obstruction*
and   on the same side:
obstructions

(a) An outside yacht shall give each yacht *overlapping* her on the inside, room to round or pass the *mark* or *obstruction,* except as provided in rules 42.1(c), 42.1(d) and 42.4, (At a Starting Mark Surrounded by Navigable Water).
Room includes room for an *overlapping* yacht to *tack* or *gybe* when either is an integral part of the rounding or passing manoeuvre.

(b) When an inside yacht of two or more *overlapped* yachts either on opposite *tacks,* or on the same *tack* without *luffing* rights, will have to *gybe* in order most directly to assume a *proper course* to the next *mark,* she shall *gybe* at the first reasonable opportunity.

(c) When two yachts on opposite *tacks* are on a beat or when one of them will have to *tack* either to round the *mark* or to avoid the *obstruction,* as between each other rule 42.1 shall not apply and they are subject to rules 36, (Opposite Tacks—Basic Rule), and 41, (Changing Tacks—Tacking or Gybing).

(d) An outside *leeward yacht* with luffing rights may take an inside yacht to windward of a *mark* provided that she hails to that effect and begins to *luff* before she is within two of her overall lengths of the *mark* and provided that she also passes to windward of it.

42.2   CLEAR ASTERN AND CLEAR AHEAD IN THE VICINITY OF MARKS AND OB-STRUCTIONS
When yachts are about to round or pass a *mark,* other than a starting *mark* surrounded by navigable water, on the same required side or an *obstruction* on the same side:

(a) A yacht *clear astern* shall keep clear in anticipation of and during the rounding or passing manoeuvre when the yacht *clear ahead* remains on the same *tack* or *gybes.*

(b) A yacht *clear ahead* which *tacks* to round a *mark* is subject to rule 41, (Changing Tacks—Tacking or Gybing), but a yacht *clear astern* shall not *luff* above *close-hauled* so as to prevent the yacht *clear ahead* from *tacking.*

42.3   LIMITATIONS ON ESTABLISHING AND MAINTAINING AN OVERLAP IN THE VICINITY OF MARKS AND OBSTRUCTIONS
(a) A yacht *clear astern* may establish an inside *overlap* and be entitled to room under rule 42.1(a), (Room at Marks and Obstructions when Overlapped), only when the yacht *clear ahead:*

(i) is able to give the required room and

(ii) is outside two of her overall lengths of the *mark* or *obstruction,* except when either yacht has completed a *tack* within two overall lengths of the *mark* or *obstruction,* or when the *obstruction* is a continuing one as provided in rule 42.3(f).

(b) A yacht *clear ahead* shall be under no obligation to give room to a yacht *clear astern* before an *overlap* is established.

(c) When an outside yacht is *overlapped* at the time she comes within two of her overall lengths of a *mark* or an *obstruction,* she shall continue to be bound by rule 42.1(a), (Room at Marks and Obstructions when Overlapped), to give room as required even though the *overlap* may thereafter be broken.

(d) A yacht which claims an inside *overlap* has the onus of satisfying the race committee that the *overlap* was established in proper time.

(e) An outside yacht which claims to have broken an *overlap* has the onus of satisfying the race committee that she became *clear ahead* when she was more than two of her overall lengths from the *mark* or *obstruction.*

(f) A yacht *clear astern* may establish an *overlap* between the yacht *clear ahead* and a continuing *obstruction* such as a shoal or the shore or another vessel, only when at that time there is room for her to pass between them in safety.

42.4   AT A STARTING MARK SURROUNDED BY NAVIGABLE WATER
When approaching the starting line to *start,* a *leeward yacht* shall be under no obligation to give any *windward yacht* room to pass to leeward of a start-ing *mark* surrounded by navigable water; but, after the starting signal, a *leeward yacht* shall not deprive a *windward yacht* of room at such a *mark* by sailing either above the course to the first *mark* or above *close-hauled.*

Rule 42 is without doubt the most commonly used and therefore the most important rule in Section C. It is a rule which to the uninitiated sailor seems to bristle like a hedgehog with clauses and sub-clauses hiding what might be called the heart of the rule. It controls the most delicate and greyest areas of the whole race, the rounding or passing of marks and obstructions.

1. Passing or rounding

There is no difference in practice between rounding and passing as far as concerns the rights and obligations arising out of rule 42. A *mark* in the sense of the definition (Part I) always has a required side on which it is obligatory to pass while an obstruction has not (and is generally only passed) and that is why rule 42 comes into force for an obstruction only in the case of two or more yachts wishing or having to pass or round on the same side.

"A starting mark surrounded by navigable water" (rule 42.4) is an exception where the other paragraphs of rule 42 do not apply. When on the other hand a starting mark *can* be rounded or passed on one side only it is virtually an obstruction and therefore is governed by the appropriate paragraph of rule 42.

Let us look for example at IYRU No. 37 (RYA 1968/6, *Howdee Doodee* v. *Sooky*). Yachts P on port tack and S on starboard tack were nearing a mark of the course to be left to port (fig. 69). In position 3 S fouled P on her port side. P protested and the protest committee considering that under rule 42 she had no obligation to keep clear of S to allow her to pass on the wrong side of the mark disqualified the latter. However, S appealed and the protest committee also

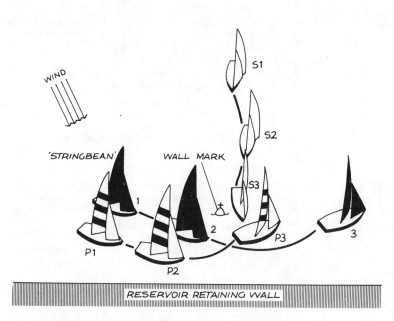

Fig. 69

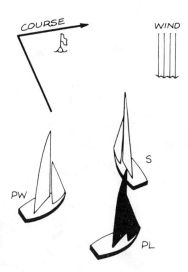

Fig. 70

asked the appeal committee under rule 77.2(a) to clarify the case and here is the decision of the RYA Council.

"1. For the purpose of interpreting the rules relating to rounding a mark, the mark can be 'removed' only when yachts either are tacking round it or are rounding it in opposite directions.

"2. The Wall mark had to be rounded to port and that was the required side. The fact that S intended rounding it to starboard had no effect on its required side. Had S either hit the mark or rounded it on the wrong hand, without colliding with P she would have infringed either rule 51.2 or rule 52.1(a)(ii).

"... S is disqualified under rule 32. Since the yachts were not 'about to round a mark on the same side' rule 42 did not apply and the situation was governed by rule 36 under which P is also disqualified."

Another case of yachts rounding a mark in opposite directions can be seen in the comment to rule 32, IYRU No. 51 (RYA 1971/4, *Hellhound* v. *Hare*).

2. Marks and obstructions   We should note here that a right-of-way yacht is considered an obstruction when she forces others "to make a substantial alteration of course to pass her on one side or the other". See for example IYRU No. 20 (RYA 1964/18, *March Hare* v. *Zest*), fig. 70, in which the yacht S on starboard had the right of way over two yachts on port tack PW and PL and therefore ranked as an obstruction because PW was obliged to make a substantial modification of her course to pass on one side or another of S. (To satisfy your curiosity PL, the outside yacht, was disqualified because she did not give water to PW, the yacht inside and overlapped.)

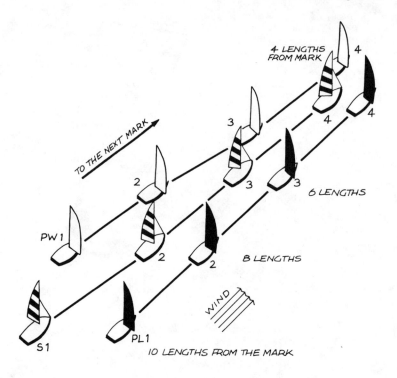

Fig. 71

Let us look at another similar case IYRU No. 45 (RYA 1970/1, *Falcon* v. *Tracey*, fig. 71). Here again we find the windward yacht PW overlapped with the leeward yacht PL. Here too a third boat arrived on starboard tack in contrast to the other two on port but in this case she sailed between them. You will also notice another difference from the preceding case in that they were all running towards the mark on slightly converging but steady courses. At a certain moment S fouled PW. The race committee disqualified both PL and PW for not having kept clear of S under rule 36.

PW did not give up and appealed maintaining that PL, once overlapped, had herself become an obstruction to PW, given that as the leeward yacht she had the right of way under rule 37.1; S, still according to PW's story, had not yet reached the two lengths distance when the overlap between PW and PL was established and therefore although she was on starboard tack she had no right to force herself between PW, the outside yacht, and the obstruction represented by PL. In conclusion PW maintained that rule 42.3(a) should have been applied and S should have gybed and passed to windward of PW without getting in her way. But the RYA dismissed the appeal observing that the correct interpretation of rule 36 was that "S held right of way over both port-tack yachts. Consequently PW did not rank as an obstruction to S and rule 42.3(a) did not apply between S and PL".

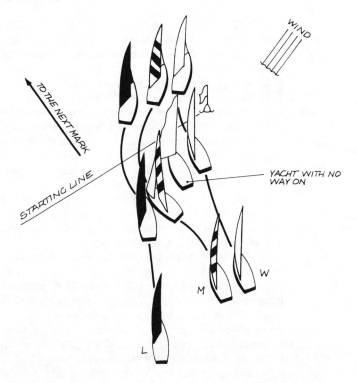

Fig. 72

It may seem that *Falcon* v. *Tracey* contradicts *March Hare* v. *Zest*. But if you look carefully this is not so. In fact in the latter case the obstruction was effectively represented by yacht S on the starboard tack and therefore with right of way. In *Falcon* v. *Tracey* PW was trying to make an obstruction out of one of the two yachts on port tack overlapped between themselves rather than the yacht (also S) which effectively prevailed over both of them under rule 36 – opposite tacks.

A yacht may also rank as an obstruction when she is obliged to keep clear and does not fulfil her obligation or indeed is stationary as in NAYRU 46 (fig. 72), where, in a collision between yachts M and L, L was disqualified for not having borne away to give room to M under rule 41.2(a); in fact the appeals committee held that the yacht O, which had purposely stayed without way on, must be considered an obstruction although they also observed that she too, overlapped as she was with L to leeward, would have been obliged to get under way to keep clear, under rule 37, by pulling in her main and thus permitting M to pass without having to bear away on L.

Rule 42.3(f) refers to the specific application of the rule in the case of a "continuing obstruction" represented by shallow water, a length of coast and such like.

**3. Yachts
subject to rule
42**

Rule 42 is applied only to those yachts which "are about to round or pass a *mark* on the same required side or an *obstruction* on the same side (and what "are about to round" means we shall see better in paragraph 4 further on). An exception (rule 42.4) is a starting mark surrounded by navigable water, that is to say it can be rounded or passed on all sides.

But this is not enough because we must also make sure whether these yachts are on the same tack or on opposite tacks and underline that rule 42 comes into force (a) for yachts on the same tack at any moment during the race, that is to say even before they have *started* in the sense of the definition; (b) for yachts on opposite tacks not only after they have *started* (and for that it is enough to cross the starting line) but after they have cleared the starting line (this is more clearly explained in the definition of starting).

The distinction is extremely important and must not be forgotten because it follows that between two or more overlapped yachts on opposite tacks about to start near a mark or obstruction, rule 36 will prevail (not rule 42) until they have all cleared the starting line completely.

Now while it is true that rule 42 applies only to yachts which are "about to round or pass a *mark* or *obstruction*" it is not equally true that it is enough to be rounding or passing a mark or obstruction for this rule to be applied inevitably. It may not be necessary for it has been said that rule 42 is one which is to be applied "only when, at a *mark* or *obstruction*, it is considered that the interaction between the yachts manoeuvring needs to be controlled because of a situation which could lead to accidents." The interpretation comes from the jury of the Nordic Cup 1968 (*Guappa II* v. *Krangel*) when they observed that in the case before them (fig. 73) the outside yacht O, which had to give room to the inside yacht I could not in any case have rounded the mark more closely than she did and therefore had absolutely no reason to invoke rule 42 with respect to yacht C which she accused of having established an inside overlap too late.

**4. The distance
at which rule 42
takes effect**

We have seen that rule 42 deals with yachts which "are about to round or pass a *mark* or *obstruction*" and from this we learn that when these particular circumstances are not present the usual right-of-way rules of Part IV remain in force and not the exception. Therefore we must see when rule 42 begins to be valid and when it ends.

Looking at it quickly you could believe that application of rule 42 starts with the establishment of an overlap between the yachts which are about to round or pass: but you must remember that basically the overlap is only one essential condition for calling on rule 42. In other words two or more yachts can already be overlapped at a longish distance from the mark or obstruction but this does not mean that they must obey rule 42 rather than rules 36, 37, or 38.

Before 1965 the distance at which the yachts were considered "about to round or pass" (with the subsequent entry into force of rule 42) had to be examined case by case and since everyone's judgement was extremely subjective it was an inevitable source of longwinded discussion and endless arguments. Now the new criterion of two lengths enforced by rule 42.3(a)(ii)

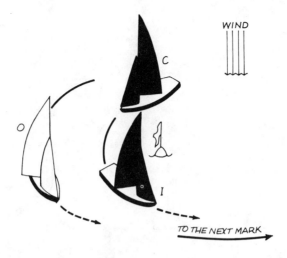

Fig. 73   Already O must give room to I and therefore cannot invoke rule 42 against C; in fact O could not round the mark more closely than she is doing anyway.

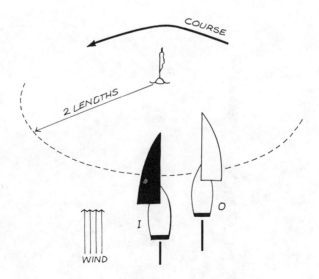

Fig. 74   At the moment she crosses the 2-length limit O, outside, must begin to keep clear of I overlapped on the inside.

Fig. 74a

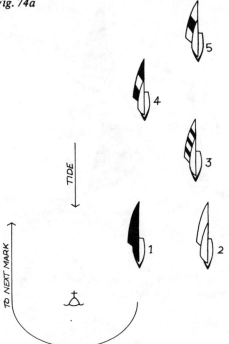

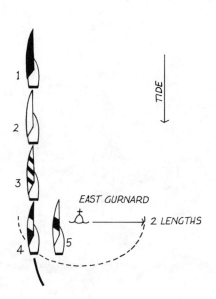

gives a distance to be taken as a basis for the point at which the yachts become "about to round or pass" and therefore must obey rule 42 (see fig. 74).*

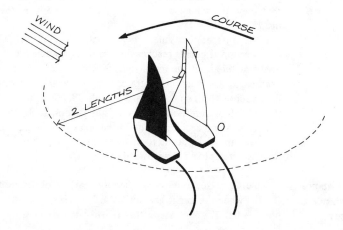

Fig. 75   As a result of O's luff the two yachts are no longer "about to round" the mark on the required side; thus, although less than 2 lengths from the mark, they are not subject to rule 42.

This is confirmed by RYA 1968/10 (*Shiralee* v. *Doodlebug*) where it was held that "rule 42.1(a) does not prevail over rules 37.1 and 38.1 until the outside or the leading yacht of two yachts overlapped reach a distance of two of their overall lengths from the mark".

Some years later this decision was officially confirmed in IYRU No. 71 (RYA 1974/9, Seaview Yacht Club). Let us look at fig. 74a. In position 1 yacht No. 4 is clear ahead of No. 5 and therefore has no problem. However (partly because she does not succeed in establishing an overlap on No. 3, ahead of her, and partly because of the current), she finishes by having to round the mark with a fairly large sweep and in fact outside the two-length circle. Being outside this fatal distance she has no right to avail herself of rule 42.2(a)(i) or (ii) with respect to yacht No. 5. It follows that "if No. 5 is within two of her overall lengths of the mark when No. 4 returns inside that distance, (see position 2) and establishes an outside overlap on No. 5, rule 42.1(a) will begin to apply and No. 5 can claim room at the mark".

* Rule 42 is always applied from the moment the yachts reach the two-lengths distance but it is possible that it could be applied even before. It cannot be excluded that in very particular cases with certain conditions of wind and sea depending on the positions of marks or obstructions a protest committee might hold that the rounding (more perhaps than a passage) was started even before the two-lengths limit. Certainly this would be a rare case, difficult to prove and to be considered with maximum caution, but you could not exclude it completely.

You must remember that a yacht cannot be considered "about to round a mark" if she is not sailing a course aimed at leaving the mark on the required side; and an application of this is the case envisaged by rule 42.1(d) since yachts which are luffing up on the wrong side of the mark certainly cannot say that they are sailing a proper course to round it on the required side (see fig. 75).

If the application of rule 42 begins only when the yacht clear ahead or one of the overlapped yachts reaches the two-lengths circle it is logical that until they arrive at this limit the usual right-of-way rules of Part IV prevail. Look for example at the situation illustrated in fig. 76: before arriving at the two-lengths limit yacht O has, on the strength of rule 38, the right to luff yacht I which has the obligation to respond to this luff but as soon as she touches the limit of the two lengths and decides to sail for the mark then O must give I, already inside and overlapped, sufficient room to round the mark (provided of course that she does not prefer to go to windward of the mark as rule 42.1(d) allows her to do).

5. The distance at which rule 42 no longer applies

Rule 42 ceases to be valid when the mark or obstruction has been rounded (that is when the yacht has put herself on her new proper course for the next mark – fig. 77) or passed, (that is when the yacht is no longer abeam of it, having passed it – fig. 78).

Doubts arise when the inside yacht instead of rounding and sailing off on her new proper course continues on her original course; but it is clear that by so

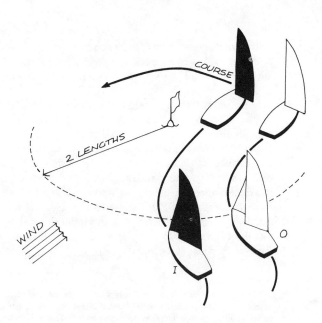

Fig. 76   O can luff I but arrived at the limit O prefers to alter course to round the mark and must give room to I, overlapped and inside.

doing she goes further and further away from the mark and cannot therefore expect to avail herself of a rule which presupposes by its very definition proximity to the mark or obstruction. This proximity can have no relation to the two lengths of rule 42.1(d) since this measurement deals only with the phase of closing the mark or obstruction and not that of getting further away from it.

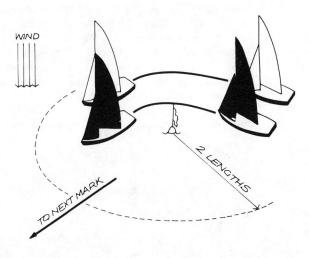

Fig. 77   Both yachts are on course for the next mark; thus they have finished their roundings and are no longer subject to rule 42 even though they are still less than 2 lengths from the mark.

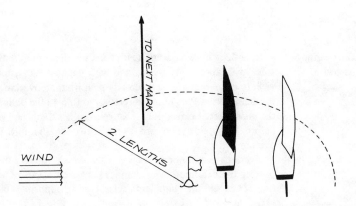

Fig. 78   Having passed the mark rule 42 no longer applies even in the 2-length limits.

The same thing is true in the case of the inside yacht that, having been given room and benefited from it, tacks in a much wider sweep than necessary because she thus indubitably forces the other to give more room than was needed (rule 42.1(a)) and therefore puts herself outside the conditions required for the application of these rules of exception at which we are looking.

A classical example is seen in IYRU No. 50 (Canadian Yachting Association 21). Looking at fig. 79 you see that yacht L has correctly given room to the inside yacht W, equally correctly overlapped, and has then continued on the same course for at least a length beyond the mark before starting to luff with the intention of putting herself on her new course to the next buoy. However, W is slower to turn and a collision results at position 3. The Canadian Appeals Committee disqualified W for violation of rule 37.1 deciding that rule 42.1(a) was no longer applicable in her favour because she had already been given sufficient water to complete her rounding and was not then hindered from keeping clear of L because the mark was too near.

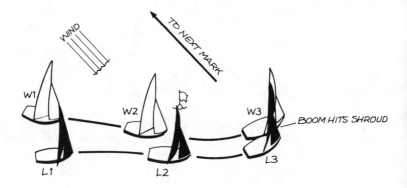

Fig. 79

6. The overlap in general

Rule 42 is in two parts: the first deals with room at marks and obstructions when overlapped and the second with yachts clear astern and ahead in the vicinity of marks. We have already seen what an overlap is when we looked at the definition in Part I, and in relation to rule 42 the obligation to give room to the inside yacht exists only if an overlap is established early enough (that is before the outside yacht arrives at the two-length limit). We must look at this overlap in detail.

Overlaps usually occur between same-tack yachts but when rounding and passing the definition even includes yachts on opposite tacks. Here rule 42, a rule of "exception", supplants rule 36 and "opposite tack" cases are ignored except in rule 42.1(c).

Having said this we can see that to have right-of-way under rule 42.1, the overlap must be established on the inside between the mark or obstruction and the other yacht, and before the other yachts (outside) finds herself at two of her own overall lengths from the mark or obstruction as in fig. 80. It is enough for any part of the hull, equipment or crew to cut – not clear – the circumference of that theoretical magic circle with its radius equal to two of her own lengths.

An inside overlap cannot be established when the outside yacht has reached the two-length limit (although an outside overlap can always be established) nor may a yacht clear astern establish an overlap when it is not within the power of the yacht clear ahead to give the required room (rule 42.3(a)i). The rule is obvious and needs no explanation. Finally it must not be forgotten that two yachts are considered overlapped when, although one of the two is clear astern of the other, a third yacht in the middle overlaps both (see definition in Part I). Examples are given in figs. 81a and b: in 81b yacht M has no overlap on O as I, the link, is not between them.

Let us look at another example of a third yacht which, because she is not in

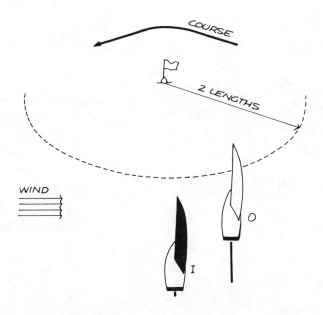

Fig. 80   I has still time to establish an overlap on O as the latter has not yet reached the 2-length limit.

the middle of the other two, cannot make a link in the chain. As you can see in fig. 82 (where A is overlapped with BO and BO is overlapped with BI) BI cannot ask for water from A because there is no overlap between them before the two-length limit from the mark. BO is not an intervening yacht, she is not between the other two, and therefore BI under rule 42.2(a) must keep clear of

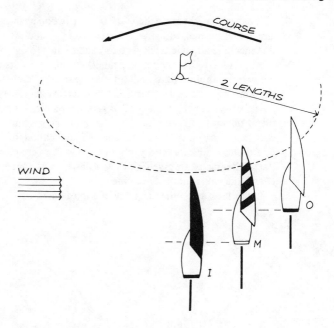

Fig. 81(a)   Thanks to M, I is overlapped with O and both M and O must give her room at the mark.

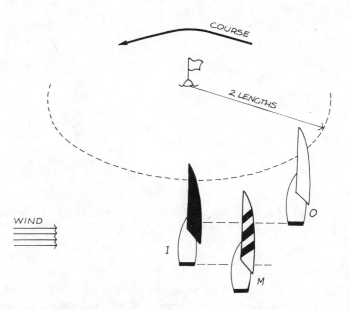

Fig. 81(b)   I is overlapped with M and O but she is not the intervening yacht; thus M cannot pretend to have an overlap on O and has no right to room from her.

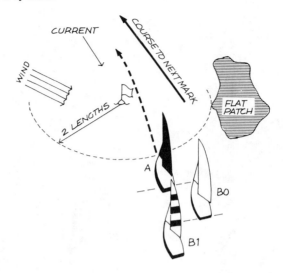

Fig. 82

the yacht clear ahead A. To be an intervening yacht BO would have had to have overlapped A on the inside that is to say on the side towards the mark. BI in her turn would have had to have overlapped with BO also on the inside between BO and the mark.

To sum up what must poor BO do seeing that BI is clearly overlapped before BO arrives two lengths from the buoy? BO must sail as if she was an outside yacht and must obey rule 42.1(a) giving the inside yacht BI room to round or pass the mark. All this is found in 1972/4 RYA Bristol Avon Sailing Club, now IYRU No. 59. The flat patch indicated in the drawing is unimportant, it did not figure as an obstruction and we only know that, being wooded, it affected the wind pattern in a way which reduced the room for the rounding still further and made the yachts calculate everything to a centimetre.

7. Overlapping on widely divergent courses

"In establishing the right to room at a mark, it is irrelevant that yachts are on widely differing courses, provided that an overlap within the definition is established". This principle is authoritatively laid down in IYRU No. 21 (RYA 1964/19 – fig. 83) Here *Nimrod*, B, while she had been overlapped correctly, did not wish to give room to *Dinah Doo*, A, maintaining that, given the enormous difference between the two courses, *Dinah Doo*, rather than establish an overlap, had in reality forced a passage but she was wrong because both the protest committee and the RYA decided rule 37.1 was not applicable and that rule 42.1(a) governed the situation.

Dealing on the other hand with yachts on parallel courses as for example in fig. 74, the determination of the moment in which a valid overlap is established does not present any difficulties. The only problem in theory would be that of the lateral distance between the yachts; but it is obvious that if this distance is small rule 42 comes into force and if large there will be no problem of room and it will not be necessary to invoke rule 42.

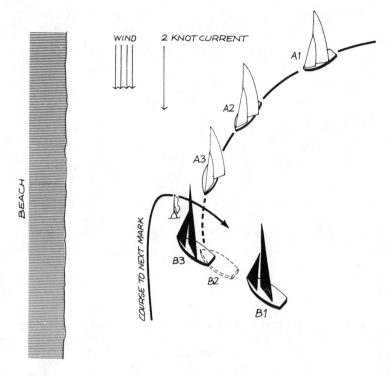

Fig. 83

However, some doubt could arise in the case of converging courses with large angles between them. That is to say somebody could maintain that yacht I (fig. 84) which will round inside can no longer ask for water from O, outside, because the latter in position 2 has already touched the magic circle while I was still outside. But this is incorrect because you can clearly see that already by position 1 neither of the two was clear astern of the other; and this means that the two were overlapped even before O touched the two-length limit and that yacht I had already acquired in time her right for room to round on the inside and maintained it until the rounding was finished.

In fact "according to the definition of overlap since neither of the two yachts is clear astern of the other, an overlap within the terms of 42.1(a) can be established at any distance" (RYA 1968/8, *Ariel* v. *Slieve Donard*).

8. Breaking an overlap and the onus of proof (42.3(c)(d))

The two-length limit, as we have just seen, is absolutely specific and unchanging. Whoever can reach it while still clear ahead cannot be forced to give room because from that moment onwards the yacht clear astern no longer has the right to establish an inside overlap (rule 42.3(a)ii). On the contrary the yacht clear ahead has not even the onus of proof, it is the other yacht which must bear the burden of convincing the race committee that her overlap has been established in time (rule 42.3(d)).

On the other hand rule 42.3(c) shows us that when an overlap exists at a

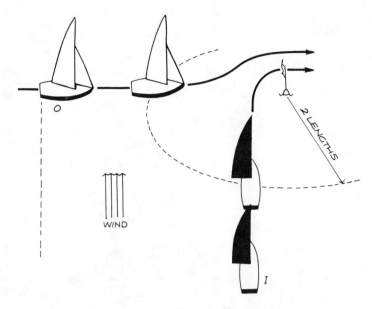

Fig. 84   I and O are already overlapped at position 1, before O gets to the 2-length limit; thus I has right to room to round the mark.

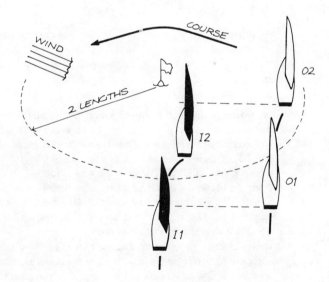

Fig. 85   Having established an overlap in time, before O arrived at the 2-length distance I then lost it (position 2); nevertheless rule 42.3(c) gives her the right to room at the mark.

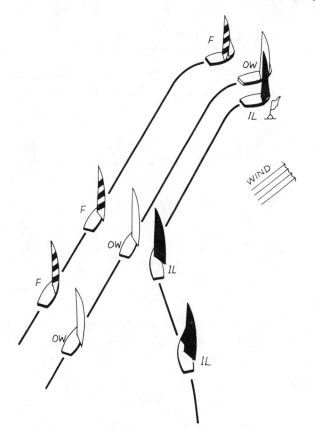

Fig. 86

considerable distance from the mark, in the absence of any corroborative evidence, the onus of satisfying the race committee that the overlap was subsequently broken is transferred to the outside yacht which makes that claim (fig. 85). This is in fact the case examined in (fig. 86) *March Hare* v. *Sugar Plum* (RYA 1967/12). The situation was as follows: at about 10 to 12 lengths from the mark, the inside yacht IL, was already overlapped with the outside yacht, OW. Starting to round the mark IL asked for water hailing "within two lengths", but OW replied "you have lost the overlap" and a collision resulted. The RYA decided the inevitable protest in second instance in favour of IL for these reasons: "It is agreed and the race committee's diagram shows that at some ten to twelve boat's lengths from the mark, IL established an overlap to leeward on OW as a result of their course converging. Clearly, IL discharged the onus laid upon her by rule 42.3(d). If the overlap was broken before OW came within the two-lengths distance of the mark (rule 42.3(a)ii), IL became bound by rule 42.2(a). If the overlap continued to exist at the time OW came within the two lengths distance of the mark and was broken thereafter, OW was bound by rule 42.3(c). In the absence of any corroborative evidence on either side the onus lay on OW to satisfy the race committee that the overlap was broken before she came within two lengths of the mark."

**9. Overlap —
tacking near a
mark or
obstruction
(42.3(a))**

Looking at fig. 87 we see B, a port-tack yacht, arriving at the mark and tacking, cutting the two-lengths limit (or indeed being within the two lengths) and thus bringing herself into a position which hinders A's passage between her and the mark (pos. 2). Strictly A cannot pretend to "be entitled to room under 42.3(a)" because the overlap began immediately after B's tack and certainly was not established before the two-lengths distance. However the addition of sub. para ii in 1969 means that now the two-length principle is not applied whenever one of the yachts in question tacks or completes her tack when she is even partly inside the magic circle. Now A has the right to enough room to complete her rounding or passage (pos. 3) and B having tacked too late must give her this room.

If rule 42.3(a)(ii) did not exist, A sailing steadily for the mark on starboard tack (pos. 1) would find herself unable to ask for room to pass inside and in fact B could reply that the overlap had not been established before the two lengths and that A therefore must keep clear of B. But the new rule requires B having tacked within the two lengths, to keep clear and well out to give adequate room to A.

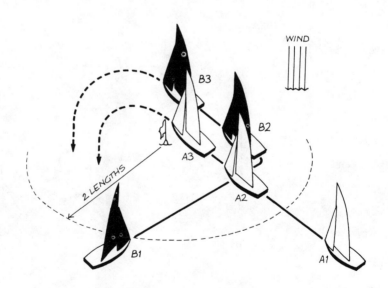

Fig. 87   It might appear that A, coming to the mark on starboard, could not have room from B as the overlap was established within the 2-length circle but rule 42.3(a) (ii) gives A the right to room when B has "completed a tack within two overall lengths of the mark".

When, on the other hand, B completes her tack outside the two-lengths zone without there being an overlap, A cannot ask for water on the inside (see fig. 88). In any case remember that rule 43.2(a)(ii) refers only to tacking and never applies to gybing.

Before we leave the subject let us look at another example, IYRU No. 59 (RYA 1972/4, Bristol Avon Sailing Club). Two yachts on opposite tacks were sailing towards a mark to be left to starboard. At a certain moment P (on port tack) tacked and put herself to windward of, and inside S. Given this situation the following question was put to the RYA: "When S came within two lengths of the mark, P was passing under her stern and clearly had no overlap. Can P claim room at the mark?" And here is the RYA's reply: "Under rule 42.3(a)(ii) the two-lengths determinative does not apply since one of the yachts 'has tacked in the vicinity of a mark'. Accordingly, if S is able to give the required room rule 42.1(a) requires her to do so on the assumption – which we take it is implicit in the question – that the overlap is established by P prior to the rounding manoeuvre." In other words the outside yacht, the other having tacked in the magic circle, loses the protection afforded by the two-length rule against last minute "barging" and must give room *as if* the overlap had been established earlier.

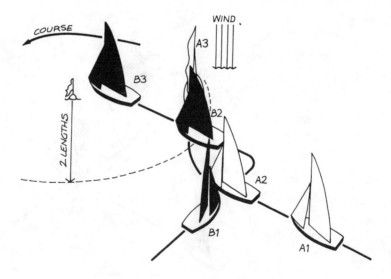

Fig. 88   B has clearly completed her tack before the two-length circle; thus rule 42.2(a) remains in force and since A has not succeeded in overlapping her before the 2-length circle (pos. 2) she is not required to give A room to round inside her.

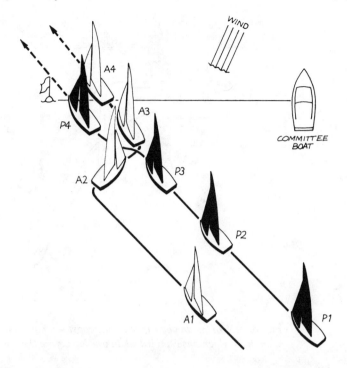

Fig. 89

FIV 1969/2 (*Pamperio III* v. *Atilo*) while not directly applying rule 42.3(a)(ii) deals with the same subject. As you can see in fig. 89, *Atilo*, A and *Pamperio*, P, were sailing towards the finishing line both close hauled on the starboard tack. In position 2 *Atilo*, to leeward but ahead, tacked and so put herself immediately ahead of *Pamperio*, she then tacked again. *Pamperio* protested under rules 41.1 and 36; but the race committee dismissed the protest and indeed disqualified her for violation of rule 42.3(a). *Pamperio* appealed, but without success, because the Italian national authority, basing its decision on the facts found in first instance, accepted that the first encounter (pos. 2) was quite in order which meant she had no recourse to rule 42.1(c) and that in the later phase (when *Atilo* went back on to the same tack as *Pamperio*) the two boats were clear ahead of each other and so that it was impossible to protest under rule 42.3(a)(ii).

"The subsequent overlap established by *Pamperio*" continued the appeal jury, "together with her bearing away towards the mark, was carried out too late and was in fact an infringement of rule 42.3(a)(ii) which forbids a yacht clear ahead of another to establish an inside overlap and thus to have the right of way (as in rule 42.1(a)) if the yacht ahead of her finds herself within the two-lengths limit from the mark."

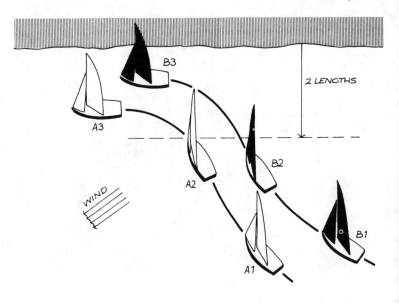

Fig. 90   Nearing an obstruction – the coast – A must under rule 42.1(a), give room to B which has established an overlap before the 2-length limit.

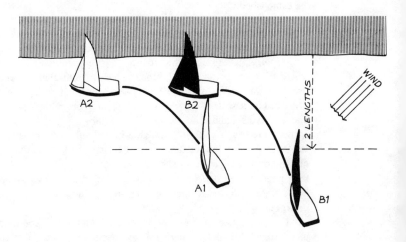

Fig. 91   Nearing an obstruction B has not established an overlap on A before the 2-length distance and has therefore no right to room. This also is governed by rule 42.1(a) and not by rule 42.3(f).

10. Overlaps at a continuing obstruction (42.2(f))

This is rarely found at sea or in open waters but common enough in more enclosed areas, above all on rivers and reservoirs or indeed where the competitor is forced to sail as close as he can to the shore to avoid stronger tides and currents.

You might ask why in such cases this particular rule 42.3(f) is necessary and why the general rule 42 is not enough, if you look carefully however, you will see immediately that you are dealing with quite a different situation.

First of all rule 42.3(f) deals only with how and when it is possible to establish an overlap in this one particular case, that is along a continuing obstruction; after which, if the overlap is in order, rule 42.1(a) will come into force, and oblige the outside yacht to give the inside one sufficient "room to pass the obstruction" for the whole of its length. Let us look at some examples: in fig. 90 we see A and B already overlapped; A on the strength of rule 38, can luff B, but as she nears the continuing obstruction constituted by the coast and comes within the two-length limit she must, in order not to infringe rule 42.1(a), give room to B, already overlapped some time earlier. On the contrary in fig. 91 B is not overlapped at the prescribed distance (that is before A arrives at the two-lengths limit) and therefore she cannot expect A to give her room under 42.1(a). These are two of the commonest cases of closing any obstruction and it does not make any difference that the obstruction later turns into a continuing obstruction along which the yachts must sail. Therefore when establishing her overlap while nearing the obstruction B must pay attention to the usual two lengths rule (42.3(a)).

It is only when the yachts are not closing the obstruction, because they are already sailing along it, and it is a continuous obstruction that we need the particular application of rule 42.3(f). If a yacht clear astern wishes to sail between the continuing obstruction and the yacht clear ahead she must respect the specific prescriptions of this rule which lays down that an overlap can only be established if there is sufficient room between the two and no danger from the manoeuvre; that is only if the yacht clear astern can pass between them in safety (figs. 92 and 93).

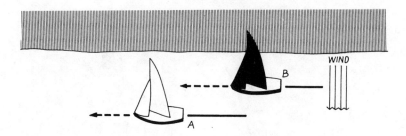

Fig. 92   B may establish an overlap over A since there is sufficient room inside to do so safely. A is under no obligation to give B room but must continue on her course without squeezing her.

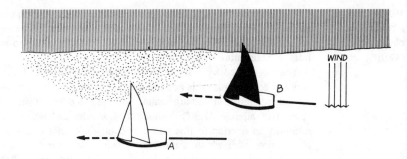

Fig. 93   B has no right to overlap A since the shallow water prevents her doing so safely. If she does so it is at her own risk and A is under no obligation to make it easy for her.

When these safe conditions do not exist a yacht establishes an inside overlap completely at her own risk and consequently an outside yacht has no obligation to give her room (always understood that if she is expressly asked – rule 35 – she must not cause the other – rule 32 – damage) but it is obvious that in such a case the yacht that is trying to establish an inside overlap is in breach of rule 42.2(f) and must retire or be penalized for having forced a passage.

IYRU No. 69 (RYA 1974/4) explains that in the situation shown in fig. 93a yacht B can establish an inside overlap only if she can do it safely, that is to say without running the risk of fouling A or running ashore. "Possibly the rules governing this situation may be more simply explained by saying that when A is sailing as close to the shore as, in the prevailing conditions, is prudent, B is not entitled to establish an inside overlap and does so at her own risk."

And if on the strength of this rule B establishes an inside overlap because there is room and because she can do it safely and if in order to defend herself

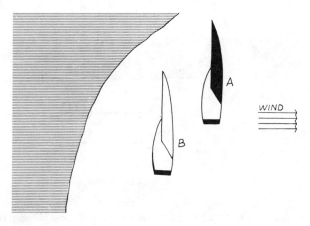

Fig. 93a

"A subsequently luffs," the RYA adds, "and B is in danger of running ashore, B, as the inside yacht under rule 42.1(a) is entitled to claim room from A to keep clear of the obstruction".

It is interesting that another yacht racing can also be a continuing obstruction. Let us look at the example given in fig. 93b IYRU No. 67 (NAYRU 163). Near the finishing line yacht W established an overlap on L and then a third yacht, M, intervened between W and L overlapping both. All three continued side by side until they crossed the finishing line without narrowing the lateral distance between them; however, W protested M accusing her of having profited from a space which under rule 42.3(a) was not

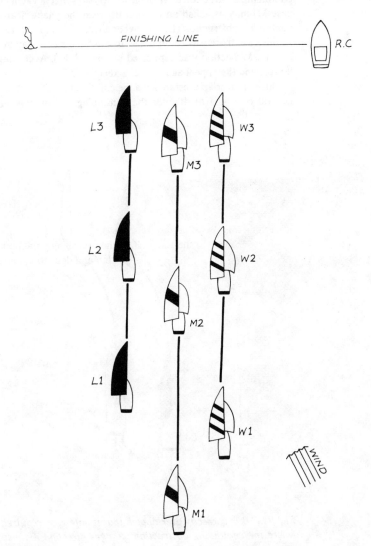

Fig. 93b

her right. The committee, noting that between L and W there was sufficient room for M as well, dismissed the protest but W appealed and here is the decision of the appeals committee: "Rule 42.3(a)(ii) says that a yacht clear astern shall not establish an overlap and be entitled to room when the yacht clear ahead of her is within two lengths of an obstruction except as provided in rule 42.3(f). L and W were within two lengths of each other. By definition, obstructions include craft underway if they are large enough, so that each of the three yachts L, M and W was an obstruction to the other two, W had established her overlap on L from clear astern and was attempting to pass her. Inasmuch as this did not occur quickly or in a short distance, L was a continuing obstruction to W. Rule 42.3(f) says that 'a yacht clear astern (in this case M) may establish an overlap between the yacht clear ahead (W) and a continuing obstruction (L) only when there is room for her to do so in safety'. In this case there was room for M to establish an overlap in safety between L and W. M's action was supported by rule 42.3(f). Accordingly, she infringed no rule and the appeal against her is dismissed."

Once an overlap is established the condition is fulfilled for the application of general rule 42.1(a). If later the continuing obstruction, instead of being a

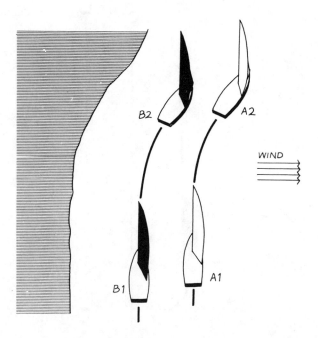

Fig. 94   B is correctly overlapped, that is safely, as required by rule 42.3(f); where the continuing obstruction changes direction A must leave B enough room to continue to pass it safely.

straight line has a kink or a curve (fig. 94), the outside yacht must continue to give the inside yacht adequate "room to pass it" and therefore must similarly change her course when and as necessary. This holds also if, after the overlap is established the water shallows (fig. 95) and if somewhere along the shore other obstructions (such as bridges, vessels, branches of trees, etc.) force a yacht to keep further off. In all these cases the outside yacht must give room if the overlap has already been established but will be under no obligation to do so if there is no overlap (or, to be precise, if the yacht clear astern cannot establish one safely).

RYA 1968/11 (*Bald Eagle* v. *Poseidon*) confirms that "A yacht which has established an overlap between a continuing obstruction and an outside yacht in conformity with rule 42.3(f) has the right to room even to pass a later obstruction which consists of a projection beyond the original obstruction (referring to a brick building sticking out from the bank along which the boats were sailing) as long as the overlap has been established before the outside yacht reached the two lengths limit from the second obstruction." The obligation of the outside yacht ends when the obstruction ends; from that moment rule 42 ceases to apply and the ordinary rules of Part IV come into play once again (figs. 96 and 97).

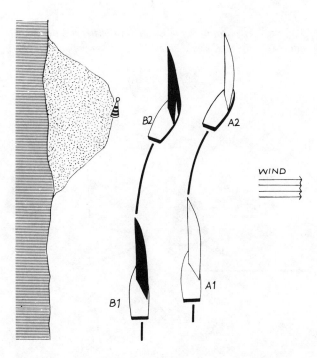

Fig. 95 Suddenly arriving at a shallow patch, B (already overlapped) continues to have right to room to pass the continuing obstruction.

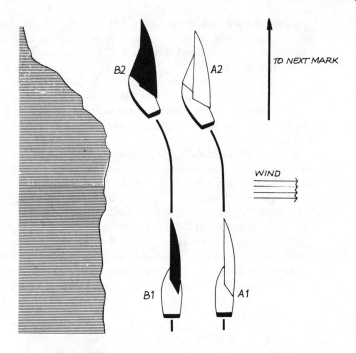

Fig. 96   At position 2 the continuing obstruction ends with respect to the course for the next mark, rule 42 ceases to apply and A can luff B under rule 38.

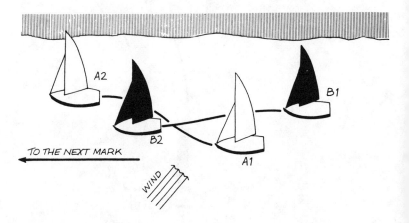

Fig. 97   When B tries to establish an inside overlap A bears away slightly (she is not prevented by rule 39) so as to hinder the establishment of an overlap and to avoid the consequences of rule 42.

11. Room to round or pass

If all the conditions required by the various sections of rule 42 are present "an outside yacht shall give each yacht overlapping her on the inside room to round or pass the *mark* or *obstruction*". Rule 42.1 itself lays down that "room includes room for an *overlapping* yacht to *tack* or *gybe* – when either is an integral part of the rounding or passing manoeuvre". This is a wide general definition because it covers a tight turn with minimum distance between the buoy and the outside yacht calculated to the nearest inch and a wide sweep and may have to include within the term "room" possible mistakes of judgement or performance in the manoeuvre itself. The IYRU was therefore asked to give, once and for all, an authoritative interpretation of this subject and replied (IYRU No. 40) as follows: "the word 'room' in rule 42.1(a) means the room needed by an inside yacht, which, in the prevailing conditions, is handled in a seamanlike manner, to pass in safety between an outside yacht and a *mark* or *obstruction*". A comparatively abstract definition and in fairness it could not be otherwise because situations of this kind must be examined case by case. So let us look at some practical examples, remembering that when examining individual cases there are three basic elements to consider: (a) the manoeuvre must be conceived, planned and carried out in a seamanlike manner; clearly it

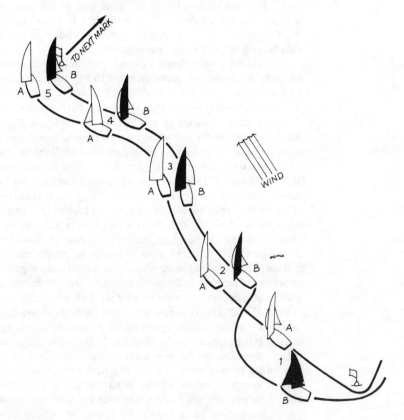

Fig. 99

is not "seamanlike" to make too large or too slow a turn; and it is wise to remember that what is good for racing is not always "seamanlike"; (b) the passage between the buoy and the other yacht must be made with a margin of safety but without an excess of prudence; (c) the two elements above must, in their turn, be considered with reference to the weather at the time, the particular place and type of boat in question; it is one thing to round a mark in a flat calm when there is plenty of space and it is quite another thing to round the same mark in bad weather with obstructions (vessels, yachts or such like) round about; and again dinghys and large offshore yachts present very different problems of manoeuvrability.

In RYA 1967/11 (*Mistoffelees* v. *Pronto*) this meaning of "room" was discussed. When rounding a mark of the course the inside 12-footer IW had 6 feet clear between her and the mark which however did not stop her boom from touching the port shroud of the outside boat OL. The race committee held that the latter had given adequate room because during the rounding the other was 6 feet from the mark but the RYA concluded that under rule 42.1(a) IW was "entitled to as much room to round the mark as she would have taken in the absence of any other yacht".

The decision is laconic but we bring it to your attention because it obviously took into consideration the tidal current and so the necessity for a bigger margin of safety for the inside yacht. From this we can draw the conclusion that "room" is not to be measured theoretically but must be estimated in each case bearing in mind all the circumstances.

To make the matter clearer we can look at another decision, NAYRU No. 64. In fig. 99 the outside yacht, A, gybes shortly before the mark (pos. 4–5) in such a way as to force the inside yacht, B, not only to let off her spinnaker boom to the forestay to avoid hitting the mark but also to haul in her main more than necessary so as not to touch A. In this case A's disqualification was inevitable because "B was under no obligation to alter the trim of her sails in order to avoid a collision with either A or the mark", she had the right to round it in a normal way, by not leaving her room to do so B was infringing rule 42.1.

Fig. 100 shows NAYRU 83, which came to the same conclusion. Here the outside yacht P instead of keeping clear of S's gybe, luffed to try to pass astern of her as she gybed but did not succeed and fouled her. The decision said that the purpose of rule 42.1(a) "is to ensure that in rounding or passing marks under the stated conditions, an inside overlapping yacht shall be given, even if on the port tack, sufficient room to handle her sheets and sails in a normal manner. This includes gybing where gybing is an integral part of the rounding or passing. Therefore S, the inside starboard-tack yacht, was entitled to gybe without interference round the leeward mark of the course."

Rule 42.1(a) lays down that an outside yacht must give room to all yachts overlapped inside. An example where a number of yachts are rounding the mark together appears in the NAYRU 22 (fig. 101). At position 2, yacht M hailed L for room; but the latter was too close to be able to do so and (pos. 3) M was forced to bear away to avoid W's stern and fouled L. At this point the appeals committee observed first of all that L had left room yes, but only enough to pass the mark and not to round it, and underlined that an inside yacht must hail for room when in her opinion she thinks she has not enough room, and that such a hail was particularly useful when there were a number of

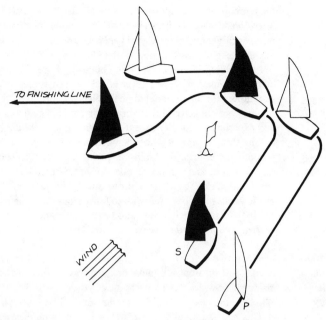

Fig. 100

yachts about to round. The committee ended by disqualifying L for "failing to allow W and M sufficient room. The outside yacht must keep sufficiently far from the inside yachts to be able to respond to a hail but also to be able to give necessary room to all the yachts with an inside overlap even without there being any hails."

These two practical examples give no idea of the infinite variety of cases which come up in the course of racing; in conclusion we can only say that

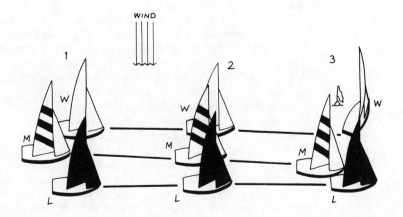

Fig. 101

judgements on "enough" or "not enough" room can only be made one at a time after considering wind, sea, current, type of mark or obstruction, the type and number of yachts involved and generally speaking anything that can influence however slightly the outcome of the manoeuvre itself.

In deciding these cases the ability and personality of the individual helmsman must, however, never be considered, a theoretical helmsman serves as a model for all; a model to be modified according to the level of racing and the average capacity of the competitors, since beginners do not have the skill and experience you may expect to find in an international championship.

One thing is sure, it is for the outside yacht to prove that the room she left was adequate, because the inside yacht, once she has shown that her overlap existed in time and that her manoeuvre was correct, has nothing to worry about and nothing else she needs to prove during the hearing. Therefore although an inside yacht must be careful not to force a passage when she has no right to do so, the outside yacht must take every precaution not to squeeze anyone correctly overlapped between her and the mark (or obstruction).

12. Obligation to gybe at first reasonable opportunity (42.1(b))

When two or more yachts are about to round a mark and when they are overlapped on opposite tacks or on the same *tack* without *luffing* rights the inside yacht which "will have to *gybe* in order most directly to assume a *proper course* to the next *mark*," must gybe "at the first reasonable opportunity".

This specific obligation aims to avoid the situation when the inside yacht does not gybe at once and maybe forces a number of others, converging on the mark to wait on the outside for their turn to gybe and round. As a result there can be dangerous crowding and confusion leading to accidents in contrast to the object of rule 42 to control the use of the room round the mark in such a way as to simplify and speed up the rounding.

The rule also blocks an unscrupulous competitor trying to abuse his right and take his adversary for a walk, perhaps in order to help a third yacht.

The obligation does not extend to an inside yacht which has to tack round the mark instead of gybing; tacking as it is carried out against the wind is easier and takes up less room and on a windward leg any close-hauled course will at least be working to windward.

For the same reasons it is clear why this obligation is not imposed when the overlapped yachts are on the same tack and the inside yacht has the right to luff; in this case the danger is less since there cannot be much of an angle between the courses of the two yachts. For example in fig. 102 the inside yacht A which is to leeward on the same tack can continue on her same course and B can in no way compel her to round or to alter course.

An interesting new case has just appeared in the 1978 additions to the IYRU case book No. 84, USYRU 195 (see fig. 103) Here two Ensigns overlapped on opposite tacks were running down to the leeward mark to be left to port. Near the two-length circle S luffed having hailed P to which P replied "You can't do that". As her bow came abreast of the mark S bore away to gybe and touched P. S protested P under rule 36 and P counter-protested S under rule 42. In their decision the appeals committee pronounced as follows: "Rule 42 is a rule of exception. In some situations at marks and obstructions outside yachts otherwise holding right of way must nonetheless yield to a yacht inside and even alter course to move far enough away from the mark or obstruction to

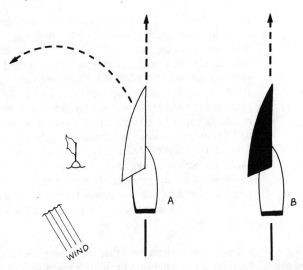

Fig. 102   The yachts are on the same tack and A, to leeward, has luffing rights and has no obligation to gybe to put herself on her new course and can continue (rule 37) in the same direction. B has an obligation to give adequate room to round the mark but, if A does not round, B cannot compel her to do so.

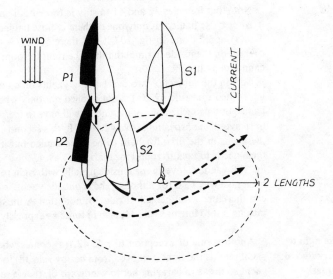

Fig. 103

give the otherwise obligated inside yacht the room she needs to pass or round it, but if the inside yacht takes more room than she needs, the basic rule rather than rule 42 is the one which applies. . . . An outside yacht which, in the absence of a mark or obstruction, would be obliged to keep clear of an inside yacht, is not relieved of her obligations to do so by rule 42 except to such an extent as may be explicitly provided in rule 42 itself." As S was starboard-tack yacht and she had been found to have gybed at the first reasonable opportunity as rule 42.1(b) required her to do, P was disqualified, showing that 42.1(b) has no force until the inside yacht passes the gybe point.

Fundamentally rule 42.1(b) is in fact an exception to rule 36 (unless the yachts are both close-hauled in which case rule 42.1(c) would apply) for even a yacht which has the privilege of being on starboard tack is compelled to gybe when faced with an outside yacht on port tack and she has no right to continue her course even a little beyond the gybe point if it is not the proper course for the next mark.

13. Yachts overlapped and close-hauled on opposite tacks (42.1)

Up to now we have seen that when there is an overlap the inside yacht has the right to room between the outside yacht and the mark or obstruction. This must be allowed even if the yachts are on opposite tacks because rule 42 is altogether an exception to the usual rules of Part IV including therefore rule 36 (see fig. 105)

However, this rule is valid up to a certain point because rule 36 (and with this rule 41 changing tacks – tacking and gybing) remains valid in the case of two overlapped yachts on opposite tacks which are close hauled that is which are working to windward as close as they can lie. Let us look for example at fig. 106, yacht B which is outside on starboard tack has the right of way over A which is inside on port; therefore B has no obligation to give water to A and A must slow down or bear away to let B pass.

Note that for rules 36 and 41 to stay in force both yachts on opposite tacks must be close hauled. If only one of them is close hauled and the other not rule 42.1(a) applies and in fig. 107 it will therefore be A (having established an overlap on the inside in time) that has the right to room round the mark and B cannot deny it to her.

Still on the subject of two overlapping yachts on opposite tacks it should be underlined that rule 42.1(a) is not applied not only when the yachts are close hauled but also when one of the yachts will have to *tack* either to round a *mark* or to avoid an *obstruction* (rule 42.1(c)). In this second case there is no need, as there was in the first, for both to be close hauled but it is enough that one of them needs to tack to round the mark or to avoid the obstruction. Therefore in fig. 108 yacht A (overlapped inside usually with right to room) while rounding must give way to B for although she is outside yacht, is on starboard tack and can therefore avail herself of rule 36; note that A must also be careful when tacking not to infringe rule 41, also in force as expressly noted in rule 42.1(c).

14. The right to luff to windward of the mark (42.1(d))

Another rule of exception to rule 42.1(a) comes when an outside leeward yacht retains the right (removed from her by rule 38) to luff the inside weather yacht so far as to carrying her to windward of, that is to the wrong side of, the mark.

But what does "to windward" actually mean? IYRU No. 55 (NARYU 145)

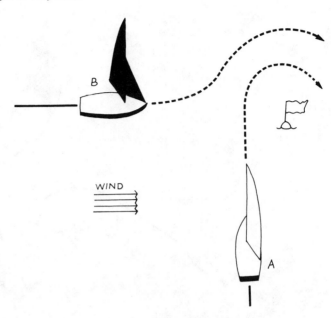

Fig. 105   A and B are on opposite tacks but not close hauled therefore B although on starboard tack must give A room to round the mark.

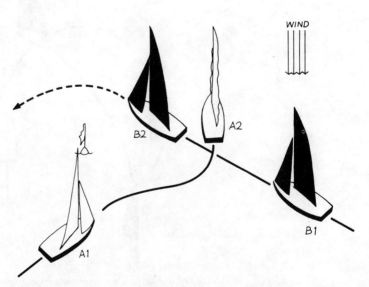

Fig. 106   Both yachts are close hauled on opposite tacks therefore rule 41.1(a) does not apply and B on starboard tack has right of way over A under rule 36.

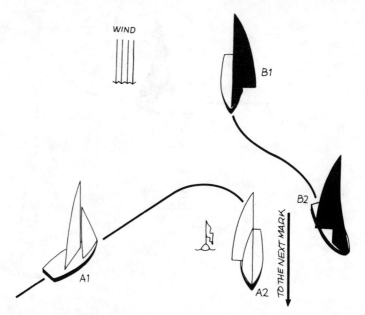

Fig. 107   Although on starboard tack B must give room to the inside yacht A on port tack. A is close hauled and therefore rule 42.1(c) does not apply.

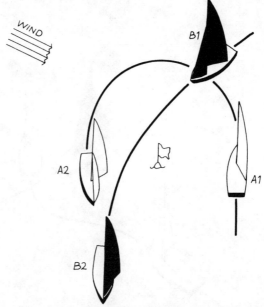

Fig. 108   A and B are overlapped on opposite tacks though not both close-hauled; A must tack to round the mark. Rule 42.1(a) does not apply and rules 36 and 41 govern the rounding of the mark. A must keep clear of the starboard-tack yacht B.

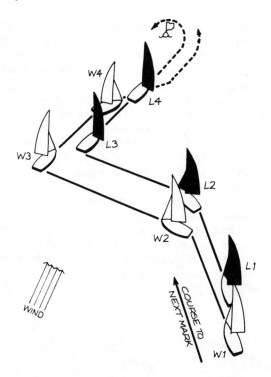

Fig. 109

gives us some idea. This dealt with two yachts broad reaching towards a leeward mark of the course. L, the leeward yacht, luffed W to windward between positions 2 and 3 and W protested under rule 42.1(d). Looking at fig. 109 we see that L, using the well-known tactics of luffing and bearing away succeeded in breaking the overlap and passed clear ahead of W before the fatal two-lengths limit. Having achieved this aim by position 3 (that is at about 6 lengths from the mark), L changed tactics and steered straight for the mark. The U.S. Appeals Committee having first of all decided that rule 42 was inapplicable because at 6 lengths from the mark with a moderate wind a dinghy was not "about to round a mark", laid down a ruling on what taking a yacht "to windward" at a mark meant, in this case taking her to the wrong side of the buoy itself, and defined precisely that it meant to take her "over a line through the mark normal or perpendicular to the direct course from the previous mark." And seeing that L had luffing rights at all times and that she had not taken W across this imaginary line she had infringed no rule by manoeuvring as she did.

At first sight it seems doubtful whether rule 42.1(d) is a true exception to rule 42.1(a) because the leeward yacht can carry out this manoeuvre only if she begins to luff before arriving at two lengths from the mark (that is to say before touching the magic circle at which rule 42 starts to apply), but looking at it more closely the exception to rule 42 appears clearly exactly at the moment when the leeward yacht enters the two-length zone: and it is in fact from that moment that she must, as outside yacht, give enough room to the inside yacht (rule 42.1(a)) and it is from that moment contrariwise that she can continue to luff under rule 42.1(d) on condition that "she also passes to windward" of the mark.

The meaning of this last sentence is that the yacht with the right to luff cannot force the other to pass to windward of the mark without going there herself; she cannot jostle her competitor up to the wrong side of the mark and then bear smartly away and slip by on the correct side leaving the other in real trouble. That is why the outside yacht if she adopts these tactics in relation to the inside yacht is obliged to carry them out herself and this enforced solidarity with her victim also explains why in each case when the outside yacht has decided to set course again for the mark she must leave the other enough room to pass on the inside (fig. 110).

It can be seen in addition (fig. 111) that an outside yacht OL luffing an inside yacht IW to carry her to windward of a mark is not obliged to pass to windward of the mark herself when IW tacks before arriving at the traverse of

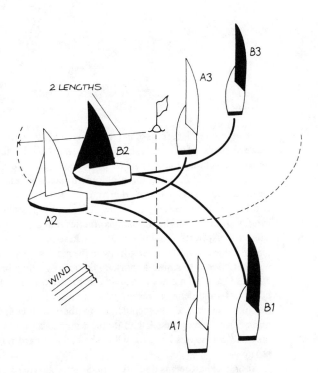

Fig. 110   B must start to luff before reaching the 2-length limit (pos. 1); she as well as A must pass to windward of the mark (pos. 2); when she resumes her proper course to round the mark she must leave sufficient room for A the overlapping inside yacht (pos. 3).

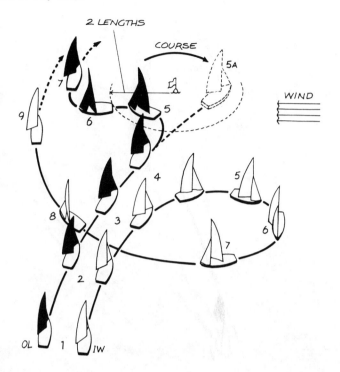

Fig. 111

the mark. This is laid down in IYRU No. 61 (RYA 1972/7, Ndirande Sailing Club, Malawi) in an incident where the windward yacht IW was the one to slip away to escape from OL's luff; then there was no longer any reason why OL should pass to windward of the mark and the particular rule had no further part to play.

It must not be forgotten that before starting this manoeuvre the leeward yacht must give notice of her intention by hailing (which is logical when you consider the difficulty caused by the nearness of the mark). It is unnecessary to add that the leeward yacht must have "luffing rights" under rule 38.

Note that rule 42.1(d) can be applied at a *mark*, not at an *obstruction* (see the respective definitions in Part I) and that the mark cannot be a starting mark because "a starting mark begins to have a prescribed side for a yacht only when she *starts*" (rule 51.3) and so rule 42 (which deals with the rounding or passage of a mark having a required side) does not apply until the yacht has crossed the starting line after the gun. It follows that before the starting signal the leeward yacht can (although only slowly – rule 40) luff until she drives the other yacht to the wrong side of the starting mark as if it were a mere obstruction, that is without having any obligation to go there herself and without having to obey this special requirement imposed by rule 41.2(d).

Finally, we would draw the attention of the reader to the fact that rule 42.1(d) can be applied only when dealing with yachts which "are about to

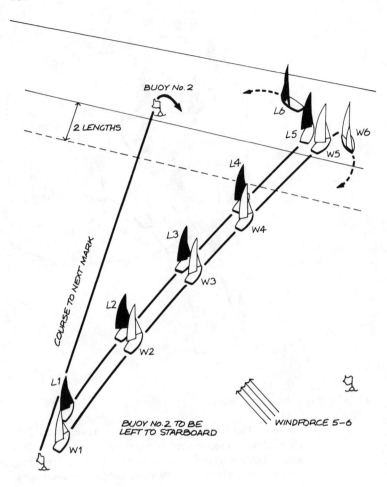

Fig. 112

round or pass a mark". IYRU No. 60 (RYA 1972/6, *Jerry Pip* v. *Teal*) is to the
point. Here (fig. 112) we see two yachts that after mark no. 1 started off on a
prolonged luffing match (L luffing W) leading them a long way from the next
mark. Having arrived at position 5 (that is to say on the perpendicular to mark
2 but more than 10 lengths away from it) W tacked to break the luff, L turned
back with a gybe and then, L in front and W behind, the two sailed along to
round the mark.

W protested, accusing L of having taken her to windward of mark no. 2
without having hailed as required. The protest committee judged that both had
in effect sailed beyond the traverse of the windward mark, and to windward of
it and therefore had to be considered "about to pass" it as is laid down in the
preamble of rule 42; and for this reason they disqualified L for violation of rule
42.1(d) because she had not given the required hail. The RYA, on appeal, upset

this decision on the grounds that the episode happened too far from the mark for rule 42 to be considered applicable and said among other things that "in open water, a leeward yacht with luffing rights is entitled to exercise them as suddenly and as unexpectedly 'as she pleases'. If, however, she delays doing so until she is 'about to round or pass a mark' rule 42.1(d) then requires her to warn the windward yacht of her late decision and to begin to luff before she is within two lengths of the mark."

15. The anti-barging rule (42.4)

Another exception to rule 42.1(a) is the so-called anti-barging rule which stops windward competitors from forcing a passage between the mark and other yachts just at the last moment before the starting signal, thus provoking confusion and collisions. Imagine a number of boats trying this when a starting line was not at right angles to the wind and the start not to windward and it is easy to understand that chaotic situations frequently arose where there was not nearly enough room for everyone. Note that rule 42.4 deals with yachts on the same tack, otherwise rule 36 applies.

The anti-barging rule is of North American origin and Harold S. Vanderbilt imagined the existence of a danger zone (fig. 113) where before the starting signal windward yachts would be obliged to keep clear of leeward yachts with right of way under rule 37.1. The result was that before the starting signal yachts in this danger zone would always be forced to pass the wrong side of the mark.

In fact rule 42.4 establishes that approaching the starting line to start a leeward yacht shall be under no obligation to give any windward yacht room to pass to leeward of a starting mark surrounded by navigable water; that is to

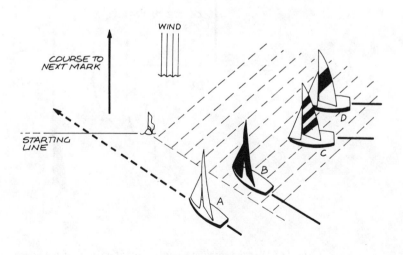

Fig. 113   B has no right to room from A to pass inside the buoy (and C need not give room to D).

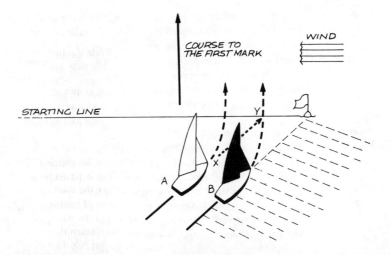

Fig. 114   Before the starting signal the outside leeward yacht, A, has no obligation to give room to the windward yacht, B, but after the starting signal (at point X) A must put herself on her course for the first mark and may not continue to "luff above her proper course". If, however, A calculates correctly so that she arrives (at point Y) just as the starting signal is given B is forced to go beyond the buoy.

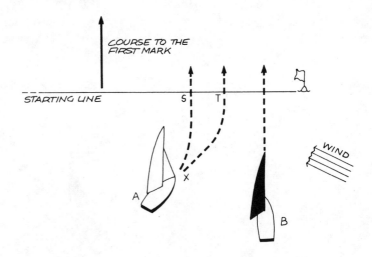

Fig. 115   At the starting signal (given at point X) A is under no obligation to put herself immediately on the correct course for the first mark (when she would cross the starting line at S) but is only obliged not to deprive B of room and therefore A can go ahead and cross the line of T if she wishes.

say, looking at fig. 113, neither has A any obligation to give room to B or to C, nor need C leave room for D.

This privilege for the leeward yacht exists only until the starting signal because once that has been fired (and it is the signal given by the committee boat and not the start made by the yacht) the leeward yacht may not deprive the windward yacht of room at such a mark by sailing either above the course to the first mark or above close hauled. Let us look at an example. In fig. 114 leeward yacht A can continue on her course under rule 37.1 and has no obligation to give water to B to allow her to pass inside the mark. When A is at point X the starting signal is fired and from that moment A cannot head up beyond the course for the first mark. Certainly if A has calculated so well that she arrives on the line at point Y at the moment of the gun, B will be forced to pass the wrong side of the mark.

On the other hand you can see in fig. 115 that A at the starting signal (once again at X) has no obligation to put herself on her course for the mark immediately but must only not hinder B. She can therefore go ahead and cross the line at point T if she so wishes without violating the anti-barging rule.

In another example (fig. 116) we can see A before the start luffing up to keep B in the danger zone (and in fact if this continues the latter would be forced to pass on the wrong side of the mark). But at the starting signal (when A is at X) she must put herself on the correct course for the first mark and can no longer head up, as she has been able to do before, beyond a close-hauled course.

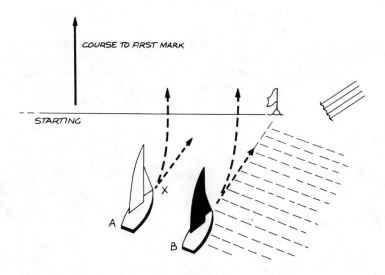

Fig. 116   Before the starting signal yacht A can luff B to windward of the buoy and after the starting signal (given at point X) A can sail a close-hauled course for the first mark but cannot luff up above close-hauled.

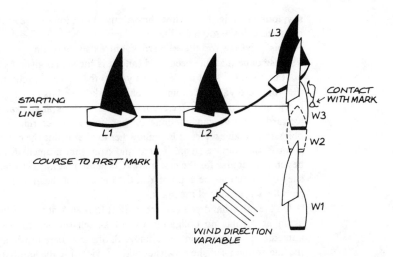

Fig. 117

Look for example at NAYRU 47. In position 3 of fig. 117 a second and a
half after the starting signal, W touched the mark and fouled L; the U.S.
Appeals Committee ended by absolving L, recognising that before the starting
signal she had no obligation, and that in the extremely brief period of time after
the signal had done everything she could to fulfil her new obligation not to
deprive W of room by sailing a course more to windward than that for the first
mark or by heading up above close-hauled position; instead they disqualified
W for an infringement of rule 37.1.

It goes without saying (as in the case of A in fig. 113) that if the course sailed
before the starting signal is the close-hauled course for the windward mark the
leeward yacht can legitimately continue on that course. She is under no
obligation to give the inside yacht sufficient room to pass the mark but is only
obliged not to deprive the windward yacht of room. That is to say she has a

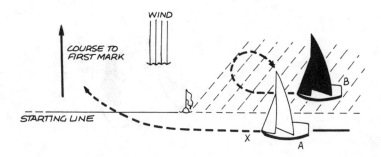

*Fig. 118   Even after the starting signal (at point X) A may continue on her
course without any obligation to give room to B, because this is her course for
the next mark.*

duty not to do anything over and above the course to the next mark which would hinder the inside yacht or deprive her of room. Even in fig. 118 in fact A can, after the starting signal has been given (at point X) continue on course without having to give room to B; even before rounding the starting mark this was the course for the first mark and even after the starting signal A was not sailing more to windward than necessary.

A recent RYA case (1976/3, *Mistral* v. *Blythe Spirit*) points out that "rule 42.4 makes no reference to 'proper course' which is a defined term. 'Course' in this rule means the most direct course to the first mark."

If we think about it, even the anti-barging rule which is basically an exception to rule 42.1(a) is reasonably coherent with the general principle. In fact it gives precedence to rule 37.1 when the starting mark is not yet a *mark* in the true sense of the definition, that is to say when it has not got a prescribed side (rule 51.3) and therefore rule 42 can not yet be valid since it refers to and governs the rounding of marks on the prescribed side. The only incongruity is that the prescribed side begins to exist under rule 51.3 at the moment the yacht starts to cut the line while in the anti-barging rule the new obligations begin with the starting signal.

In the first edition of this book we observed that a certain common parentage undeniably exists between the two rules. Now IYRU No. 54 (NAYRU 143) has confirmed this observation declaring explicitly that the anti-barging rule is perfectly compatible with rule 37.1 and underlining indeed that they are complementary. This case referred to two overlapped yachts, L and W, converging on the starboard end mark of the starting line. Looking at fig. 119,

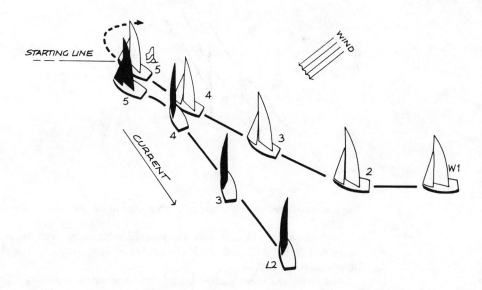

Fig. 119

you can understand why the U.S. Appeals Committee decided that yacht L was robbed of her right of sailing as near to the buoy as she wished, the right due to her under rule 42.4 and decided that W forced a passage which she had no right to thus rendering herself liable to disqualification "on the strength of rule 37.1 for failing to keep clear of a leeward yacht."

It is also interesting to look at NAYRU 38 (fig. 120). At the starting signal yachts M and W were nearing the line on courses which forced a passage inside the mark, so much so that L, on the wind, was forced to bear away (you should know that M did not know of the existence of the anti-barging rule and considered wrongly that she had to leave room for W at the mark and that she had in her turn the right to have room from L; W on the contrary knew perfectly well that she had no right to room and in fact she did not ask for it, she just profited from the circumstances to pass between M and the mark). The U.S. Appeals Committee disqualified M for violation of rule 37 and the anti-barging rule, and as to W pronounced: "It is an established principle of yacht racing that when a yacht voluntarily or unintentionally makes room available to another yacht which has no right under the rules to such room nor makes or indicates any claim to it, such as to pass between her and a mark or

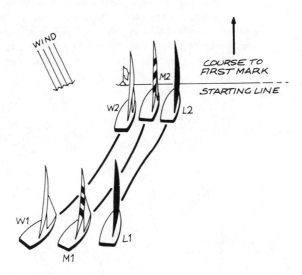

Fig. 120

obstruction, the other yacht may take advantage, at her own risk, of the room so given."

The anti-barging rule deals only with yachts overlapped between themselves (otherwise rules 37.2 and 37.3 prevail before the start and rule 42.2 afterwards).

And finally remember that the mark in question must be a starting mark in the sense described by rule 6 and must be a mark surrounded by navigable water that is a mark which allows the windward yacht to pass if need be on the

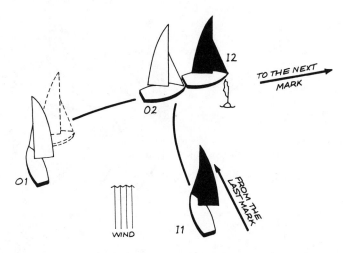

Fig. 122

wrong side of the mark without running into danger. If this is not so (whether because of shallow water or other yachts blocking the passage or indeed because such a mark is in fact the end of a breakwater – see definition Part I) the leeward yacht must keep to rule 42.1(a) because even before the starting signal this "mark" deliminates an extremity of the starting line and must be considered as a real and proper "obstruction which has to be rounded or passed on the same side".

16. Yachts clear ahead and clear astern (42.2)

If there is no overlap when the yacht clear ahead reaches the two-length limit from the mark she has the right not to be disturbed by the yacht clear astern while she rou... ds the mark or obstruction. IYRU No. 5 (NAYRU 87) serves very well to remove some fundamental misunderstandings on the rights of the yacht ahead. As you can see in fig. 122 two port-tack yachts (O on the outside and I on the inside) off the wind are nearing a mark which is to be left to starboard. You can see that in position 1 yacht O is clear ahead of I. When O comes more or less abeam of the mark she gybes to starboard and at this point (dotted position) the two yachts are overlapped. Shortly afterwards I gybes too and is so much nearer to the buoy that in position 2 she becomes clear ahead of O.

O protested I for violation of rules 42.2(a) and 42.3(a) and maintained that I should have given way to her rounding the mark because in position 1 (that is when they were both on port tack), she was clear ahead of I. The U.S. Appeals Committee dismissed the protest observing that: "rule 42.2(a), in conformity with rule 42.3(a), does not apply unless and until the yacht clear ahead is 'within two of her overall lengths of the *mark* or *obstruction*', and while O, on a direct course from the preceding mark, had come abreast of the mark she was about to round, she was still well over two lengths from it. When O altered course to gybe, the yachts became overlapped and rule 42.1(a) began to apply. Under it O was obligated to give I room, which included room to gybe since gybing was an integral part of the rounding manoeuvre."

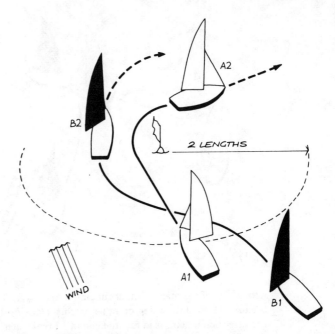

Fig. 123   A (clear ahead of B) rounds the mark and "remains on the same tack": B must keep clear before and during the rounding.

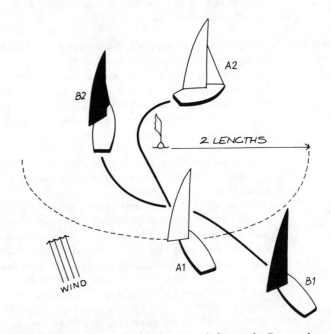

Fig. 124   A (clear ahead of B) gybes round the mark: B must keep clear before and during the rounding.

In other words the yacht clear astern, that is the following yacht, can no longer establish an overlap on the inside and thus have the right to a passage under rule 42.3(a) but she must herself keep clear during the rounding or passing (rule 42.2(a)).

However, this obligation to keep clear is subject to the condition that the clear-ahead yacht, in order to round or pass, remains on the same tack (fig. 123) or gybes (fig. 124). It follows that if the yacht ahead tacks (fig. 125) she no longer has an unconditional right to a passage (rule 42.2(a)) but must obey rule 41 tacking or gybing (fig. 126).

IYRU No. 26 (RYA 1966/8 the Skefco Sailing Club) illustrates the point (fig. 127). Here AN has the right to maintain close-hauled course and AD may tack only if she can do so without infringing rule 41.

Let us look now at a more complicated situation described in IYRU No. 71 (RYA 74/9 Seaview Yacht Club). In position 1 (fig. 127a) yacht A must round the buoy leaving it to port but the wind is strong and she dare not risk a capsize and considers it safer to change tacks by tacking instead of gybing. As a result of this manoeuvre (pos. 2) A is within the two lengths on port tack while B is still on starboard. What happens then at this point? Must B give way to A

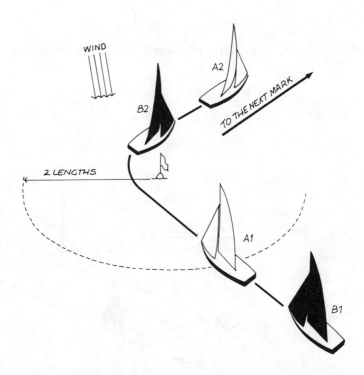

Fig. 125   A (clear ahead of B) tacks to round the mark: she can do so only if she does not infringe rule 41.

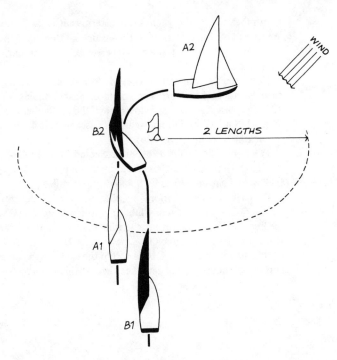

Fig. 126   If A's tack forces B to change course to avoid her, A has infringed rule 41.

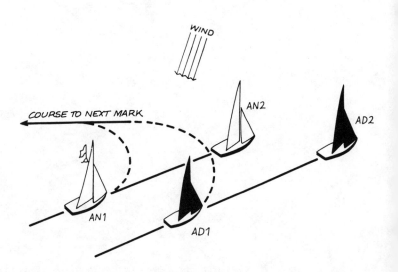

Fig. 127

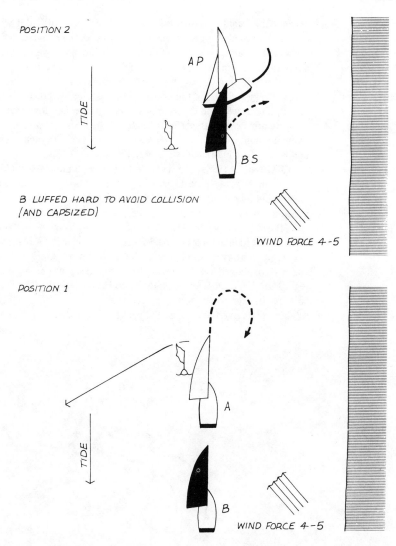

POSITION 2

TIDE

A P

B S

B LUFFED HARD TO AVOID COLLISION
(AND CAPSIZED)

WIND FORCE 4-5

POSITION 1

TIDE

A

B

WIND FORCE 4-5

Fig. 127a

because the latter is rounding a mark? The reply is "No. Rule 42.3(a) applies
only to a yacht clear astern, B, provided that the yacht clear ahead, A, does not
tack. A having tacked, rule 36 applies". In other words the yacht clear astern,
B, must leave room for the yacht clear ahead, A, only when the latter while
rounding the mark "remains on the same *tack* or *gybes*" (rule 42.2(a)). If on the
other hand A tacks she loses her right-of-way, the rule of exception 42 ceases to
apply and we are back with basic rule 36 by which port tack must give way to
starboard.

    Still on the subject of the case where the yacht ahead has to tack, the yacht
astern for her part has the obligation not to "*luff* above *close-hauled* so as to

prevent the yacht *clear ahead* from *tacking*" (42.2(b)). But what does "luff above close hauled" mean? The reply, given in the relevant definition, is that the yacht clear astern can "sail by the wind as close as she can lie with advantage working to windward." That is to say she is free to sail on any course which permits her most to improve her position relative to the next mark. Every luff above the course which is considered the fastest and most advantageous while on the wind will not only slow her down but will also be an open demonstration that she is hindering (it does not matter whether she is doing it voluntarily or through mere incompetence) the yacht which was ahead and is therefore in breach of rule 42.2(b) (see fig. 128).

IYRU No. 27 (RYA No. 1966/9, St Mawes Sailing Association) shown in fig. 46 on page 133 deals with a group of boats nearing an obstruction constituted by a headland to be left to port (pos. 2). Yachts X, Y and Z helped by squalls have caught up and are overlapped with C and respectively with E, F and H. But they have not enough room to pass through if the yachts in front of them do not haul in their booms. In this situation the RYA held that, since X, Y and Z did not have room to pass, rule 42.2(a) must apply and therefore X, Y and Z were obliged to keep clear before and during the passing manoeuvre with regard to C and D, E and F and G and H respectively. The decision is more comprehensible when you consider that X, Y and Z ought not to have established an overlap because the yachts clear ahead of them was not "able to

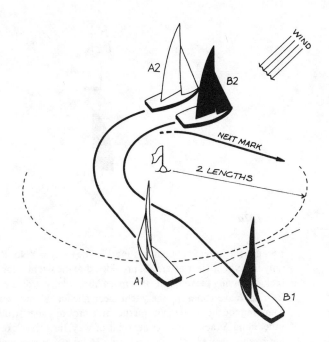

Fig. 128   To round the mark A (clear ahead of B) must tack taking care not to infringe rule 41. B on her part may not luff above close hauled thus obstructing A from getting on her new course to the next mark.

give the required room" (rule 42.3(a)i); it follows that because an overlap is not possible the yachts had to consider themselves as "clear" between each other and for this reason had on passing an obstruction to obey rule 42.2(a) with all its implications.

Rule 43. Close-hauled, hailing for room to tack at obstructions

HAILING

When two *close-hauled* yachts are on the same *tack* and safe pilotage requires the yacht *clear ahead* or the *leeward yacht* to make a substantial alteration of course to clear an *obstruction,* and when she intends to *tack,* but cannot *tack* without colliding with the other yacht, she shall hail the other yacht for room to *tack* and clear the other yacht, but she shall not hail and *tack* simultaneously.

43.2   RESPONDING

The hailed yacht at the earliest possible moment after the hail shall: — either

(a) *tack,* in which case the hailing yacht shall begin to *tack* either: —

  (i) before the hailed yacht has completed her *tack,* or

  (ii) when she cannot then *tack* without colliding with the hailed yacht, immediately she is able to *tack* and clear her;

or

(b) reply "You *tack*", or words to that effect, when in her opinion she can keep clear without *tacking* or after postponing her *tack.*

In this case: —

  (i) the hailing yacht shall immediately *tack* and

  (ii) the hailed yacht shall keep clear.

  (iii) The onus of satisfying the race committee that she kept clear shall lie on the hailed yacht which replied "You *tack*".

43.3   LIMITATION ON RIGHT TO ROOM WHEN THE OBSTRUCTION IS A MARK

(a) When the hailed yacht can fetch an *obstruction* which is also a *mark,* the hailing yacht shall not be entitled to room to *tack* and clear the hailed yacht and the hailed yacht shall immediately so inform the hailing yacht.

(b) If, thereafter, the hailing yacht again hails for room to *tack* and clear the hailed yacht she shall, after receiving room, retire immediately or exonerate herself by accepting an alternative penalty when so prescribed in the sailing instructions.

(c) When, after having refused to respond to a hail under rule 43.3(a), the hailed yacht fails to fetch, she shall retire immediately, or exonerate herself by accepting an alternative penalty when so prescribed in the sailing instructions.

Another exception to the rules of Section B only applied in particular cases is rule 43. This comes into force when a yacht has to tack to avoid an obstruction and cannot do so without colliding with another or without violating rule 41.1 (changing tacks — tacking or gybing).

Hailing for room to tack (3.1)

No yacht can benefit from this special rule until the following conditions are fulfilled:

(a) "Two *close-hauled* yachts are on the same *tack*". The respective definitions in Part I underline that there is no need for the yachts to be overlapped since the rule talks about leeward or clear ahead. The rule speaks of "two yachts" but there may be a third to windward or astern of the hailed yacht and a fourth to windward of her and so on. Then when the first yacht hails for room to tack the second must ask in turn for room from the third and so on down the line. It is important for the first to remember that her hail must reach the outside yacht and make it in enough time for all to respond.

(b) One of the two yachts must be forced to alter her course substantially; this means that a small alteration such as might arise from passing wind shifts is not enough, it must really change her course from what it has been: and this is made clear by the fact that the alteration must give rise to a tack.

(c) This substantial alteration of course must be made "to clear an *obstruction*" and for no other reason. The definition in Part I tells us that an obstruction is any object compelling a yacht to alter course to pass on one side or the other, or which can be passed on one side only, as for instance a coastline (fig. 129).

Just as "vessel under way", even a right-of-way yacht, can be an obstruction

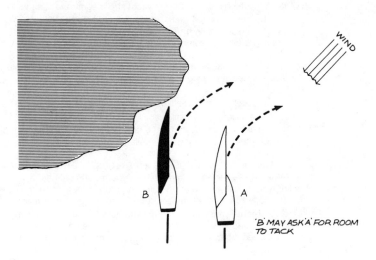

Fig. 129

(see rule 43.3), so can an object designated as a *mark* when it is impossible to pass it on both sides (for example, the end of a breakwater or jetty or a committee boat if it is cluttered up with spectator boats giving rise to a dangerous situation forcing a yacht to tack. See for example NAYRU 8 fig. 135).

(d) This substantial alteration of course, other than having as its object the avoidance of an obstruction, must be essential for safety. You cannot make use of the exceptional facility conceded by rule 43 (or oblige the other yacht to renounce the protection of rule 41), if you are not unavoidably compelled to tack to escape an accident such as a grounding or a collision. The looming accident need not be serious nor such as would be likely to cause damage. On the contrary, this rule like the others follows the fundamental object of encouraging safe navigation which must be based on safe pilotage, and certainly this requirement would never be met if there was any possibility of an accident, even if without material damage.

(e) To achieve the substantial alteration of course the yacht must be compelled to tack and must in addition find herself in a position in which she "cannot *tack* without colliding with the other yacht". When therefore she gybes, instead of tacking, to avoid collision rule 43 does not apply and she cannot call it in aid but must stick carefully to rule 41 to stay out of trouble.

Why is so much help given to the yacht which has to tack and none to that which must gybe? Gybing is generally (but not always) easier or more possible than tacking since the latter forces a yacht to change direction by 90° and brings her directly on top of any yacht to windward on the same course. But the real moral is never to get into a position where the final and only escape is a gybe, because then no-one need help you. To put it bluntly it would be equivalent to throwing yourself from a balcony knowing perfectly well that there is no mattress underneath.

Neither does rule 43 apply when the yacht in question is capable of tacking without running into or hindering the other in any way. However, it is only the first yacht (the one in difficulties, real or presumed as they may be) that may judge if she is in such a position that she must effectively call upon rule 43 because there is no other way out. In fact the second yacht cannot dispute the first's hail and, as we shall see in a moment, has no other alternative than that of accepting the hail and tacking (rule 43.2(a)) or, at any rate, keeping clear of her in some other way (rule 43.2(b)). But no one can take away from her the right to protest if she believes that the hail was misconceived and ill-founded and in the case of controversy the onus is on the first yacht to prove that her hail was legitimate, in as much as all the conditions we have been looking at effectively existed. And you can be sure her job will be anything but easy. You will finally notice that the yacht which has to avoid the obstruction can ask for room to tack even if she is able to avoid it by bearing away. In other words when protected by rule 43 there is no obligation on her to bear away instead of tacking unless she is obliged to do so because of the other's lack of response.

(f) If all the above mentioned conditions exist, *all* of them, and she thinks she therefore has the right to avail herself of the privilege provided by rule 43 then our yacht shall hail the other asking "for room to tack and clear the other yacht". Notice that the actual wording of the rule uses the imperative form "shall" instead of the optional "may" which existed until 1961; this means that the hail is mandatory and that without a hail there is no obligation to let her tack. Obviously the hail must be loud and in intelligible terms, not too generic, and announce expressly and clearly that she is calling for room to tack. Further it should be noticed that this request must be made in good time, because it is no good expecting that the other yacht will or can respond immediately and make room at once. On the contrary it is worth while remembering that the latter has no obligation to listen out for a hail and be on the alert; she may well be taken by surprise and be unready to carry out the required manoeuvre.

Here is a typical case, IYRU No. 16 (RYA 1963/24) (fig. 130). Three overlapped yachts were nearing the bank of a river when L hailed M for room to tack; M therefore did the same and hailed W but W did not give the necessary room in time and her failure to do so led to a collision between L, which had nowhere else to go and had to tack, and M, which was hindered by

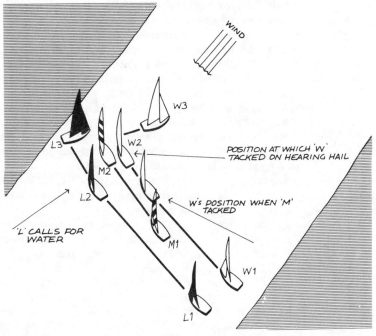

Fig. 130

W. It is no surprise to learn that W ended up by being disqualified for violation of rule 43.2.

We can learn a lot from IYRU No. 6 (RYA 1962/37, *Seahawk* v. *Fundi*) (fig. 131). Yacht S, close-hauled on the starboard tack, was sailing towards two other overlapped yachts both on port tack, PL to leeward and PW to windward. Closing, S hailed PL "starboard tack" and PL hailed PW at least three times for room to tack. But PW hesitated and responded only at the third

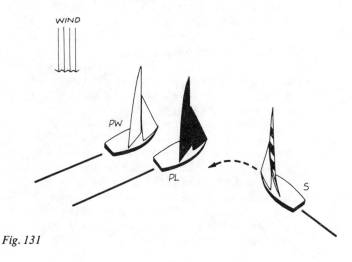

Fig. 131

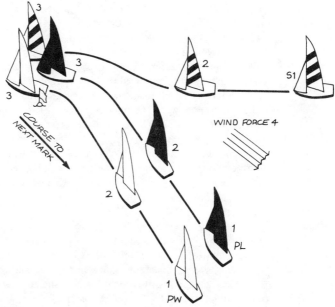

Fig. 132

hail so that S was forced to bear away to avoid a collision with PL. S protested PL under rule 36 (PW retired). The protest committee accepted the protest and disqualified PL but the latter appealed and with success because the RYA, having underlined that she had hailed PW three times, decided that nothing in the rules compelled PL either to bear away and go under S's stern or to anticipate PW's failure to comply with rule 43.2(a). In other words the council recognized that PL had done everything that she should have done and had done it in time.

A similar situation is dealt with in NAYRU 11 (fig 132). Here too PW did not respond to PL's hail (indeed she was disqualified in the end) and S was forced to luff to avoid PL. Here too PL was protested and disqualified in the first instance for infringement of rule 36 but in this case, unlike the preceding one, her appeal was unsuccessful. The appeals committee held that first of all it was necessary to examine whether PL, which "claimed that she did not bear away under the stern of S because she thought . . . a collision would result", could be "exonerated as the victim of another yacht's foul". But having realized that the protest committee had found as a fact that it had been possible to bear away, concluded that PL's error on this point was evident.

Having decided this first point the appeals committee considered it necessary to face up to a second question; whether PL had got mixed up in the incident through her own fault or not; and they decided that she had, observing, "it is reasonable to assume that all yachts in a race know and will obey the rules but discreet to anticipate that in some circumstances they may not". They went on to say that PL should have hailed PW in time so that, if PW had failed to tack, PL would have had the opportunity of passing astern of S, but she did not do so and as a result wrongly forced S to alter course; and they disqualified PL.

The meat of this decision is that now to justify using the escape route offered by rule 43 you must hail in adequate time and the lack of a response by the hailed yacht is not automatically a valid reason for justifying your own wrong doing with respect to any third yacht with right of way.

The above two decisions, however, are contradictory. The British one holds in fact that "nothing in the rules compelled PL to anticipate PW's failure to comply with rule 43.2(a)". Yet the American decision is fairer, when it affirms that it is no good expecting everyone to observe the rules. In fact PL first and foremost had a duty to keep clear of S on a starboard tack, and her first consideration should have been that of maintaining her ability to do so, keeping in hand a second escape way if (as she should have foreseen) PW did not respond according to the requirements of the rules.

2. The response of the hailed yacht (43.2)

The yacht which is hailed for room to tack must respond without hesitation and may not refuse to do so for any reason (with the limited exception as we shall see allowed by paragraph 3 below). Rule 43 starts from the premise that the hailing yacht, since she is nearer to the obstruction, can more easily recognize a dangerous situation (typically, shallow water or rocks) which the other cannot see and is therefore better able to judge whether it really is necessary to tack. Rule 43 is intended to lead to safe sailing and while racing you often have to hold a tack right up to an obstruction in order to enjoy a special wind or to keep out of tidal currents and so on. If the rule allowed the hailed yacht to decide on the correctness of the hail (and therefore perhaps choose not to respond to it) then clearly, when the two boats had different opinions, precisely the accident that the rule wished to avoid would result.

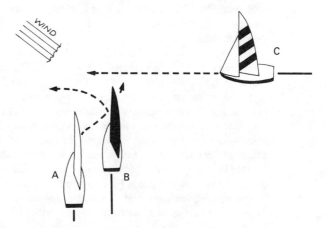

Fig. 133   B is obliged to tack to avoid the obstruction, C (starboard-tack yacht), and A must give her room (rule 43). To fulfil her obligation A must tack too or bear away to pass astern.

Naturally whenever the hail appears unfounded the hailed yacht can protest afterwards but she can do so only when she has immediately conceded the room asked for. Not to do so would at once put her in the wrong.

The hailed yacht need not tack; it is enough for her to enable the hailing yacht to tack somehow or other and get clear away (such in fact is the meaning of the phrase "to clear"). The hailed yacht may, for example, luff until she is head to wind and slow down to let the other pass, or she may bear away and pass astern of a hailing yacht which is ahead (see fig. 133) as long as she does it "at the earliest possible moment after the hail". With this alternative there are two cases: 1. The hailed yacht responds by tacking (43.2(a)) whereupon the hailing yacht must in her turn begin to tack as soon as possible, even "before the hailed yacht has completed her tack" (43.2(a)i) or if she cannot do it at this stage she must at any rate start to tack "immediately she is able to *tack* and clear her", that is to say just as soon as she has enough space to carry out the manoeuvre (43.2(a)ii). To sum up: the hailing yacht must get a move on and must not delay even for a moment, a manoeuvre which she enjoys only as a very particular concession and which in no way gives her the right to damage the interests of other yachts when she carries it out. 2. The hailed yacht responds "without *tacking* or after postponing her *tack*" (rule 43.2(b)) and then the hailing yacht "shall immediately *tack*" (43.2(b)i) while the hailed yacht must equally quickly keep clear in whatever way she considers most suitable (for example: heading up, slowing down, bearing away, changing her course as much as is necessary, tacking but a bit later and even, if she can manage, just continuing her course, if she has calculated better than the hailing yacht).

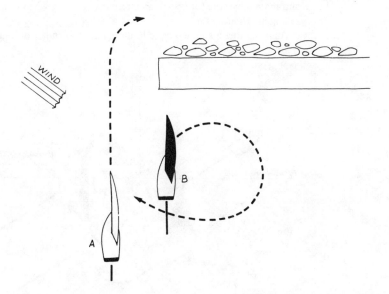

Fig. 134   A can lay the mark. B cannot lay it without tacking, and cannot expect A to give her room to do so (rule 43.3(a)). Note that B cannot invoke rule 42 because she has to tack.

IYRU No. 80 (*Gemini* v. *Outrageous* USYRU 189) is a recent case on the subject.

It is clear that in order to make it known to the hailing yacht that she has chosen this second alternative and in order not to keep her waiting unnecessarily the hailed yacht must communicate with her immediately shouting, in reply to the original hail, "you tack" or similar words. In this case, however, the onus of proof that the choice was correct (in the sense that it was enough to enable her to "keep clear without *tacking* or after postponing her *tack*" will fall on the hailed yacht if there is a protest.

3. Limitation on right to room when the obstruction is a mark (43.3)

Up to now rule 43 has seemed simple but we must not rely on appearances because, rather like a scorpion, its sting lies in its tail and has a rare poison and this is when "the hailed yacht can fetch an obstruction which is also a *mark*" (fig. 134). In such a case it is obviously unfair to force the hailed yacht to lose her advantage, and therefore the hailing yacht is denied the right to ask for room to tack. It is equally obvious that in such an event the hailed yacht which wishes to reach the mark must "immediately so inform the hailing yacht" so that she can do something different.

It may happen (43.2(b)) that the hailing yacht has got herself into such an awkward position that her only way out is by the tack she is asking for, and since the first aim and end of the rule is that of avoiding accidents in this situation the hailing yacht is authorized to hail again for room to tack and the other cannot then refuse it to her.

But even this coin has its reverse because once she has obtained enough room to get her out of her troubles the hailing yacht must immediately and automatically retire (or accept an alternative penalty when so prescribed in the sailing instructions).

As usual there is an example to illuminate this rather obscure point. Let us

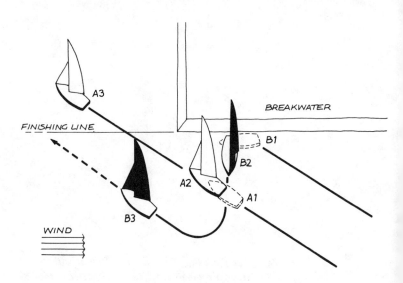

Fig. 135

look at NAYRU 8 (fig. 135). Yacht B was correctly disqualified by the protest committee (on A's protest under rule 41.2) because she threw herself on top of A after tacking too close to her so as to avoid the breakwater. Before tacking B did not hail A for room to tack as required by rule 43 and B had no right to room to tack because the *obstruction* was also a *mark* which A could fetch (rule 43.3(a)). "B did not take advantage of the alternatives to sailing herself into an impossible situation such as: bearing away, or luffing, or easing her sheets before reaching the breakwater so as to obtain room to tack without fouling A and thereafter establishing starboard tack rights on A or passing astern of her. Since the breakwater consituted a mark which A could fetch as well as an obstruction, B did not have the right to hail A about as provided in rules 43.1 and 43.2. In such a situation rules 43.3(a) and 43.3(b) were applicable and A, after being hailed twice, would have been obliged to give B room to tack and B, upon receiving it, would have been required to retire immediately."

The case is interesting because as well as illustrating rule 43.3(b) it furnishes us with an example of an *obstruction* represented by "a *mark* which the hailed yacht can fetch" and indeed a mark which because it is big and not completely surrounded by navigable water can at a certain moment offer no other escape than that of asking insistently for room from a yacht which has under rule 43.3(a) no obligation to give it.

If after this the hailed yacht does not accept the hail because she can fetch the mark and is then shown to be mistaken because (victim of the tide or wind change or just bad judgement) she cannot reach the mark she is then really hoist with her own petard. Indeed rule 43.3(c) says that "when after having refused to respond to a hail under rule 43.3(a) the hailed yacht fails to fetch, she shall retire immediately". This is simple and constructive because it shows that you must never follow the letter of the rule too closely if you are not absolutely certain of being right. When in doubt it is always better not to look for trouble and to try to arrive at the finishing line intact and with the thanks of any competitor who got out of his problems at little expense.

New light is thrown on this point by RYA 1977/8 *Electron of Portsea* v. *Combat*. Here *Electron* hailed for room to tack and *Combat* replied "you tack". *Electron* tacked, then thought she could not clear *Combat* and as *Combat* continued on her course tacked again and finally ran ashore. The race committee dismissed *Electron*'s protest, ruling that it was satisfied that *Combat* was able to keep clear by maintaining her course; however, *Electron*'s appeal was upheld, the council stating "the hailing yacht is the sole judge as to whether or not it is safe for her to bear away so as to pass astern of the hailed yacht and the latter must give her room; if she deems the hail to have been improper her only remedy is to protest".

Rule 44.
Returning to
start

44.1

(a) After the starting signal is made, a premature starter returning to *start*, or a yacht working into position from the course side of the starting line or its extensions, shall keep clear of all yachts which are *starting* or have *started* correctly, until she is wholly on the pre-start side of the starting line or its extensions.

(b) Thereafter, she shall be accorded the rights under the rules of Part IV of a yacht which is *starting* correctly; but when she thereby acquires right of way

over another yacht which is *starting* correctly, she shall allow that yacht ample room and opportunity to keep clear.

44.2 A premature starter while continuing to sail the course and until it is obvious
that she is returning to *start,* shall be accorded the rights under the rules of
Part IV of a yacht which has *started.*

At the starting signal yachts finding themselves in the wrong place lose (at
that moment) all their rights of way with respect to the other competitors and
must conform to the dictates of rule 44. The outlaws are, to be precise, those
found among the following two categories.

(a) Premature starters returning to *start.*

"Starters" is not used in the sense of the definition but only to mean yachts
which have cut (take note here, just cut perhaps only by a centimetre not
crossed and cleared) the starting line before the starting signal. But to be
subject to rule 44.1 they must also "be *returning* to start". Indeed it must be
"clear" that they are returning to do so; otherwise, that is if they continue
racing unperturbedly and notwithstanding a recall do not turn back, under
para. 2 of the same rule they will be accorded the rights of way under the rules
of Part IV owed to a yacht which has started correctly. Except of course they
will not appear on the list of finishers.

(b) Yachts which are working into position from the course side of the
starting line or its extensions.

A yacht on the wrong side of the starting line is no surprise because in the
rule there is absolutely no obligation to wait for the starting signal on the pre-
start side of the line (except with rule 51.1(c) or unless the sailing instructions
call for special rules such as the so called "one minute rule" "two minute rule",
etc). Remember that the course side of the line is the side in the direction of the
first mark of the course and you can check this in the definition of starting and
also in rule 6 (Starting and finishing lines).

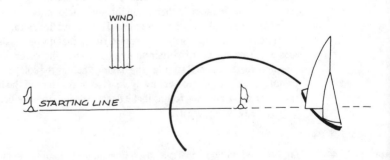

*Fig. 136   The yacht which has crossed the line prematurely may return by
passing outside the limit mark. As soon as she has wholly crossed the
theoretical extension of the line she is in correct position to start and is no
longer subject to rule 44.*

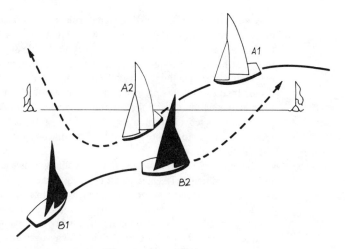

Fig. 137   As soon as she has completed her return (pos. 2), A acquires starboard-tack rights and now B, up to that moment under no obligation to change course to avoid her, must begin to keep clear under rule 36.

You will notice also that this "course side" refers not only to the starting line true and proper between the two limit marks but refers also to the theoretical extensions of this line outside the limit marks. We have gone into detail here because, as we shall see shortly, if a yacht at the starting signal finds herself over the line and must get back to the pre-start side of the line in order to start she can either recross between the two limit marks or bypass one of them until she finds herself completely beyond the line or its extension (fig. 136). In fact only in the case governed by rule 51.1(c) is it necessary for her return outside the limit marks.

You must be careful, however, after the preparatory signal, to go to the pre-course side of the line at least once otherwise you run the risk of not getting a recall because you have never started prematurely.

The obligations that from the starting signal fall on the yacht we have been looking at, the yacht in the wrong place, consist of her having to keep clear of all yachts which are starting or have started correctly. In other words the rights deriving from, for example, being on starboard tack (rule 36) being to leeward or clear ahead (rule 37), of being on a tack (rule 41) and so on no longer apply. These yachts must absolutely and with no exceptions make room for all the other competitors who are sailing towards the starting line in order to cross it (are starting) or who have already cut the starting line (have started).

The loss of every right of way and the obligation to keep clear of all the other yachts ends only when the yacht has purged herself that is to say when she has recrossed with every part of her hull, equipment and crew to the pre-start side of the line or its extensions (fig. 136). From this moment (rule 44.1(b)) she shall be accorded the rights under the rules of Part IV of a yacht which is starting correctly (fig. 137).

Note that, before the starting signal, rule 44 has no existence. FIV 1966/5 gives a good example (fig. 1a). Here we see that yacht A on the course side of the line has the right of way over yacht B under rule 36, and she can insist on this right because the starting signal has not yet been given. If therefore, still before the starting, there is a collision between A and B the latter must be disqualified for not having given room to a starboard tack yacht. As soon as the starting signal is given the situation is reversed and A, being in the wrong place, must keep clear of everyone including B; but as soon as she has recrossed wholly to the pre-start side of the line A's position will be regularised with all that follows.

You must not think, however, that the yacht which is no longer in the wrong place can immediately exercise all her acquired rights of way in the sense of being able to use them at the very moment she has returned over the line. On the contrary the black sheep must be patient for a moment and cannot expect to change suddenly into a wolf and attack whoever must give her room for rule 44 adds "if she thereby acquired right of way over another yacht which has started correctly she shall allow that yacht ample room and opportunity to keep clear".

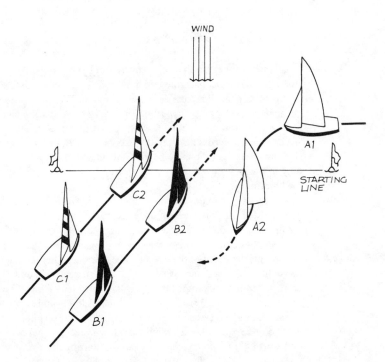

Fig. 138   At the starting signal (pos. 1) A is over the line and is recalled. Until A "wholly" returns B and C, although they are on port tack, have no obligation to alter course to keep clear. In position 2 A has wholly returned and has re-acquired her right of way under rule 36; but she cannot expect B (obstructed and incapable of doing so) to keep clear of her immediately (rule 44.1(b)).

This is because the yacht which is starting correctly (for example B in fig. 138) has above all no obligation to begin to keep clear until the other has completely returned and even then she may not be able to do so immediately (for example she could be hindered by other competitors or by the nearness of the yacht which has just returned).

Up to this point we have been considering the case of a yacht or yachts in the wrong place in front of others which are starting or have started correctly. What happens in the case of two yachts which are both in the wrong place? The problem is not difficult to resolve because it is enough to remember that both are *racing* from the moment of preparatory signal, and that they must continue to be so until they retire (rule 33); it follows that they are both subject to the rules and must keep them between themselves with the sole exception of having to keep clear of all those which are starting or have started correctly.

Once again there is a law even for the outlaw and he must respect it; it is not true that the thief can with impunity steal from another thief.

Further, as soon as the first of the two (for example A in fig. 139) has succeeded in returning completely the other, while still on the wrong side of the line, must keep clear under rule 44.1. To follow our metaphor from crime, with respect to the competitors, the thief that has paid the penalty can now hold his head high and need no longer live on the fringe of society as must the other who has not yet paid his account with justice.

The premature starter generally returns as a result of a recall (see rule 8) but quite possibly she does it of her own accord having realized that she was in the wrong (and is sporting). But it may also happen that a yacht (because she has not heard or seen the recall or because she had not noticed her mistake or even because in perfect bad faith she hopes to get away with it) sails on instead of returning and puts herself on course for the next mark. Obviously the other competitors may not turn themselves into judges and decide that she has made a mistake and take away all her rights. The rule always tries to avoid confused contradictory situations which lead to accidents and has generally established

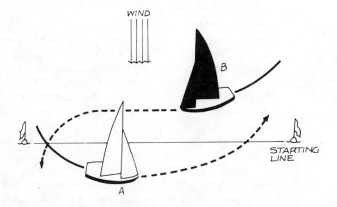

Fig. 139 A returns wholly before B, thus B, not yet in order, must give her room.

(see Section A of Part IV), that if a yacht does not retire "other yachts shall continue to accord her such rights as she may have under rules of Part IV". This general principle is repeated here (rule 44.2) detailing that "a premature starter while continuing to sail the course and until it is obvious that she is returning to *start* shall be accorded the rights under the rules of Part IV of a yacht which has *started*".

This position is clear and needs no explanation. In fact if a yacht sails calmly on with all the other competitors, deaf and blind to all recalls, it will be clear that she is doing anything but "returning to start" and it only remains therefore for her adversaries to allow her to cross the finishing line and then, when the race is over let the race committee deal with her.

Rule 45. Re-rounding after touching a mark

A yacht which has touched a *mark,* and is about to exonerate herself in accordance with rule 52.2, (Touching a Mark), shall keep clear of all other yachts which are about to round or pass it or have rounded or passed it correctly, until she has rounded it completely and has cleared it and is on a *proper course* to the next *mark.*

45.2   A yacht which has touched a *mark* while continuing to sail the course and until it is obvious that she is returning to round it completely in accordance with rule 52.2, (Touching a Mark), shall be accorded rights under the rules of Part IV.

This rule, in existence since 1969, relates to rule 52.2, introduced at the same time, which permits a yacht that has touched a mark to exonerate herself by making a complete rounding of it leaving it on the prescribed side without touching it, in addition to the rounding or passing required to sail the course. Here too, as in the case of rule 44 (Returning to start) the yacht doing a penalty turn loses every right she might have in relationship to the other competitors who are rounding or passing or who have rounded or passed correctly.

Her inferior status begins at the moment in which she touches the mark and lasts until she has re-rounded it completely, has cleared it and is on her proper course to the next mark, that is she has fully complied with rule 52.2. It is clear that a guilty yacht gets her rights back neither when she has completed her penalty turn nor her successive manoeuvre of rounding or passing needed to complete the course (rule 52.2(a)) but only when she has put herself "on a *proper course* for the next *mark*".

Although it is easy to distinguish the beginning of such an incident it can be in practice very difficult to establish the final moment when the ex-culprit gets onto her proper course. When there is any doubt yachts which have not made a mistake will be favoured rather than a yacht which has had to re-round the mark. It might be worth while to look again at the comment to the definition of "proper course" and also at the references in points 1 and 5 of the comment on rule 42. In the not improbable case that there are two guilty yachts or even more you must remember that they are still *racing,* until they retire (see rule 33). Therefore they must obey in full the rules governing the relationships between them while they still have an obligation to keep clear, whatever happens, of third parties who have sailed or are manoeuvring correctly. There is no paradox and we can repeat that between outlaws the rule continues to be enforced while on the contrary it no longer protects them against others.

We must, however, add that a man remains free and innocent until he has been condemned or until he has of his own accord put on sack cloth and ashes (as rule 52.2 might be described). Because, as in rule 44.2, rule 45.2 accords all the "rights under the rules of Part IV" to a yacht that although she has touched a mark nevertheless continues racing unless it is obvious that she is returning to round it properly in accordance with rule 52.2. Here too the rule does not wish other competitors to judge whether there has been an infringement on the part of a yacht which has touched the mark or whether she has been wrongfully forced to touch it by another yacht (rule 52.1(b)i).

Rule 46. **Anchored,** **aground or** **capsized**	46.1	A yacht under way shall keep clear of another yacht *racing* which is anchored, aground or capsized. Of two anchored yachts, the one which anchored later shall keep clear, except that a yacht which is dragging shall keep clear of one which is not.
	46.2	A yacht anchored or aground shall indicate the fact to any yacht which may be in danger of fouling her. Unless the size of the yachts or the weather conditions make some other signal necessary, a hail is sufficient indication.
	46.3	A yacht shall not be penalized for fouling a yacht in distress which she is attempting to assist or a yacht which goes aground or capsizes immediately ahead of her.

The final rule makes an exception to the other rules in Part IV (but not those in Section A, which always apply) and refers to situations which in practice every good seaman should know how to resolve. It is intuitive that a yacht under way must avoid a yacht which is anchored, aground or capsized and is therefore not in command and cannot get out of the way (rule 46.1). Bear in mind that the wording "anchored, aground or capsized" is not definitive but exemplary, that is to say other similar cases can be included. The Italian Appeals Committee (FIV 1971/7, *Meltemi* v. *Sciria*) dealt with an incident where a yacht was left hanging by her main sheet on a mark of the course. There was a discussion about whether she could be considered to fall within the cases envisaged by rule 46.

It stated "It is clear that the intention is to lay an obligation on a yacht underway to avoid a yacht which cannot move. For this reason the obligation is not limited to the three examples indicated in the clause, but should be extended to those cases (and this is the spirit of rule 46) where a yacht is static because it is out of control."

It is also obvious that, of two anchored yachts the last one to anchor must avoid the one already in position which cannot move (rule 46.2). It is equally clear that a yacht anchored but dragging must, just because she has got herself into a difficult and unacceptable situation be the one to worry about keeping clear and out of the way of the stationary better-anchored yacht that is not annoying anybody.

It is also logical that a yacht which is anchored or aground (and we would add even the yacht about to anchor or, as sometimes happens, that realizes she can no longer avoid going aground) must warn others that she is no longer capable of avoiding an accident. This information, rule 46.2 says, can be signalled by a simple hail and in normal conditions this will be sufficient. Sometimes, for example with reduced visibility, a simple hail will not be enough and other methods must be used (flags, fog horns, lights, rockets, smoke, etc.).

Rule 46.3 envisages finally the case of a yacht which while racing goes to try and help a yacht in difficulties (see also rule 58), and it is logical that since it may not be possible to do this without touching, the good samaritan must not pay for his virtue but must be exonerated from any penalty normally resulting from cases involving collision (rule 31) or even touching a mark (rule 52) when rescue operations are going on.

Equally a yacht that has failed to avoid running into another competitor aground or capsized immediately ahead of her is protected in the same way. Here too the innocent yacht must be able to go on her way without being penalized. It should be underlined that the accident must be unavoidable because it happens close to, and is unexpected and unforeseeable, and if these conditions did not in fact exist in the actual case under examination (and it is up to the yacht which has run into the other to provide the evidence) it is obvious that there is no exception and that the infringing yacht must be punished.

Other rules which have a bearing on rule 46 and must be borne in mind are 53 (Fog signals and lights), 56 (Boarding), 57 (Leaving, man overboard), 58 (Rendering assistance), 59 (Outside assistance), 62 (Manual power), 63 (Anchoring and making fast) and 64 (Aground or foul of an obstruction). And remember that rule 46 of which we are talking, is part (although as an exception) of those rules united in Part IV which serve to regulate encounters between yachts in such a way as to prevent collisions between them. The rules of Part V on the other hand which follow are about other possible situations in racing which have nothing to do with the dispositions of Part IV.

Part V
Other sailing rules

Obligations of Helmsman and Crew
in Handling a Yacht

A yacht is subject to the rules of Part V only while she is *racing*.

As was suggested at the end of the last chapter, Part V is in a certain sense a continuation of Part IV; it too contains rules applied only during the *race* (in the strict sense of the definition) with the difference that the regulations of Part IV are directed at the helmsmen and deal with the sailing rules that these must obey, while those of Part V are for all members of the crew dealing as they do with such matters as setting of sails, embarking and disembarking and anchoring.

In practice the rules of Part V relate to the period from the preparatory signal to the moment when a yacht finishes and clears the finishing line or retires, or until the race is postponed, abandoned or cancelled. Remember that Part V controls all aspects of the progress of a race which are not right-of-way rules in the strict sense.

50. Ranking as a starter
A yacht whose entry has been accepted by the race committee, which does not *start* but sails about in the vicinity of the starting line between her preparatory and starting signals shall rank as a starter.

This short rule can be considered as one of those which, although not part of the right-of-way rules of Part IV, are nevertheless logically connected with *racing* (in the sense of its definition). It provides a useful criterion in those races where the number of competitors is a basic element for calculating points and serves to establish the validity of a race which is subject to a minimum number of starters. It also helps decide the number of starters when prizes depend on this number. This is the reason for a rule that otherwise would be contradictory by ranking as a starter precisely that yacht which has not in fact started, that is to say which has not crossed the starting line as required by the relevant definition.

However, the rule as laid down is in perfect accord with what the definition of *racing* terms the beginning; indeed the class preparatory signal is taken as the beginning of the race in both these rules (see rule 4.4(a)). This explains why a yacht which sails about in the vicinity of the starting line between her preparatory and starting signals ranks as a starter even if she deliberately retires (that is telling the committee or lowering her distinguishing flag or hoisting her ensign) before the starting signal or at any rate before crossing the starting line.

But what does the phrase "sailing about in the vicinity of the starting line" mean? It is not possible to lay down a general rule which will permit you to establish whether such a "vicinity" exists or not, and the decision must be left to the wise judgement of the race committee. In any case this vicinity will depend on the size and character of the yacht (and therefore her speed and her ability to arrive at the line within reasonable time) as well as her apparent intention to take part in the race (an intention which usually is then frustrated by some accident).

Sometimes a yacht can be considered *racing* even before the preparatory signal (see comment to the definition of *racing*, para. 2); but this has no consequences as far as rule 50 is concerned which takes effect only after the preparatory signal that is to say only five minutes before the start.

To finish let us look at a curious case which was the subject of IYRU No. 34 (NAYRU 112). In a race for the L36 class the start, fixed in the programme for 11.15, was correctly postponed with the right signals under rule 4.1 about 30 seconds before the original start time. Four yachts did not notice the postponement signal and crossed the line at 11.15, sailed the course and arrived after about four hours. The race committee considered them to be non-starters but one of them sought redress maintaining that they should have been disqualified as premature starters. The protest was dismissed by the race committee, observing that while it could not be denied that the yachts had obviously every intention of taking part in the race, they had not started according to the definition nor could they rank as starters under rule 50; this rule refers only to a start which has actually happened and not to one which has been postponed. This decision was upheld by the U.S. Appeals Committee which observed: "a yacht which neither starts nor sails about in the vicinity of the starting line between her preparatory and starting signals is not a starter, unless the scoring system in use so ranks her – a point which is not at issue in this case".

Rule 51. Sailing the course	(a) A yacht shall *start* and *finish* only as prescribed in the starting and finishing definitions.
51.1	(b) Unless otherwise prescribed in the sailing instructions, a yacht which either crosses prematurely, or is on the course side of the starting line or its extensions, at the starting signal, shall return and *start* in accordance with the definition.
	(c) Unless otherwise prescribed in the sailing instructions, when after a general recall, any part of a yacht's hull, crew or equipment is on the course side of the starting line or its extensions during the minute before her starting signal, she shall return to the pre-start side of the line across one of its extensions and *start*.

(d) Failure of a yacht to see or hear her recall notification shall not relieve her of her obligation to *start* correctly.

51.2 A yacht shall sail the course so as to round or pass each *mark* on the required side in correct sequence, and so that a string representing her wake from the time she *starts* until she *finishes* would, when drawn taut, lie on the required side of each *mark*.

51.3 A *mark* has a required side for a yacht as long as she is on a leg which it begins, bounds or ends. A starting line *mark* begins to have a required side for a yacht when she *starts*. A starting limit *mark* has a required side for a yacht from the time she is approaching the starting line to *start* until she has left the *mark* astern on the first leg. A finishing line *mark* and a finishing limit *mark* cease to have a required side for a yacht as soon as she *finishes*.

51.4 A yacht which rounds or passes a *mark* on the wrong side may exonerate herself by making her course conform to the requirements of rule 51.2.

51.5 It is not necessary for a yacht to cross the finishing line completely; after *finishing* she may clear it in either direction.

Rule 51 lays down how to start (or return in the case of a premature start), how to complete the course round the various marks (and correct any errors) and how to finish.

At first sight it may seem that great confusion is caused by fragmenting one subject into many prescriptions and much of the material (for example rule 4.2 (Signalling the course), rule 4.3 (Changing the course), rule 4.4 (Signals for starting a race), rule 4.5 (Finishing signals), rule 6 (Starting and finishing lines), rule 7 (Start of a race), rule 8 (Recalls), rule 9 (Marks), rule 10 (Finishing within a time limit), etc.), is met again in other parts of the rule. However, the examples above belong to Part II as they are directed at the organizers and lay down how the essential elements of the race must be prepared and organized; while those in Part V including rule 51 are addressed to the competitors instructing them how to sail correctly round the course. Having cleared up this point let us look at the various sectors of the rule in the same order as is followed by a yacht when racing.

1. The way to start. The starting line wrongly laid or erroneous sailing instructions (51.1(a))

Until 1973 the competitor was explicitly told not to concern himself about the possibility of the committee boat being anchored on the opposite side of the mark to that laid down in the sailing instructions. The rule laid down that even in such cases he only had to follow what was prescribed in the relevant definition in Part I: in the sense that it is compulsory to cross the starting line in the direction of the first mark. This detail about the committee boat is now considered superfluous in view of the clarity of the definitions of *finishing* and *starting*. However, we think it may still be useful to reprint the text and diagrams from the old edition of this book because they are still useful for explaining rule 51.1(a) (see also rule 6 – Starting and finishing lines).

In what circumstances can a committee boat be said to be anchored on the side of a mark opposite to that laid down in the sailing instructions? Lines where possible should be laid at right angles to the direction of the first leg of the course when starting and to the last leg of the course when finishing. Fig.

141 shows three cases where you can see that if you start in a different way
from that prescribed in the definition (either because the sailing instructions are
wrong or because the committee boat is not in its proper place) the course to
the first mark goes round one of the limit marks, thus creating a greater chance
of accidents – exactly what the rule has always tried to avoid.

To repeat, no yacht is considered to have *started* if she crosses the line in a
direction which is other than that leading to the first mark of the course even if
the sailing instructions erroneously lay down the contrary or even if the
committee boat is anchored on the opposite side to that laid down correctly by
the sailing instructions.

Fig. 141 (1)

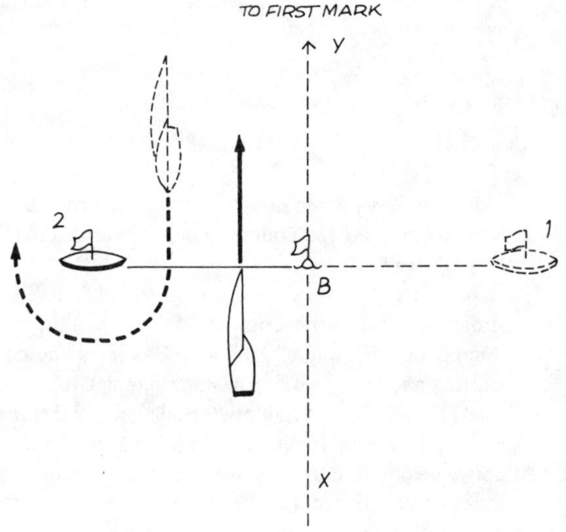

(2)

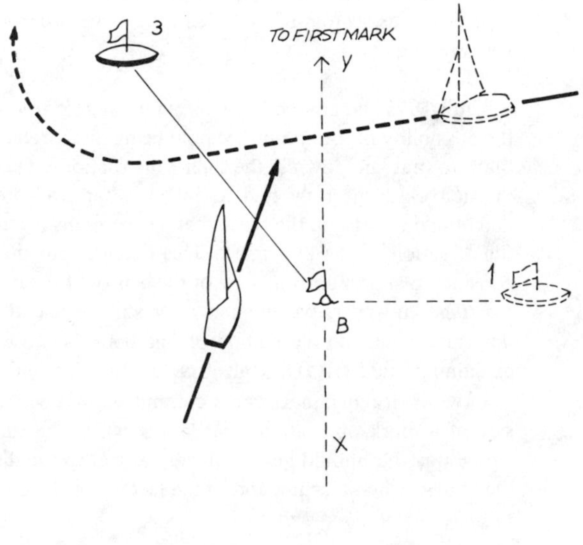

(3)

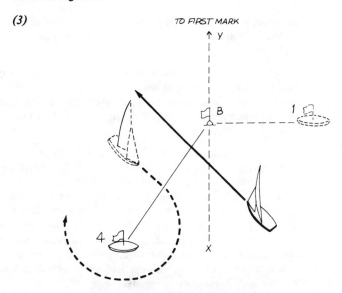

Fig. 141   Starting: in these examples (1, 2 & 3) the sailing instructions prescribe a course with marks to port and a starting line between buoy B and the committee boat at position 1. However the boat mistakenly anchors at position 2, 3 or 4. Nevertheless competitors, in accordance with the definition of starting must ignore the mistake, and in each case cross the line "in the direction of the first mark" leaving the buoy to starboard (rather than crossing the line the opposite way as shown by the dotted line).

2. A premature starter or a yacht which finds herself on the course side of the line; recall signals

(51.1(b)(c))

We have already spoken of yachts at fault in these two situations in the commentary to rule 44 (Yachts returning to start), so just remember:

– that to be a premature starter it is enough for any part of the hull, equipment or crew even in an abnormal position to be on the course side of the line at the starting signal (see the definition of starting in Part I);
– that the course side of the line is that on the side of the direction of the first mark of the course (see definition of starting and rule 6 – Starting and finishing lines);
– that in both the above cases the "fault" begins only at the starting signal and not before, unless sailing instructions prescribe the contrary and anticipate this moment (as for example with the so called "minute rule" see the comment to the definition of starting, para 3 and rule 8, para. 4).

We have already spoken about the obligation to return and start in accordance with the definition in the comment to Part I, rule 8 (Recalls) and rule 44 (Returning to start). Readers should go back if they have any doubts on these and we would only remind you: that a yacht is considered to have recrossed when she has completely passed from the course to the pre-start side of the line or its extensions. That is to say with every part of her hull, equipment and crew;

– that a yacht until she has returned loses every right of way relative to the yachts which are starting or have started correctly;
– that nevertheless a premature starter which instead of turning back continues to sail on temporarily enjoys all the rights which Part IV accords to a yacht which has started correctly.

In 1969 the rules codified in the mildest form the so called "minute rule" or "last minute rule" which had already been widely adopted by race organizers when a particularly large number of competitors made identification and recall of premature starters difficult (see comment to rule 8). For this reason rule 51.1(c) (adopting a system of dubious worth perhaps from certain points of view of pure sport, but in practice useful) now establishes the starting procedure to follow a general recall (rule 8.3); a yacht is forbidden to cross the starting line "during the minute before her starting signal" (an exception of course to the various procedures laid down by rule 8.2 which enter into function only at the starting signal).

At the starting signal (and only at that moment) the race committee must show the recall number or letter (or put into action any other prescribed recall system) to advise a yacht, caught by rule 51.1(c) during the last minute, that she has not come back to the prestart side of the line round the limit marks. Rule 8.2(a) applies in such cases and the yacht in question will therefore have the right to an ordinary individual recall (subject to the sailing instructions).

In fact a yacht that during this one-minute period has crossed the starting line with any part of the hull, crew or equipment is not automatically and irredeemably disqualified (as the strictest version of the minute rule prescribes), but is given a way of getting herself into the right again. To do so the culprit must first of all get to one side in such a way as not to hinder yachts starting correctly and once clear she must come back to the prestart side but across an extension of the line, outside the limit marks (fig. 136). It is clear that while carrying out such a manoeuvre she must keep clear of all yachts which are starting or have started correctly and so until she has completely re-entered as laid down by rule 44.1(a). Rule 51 does not specify this (and indeed to be precise rule 44 enters in function only when the starting signal is given) but our own opinion is that in the case of rule 51.1(c) this obligation to keep clear of all the others whilst she is returning must already exist in the minute preceding the starting signal; if this were not so it would be contrary to the aim of the prescription automatically and immediately to outlaw anyone who crosses the line during that minute.

Rule 51.1(c) as we have already explained serves above all in races with a large number of competitors particularly if they are indisciplined but sailing instructions can specifically omit rule 51.1(c) and keep to the normal rules under rule 8 (Recalls).

However, note that "failure of a yacht to see or hear her recall notification shall not relieve her of her obligation to *start* correctly" (rule 51.1(d)). It really would be iniquitous to pardon for any reason a mistake that gives a great advantage to an erring competitor as against all the others who had started correctly and if such mistakes were condoned it would not be long before someone would try to justify themselves affirming perhaps falsely that they had not noticed the recall signal.

3. How to sail the course; the piece of string and correction of any errors (51.2 and 57.4)

To understand rule 51.2 better remember that the sailing instructions have to specify (rule 3.2(a)ii) the course to be sailed, "describing all *marks* and stating the order in which and the side on which each is to be rounded or passed".

Rule 51.2 lays down how mistakes in the course can be rectified; it

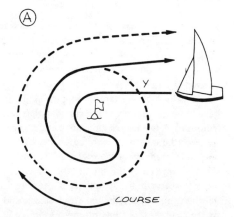

Fig. 142(a)   Buoy to starboard: the yacht realizing that she has mistakenly left the buoy to port returns along her wake but then omits to round it on the required side as she should have by following the dotted line. Pulling the imaginary string represented by her wake it is clear that the buoy has remained to port, the wrong side.

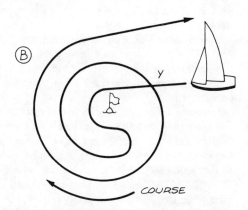

Fig. 142(b)   A yacht having returned the way she came to where she began to go wrong (y) correctly leaves the buoy on the required side. The piece of string test shows that she has now left it to starboard.

prescribes how a yacht that has made a mistake, must first of all retrace her steps (indeed her wake), resailing completely her erroneous track in the opposite sense. It adds that only after she has thus returned to where she went wrong can she restart the correct course, rounding or passing the mark on the prescribed side. In addition the rule provides a way to check out her course (including the righting of any error). It imagines that the wake of a yacht is represented by a piece of string and tells us that if we pull this string tight we can easily see whether the buoy remains on the correct side, as prescribed by the sailing instructions. Fig. 142a and b show how a mistake is corrected and how the check works with a mark that must be left to starboard.

4. The required side of a mark (51.3)

We saw (rule 3.2(a)ii) that sailing instructions indicate the order and the side on which each mark of the course is to be left. Rule 51.3 explains that this obligation does not hold good for the whole of the race, but only for the period in which the buoy effectively functions as a course mark when it "begins bounds or ends" a leg on which a yacht is sailing.

Let us look at an example on a triangular course in which buoys A, B and C have to be left to port. On the first leg that is to say where the yachts are sailing from A to B, C has no significance and no prescribed side; it is not a *mark* in the sense of the definition although it may be a simple *obstruction*. Later A will loose its significance as a *mark* to be rounded or passed on a required side and this will happen at the moment in which a yacht, having rounded or passed mark B, starts on the second leg of the course towards C and simultaneously C will become a *mark* in the strict sense, and so on. There is no difficulty in understanding this rule and the reason for it, *marks* serve to limit legs of the course and therefore are of no interest once a leg has been completed or before it has been started. The same holds good for the two *marks* which limit a starting or finishing line. Rule 51.3 states that "a starting line *mark* begins to have a required side for a yacht when she starts", that is when she cuts the line for the first time after the starting signal in the direction of the first mark of the course (see definition Part I). Therefore before crossing the line a yacht can pass the mark as she wishes without any consequences even if the starting signal has been given.

This explains why a premature starter, or a yacht on the wrong side of the line, is allowed to come back passing inside the two limit marks (that is to say leaving them on the opposite side to that laid down for the start, unless of course there are contrary sailing instructions requiring her to return only outside them).

It is quite a different story for marks marking the outer limit of a transit line laid in accordance with rule 6(c) that is with two fixed posts ashore. In this case the buoy is called "starting limit *mark*" instead of a "starting line *mark*" and it has a required side for a yacht from the time she is approaching the starting line to start until she has left the mark astern on the first leg. This new prescription from the 1973 edition will, it is hoped, eliminate the problems which arise at the start when the limit buoy is badly laid, that is, when it is not on the line or on the course side but on the prestart side (as we have shown in our comment to rule 6(c)).

Once a yacht has crossed the starting line and has therefore *started* one of the two limit marks of the line will as far as she is concerned continue to be a *mark* because it automatically becomes the mark which begins the first leg of the course. The other line limit mark will lose its significance as a *mark* in the technical sense (that is to say which has to be left on a required side and which cannot be touched without disqualification) once the yacht has cleared the starting line and sailed away. Since the criterion is the same for the start and the finish we can look at an example offered us by NAYRU 70. The sailing instructions laid down that the finishing line was between the committee boat (to be left to port) and a buoy with a flag. One yacht arrived, from the direction of the last mark, made an ample circle (fig. 143) altering course by almost 180°, continued on round the committee boat leaving her to port and, still turning in the same direction, crossed the line between the two marks in the prescribed direction.

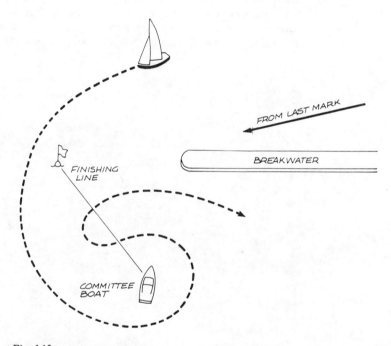

Fig. 143

The appeals committee's decision reads as follows: "Rule 51.3 states in part 'a mark has a required side for a yacht as long as she is on a leg which it begins, bounds or ends'. Thus a finishing mark 'has a required side for a yacht as long as she is on' the last leg of the course.

"The marks at the two ends of a line have opposite required sides. In this case the committee boat was to be left to port and the buoy to starboard. Yacht G, however, left the buoy to port and although rule 51.4 permits 'a yacht which passes a mark on the wrong side' to correct her error by making her course conform to the requirements of rule 51.2, she did not do so. As can be seen from the diagram of G's course at the finish, 'a string representing her wake from the time she started until she finished would, when drawn taut, lie' on the wrong side of the buoy so that she not only passed the buoy on the wrong side but failed to 'correct her error' by retracing her course in conformance with rule 51.2". However, the race committee decided that she had not *finished* and this decision was confirmed in second instance.

A similar decision some years afterwards appeared in IYRU No. 28 (RYA 1966/11, *Volvo* v. Race Committee, (fig. 144). The sailing instructions laid down that the finishing line was between the inner and middle buoys and that yachts were to pass between the inner and middle buoys in a south-westerly direction. However, *Volvo*, while sailing south-west, passed between outer and middle buoys leaving the latter to starboard; she then, by mistake, made a complete turn so that she left the inside mark to starboard as well and then finally she sailed south-westerly again crossing the finishing line as prescribed between the inner and middle marks. The race committee held that she could not be considered to have finished correctly. *Volvo* appealed maintaining that she was under no obligation to correct an error by unwinding since nothing

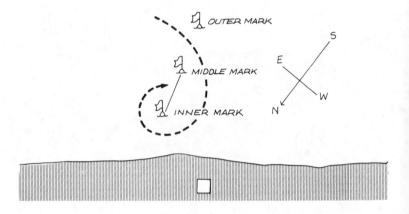

Fig. 144

prevented her from passing either of the two limit marks indifferently to port or starboard before she actually finished. But she was wrong because in this case too a mistake had been made which could have been corrected (rule 51.4) but only in the way laid down by rule 51.3. The finishing-line limit *mark* could be treated only as such and not as if it was also the last mark of the last leg of the course; and *Volvo*'s reasoning was proved wrong by the string test. This case is no longer published, since it is covered by the '77 rules.

A finishing mark and a finishing limit mark cease to have a required side for a yacht as soon as she finishes. That is when she cuts the line coming from the direction of the last mark of the course (see definition Part I). Note in addition that this refers only to the required side and that even after cutting the line she is considered to be still *racing* until she has cleared the line. This explains why she may not touch these finishing marks without disqualification (rule 52.1(a)iii).

5. How to
finish; the
finishing line
laid wrongly
(51.1(a) and
51.5)

Rule 51 makes it mandatory (that is to say even if the sailing instructions try to alter it or when the committee boat is anchored on the opposite side to that stated in the sailing instructions), that when finishing a yacht must cross the line "in accordance with the definition of finishing"; that is to say coming from the direction of the last mark (fig. 141).

Since the finishing line is more often badly laid or badly designed than you might think, some classical examples must be given. Let us begin with IYRU No. 22 (RYA 1965/1) *Polly* v. the Royal Northern Yacht Club (fig. 145) In this case the yacht *Polly*, even though the sailing instructions prescribed (as they could not) that the finishing line should be crossed leaving the mark to starboard, crossed the line in accordance with the definition, from the direction of the last mark (A in the figure). Stating that her way of finishing was correct the RYA explained that "the IYRU prefers a 'straight through' to a 'hook round' as being simpler and fairer". As to the excuses put forward by the organizers, who pointed out certain particular problems of the course the RYA suggested: "it is therefore suggested that the local requirement, that all yachts

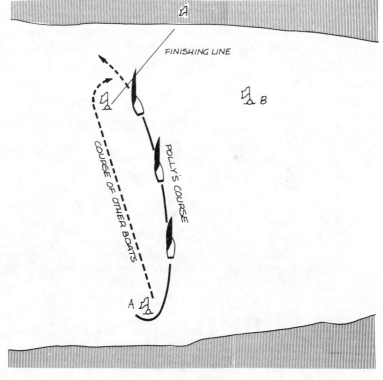

BOOM TOUCHED MARK AT THIS POINT

Fig. 145

should cross the finishing line in the same direction at the end of each round, might be met by laying an additional mark (B) and requiring yachts to round it on the port hand before crossing the finishing line."

Still on the same subject the reader should look at a similar decision FIV 1966/3, under the definition of finishing. Here too the terms of the definition prevailed over contrary sailing instructions which were given to the yachts.

It is important to notice that by "last *mark*" is meant the last mark that has been rounded or passed before the finishing line; this is contained in NAYRU 84 which decided a similar case along the same lines.

Before leaving rule 51 look at the last phrase of rule 51.5. It permits a yacht to finish without crossing the finishing line completely (see the definition of finishing) and she can therefore clear it in either direction. She can either sail on, crossing the line completely, or she can turn back on to what might be called the course side of the finishing line. Thus yachts that have finished can get out of the way of others as quickly as possible. There is no contradiction here to the definition of *racing* which says that a yacht is under the rules after she *finishes* until she has effectively cleared the line.

Rule 51.5 is in full accord with rule 52.1(a)(iii) which penalizes touching a mark of the finishing line even when this happens after the yacht has *finished*. And it is also in accord with rule 31.2 which permits the disqualification of a yacht that has already *finished* but seriously hinders a competitor still *racing* (for example yachts that have finished the race often enjoy watching on or by the line and get in the way of those still trying to finish).

Rule 52.   52.1   A yacht which: —
Touching a
mark   either
                     (a) touches: —

                            (i) a starting *mark* before *starting;*

                            (ii) a *mark* which begins, bounds or ends the leg of the course on which she is sailing; or

                            (iii) a finishing *mark* after *finishing;*
                     or
                     (b) causes a *mark* or *mark* vessel to shift to avoid being touched,
                     shall immediately retire, unless either:

                            (i) she alleges that she was wrongfully compelled by another yacht to touch it or cause it to shift, in which case she shall act in accordance with rule 68.3, (Protests), unless the other yacht exonerates herself by accepting an alternative penalty when so prescribed in the sailing instructions, or

                            (ii) she exonerates herself in accordance with rule 52.2.

        52.2   (a) When a yacht touches a *mark* surrounded by navigable water, she may exonerate herself by completing one entire rounding of the *mark*, leaving it on the required side and thereafter re-rounding it or re-passing it without touching it, as required to sail the course in accordance with rule 51.2, (Sailing the Course), and the sailing instructions.

                (b) When a yacht touches:

                            (i) a starting *mark*, she shall carry out the rounding after she has *started;* or

(ii) a finishing *mark,* she shall carry out the rounding, and she shall not rank as having *finished* until she has completed the rounding and again crosses the finishing line in accordance with the definition of *finishing.*

Even beginners who certainly do not know of the existence of rule 52.2 know that when racing you must not touch competitors or marks and this means that you must not touch them with any part of the hull, equipment or crew (including a hand pushed out as a fender).

What beginners do not know (nor sometimes even experienced competitors) is the exact duration of the period when objects are *marks* and cannot be touched (see definition Part I). A *mark* is "any object specified in the sailing instructions which a yacht must round or pass on a required side"; and when it is no longer such (see rule 51.3) it becomes a mere *obstruction* so that a yacht may touch it without being caught by rule 52.

Rule 52 specifies that the ban on touching marks is in force:
1. for starting marks (see rules 6 and 7) from the preparatory signal (see the preamble to Part V and definition of racing) until the moment in which the mark ceases to have a required side (that is until it has been rounded or passed, remembering that it may be the mark which begins the first leg of the course when it must be treated as a mark, not of the start, but of the course itself).
2. for a mark of the course while it begins, bounds or ends the leg of a course (rule 51.3).
3. for any finishing mark from the moment in which a yacht having rounded or passed the last mark of the course is sailing on the last leg; until she has finished *racing* (preamble to Part V) and cleared the line and the finishing mark (definition of *racing,* para. 7 of the comment).

In addition if the occupants of a mark boat, seeing a competitor sailing right on top of them, think it wiser to move to avoid being hit, it logically follows that a collision, even though it has been avoided materially, has taken place theoretically from the point of view of the rule (rule 52.1(b)). This holds for any occasion even if the collision is avoided by the mark boat's own means or her crew's hands.

Breach of rule 52 does not lead inevitably to a disqualification (or retirement) for rule 52.2 allows a yacht to exonerate herself, but may in its turn be excluded from operation by the sailing instructions (see rule 3.1).

In fact in 1976 the new 1977 rules made it impossible for organizing clubs to exclude rule 52.2, it was then realized that, in some crowded waters with big boats, the rule was really not acceptable and could make matters even worse; at the eleventh hour then the rule was changed and competitors should be aware of this as the very first copies of the '77 rules were printed without correction.

Let us look then first at what happens when rule 52.2 is not in action and when the yacht touching a mark feels that it was not her fault. First of all rule 52.1 calls for "immediate retirement" if she is not to be disqualified (however, a yacht continuing to race will continue to be accorded her rights under Part IV as in rule 33).

Rule 52 would be terribly severe if every yacht had to retire or was disqualified whenever she hit a mark, and it is obvious that a yacht that alleges that she was wrongfully pushed on to a mark by another yacht can continue to race in spite of the collision as long as she immediately asks the race committee to look into the incident and clear her by acting according to rule 68.3: that is she must protest (unless the other yacht accepts a penalty when Appendix 3 is specified in the sailing instructions).

To this end, immediately after the incident, she must hoist her protest flag and then complete a written protest, otherwise the race committee cannot help her. On this subject there is an important decision, NAYRU 49 dealing with a case of a yacht A which ended up on a mark through the fault of another yacht B. After the incident A hoisted her protest flag immediately and flew it until after she finished but then did not put in a written protest. Here is the part of that sentence which deals with the rule which we are looking at: "Rule 52.1 is the only rule that requires a yacht once she has hoisted a protest flag to follow it up with a written protest, and requires a yacht, in effect, to disqualify herself by retiring if she fails to follow the imperative provisions of the rule.

"It is regarded as important that the provisions of rule 68 be strictly complied with and any deviation, unless specifically provided for in the sailing instructions, is not permitted. While not subject to disqualification in the circumstances, A has placed herself in an unsportsmanlike position for which there is no specific penalty. Her failure to observe the spirit of the rules will be reflected in the adverse opinion of the race committee and fellow yachtsmen and there is always the prospect that one who makes a practice of such behaviour may be confronted in future events with the power of the race committee in rule 1.4, to reject any entry without stating the reason."

A similar incident characterized IYRU No. 41 (RYA 1969/10, *Crest* v. *Cloud*), with some precedural complications added. Here too a yacht, *Cloud*, touched a mark but did not retire and did not protest anyone else. *Crest*, having seen the incident, protested against *Cloud*. A third yacht *Kelpie* discovered all this later and quite correctly hastened to declare that she had forced *Cloud* onto the mark and retired excusing herself for not having done so immediately because she did not know that she had caused an incident. However, the race committee, while realizing that the fault was *Kelpie*'s, disqualified *Cloud* for violation of rule 52.1 because she neither retired nor protested.

Cloud was not best pleased with this decision and appealed, explaining that she had hoisted her protest flag but had not then presented a written protest because she had learnt that *Kelpie* intended to retire because it was her fault. However this argument was not held sufficient, and the appeal was dismissed and the RYA underlined that "rule 52.1 is the only rule which requires a yacht to disqualify herself (by retiring) if she fails to comply with mandatory provisions of that rule"; and specified that *Cloud*'s failure in this regard was "breach of both the letter and the spirit of the racing rules" explaining that *Cloud* had to be disqualified "not for touching the mark but for failing to implement her protest flag by lodging a written protest as required by rule 52.1".

Re-rounding a mark

The rule seeks to penalize a culprit by making her lose time with respect to the other competitors.

IYRU No. 42, now no longer published, stated in clarification of this rule that the rule of the piece of string – 51.2 – can be usefully applied here. When a mark is touched and the yacht completes her extra turn and then rounds the mark the string representing her wake will have one turn round the mark (fig. 145a).

More help comes from IYRU No. 59 (RYA 1972/4, Bristol Avon S.C. question no. 3). Here the mark has to be left to starboard and a yacht broaching upwind of it is pushed against it by the tide in the exact point shown in fig. 146. The question is: "Should this boat follow the requirement of the solid line course before proceeding or could she have continued from point A as shown by the broken line?" The RYA answers: "The boat must follow the solid line course as shown"; only thus would she leave her piece of string wrapped once round the mark as laid down. A 360° turn is asked for, not a complete turn after having touched the mark; among other things this would be virtually impossible because the helmsman could not judge accurately when she had got back to the point of impact.

The rule requires that the final rounding or passage is completed without touching it, that is to say that it is carried out as if the mark were being rounded or passed for the first time.

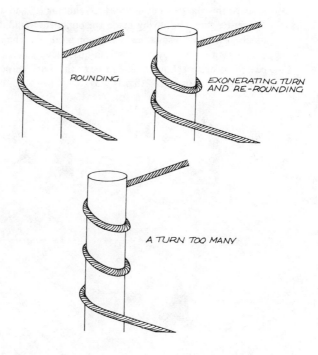

Fig. 145a

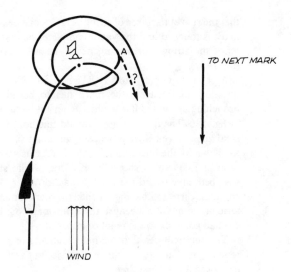

Fig. 146

On this point a look at NAYRU 149. Here a yacht was accused of having touched the mark "while she was re-rounding it" and disqualified by the race committee "for not having made one complete rounding of the mark without touching it". The disqualified yacht appealed, underlining that she had been in contact with the buoy for nearly a quarter way round but that contact had ceased before reaching "a line through the mark perpendicular to the course from the previous mark" (fig. 147/3).

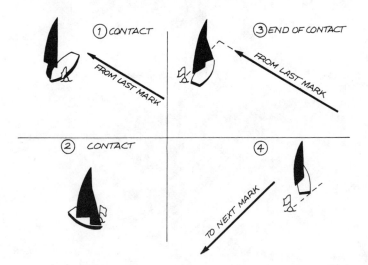

Fig. 147

The U.S. Appeals Committee upheld the appeal observing that the penalty turn was carried out (even though touching the mark for 180° of it) and that the subsequent rounding had also been completed but without touching the mark, and she therefore had properly fulfilled the requirements of rule 52.2 to re-round or re-pass without touching the mark.

Since the intention of the penalty turn is to make a yacht lose time, and therefore places, and if she loses this time while still rubbing up against the mark, that is her affair. IYRU No. 64 (RYA 1973/6) bears this out. When the mark touched is a starting mark the penalty turn can be made only after the culprit has *started* in the sense of the definition (rule 52.2(b)i). The reason is clear, because if she could re-round immediately (imagine that she touches it two or three minutes before the starting signal) the aim of making her lose time in respect of the other competitors would not be achieved.

Whenever a finishing mark is touched the opposite is true and for the same reason: that is to say the culprit must first make the penalty turn and only afterwards can he cut the finishing line in accordance with the definition and so *finish*. In any case (that is with a mark of the course a starting mark or a finishing mark) the penalty turn must be made leaving the mark on the prescribed side (fig. 148).

IYRU No. 42 which we have already mentioned furnished an imaginary case where at the starting signal a yacht's bow was over the starting line and touching the mark. "As a premature starter", explained the IYRU, "this yacht is first of all obliged by rule 51.1(b) to return to the prestart side of the line; afterwards she must make a complete turn of the starting mark as a penalty turn and then she must re-cross the line in the direction of the first mark of the course. Only thus will she have completed her supplementary turn in conformity with the piece of string test and can thereafter *start*."

The matter does not finish here because (as we have seen in the comment to rules 8 and 44) returning can normally be carried out across the line, that is passing between the two limit marks. But when the round-the-ends rule is in force a yacht must come back outside the marks and across the extensions of

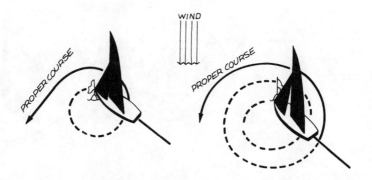

Fig. 148   *After touching the buoy the yacht (leaving it always on the required side) completes one entire rounding as a penalty and then must re-round or re-pass it without touching it as laid down by sailing instructions.*

the line rounding one of the limit marks. In the first case (returning as she likes fig. 149a) she must first of all return to the prestart side of the line by continuing round and outside the mark or she can sail or drift backwards across the line. If however, she is subject to the round-the-end rule she can only sail on round the mark (fig. 149b).

Things do not change when the mark is touched before the starting signal because here too the culprit must do three things (a) return in the way prescribed (if she has cut the line of course), (b) complete a penalty turn of 360° leaving the mark on the prescribed side and (c) start. It makes no difference whether the starting signal is fired while she is re-entering or re-rounding: you will see that in all cases she will sail the same course; she will make one turn more than those (whether they are over the line or not) that have not touched the mark. Theoretically a yacht which, sailing under the round-the-ends and one-minute rules, crosses the starting line in the fatal last minute and realizes what she has done but at that moment touches the starting mark must act as follows: for the first infringement (over the line in the last minute) she clears herself by immediately rounding one of the starting marks and returning to the prestart side; for the second infringement (touching the mark) she can re-round but only after she has *started*, not immediately.

If the mark she has touched is not a starting but a finishing mark there is practically speaking little difference (except that there is no question of a starting signal or a prematurely-cut line). It sometimes happens that the finishing mark is touched after the yacht has *finished* the race in the sense of the definition. But rule 52.1(a)(iii) incriminates also any yacht touching the mark after she has finished and so even in this case she must return to the course side of the finishing line rounding outside the touched limit mark and must again cross the finishing line from the direction of the last mark that is to say she must repeat her *finish*.

Finally it must be remembered that a yacht completing a penalty turn must keep clear of all other yachts that are rounding or passing the mark or that have

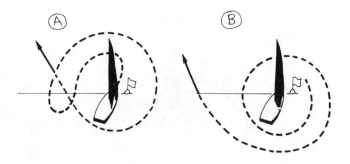

Fig. 149(a)   Touching the mark by a premature starter; "free" return, start and penalty turn.

Fig. 149(b)   Touching a mark by a premature starter; return over an extension of the line, start and penalty turn.

rounded or passed correctly. Rule 45 (Re-rounding after touching a mark) prescribes this and further details are given there.

Rule 53. Fog signals and lights

Every yacht shall observe the International Regulations for Preventing Collisions at Sea or Government Rules for fog signals and, as a minimum, the carrying of lights at night.

Little need be said here on this subject. Those classes which are likely to sail offshore where fog signals are required, or at night, normally sail under special regulations specified in the sailing instructions which lay down the gear to be carried.

Of course, at sea all the IRPCS should be observed except for the right-of-way rules between yachts racing. So it is hard to understand why this rule which refers to fog and light signals only should have found its way into the racing rules.

Rule 54. Setting and sheeting sails

54.1

CHANGING SAILS
While changing headsails and spinnakers a replacing sail may be fully set and trimmed before the sail it replaces is taken in, but only one mainsail and, except when changing, only one spinnaker shall be carried set.

54.2

SHEETING SAILS TO SPARS
(a) Unless otherwise prescribed by the national authority or by the class rules, any sail may be sheeted to or led above a boom regularly used for a working sail and permanently attached to the mast to which the head of the working sail is set, but no sails shall be sheeted over or through outriggers.
(b) An outrigger is any fitting so placed, except as permitted in the first sentence of rule 54.2, that it could exert outward pressure on a sheet at a point from which, with the yacht upright, a vertical line would fall outside the hull or deck planking at that point, or outside such other position as class rules prescribe. For the purpose of this rule: bulwarks, rails and rubbing strakes are not part of the hull or deck planking. A boom of a boomed headsail which requires no adjustment when *tacking* is not an outrigger.

54.3

SPINNAKER; SPINNAKER BOOM
A spinnaker shall not be set without a boom. The tack of a spinnaker when set and drawing shall be in close proximity to the outboard end of a spinnaker boom. Any headsail may be attached to a spinnaker boom provided that a spinnaker is not set. A sail tacked down abaft the foremost mast is not a headsail. Only one spinnaker boom shall be used at a time and when in use shall be carried only on the side of the foremost mast opposite to the main boom and shall be fixed to the mast. Rule 54.3 shall not apply when shifting a spinnaker boom or sail attached thereto.

1. Changing sails (54.1)

This first paragraph accepts for obvious reasons the necessity of not losing sail area and therefore drive. Two similar sails may be hoisted simultaneously for the shortest time necessary for a sail change even when class rules allow only one to be set. However, only headsails and spinnakers may be changed in this way and bear in mind that a sail tacked down abaft the forward mast is not a headsail (rule 54.3). These are general rules, which apply only when there are no other contradictory class rules, sailing instructions or national prescriptions.

2. Sheeting sails
to spars
(54.2)

If instead of passing over or under the main boom or indeed being fixed to it the sheet is kept out by other means we arrive at an outrigger, which is prohibited: This is a fitting, which normally consists of a stick or pole fitted, not as permitted by 54.2(a) above, and exerting "outward pressure on a sheet", so that it tends to push the sheet further out.

After this the rule states that an outrigger can be defined as such (that is a gadget prohibited because it sticks outboard) only whenever by means of it the sheet lead is "at a point from which, with the yacht upright, a vertical line would fall outside the hull or deck planking at that point" or "outside such other position as class rules prescribe".

Rule 54.2 details also that, for the purpose of this rule, bulwarks, rails, and rubbing strakes are not part of the hull deck planking. That is to say that these parts of the hull may stick out further than the "true" side of the boat.

Some years ago the new edition of rule 54.2 omitted the phrase "no part of the body of a crew is an outrigger", and it was asked whether this omission meant that it was now not permissible for a crew to hold a headsail sheet or spinnaker sheet outboard of the hull. The reply was given in IYRU No. 7 (RYA 1962/41, Royal Lymington Y.C.) where it was laid down that "rule 54.2 defines an out-rigger as any *fitting*. It is, therefore, permissible for the crew to hold a sheet outboard of the hull".

3. Spinnaker;
spinnaker boom
(54.3)

The third paragraph of rule 54 tells us:

(a) that the spinnaker must not be used without a spinnaker pole, that is to say it must be tacked down to it;

(b) that the tack must be in close proximity to the outboard end of the spinnaker boom when set and drawing (this latter phrase "set and drawing" permits, while gybing, the use of a spinnaker sheet running through a sheave or a block at the end of the spinnaker boom and thus allows the sail for a short time to be distant from the end of the boom);

(c) that any headsail (that is to say any sail that is not tacked down abaft the foremost mast) can be fixed to the spinnaker boom as long as the spinnaker is not hoisted as well;

(d) that only one spinnaker boom may be used at a time and that it can only be carried on the foremost mast;

(e) that it must be carried only on the side opposite to that of the main boom (that is to say on the weather side);

(f) that it must be fixed to the (foremost) mast; which does not mean that it must be tied or attached to the mast, but that the boom may not be fixed to any other point of the yacht, forestay, shrouds, etc., or held in the hand.

Finally the rule adds that none of these regulations is applied when gybing and so you can then pass the spinnaker boom from one side to another if there is only one, or the sail which is fixed to it if you have twin spinnaker booms. You can have a moment or two when the spinnaker is not led to the spinnaker boom at all or when the tack is not close to the end of it or indeed when the spinnaker is fixed to two booms at the same time or when it is on the same side as the main or when the spinnaker boom is not fixed to the mast; in fact you can for this brief period do as you wish.

It must be underlined that there may well be overriding class rules.

Rule 55. Owner steering another yacht

An owner shall not steer any yacht other than his own in a race wherein his own yacht competes, without the previous consent of the race committee.

This rule has been put in with the object of preventing one yacht helping another (and to avoid any suspicion of wrongdoing and the inevitable gossip which follows such suspicion).

It forces an owner or co-owner who wishes to steer another's yacht in a race in which his own is taking part to declare his interest and ask permission from the race committee. Bearing in mind the similarity with rule 20 (Ownership of yachts) there is no doubt that this control is directed equally at someone who has chartered (perhaps only partially) a yacht which is taking part in the same race.

Since the yachts must compete in the same race the rule will not come into force merely for entering a yacht, the yacht of the owner in question must at least be seen manoeuvring near the starting line after the preparatory signal even if she did not then *start*.

There is no mandatory prohibition for if there is a valid reason the race committee at its discretion may permit the owner to race without risk of being protested under this rule.

Finally you will notice that rule 55 deals with steering a yacht in a race (and is indeed included in part V – Obligations of a helmsman and crew) while rule 20 deals with ownership and being limited to the purely preparatory phase of the race is included in Part III (Owner's responsibilities for qualifying his yacht).

Rule 56. Boarding

Unless otherwise prescribed by the national authority or in the sailing instructions, no person shall board a yacht except for the purposes of rule 58, (Rendering Assistance), or to attend an injured or ill member of the crew or temporarily as one of the crew of a vessel fouled.

Applying equally to classes where the number of crew is fixed and to those where the number can be varied, this rule is intended to prevent the numbers changing during a race, and it holds good from the preparatory signal (rule 4.4(a)) until *racing* (definition Part I) is over.

It would be against the general aim of keeping things equal and fair between competitors if they were allowed to embark extra crew either for more weight and more hands when the weather gets worse, or when someone with particular skill was felt to be needed.

This logical rule can be altered by a prescription by the national authority or by sailing instructions but otherwise can be ignored only in three well-defined and clearly specified situations:

(a) to fulfil the requirements of rule 58 (Rendering assistance);
(b) to help a member of the crew who is injured or sick;
(c) in the case of collision to help the other boat involved in the incident;

but note that while in cases (a) and (b) the newcomer can stay on board for the rest of the race (perhaps because the injured person needs continuous aid) in the third case the boarding may only be temporary, that is only as long as is required to give help.

Unless otherwise prescribed by the national authority or in the sailing instructions, no person on board a yacht when her preparatory signal was made shall leave, unless injured or ill, or for the purposes of rule 58, (Rendering Assistance), except that any member of the crew may fall overboard or leave her to swim, stand on the bottom as a means of anchoring, haul her out ashore to effect repairs, reef sails or bail out, or help her to get clear after grounding or fouling another vessel or object, provided that this person is back on board before the yacht continues in the race.

For the same reasons as those which give rise to rule 56, rule 57 prohibits disembarking crew from the preparatory signal until the end of the race; it would be too easy a way to get rid of superfluous weight in a calm. The 18-ft skiffs, professionally sailed in Sydney Harbour, do exactly this, arriving at the windward mark a number of the crew jump into the water and swim ashore, but not under IYRU rules. However, this rule too can be altered by prescriptions of the national authority or the sailing instructions and here too special exceptions are made which as in rule 56 are specific and can not be extended to similar cases.

To define them a person may be put ashore during a race in the exceptional cases:

(a) when the crew is injured or sick;
(b) to fulfil the requirements of rule 58 (Rendering assistance);
(c) man overboard;
(d) to swim, even for pleasure, provided it does not infringe rule 60 (Means of propulsion);
(e) to keep the boat "anchored" by standing on the bottom of the sea (see rule 63.2);
(f) to haul the boat out ashore in order to "effect repairs, reef sails or bail out" (see rule 63.1);
(g) to free the boat "after grounding or fouling another vessel or object".

The last phrase of the rule is not absolutely clear but it seems logical that the proviso at the end "provided that this person is back on board before the yacht continues in the race" cannot relate to the case of someone injured or sick. Indeed a doubt could arise even in the case of disembarking to give help but we believe that in this case the obligation to reboard exists because, as we shall see in rule 58, a yacht which has given assistance may ask for the race to be resailed.

While dealing with re-embarking let us look at IYRU No. 1 (RYA 1962/22, Bosham Sailing Club). A question was put to the RYA about an incident twenty yards or so before the finishing line when an Albacore dinghy capsized but nevertheless, thanks to the tide, crossed the finishing line even though her keel was up in the air with her two crew members swimming alongside. The RYA replied that in such cases the boat must be considered to have finished regularly provided the complete crew remained with the boat.

Another conclusion, however, was reached in RYA 1967/14 (Port of Falmouth Sailing Association) which also dealt with swimming. Here the helmsman of a dinghy, *Buccaneer*, fell overboard two lengths from the finishing line, but the crew member immediately took his place and succeeded in crossing the finishing line, followed shortly afterwards by the helmsman swimming. The advice of the national authority was asked and pointing out that rule 26 of the class rules of the International 14-footers said literally "*Crew*: two, including the helmsman. If a member of the crew during the course of a race leaves the boat voluntarily he shall be deemed to have been lost over-board within the meaning of rule 57".

And here is the RYA's opinion: "IYRU rule 1.5 empowers a race committee to refuse to recognize any class rule which conflicts with the racing rules.

"The fact that International 14-foot dinghy class rule 26 says that a member of the crew leaving voluntarily shall be deemed to have been lost overboard merely ensures that, in accordance with rule 57 he must be back on board before the yacht continues in the race. If this requirement must be fulfilled when a crew leaves voluntarily it must apply with even more force when he leaves involuntarily.

"Furthermore," continued the RYA, "as *Buccaneer* has lost her helmsman overboard he must be regarded as being in peril. *Buccaneer* being in a position to render all possible assistance apparently failed to observe rule 58, and preferred to finish." For these reasons the RYA considered that *Buccaneer* had violated both rule 57 and rule 58.

Another case of a crew member falling overboard and being rescued by third persons is reported in the comment to rule 59 (IYRU No. 66).

Rule 58.
Rendering
assistance

Every yacht shall render all possible assistance to any vessel or person in peril, when in a position to do so.

The traditions of the sea demand help for anyone in danger, vessel or person as may be. Thus rule 58 makes it the duty of a competitor to help any vessel or person whether racing or not. This duty only arises when there is a situation of actual danger (there is none for example if someone falls overboard near the coast in fair weather close to other vessels ready to help them in an area where there are no squalls etc.). In each case the facts must be investigated and the race committee will use its common sense and bear in mind the strength of the sea and wind, the place, the type of yachts involved and the capacity of the individuals concerned. Similar judgement must also be exercised from the point of view of the possibility of giving help; a would-be samaritan merely makes matters worse if he risks getting into the same danger as the person he was going to help. At any rate a yacht seeing a situation which raises even the smallest possibility of peril must forget the race immediately and go and help.

An out-and-out racing man might well turn his head so as not to see an incident, and sail on, and to discourage this the rule has already provided (rule 12) for a race committee to "make such arrangement as it deems equitable" – when it decides a yacht's finishing position has been materially prejudiced by rendering assistance in accordance with rule 58. These equitable arrangements may consist of re-sailing the race under rule 13 or indeed the presentation of a special prize. There is no obligation, a facility is all that is necessary which is evident when, for example the rescuer is placed one of the last in her race and has absolutely no possibility of recovery.

Interesting points on rule 58 were made in IYRU No. 38 (RYA 1968/14, *Francessa II* v. The Sussex Yacht Club). First of all it was said that the fact that the person in danger had not asked for the help offered to him was irrelevant to the effects of the application of the rule. It was also stated that the yacht which came to give assistance had the right to the benefits provided by rule 12 "even if a later examination of the events had shown that there had been no danger".

In face of the obvious possibility of abuses (the example was given of a competitor who asked for help from someone else even though he was not in danger and as a result made the race committee re-sail the race) the RYA gave the following judgement: "So far as the fears expressed by the race committee are concerned regarding the possible exploitation of such a situation by an unscrupulous helmsman, the rules are framed to ensure that, as far as is possible, yachts compete against one another safely and equitably. The rules are not based upon contemplation of misuse. No attempt whatever is made to prevent misuse, because it is almost unknown. Should isolated instances of misuse occur, the Fair Sailing Rule and rule 1.4 suffice."

Never forget that while rule 58 lays a duty on every yacht racing, it in no way exonerates the aided yacht (when she is also in the race) from the observances of the racing rules in general and in particular of rules 59 (Outside assistance), 60 (Means of propulsion), 62 (Manual power), 63 (Anchoring and making fast), 19 (Certificates) and 22 (Shifting ballast).

Rule 59.
Outside
assistance

Except as permitted by rules 56, (Boarding), 58, (Rendering Assistance), and 64, (Aground or Foul of an Obstruction), a yacht shall neither receive outside assistance nor use any gear other than that on board when her preparatory signal was made.

Rule 59 follows the same principle as rules 56 (Boarding) 59 (Leaving, man-overboard), 63 (Anchoring and making fast) and 64 (Aground or foul of an obstruction). It lays down that a competitor must take part in the race by his own means only, he may not receive any help from other vessels or people and he may not modify any equipment on board (see also rules 19 – Certificates, 22 – Shifting ballast and 23 – Anchor).

This obligation which begins (see the preamble to Part V) at the preparatory signal (rule 4.4(a)) and ends when the yacht is no longer *racing* (definition Part I), covers ground which appears unlimited, for the rule in very clear terms forbids a yacht to "receive outside assistance" in general and to "use any gear other than that on board when her preparatory signal was made". Because the rule makes no distinction of any kind the ban must be considered overriding and to include outside assistance in all its varieties and gradations, from what can be supplied offshore by a salvage tow right down to the loan of a screwdriver. There is a benevolent tendency to overlook minor episodes (as for example that of the screw-driver), but in our opinion if the rule makes no distinctions we must not make them either; thus strictly giving someone a bottle of beer should be considered equally culpable as the loan of a sail to replace one that has been blown out.

What is rule 59 really aiming at? It requires each competitor to ensure that he is self sufficient, to know how to prepare the boat and crew adequately, to foresee every eventuality and to be ready to confront it competently, one of the first necessities for anyone going to sea. If the competitor knew, like a cyclist or as in motor racing, that he could count on the possibility of re-stocking, getting repairs done, or obtaining new equipment, all the virtues which rule 59 upholds would be lost by helping the unprepared and incompetent competitor.

The Italian Appeals Committee confirmed the spirit of this rule in a decision (FIV 1967/5) which forbade even verbal suggestions to be given to a competitor (they were dealing with a cadet race and precisely at an incident which happened at the round of a mark at the advice of a coach). "In fact", says the sentence "it is intuitive that competition between individuals must be based on the individual power and skill of the competitor, the cases covered by rule 59 must not be (as might mistakenly be thought from a superficial examination of its literal tenor) limited to purely material help but must also comprehend any suggestion or information furnished during the race to the competitor on the part of third persons who can be held to have some connection (to be judged case by case) with the competitor himself and which places those who use it in a situation of unfair advantage with respect to the others."

In the same appeal it was pointed out that the shouted advice was in fact quite audible and therefore useful to all nearby yachts and the appeals committee added the following judgement: "Consequently the inacceptability of the first grounds for appeal becomes crystal clear seeing that the advice could have been of value to only those who at that moment were near the buoy and not to all the competitors in the race." As far as it concerns the rule the fact that the external help has not been useful is of no importance; it is enough that the advice has been received. Naturally exceptions are made for such non-material help as for example advice or information given orally which has not been asked for but which it has been impossible not to hear.

While still dealing with non-material help the increase of radio, which has spread to racing, raises problems and in our opinion the international jury of the 19th Olympiad thought the same when they ruled on the use of radio (Acapulco 1968 confirmed at Kiel 1972); "that since the use of a radio would be a violation of IYRU rule 59 there was not to be any radio on any boat during the race". At the Kingston Olympics of 1976 further precautions were taken, to prevent an infringement of rule 59, even access for team support boats to the race area was banned.

RYA Cases 1963/27 and 1963/28 also dealt with the same subject, the latter finished with the words "the council . . . did not consider oral advice volunteered by a third party to be within the intention of rule 59. Each case, however, is for the race committee to decide on its merits."

Leaving clandestine radios on one side and passing briefly to those permanently carried by offshore yachts, while reception of news and weather bulletins for general use are permitted every radio communication which is not purely private and personal with the strictest exclusion of any reference to the race is forbidden and, it must be underlined, it follows that any prearranged transmission to the benfit of a single competitor is prohibited too. Sometimes in ocean races, sailing instructions permit communications with an escort ship for emergencies and, at predetermined times. However, these are exceptions to the rule which must be expressly permitted by the sailing instructions and which must clearly benefit everyone equally.

The all-embracing prohibition laid down by rule 59 is attenuated by three exceptions in rules 56, 58 and 64 which permit:

(a) outside help by anyone for a member of the crew who is injured or ill (rule 56);
(b) outside help by anyone for yacht and crew in the case of danger (rule 58);
(c) outside help for a yacht that has been fouled (rule 64);

but only by the crew of the other yacht involved in the incident and only temporarily and for that purpose (rule 56).

For any exception to rule 59 to be valid the outside help must fall strictly within the limits outlined in the cases above and may be provided only by the people indicated above. A decision in the United States gives a typical example (NAYRU 75) where a well-meaning spectator jumped quickly into the water to help a capsized catamaran to right herself, but she was then immediately disqualified "seeing that rule 59 provides that a yacht must not receive outside help except in the exceptional cases of rules 56, 58 and 64, none of which arose on this particular occasion".

Another case of outside help was examined in IYRU No. 66 (NAYRU 161). Here it was established that a yacht must be classified as finished even if one of the crew, who had fallen overboard, was fished out by a spectator boat and was therefore helped by a third person. "Man overboard" says the judgement "normally should be considered to involve some degree of peril"; and for this reason rule 58 is applicable unless other particular circumstances exclude that there had been a dangerous situation.

To give some example of actions not permitted by rule 59, a tow to get off the mud is not permitted, nor, in the case of a collision, is help given by others unless the crew of the other yacht involved, neither may help be taken from anyone when there is no danger. Under rule 58, a yacht must retire, in order to avoid disqualification, whenever the help given to the competitor in danger is carried out by means (for example a tow) that cannot fail to infringe the principles of rule 60 or even with those of rule 59 itself (as it would for example if a crew member were put back on board, or a part of the yacht repaired or substituted). To sum up, rule 58 is limited to imposing an obligation to help whoever is in danger and does not justify any infringement of the rules by the assisted yacht, which she may commit by receiving the help.

Rule 60. Means of propulsion

60.1   A yacht shall be propelled only by the natural action of the wind on the sails, spars and hull, and water on the hull, and shall not promote or check way by abnormal means, except for the purposes of rule 58, (Rendering Assistance), or of recovering a person who has accidentally fallen overboard. An oar, paddle or other object may be used in emergency for steering. An anchor may be sent out in a boat only as permitted by rule 64, (Aground or Foul of an Obstruction).

60.2   "Pumping", "ooching" and "rocking" shall be prohibited except under conditions established and defined in Appendix 2.

Note *(Experimental rule for possible replacement of rule 60.2 and Appendix 2 before 1981.*

60.3   When so prescribed in the sailing instructions, rule 60.2 and Appendix 2 will be replaced by:

(a) The following actions by a helmsman or crew shall constitute an infringement of rule 60.1:

    (i) Repetitive frequent trimming and releasing of any sail(s).

    (ii) Repetitive forceful movement of the helm.

    (iii) Repetitive changing of the lateral or fore and aft trim of the yacht.

    (iv) Sudden movement of the crew weight fore and aft.

(b) When conditions of wind and water are such that the actions described in this rule are considered by the race committee to be a normal part of yacht racing, a signal to this effect (to be prescribed in the sailing instructions) shall be made by the race committee. When such a signal is made and for as long as it continues to be displayed, the actions described above shall not be prohibited. When the race committee considers that the conditions have changed sufficiently to prohibit these actions, a second signal (also to be prescribed in the sailing instructions) shall be displayed at the next rounding *mark* about to be rounded by the class to which the signal applies. Such visual signal shall be accompanied by a repeated sound signal.

60.4   A yacht which hails before protesting under this rule helps to support her case.

1. Use of the rudder

It can come as no surprise that in a sailing race the competing yachts must be driven only by their sails. And yet in company with many who know how to cheat by working the tiller and rudder (even if not their hands or a paddle) there are a number of helmsman who in good faith think that the use of the tiller as a means of propulsion is permitted for a short period (for that little tiny kick ahead round a mark) or to escape from imminent disaster (in a flat calm from the tide near a rock) but they are wrong.

In FIV 1966/2 a competitor (penalized for having continually worked the tiller to get his boat along in the lightest of breezes) disagreed with the decision of the race committee maintaining that there had been no violation of rule 60 because it does not mention the tiller; indeed he added that since the tiller was part of the hull it would be permissible to exploit the action of water on it. This was clearly nonsense but the definitions below laid down on this occasion by the Italian Appeals Committee are worth looking at.

"If in certain circumstances (to be looked at case by case) some slight jerk of the rudder is acceptable when it helps to change or to maintain the direction of the yacht it is not admissible to work the rudder repeatedly so as to propel the yacht ahead as happened in the case under examination. And it is hardly necessary to point out that this sort of action (that is of rudder blade on water) cannot be compared to that, foreseen by rule 60, of water on the hull" (as could be for example a comparable action freely allowed and deliberately aimed at when planing or surfing).

A classic definition of what must be "the limit of the action of the rudder" has been given by the NAYRU 56 when judging a case of a yacht which, almost in a flat calm was nearing a mark and saw that she could only round it if she succeeded in luffing a little more. At this moment the helmsman (here it is opportune to give the exact words of his actions) "put her tiller to starboard but by reason of the spinnaker and her slight headway response was very slow. In order to bring her up faster her skipper returned the tiller to approximately midships several times, the testimony indicating three to six times and then pushed it hard to starboard in an effort to clear the mark. The mark was cleared by about 18 inches. Thereupon the helmsman put the tiller to port to bring her around to the new course. The response was slow and her skipper then returned the tiller to approximately midships and back to port several times to bring her around."

The race committee disqualified the competitor for violation of rule 60 but the appeals committee was of other opinion and expressed themselves as follows: "In view of the facts found by the race committee that the yacht did not resort to 'sculling' and that her skipper while moving the tiller to starboard several times before reaching the mark and to port several times after reaching it, did not bring it beyond amidships, the purpose and result of his actions being only to alter the course of his yacht and not to give her headway his actions did not constitute an infringement of rule 60."

There are some cases in which, exceptionally, the rudder can be moved from one extreme to the other without contravening rule 60. Here is an example (which involves the already mentioned legitimate exploitation of wave motion), from IYRU No. 14 (NAYRU 91). "A helmsman moved his tiller across the centre-line of his yacht in a series of alterations of course which were rhythmically timed to the passage of each wave under his yacht . . . he only performed this act with his tiller during the time in which his yacht was encountering the waves generated by the nearby passage of a power cruiser."

Both the race committe and the Small Boat Racing Association of Southern California disqualified the yacht but the appeals committee reversed these decisions and absolved him. In fact the sentence observed that "in the case of *El Toro* 2468 which was sailing in a ten-knot breeze at about hull speed, sculling would have had the effect of slowing her speed, not of propelling her ahead faster.

"Taking advantage of wave action is well accepted as a part of yacht racing which is recognized by the statement in rule 60; 'a yacht shall be propelled only by the natural action of wind on the sails, spars and hull and the water on the hull. . . .'. The skipper of 2468 made no rhythmical movements with the tiller in the absence of the power-boat waves. When a yacht is going at about hull speed such an operation as sculling is impossible. In taking advantage of waves a skipper may move his tiller as he thinks best to accomplish that purpose."

This is a good example of what is meant by exploiting the natural action of water on the hull and it does not need much imagination to understand the meaning of natural action of wind on the sails, spars and hull. Therefore it is sufficient to underline the meaning of the adjective "natural" by saying that this is intended to prohibit any artificially induced action (by the competitor or by third parties) which is of assistance; with a further hint that the wave of the motor boat's wake, in the example quoted, cannot by this be considered artificial within the meaning of the rule since it is an undesirable casual

movement of the sea commonly met with while racing where other vessels
happen to be passing.

2. "Pumping", "ooching" and "rocking"

If as we have seen it is possible to create an artificial wave movement to help
a competitor, it is impossible with the wind. Even if you cannot make the wind
act on the sails the opposite is often found (also a violation of rule 60) which
consists in what might be called sculling with the sail in the air; carrying out this
action is called "pumping" and it consists of "frequent rapid trimming of sails
with no particular reference to a change in true or apparent wind direction".
This action, recalling that of a bird's wing in flight, is almost always
accompanied by artificial rocking which consists of persistently rolling a yacht
from side to side and which opportunely co-ordinated with pumping exploits
the situation even better (see Appendix II).

A lively description of this technique is found in the old IYRU No. 15
(NAYRU 92) "keeping the centreboard up and remaining seated in the normal
position the helmsman of the dinghy with determined regularity at intervals of
about ten seconds made the boat heel about ten degrees from the perpendicular
to windward and then he made it heel the same amount to leeward and every
windward heel the helmsman pulled in the sheet and therefore the mainsail by
about a foot and half to two feet, and at every leeward heel he let it go back to
its first position. No movements of the helm were noted or measured except
that which consisted in small changes necessary to maintain his proper
course".

In fact one is dealing with actions which are prohibited because they are
contrary to rule 60 originally laid down by the IYRU in 1962. In the 1969 rule
Appendix 2 was inserted which furnishes an official explanation of these illegal
methods. It is clear and complete and therefore worthwhile printing here:
"Where surfing or planing conditions exist, however, rule 60 allows taking
advantage of 'the natural action of water on the hull' through the rapid
trimming of sails and adjustment of helm to promote (initiate) surfing or
planing.

"The test is whether or not the conditions are such that by rapid trimming of
sails a boat could be started surfing or planing. A skipper challenged for
'pumping' will have to prove, through the performance either of his own boat or
of other boats, that surfing or planing conditions existed, and that the fecuency
of his rapid trimming was geared to the irregular or cyclical wave forms rather
than to a regular rhythmic pattern.

"Note that the interpretation refers to 'promoting' and not to 'maintaining'
surfing or planing. Once a boat has started surfing or planing on a particular set
of wave forms, from then on she must let the natural action of wind and water
propel her without further rapid trimming and releasing of the sails.

"Rapid trimming when approaching marks or the finishing line or other
critical points should be consistent with that which was practised throughout
the leg."

At the end of Appendix 2 "ooching" is mentioned as one of the prohibited
methods of sailing; it consists of "lunging forward and stopping abruptly", in
such a way as to give the boat an impulse; an action obviously very different
from that of the wind or the sea, and which therefore falls "into the same
category as pumping". "Similarly, frequent, quickly-repeated gybing, roll-

tacking in calm and nearly calm conditions falls into the same category as 'pumping'".

IYRU 82 (USYRU 193) also deals with pumping, rocking and ooching with reference to planing by boats such as Lasers and Finns.

3. Abnormal means of stopping the boat

We have already seen the methods forbidden to drive the yacht ahead and now must look at the other ban in rule 60 which deals with abnormal means to "check way". The reasons for this are perhaps less evident, but it has been thought necessary to ban any means not resulting directly from sails, mast and hull, that is to say from those special parts of a yacht which may be used exclusively to move her while racing.

Therefore you may not brake a boat by using the resistance of an oar, paddle, bucket, stone, a hand or a foot in the water or any other similar stop.

However, a sail may be backed and the tiller given one or two kicks to swing the hull and slow down her way. The anchor is absolutely forbidden for reducing speed (but not to keep the boat still, see rule 63) and rule 61 ensures that a depth-sounder is not used in lieu. In our opinion it is, however, permissible to use one or more warps astern to create a resistance to stop broaching in a big sea, they are safety measures rather than a brake (so that a sea anchor would be acceptable too).

As with all the rules of this world rule 60 has its exceptions. One of these (which does not really soften the ban but deals with the way to get free after grounding) permits an anchor to be sent out in a boat within the requirements of rule 64 (Aground or foul of an obstruction). And while on the subject of anchoring it is no violation of rule 60 to get an anchor up as long as when it was thrown overboard it was not thrown or carried out ahead (RYA 1968/44, see comment to rule 63).

Note also that it is considered an infringement to use the centreboard blade lowered into the mud to keep the boat still while waiting for the starting signal (RYA 1954/16, see comment to rule 63).

Exceptionally the use of means of propulsion which would otherwise be forbidden, such as oars or even engine is permitted where it serves to help someone under rule 58 or to recover a man overboard. The yacht which has used such means for these ends may continue the race but naturally must inform the race committee (generally in her declaration – see rule 14); thus the race committee can deal with the matter as necessary. An odd case was examined by the RYA in 1964/24 (Steel Company Wales Yacht Club) when they were asked a question about a capsized yacht hauled ashore by her crew whilst still afloat prior to grounding for the purpose of bailing out. The RYA laid down that this was permissible under rule 63.2 and did not contravene rule 60 as "after a capsize, rule 63.2 over-rides rule 60".

Finally rule 60 states "an oar, a paddle or other object may be used in emergency for steering" without a yacht having to retire from the race or being accused of infringement. This too, however, is not a real exception to the general ban laid down by rule 60, but merely permits the use of *ad hoc* methods of directional control in an emergency and this has nothing to do with means of propulsion or braking.

Rule 61.
Sounding

Any means of sounding may be used provided that rule 60, (Means of Propulsion), is not infringed.

It is enough to say here that this rule prohibits the use of any method of measuring the depth of water in such a way that it contributes any forward impulse to the yacht (or indeed reduces her speed).

To give an example, one of the most notorious depth sounders is of course the pole (or its substitute such as a boom, a boat hook or oar); it serves to touch the bottom to measure depth but in the hand of a cheat it can all too easily be used to push a boat forwards or sideways or to brake.

The same must be said about all those bits and pieces which can be thrown out ahead as far as possible and which are excessively heavy (or have a special shape) and therefore can, up to a point, stick to the bottom and so drag the boat ahead, or be used to put the brakes on perhaps just by being dragged along the bottom. The results of these ambiguous operations are not conspicuous, but we all know that every centimetre gained in a calm is worth a metre in normal weather. And that is why rule 61 (which is really a corollary to rule 60 – Means of propulsion) definitely makes even these small gains illegal.

Rule 62.
Manual power

A yacht shall use manual power only, except that when so prescribed by the national authority or in the sailing instructions, a power winch or windlass may be used in weighing anchor or in getting clear after running aground or fouling any object, and a power pump may be used in an auxiliary yacht.

Winches may not be motor driven even when used to free a yacht after grounding or collision, except that national prescriptions and sailing instructions can permit power winches or windlasses in such circumstances. The same concession can be made, if published as above, for normal anchor winches, but outside these three carefully circumscribed cases, no exception is allowed.

Any motorized equipment, however, which is not connected with the race itself, is allowed on any boat (for example to work refrigerators, ventilators, generators, pumps for loos, etc.); and even while dealing with apparatus which serves to maintain the safety of the hull (which therefore has a direct relevance to racing) in practice everyone may use a powered bilge pump, since the generic ban in rule 62 contains an explicit exception for yachts with auxiliary engines, that is all those or almost all of those which race offshore and which are fitted with pumps working from the engine.

The term "manual power" used in rule 62 should be understood in its general sense, that is to say the force generated by a man even for example by his legs. While motors are forbidden, the use of other systems is not (as for example hydraulics) which serve to transmit a manual driving force. Methods which accumulate power, even manual power, are excluded.

Rule 63. 63.1   A yacht shall be afloat and off moorings before her preparatory signal, but
Anchoring and   may be anchored, and shall not thereafter make fast or be made fast by
making fast   means other than anchoring, nor be hauled out, except for the purpose of
rule 64, (Aground or Foul of an Obstruction), or to effect repairs, reef sails or
bail out.

      63.2   A yacht may anchor when racing. Means of anchoring may include the crew
standing on the bottom and any weight lowered to the bottom. A yacht shall
recover any anchor or weight used, and any chain or rope attached to it,
before continuing in the race, unless after making every effort she finds
recovery impossible. In this case she shall report the circumstances to the
race committee, which may disqualify her if it considers the loss due either to
inadequate gear or to insufficient effort to recover it.

    The prohibition against making fast arises from the principle that it is an
absolute duty of a yacht to keep clear of everything except water. Yet she may
use her own anchor, in calms when there is a current, or in other circumstances,
for instance to repair sails.

    The "anchor" foreseen by rule 63 need not be a traditional one with flukes. It
may consist of any weight capable of fulfilling the same function under the
water (an anchor put out ashore, out of the water, is the same as making fast
and is not allowed). This wide interpretation is described in 63.2 and leads us to
believe that similar equipment can be covered by the term "anchor" where used
in rule 23 (Anchor) unless class rules or sailing instructions prescribe
otherwise.

    The vagueness as to what can be considered an anchor is such that the rule
in addition to "any weight lowered to the bottom" includes "the crew standing
on the bottom". A curious case occurred in RYA 1954/16 (Cambridge
University Cruising Club) where a yacht was disqualified for her actions while
waiting for the start. She got to a protected position out of the wind and current
and well tucked into the bank of the river and then lowered her centreboard into
the shallow mud where it held her until the starting signal; after which she
hauled up her centreboard, sailed off and crossed the starting line. Note,
however, that this ruling was made ("bearing in mind the principles laid down
by the fundamental rule for fair sailing" says the decision) not for violation of
rule 63 (then rule 23) but for an infringement of rule 60 – Means of propulsion
(then rule 24) because the yacht was considered to have "checked way by
abnormal means".

    It may seem strange that in this episode the question of anchoring did not
arise seeing that all-in-all the means used consisted merely of something under
water which held her to the bottom. However, we must not forget that the
object of rule 63 is to make sure that the competitors do not, as in the above
case, gain any unfair advantage; and we say unfair because there is a distinct
difference between just lifting a centreboard enough to free a dinghy and
complete recovery of an anchor and cable as prescribed in the rule under
examination.

    Rule 63.2 requires that in all cases the anchored yacht "shall recover any
anchor weight used, and any chain or rope attached to it, before continuing in
the race". This duty (which fits in with the requirements of rule 23 to have an
anchor on board) is linked to the general principle which forbids any change in

positioning weight and how much there is aboard during the race (see rules 19, 22, 56, 57 and 64).

When recovery is impossible the yacht may avoid disqualification only if the race committee (informed in detail by the competitor) holds that every reasonable effort has been made and that the loss results from no fault of the competitor (as when for example the anchor cannot be freed from the bottom) and this will not be so if it is held that the loss is due to inadequate equipment, (e.g. inadequate cable) or to insufficient effort for recovery.

Weighing anchor, as we have said, constitutes no violation of rule 60 (Means of propulsion) as long as the anchor was not thrown ahead or, worse still, taken ahead by the dinghy. If you have anchored by letting the anchor go straight down, the little that the yacht then drops back is equivalent to the little which she will move ahead when she up-anchors. Thus the RYA laid down in IYRU No. 9 (RYA 1962/44, Liverpool Sailing Club) in answer to a question about dinghies which to avoid drifting backwards in a contrary current were forced to anchor almost on the starting line waiting for more wind or for the tide to weaken in order to start. However, a very recent case (RYA 1978 Royal Lymington Y.C.) states: "a yacht which recovers her anchor so quickly that she gains appreciable way over the ground at the point where the anchor is broken out infringes rule 60". So it is possible to overstep the mark.

Every yacht begins *racing* at the preparatory signal (rule 4.4(a)) and from that moment on must therefore be "afloat and off moorings" meaning that her hull, crew and equipment must no longer have any contact with the ground or with other vessels or with the moorings. However, rule 63 allows a yacht *racing* to be hauled out in the following cases:

(a) for the purposes of rule 64 (Aground or foul of an obstruction);
(b) to effect repairs;
(c) to take reefs;
(d) to bail out.

This deals with typical emergencies which justify exceptions to the general rule, but take care, just because they are exceptions they are strictly specific and cannot be applied to analogous cases even if these only differ slightly. As the greater includes the less we are of opinion that (only of course for the reasons listed above) you can also tie up along side another ship or a quayside.

And do not forget RYA 1964/24 (Steel Co. of Wales Y.C.) discussed in the comment to rule 60, where a capsized yacht, still afloat, was pushed ashore by her crew swimming, in order to bail out and this was held to be in order.

The sailing instructions for offshore racing may permit yachts to remain moored after the five-minute gun. Inevitable hold ups occur and it is sometimes impossible for a yacht to start, say, a Fastnet Race exactly on time owing to totally unforeseen circumstances. It seems to many unfair to penalize a yacht already late for what is a technical offence and therefore, with various precautions, she may be allowed to collect crew or vital equipment and then come late to the start without infringing rule 63.

Rule 64.
Aground or foul
of an
obstruction

A yacht, after grounding or fouling another vessel or other object, is subject to rule 62, (Manual Power), and may, in getting clear, use her own anchors, boats, ropes, spars and other gear; may send out an anchor in a boat; may be refloated by her crew going overboard either to stand on the bottom or to go ashore to push off; but may receive outside assistance only from the crew of the vessel fouled. A yacht shall recover all her own gear used in getting clear before continuing in the race.

We have seen that while *racing*, that is from the preparatory signal (rule 4.4(a)) until the yacht has crossed and cleared the finishing line and its marks nobody can embark or disembark (rules 56 and 57) and a yacht may not receive help from third persons (rule 59), use means of propulsion other than natural action of wind and water (rule 60) and can make fast only by anchoring, letting the anchor drop directly down without throwing it ahead (rule 63).

All these prohibitions are over-ruled in cases of accidents that consist of involuntary grounding or fouling another vessel or object. Then while the principle remains that the crew of the yacht in the accident must fend for themselves without outside help, the following exceptions are allowed, she may:

(a) use her own anchors, boats, ropes, spars and other gear to get clear, that is to say means of propulsion which would otherwise be prohibited by rule 60;

(b) send out an anchor in her own boat (otherwise prohibited as an infringement of rule 60);

(c) disembark members of the crew at sea or ashore to carry out this operation of refloating or pushing off.

Only in the case of a collision with another vessel, even if not *racing*, may one crew be helped by the other without it being considered a breach of rule 59. Rule 64 places no limits on the assistance provided, but it follows that there must not be more help than is necessary to free the yacht and perhaps a temporary loan of some tool or bit of equipment for freeing her or for making summary repairs; excluding loans or substitutions of crew or sails or undamaged equipment or parts or the yacht generally; finally this help may consist of towing or of action which for as far as it concerns the yacht racing is not in accordance with rule 60, (Means of propulsion) and rule 62 (Manual power).

It will come as no surprise that before continuing the race the yacht must recover all her own gear that was used for clearing her. This agrees with the general principles of maintaining weights during the race and ensures that her equipment is unchanged and that she therefore continues to keep within rules 19 (Certificates), 22 (Shifting ballast), 23 (Clothing and equipment), 56 (Boarding), 57 (Leaving, man overboard) and 63 (Anchoring and making fast).

Rule 65. Skin friction

A yacht shall not eject or release from a container any substance (such as polymer) the purpose of which is, or could be, to reduce the frictional resistance of the hull by altering the character of the flow of water inside the boundary layer.

This rule was introduced in 1969 (but already adopted previously in the Olympic Games in Acapulco in October 1968) and arose from the realization that certain chemical substances (or precisely certain polymers) reduce the friction between the water and the wetted surface of the hull in the most remarkable way. They reduce that element which together with the shape of the hull and with the energy spent in wave formation generates the overall resistance of the hull to moving ahead.

It was noted in fact that certain substances produced by salt- and fresh-water algae and the mucus secretion of the skin of many fish, by a molecular mechanism as yet not absolutely understood, reduce the resistance arising from the adhesion of water to the hull and from its viscosity.

Once these chemicals were identified it was quickly realized that if they were released into the water near the hull, very small quantities indeed would greatly augment the speed of the boat at low speeds. In practice this called for either a special under-water paint containing these polymers to disperse them in the water or apparatus designed to release them when suitable. Once the trick had been learnt it was necessary to create a rule to stop it. The ban on "hull doping" covers only emissions from a container and not paint with polymers in it because it appeared that its efficacy is limited to a few hours and the experiments were ended by insisting that the boats were in the water the evening before the race.

**Rule 66.
Increasing
stability**

Unless otherwise prescribed by her class rules or in the sailing instructions, a yacht shall not use any device, such as a trapeze or plank, to project out-board the weight of any of the crew, nor, when lifelines are required by the conditions for the race, shall any member of the crew station any part of his torso outside them, other than temporarily.

This rule, like the last, came into force with the 1969 edition of the Rules and is directed particularly at offshore boats with lifelines. It aims to stop the crew who want to augment the righting moment of the hull, leaning out with the upper heavier part of their body, outside the lifelines which have been especially put there to stop them falling overboard.

The use of artificial means to augment the arm of the lever of this righting force (defined by rule 66 as trapezes and planks) is extremely common in small boats (those without lifelines) and is expressly provided for and permitted by their respective class rules.

In conclusion:

(a) the crew of any boat without lifelines can lean out as far as they wish so long as they only use those trapezes, planks and similar apparatus permitted by class rules;

(b) in yachts with lifelines such as the IOR class, no crew may station any part of his torso outside the hull except for short temporary periods called for by some particular work, and no trapezes or planks are allowed. Slack lifelines are also prohibited as they lead to virtually useless lifelines from the point of view of safety.

Part VI
Protests, disqualifications and appeals

Up to this point the Rules set out the various regulations controlling the running of a race, laying down mandatory official definitions of the technical terms used (Part I) the duties of organizers (Part II), the duties and responsibilities of owners (Part III) and providing the helmsman with right-of-way rules to observe when yachts meet (Part IV), as well as setting out other rules of navigation crews must respect during the race (Part V).

Unfortunately, in this world forbidding something does not necessarily lead to the law being respected, and rules have to be strengthened by the threat of punishment when necessary. The thankless task of enforcing penalties is the responsibility of "judges" who, and note how unusual this is, act almost always at the request of a competitor and only in exceptional, rare cases (see rule 73.1 – disqualifications without hearing) on their own initiative or on the reports of other people, thus beginning the very last phase of the race which consists in the clarification of any infringements of the rule and their penalization.

This is a less familiar aspect of racing since it takes place not at sea under the sky but in a closed room, no longer in the exciting atmosphere of competition with buffeting winds or long calms but round a table where "experts" pontificate on minor details and where the yachts become tiny motionless models. Perhaps for this very reason many people scorn protests and consider them unsporting. Such people are wrong because this attitude benefits certain competitors who will continue to believe they have rights that in reality they have not got.

That is why a protest must be considered a routine for it serves to discourage sea-lawyers and teaches manners to anyone who ignores the rules and without wishing it treads on their neighbour's toes.

Rule 68.
Protests

68.1   A yacht can protest against any other yacht, except that a protest for an alleged infringement of the rules of Part IV can be made only by a yacht directly involved in, or witnessing an incident.

68.2   A protest occurring between yachts competing in separate races organised by different clubs shall be heard by a combined committee of the clubs concerned.

68.3   (a)   (i) A protest for an infringement of the rules or sailing instructions occurring during a race shall be signified by the protesting yacht conspicuously displaying a flag (International Code flag "B" is always acceptable, irrespective of any other provisions in the sailing instructions) at the first reasonable opportunity and keeping it displayed until she has *finished* or retired, or if the first reasonable opportunity occurs after *finishing*, until acknowledged by the race committee.

(ii) In the case of a yacht sailed single-handed, it will be sufficient if the flag be displayed at the first reasonable opportunity after the incident and brought to the notice of the race committee when the protesting yacht *finishes*.

(b) A yacht which has no knowledge of the facts justifying a protest, including the failure of another yacht to lodge a required protest, until after she has *finished* or retired may nevertheless protest without having displayed a protest flag.

(c) A protesting yacht shall try to inform the yacht protested against that a protest will be lodged.

(d) Such a protest shall be in writing and be signed by the owner or his representative, and include the following particulars:

.(i) The date, time and whereabouts of the incident.

(ii) The particular rule or rules or sailing instructions alleged to have been infringed.

(iii) A statement of the facts.

(iv) Unless irrelevant, a diagram of the incident.

(e) Unless otherwise prescribed in the sailing instructions a protesting yacht shall deliver or, when that is not possible, mail her protest to the race committee:

(i) within two hours of the time she *finishes* the race or within such time as may have been prescribed in the sailing instructions under rule 3.2(b)(xv), (The Sailing Instructions), unless the race committee has reason to extend these time limits, or

(ii) when she does not *finish* the race, within such a time as the race committee may consider reasonable in the circumstances of the case.

A protest shall be accompanied by such fee, if any, as may have been prescribed in the sailing instructions under rule 3.2(b)(xv), (The Sailing Instructions).

(f) The race committee shall allow the protestor to remedy at a later time:

(i) any defects in the details required by rule 68.3(d) provided that the protest includes a summary of the facts, and

(ii) a failure to deposit such fee as may be required under rule 68.3(e) and prescribed in the sailing instructions.

68.4 (a) A protest that a measurement, scantling or flotation rule has been infringed while *racing*, or that a classification or rating certificate is for any reason invalid, shall be lodged with the race committee not later than 18.00 hours on the day following the race. The race committee shall send a copy of the protest to the yacht protested against and, when there appears to be reasonable grounds for the protest, it shall refer the question to an authority qualified to decide such questions.

(b) Deviations in excess of tolerances specified in the class rules caused by normal wear or damage and which do not affect the performance of the yacht shall not invalidate the measurement or rating certificate of the yacht for a particular race, but shall be rectified before she *races* again, unless in the opinion of the race committee there has been no practical opportunity to rectify the wear or damage.

(c) The race committee, in making its decision, shall be governed by the determination of such authority. Copies of such decision shall be sent to all yachts involved.

68.5   (a) A yacht which alleges that her finishing position has been materially prejudiced by an action or omission of the race committee, may seek redress from the race committee in accordance with the requirements for a protest provided in rules 68.3(d), (e) and (f). In these circumstances a protest flag need not be displayed.

(b) When the race committee decides that such action or omission was prejudicial, and that the result of the race was altered thereby, it shall make such arrangement as it deems equitable, which may be to let the results of the race stand, to adjust the points score or the finishing time of the prejudiced yacht; or to *abandon* or *cancel* the race, provided that the race committee shall not act under this rule before satisfying itself by taking appropriate evidence that its action is as equitable as possible to all yachts concerned, for that particular race and the series, if any, as a whole.

68.6   A protest made in writing shall not be withdrawn, but shall be decided by the race committee, unless prior to the hearing full responsibility is acknowledged by one or more yachts.

1. Yachts permitted to protest (68.1)

We have already noted that a peculiarity of the sport of sailing is that, when a rule is infringed, a jury or race committee acts on its initiative only in exceptional cases, because the rule itself so lays it down and because sometimes – let us admit – it is convenient and shrewd not to see or hear. This will be looked at under rule 73 (Race Committee's action against an infringing yacht). Usually a "judge" only intervenes at the request of a competitor who feels himself harmed by another's breach of a rule or who has seen a breach. This first point needs some explanation.

Applying the above principle rule 68.1 states, that "a yacht can protest against any other yacht"; but it is as well to underline at once that she cannot always do so. In fact the rule hastens to point out that "a protest for an alleged infringement of the rules of Part IV can be made only by a yacht involved in, or witnessing an incident". What is the reason for this distinction? The innovation (which goes back to 1961, before that everyone could protest everyone else) was introduced to stop protests being lodged by competitors who had not been involved in or were out of sight of the incidents, but nevertheless wished to profit from them even when they only heard about them later, with the object of eliminating by protest a competitor who was difficult to beat in any other way.

It could be said that with the new form of rule 68.1 the possibility of tracking down competitors who have little respect for the rule (always to be encouraged) has now been reduced too much and this may be true. It was hoped that this qualification would stop any competitor with "no knowledge of the facts justifying a protest . . . until after she has *finished* or retired" from protesting "without having displayed a protest flag" (as rule 68.3(d) would, in fact, give her).

And this is why only the yacht that has been involved in the incident or has witnessed it directly without being mixed up in it herself can lodge a protest for a breach of a rule of Part IV. The limitation affects only those infringements of the rule which can happen on the race course and therefore require immediate display of a protest flag as described by rule 68.3(a).

It follows that any other infringement not concerning Part IV can be freely protested by any competitor even if she is not present at, or involved in, the incident.

The right to protest belongs also to a yacht which has retired (see comment to point 4 to follow).

Further it is clear that a protest lodged by a yacht which is disqualified for a previous breach of the rules remains valid (IYRU No. 2. RYA, Chipstead S.C. 1962/25).

2. Protests between yachts competing in separate races sponsored by different clubs (68.2)

This deals with the particular case of yachts competing in different races (a situation already envisaged in the preamble to Part IV) and involved in an incident because they are racing in the same area or in areas very close to each other. This is not a case of races for different classes organized by the same club but races organized by different clubs. It is not laid down which of the two clubs must receive the protest under rule 68.3 nor in what form (time-limit, etc.) but our advice would be to lodge a protest with the organizing club of the race in which the protested yacht took part and in the form prescribed by their sailing instructions. However, at the same time it would be as well to inform the committee of the other club so as to put them in a position to comply with the requirement of rule 68.2 – a combined committee of the clubs concerned.

3. Displaying a protest flag (68.3(a)(b))

First of all it must be stressed that this paragraph applies only when "an infringement of the rules or sailing instructions occurs during a race" and this is obvious because a protest flag, even if it could be conspicuously displayed, would serve no purpose for infringements which do not happen in the race area. The obligation begins when the boat, in the water and "intending to race, begins to sail about in the vicinity of the starting line" (see preamble to Part IV; for breaches of Part V it begins only at the preparatory signal – rule 4.4(a)) "until she has either finished or retired and has left the vicinity of the course".

The rule lays down that the protest should be signalled by a flag. No flag is categorically specified but, because red is so clearly visible, international code flag B is recommended and while not mandatory, it is *always* acceptable irrespective of any other provisions in the sailing instructions. This is confirmed in rule 3.1 (Status).

Strictly speaking a flag is rectangular in shape but the rule does not go into such detail and by this word implies, in a general sense, any signal that falls within the description (whether made of stuff or not) having the capacity to attract the attention of others. For example the decision in NAYRU 88 explicitly affirmed "that, for the purposes of rule 68, "flag" should be broadly interpreted and may include makeshifts such as a handkerchief, provided the sailing instructions do not specify a particular flag. Accordingly the prompt display of a red cellophane tell-tale met the local requirements for a "red flag".

This flag, continues the rule, must be "conspicuously" displayed and, if the protest is to be accepted at all, at "the first reasonable opportunity". On this point (which in our opinion is a question of fact to be left to the wise judgement of the race committee) listen to the words of the appeals committee in NAYRU 3: "while the phrase 'at the first reasonable opportunity' used in rule 68.3(a) is not synonymous with 'immediately', it implies that a protest flag must be displayed within a reasonably short time after a contestant has infringed a racing rule while racing. . . . In fairness to such a competitor he should be notified promptly of his alleged infringement of the rules."

But that is not all because to emphasize the importance of this signal the U.S. Appeals Committee quoted other precedents confirming that the rule was mandatory and went on: "in all ordinary circumstances when a flag could be flown, if it was not flown, the race committee should refuse to hear the case. The spirit of the rule is that the protesting party must signal his intention at the time prescribed."

A protest should at once be proclaimed publicly; to the adversary and any witnesses so that they can think about the incident while it is clear in their minds; to the race committee on each round so that they know what is going on and at the finish to those doing the results so that they know they must wait. For these reasons rule 68.3(a) prescribes that the flag must be "displayed until the yacht has *finished* or retired, or if the first reasonable opportunity occurs after *finishing*, until acknowledged by the race committee".

Sometimes it may be that the "reasonable" time which the rule requires is equally "reasonable" much later. On this subject Appeal No. 4 of 1970 of the Dutch Federation (*Flevo Jrn.* v. Race Committee) is relevant. *Flevo Jrn.*, a light centreboard boat, wished to protest about an incident at the gybe mark but delayed displaying her protest flag. This delay lasted the whole length of the leg after the buoy because of the very strong gusty wind for the crew were fully occupied keeping her upright, sitting her out and continually trimming sheets. The Dutch national authority held that it would have been "unreasonable to expect to see a protest flag immediately after the incident when this would certainly have caused the protester considerable loss of speed and position since to display a flag requires two hands".

That is why the "first reasonable opportunity" is not always synonymous with "immediately" but must be evaluated by a protest committee investigating in each case all the actual circumstances of place and time.

The last part of rule 68.3(a) allows that "in the case of a yacht sailed single-handed it will be sufficient if the flag be displayed at the first reasonable opportunity after the incident and brought to the notice of the race committee when the protesting yacht *finishes*". This arises naturally from the fact that a single-handed helmsman has not got four hands; and so instead of displaying his flag continuously he need show it only twice but these two occasions are mandatory. It is interesting to note that the last sentence in this rule finally confirms that the object is to have the flag seen both by the adversary and by the race committee.

The inflexibility of the rule which insists that the flag be hoisted immediately and (except for singlehanders) continuously is underlined by a well-known decision in NAYRU 60. Here two yachts '60' and '45' both protested about an incident at the start; however, the race committee "refused to hear the protests because neither yacht had complied with the requirements of rule 68.3(a), that a protest flag be shown at the first reasonable opportunity and kept flying until she had finished. It was found that '45' had shown a flag following the incident but it had blown overboard and neither she nor '60' were flying a protest flag when they finished." It might seem unreasonable to have expected a small boat to carry more than one flag but since she did not put up some other object it was held that the race committee had been correct to invoke rule 68.3(a) and to refuse to examine the protest.

4. Protest without a protest flag (68.3(b))

Very exceptionally the protesting yacht "has no knowledge of the facts justifying a protest . . . until after she has *finished* or retired instanced by "the failure of another yacht to lodge a required protest"; a yacht which had witnessed or been involved in the incident and had flown a protest flag thus showing that she intended to act under rule 68 against the infringing yacht.

First of all this must refer to an infringement of a rule *not* in Part IV (see rule 68.1) because otherwise only a yacht directly involved or witnessing an incident can protest, both circumstances which carry a duty (rule 68.3(a)) to hoist a protest flag "at the first reasonable opportunity".

For example an occasion might arise from some error in sailing the course (rule 51) or hitting a mark (rule 52) or lack of navigation lights (rule 53) or incorrect setting of the sails (rule 54) or the use of prohibited means of propulsion (rule 60) or outside assistance (rule 59) and so on just as it might also arise from incorrect ratings or lack of required equipment (rules 19, 22, 23, 24), etc. What counts is that in each case the protester has learnt about it after he had finished and after he has sailed away from the finishing line and from the area where the race committee is timing in the boats because otherwise he would still be under the rule that obliges him to display a protest flag.

In RYA 1967/15 (Stock Exchange Sailing Club), the British national authority replied to some interesting questions as to whether a yacht which has retired may lodge a protest without having flown a protest flag. Naturally the answers which follow also hold good for a yacht which does not retire but finishes and then learns of the facts justifying a protest either when the crew get ashore or indeed later still.

First they were asked whether a crew seeing an incident after retiring could protest under rule 68.3(b), even if they had already come ashore. The reply was that in these circumstances rule 68.1 permits a protest without a flag, including a protest under Part IV.

It was then asked whether the same yacht, once she had retired could protest if the incident came to her notice only indirectly through information from others, the reply was "no" since rule 68.1 prohibited a yacht "from protesting on hearsay evidence".

Then they asked whether in the two cases above the situation would change in a case of team racing and the answer here too was negative. Finally it was asked whether the situation would change when the protester first retires and then sees the incident while she continues to sail along with the other competitors; but here it was held that she had the ability to display her protest flag at the first reasonable opportunity like the others and so must do so.

The expectations of some competitors are illustrated in IYRU No. 47 (RYA 1970/5, *Hocus Pocus* v. *Star-Kus* and others). *Hocus Pocus* protested three yachts accusing them of having started outside a limit mark. But the race committee declared that the protest was inadmissible (and would not hear it) because no protest flag had been flown; and it was no good *Hocus Pocus* justifying this omission by saying that her helmsman had been able to look at the sailing instructions only after coming ashore and that only then had it been possible to make sure that the three yachts had infringed the rule.

The council dismissed *Hocus Pocus*'s appeal, saying "all competitors are presumed to be aware of the provisions of the sailing instructions.

"A yacht which has reason to believe that another yacht has infringed a rule or sailing instructions and wishes to protest must show a protest flag in accordance with rule 68.3(a). If, after finishing she is satisfied that no infringement occurred, she need take no further action, other than to explain to the race committee why she showed a protest flag."

Remember that rule 33.2 does not require a protest flag from a yacht which has witnessed an incident in which the protagonists have flown their flags and later comes to learn that neither of the two had either protested or retired.

Displaying the protest flag is not essential where a yacht seeks redress against the committee (rule 68.5(a)) when involving acts or omissions that cannot be appreciated immediately.

5. Duty to inform the protested yacht (68.3(c))

The fact that a yacht has flown her protest flag at the first reasonable opportunity after the incident is not enough to ensure that the other yacht involved knows without doubt that the protest was against her. In fact this certainty is given only by the contents of the protest itself, that is on reading it, a right reserved by the race committee.

Bear in mind further that a protest can legitimately be presented at the very last moment of the time limit and so the presumed protested yacht might be forced to wait for a long time before knowing if she was to be the object of an enquiry and therefore must prepare her defence. In the meanwhile the protester would have the advantage of going and looking for witnesses, begging them not to go away because there was going to be a hearing, and would have been able to take advice from his friends and so on.

This is why an elementary rule of good sporting behaviour, written into rule 68.3(c), obliges the protesting yacht to "try to inform the yacht protested against that a protest will be lodged"; and it must be understood that this must be done as soon as possible because if it is done only at the last moment the protester will really have avoided doing his duty.

Do not imagine that the poor protested yacht is unprotected when faced by an unfair protester who does not give a damn about this rule and who informs her only when it is already too late; in fact rule 70 (Hearings), as well as laying down that the race committee must inform both parties of the time and place of the hearing and make the protest available to the interested parties, says "a reasonable time shall be allowed for the preparation of the case"; and it is easy to understand that "reasonable time" will also depend among other things on the care taken by the protester in informing her adversary.

Rule 68.3(c) does not specify how the communication must be made and it follows therefore that theoretically a homing pigeon would be as good as direct speech, as long as the information got to the interested party and, what counts, arrived in time. As far as the protesting yacht is concerned she would do well to give this warning in such a way as to be able to show the race committee if necessary that she has done so since "a protest cannot be declared inadmissible by reason of the absence of the protested yacht especially if the protesting yacht has not been given any chance to prove that the protested yacht has been regularly informed", FIV 1961/4 (*Maccabeo* v. *Turbine*). Indeed, the saying that the absent are always wrong is not to be relied on because a good protest committee will always be uneasy when the protested yacht is not represented (more than ever if the protesting yacht has not bothered to get hold of her as so often happens) and for this reason will unconsciously tend to deal more gently in her regard.

What then do the words "try to inform" really mean. It is clear that one is dealing with a question of mere fact, which only the protest committee can investigate and decide case by case according to the circumstances; and that can be very varied, according to whether you are dealing with a short race on a small lake between four boats or a large offshore entry where more than a hundred competitors finish hours, if not indeed, days apart.

6. Form and contents of a protest

(68.3(d)(f))

Two essential conditions for the validity and admissibility (see rule 69) of a protest are that it shall be in writing and signed by the owner of the yacht (even if he has not been racing) or by his representative.

Who may appear as the representative of the owner? The rule does not lay it down precisely but (referring to rules 14 – Award of prizes, 21 – Member on board, 70 – Hearings, which use the same words or refer to the person "responsible for the yacht") he may or may not be a member of the crew; but at any rate if he was not on board he should perhaps, unless he is a close relation or well known to be closely connected with the owner, have a letter of appointment.

As to the real contents of the protest, it must first of all be underlined that the list under (d) is not absolute as appears, since it is modified by 68.3(f) later on. In fact the U.S. Appeals Committee (NAYRU 88, *Simba* v. *Kandu*) observed that the changes introduced into the rule (in 1961) permitted a protest committee not to invalidate a protest for mere technicalities.

In fact if the details were mandatory and this was applied literally it would end by invalidating nine out of ten protests. "A protest should identify the incident, designate the rule believed to have been infringed (not necessarily by its number or rule book name) and give enough of a description of the incident so that the race committee can form a picture of what happened. This is what the items listed in rule 68.3(d) are designed to provide."

After this general statement the appeals committee examined the case before them and observed "the written protest before us adequately met the minimum requirements, it identified the incident by date (Saturday 16.9.1961), approximate time (the leg from mark 7 to mark 16 in the race starting at 11.40) and whereabouts (off the Army Docks at Aquatic Park). It clearly designated the rule believed to have been infringed as the Opposite Tack Rule. It gave a brief clear statement of the facts which was not disputed. It did not contain a diagram of the incident and while a diagram was certainly relevant, its omission in this case did not invalidate the protest since the essential facts were clear without it. The race committee was correct (see rule 68.3(f)) in asking for and accepting a diagram at a later date."

Their decision authoritatively and exhaustively illustrates rule 68.3(d). We therefore only need add a detail taken from IYRU No. 29 (RYA 1966/12 RYA of India). Here it was held that not even the lack of a written statement invalidates a protest when substance of the alleged infringement of the rules is made clear to the protest committee in some other way (for example by a diagram). They went on to say that rule 68.3(f) made it mandatory for the race committee to allow any relevant omission to be remedied at any time until the hearing is opened. The RYA referring this "later time" within which the rule itself permits minor defects to be remedied or fees which have not been deposited to be paid, then laid down that the "later time" terminated at the opening of the hearing. The new wording of rule 68.3(f) has given official confirmation to the cases mentioned above thus sanctioning what good sense had already prompted.

7. Time limit for lodging a protest (68.3(e))

Sailing instructions can establish special time limits for lodging protests, specifying where they should be handed in and any fee which must be deposited with them. (It seems this fee is meant to give a certain amount of seriousness to the protest although in our opinion this monetary control is unfitting in a sporting competition unless you think of it as paying for the drinks which the protest committee will consume while hearing the protest).

If, however, the sailing instructions say nothing different on the subject the general disposition contained in rule 68.3(e) will prevail; that is the time limit will be two hours with no money. This time limit will begin to run from the moment a protesting yacht *finishes*. If she has not finished the race (because she retired or finished after the time limit) she must protest within two hours maximum from her arrival in harbour or within such time as is considered reasonable.

When it is impossible to hand in the protest (for example because a yacht has ended up after the race miles from the race committee) it can be sent by post provided that it is posted within the correct time limit (and in this case the postal stamp time will count and not that of its arrival). It is obvious that in such cases the fastest post available must be used and, above all, the protest committee must be advised immediately in some other way, probably by telephone, of the existence of a protest.

In the case of a yacht which has *finished* (rule 68.3(e)i), and only in this case, unusual circumstances may make delivery of a protest within the required time of two hours (or whatever is fixed by the sailing instructions) difficult or impossible (perhaps because there is no-one to receive at the nominated place or because the return to harbour has been delayed by bad weather or by an accident or because the race has finished very late etc.) and then the protest committee may extend the time limit.

"The protest committee may decide to lengthen the time limit at any time" explained the U.S. Appeals Committee in NAYRU No. 88 already mentioned on p. 275 "and this need not necessarily be decided before the end of the time limit. Indeed the fact that a protest committee is informed of a valid reason for lengthening the limit only after the time has passed must not deprive a yacht of her right to present a protest. On the other hand this does not mean that the protest committee has unlimited power to prolong the time limit for the presentation of a protest for the reason for arriving at the decision may not be capricious or arbitrary."

To whom must you give the protest if the sailing instructions lay down no particular rules on this subject? It must be lodged with the race committee (see the comment to rule 1) or to the protest committee (into the hands of a member of it or someone specifically named for that job) in any particular place they may have or, lacking anywhere else, the secretariat of the organizing club for the race. The protester would be wise to check the time it is lodged and write it on the protest itself and get the person taking it to sign it, because this will be evidence to the protest committee that it was lodged in time.

8. Protests on a measurement rule (68.4)

To understand this part of the rule it will help the reader to remember the comment to rule 19 (Certificates); then he will understand rule 68.4 which deals with protests about the following two categories of infringements;

(a) that a measurement, scantling or flotation rule has been infringed while *racing*. These three cases must refer to infringements arising during a race, though they have usually arisen from temporary commissions or omissions, such as can be checked in an inspection before or after a race and which can therefore be corrected or modified. For example infringments might concern the minimum or maximum weights of the boat, and the length of the spinnaker pole, boom, or battens the sizes of stamps on the sails, the ballast and the special equipment or the relationship between trim and waterline length.

Rule 68.4(b) allows the committee to disregard (but only once unless it has been impossible to repair or correct mistakes before the next race) deviations in excess of tolerances caused by normal wear or damage. But this refers to minor differences that have no bearing on the performance of the boat compared with that of other competitors who are in order.

(b) that the classification or rating certificate is for any reason invalid. Unlike (a) this infringement can exist and can be protested even before the race, because it deals with an irregularity that consists, not of some rare transitory episode, but of a substantial and permanent fault (for example differences between the measurements of the boat and those on the certificate whether by mistakes in measurement or in writing down the measurement or because of changes to the yacht, or because the figures are incomplete or because the certificate itself is out of date).

Protests of this kind, called measurement protests for convenience, can be lodged very much later than normal since the time limit falls at 6 p.m. on the day *after* the race mistakes in measurement cannot always be discovered during the race; they may consist of technical errors which are not easily checked and become apparent only after the end of the race (indeed we would say that the second case is much more probable because when the boats come ashore they are easier to look at and the sharp eye of a knowledgable and keen competitor may well see something awry).

Faced with a measurement protest the protest committee must first of all "send" (and not only "make available" – see rule 70) a copy of the protest to the protested yacht so that the latter is fully informed, very necessary with questions of a technical character which probably need precise detail. Then the protest committee must immediately (as required by rule 70 in the presence of the parties) hold a summary hearing on the technical basis of the protest; and if at this first meeting "there appears to be reasonable grounds for a protest" then the race committee must "refer the question to an authority qualified to decide such questions".

The rule does not lay down who this competent authority should be and so each national authority does as it thinks fit. Generally the matter is first referred to an official measurer, and, on appeal, to the body which issued the certificate. The experts called by the protest committee complete their checks and then reply to questions put to them. Thereafter the technical questions having been clarified (the measurers having certified whether there has been an infringement of the certificate) the protest committee can make their decision penalizing – or not – the protested yacht.

Rule 68.4(c) says that the race committee "in making its decision shall be governed by the determination of such authority". It is very important not to confuse the two quite distinct sectors and powers of the protest committee and the technical experts because "a jury of any grade and only a jury has the power to pronounce final judgement on the protest while the technical expert, and only he, can check and control a technical point of measurement; with the consequence that the judicial body (protest committee) must follow the expert's advice in all relevant decisions" thus the Italian Appeal Jury in FIV 1965/2, *Cigno Nero* v. *Mila II.*

Finally just as a copy of the protest has to be sent immediately to the protested yacht, copies of the final decision of the protest committee must be sent to all the yachts involved.

9. Seeking redress against the race committee* (68.5)

A jurist might well think that rule 68.5 was very strange, not least for the fact that it permits a "protest" against the race committee in spite of the fact that the question will be judged by the body that is protested. In fact it is called a "protest" in common parlance because it follows the same procedure, but it should really be called "seeking redress", the phrase used in the rule itself. But rather than looking at it as a contradiction, the judicial point of view, it is better to consider it as a demonstration of faith towards a body whose impartiality must stretch to disowning even its own acts.

After all it is only too common for the race committee to make a mistake; think only of the number of times starting and finishing lines and course marks are laid wrongly, how many mistakes are made in calculating times and in starting procedures in recalls and in all the other signals laid down by the rule or in the sailing instructions in cancelling, abandoning and shortening courses, in counting the points and in the final results, in giving prizes etc.

The scope for error is large and varied; what counts as far as rule 68.5 is concerned is that the race committee have done or have failed to do something required by the rules or the sailing instructions so that a yacht's finishing position has been "materially prejudiced", (finishing position in a single race or the points won in a series). The right of recourse to the protest committee can never be denied not even if, to quote the appeals committee in FIV 1972/6, "the sailing instructions have, by partially modifying rules 8.1 and 8.2 excluded individual recalls, or if they have empowered the protest committee to disqualify without a hearing any competitor who infringes some well-determined rules (for example crossing the line in the minute before the start).

"This inalienable right of recourse to a protest committee is reasonable because the possibility of a mistake cannot be excluded, and in that case the

---

* This particular problem does not exist when the committee is divided into race committee and protest committee or jury (see point 2 of the comment to rule 1). Here the protest committee may well have the power to control and therefore to judge the work of the race committee. This does not remove the right, in theory, to ask for redress against the protest committee too for any action or omission but it must refer to something which has influenced the outcome of the race and not arisen from the decision which they have pronounced as a result of a regular protest procedure.

competitor must be able to demonstrate that he has been unfairly penalized by asking under rule 68 for a hearing under rule 70."

The action or omission of the race committee must have damaged only one or two competitors; because if on the contrary the mistake has affected everyone equally, helping or harming no one yacht more than another, the competitor will have no recourse. We can see this in the decision of the Olympic Games Jury at Acapulco where a competitor protested because he thought that the direction of the starting line left something to be desired; "It is normal for sailing instructions to show the nature of the course, but once put into effect few courses are in the end perfect. Presuming that the version given by the protesters about the length and angulation of the line is correct and accepting the direction of wind and even realizing that in this respect there is some foundation, the jury holds nevertheless that there is no justification for abandoning the race or for taking any other step in favour of the protester since he had the same chances as anyone else and therefore he had not suffered that prejudice which rule 68.5 requires". It must be added however that this criterion can only be followed while dealing with minor deficiences because otherwise you might as well say that a horse that is lame in all four legs must be considered sound because all four legs are in the same condition.

Rule 68.5 lays down that this "seeking of redress" must be in accordance with the requirements in rule 68.3 (d), (e) and (f) that is with the usual protest procedure (and the successive phases, a hearing (rule 70) and decisions (rule 71) will also be followed). The aim is to avoid going to appeal against acts of the race committee and so the committee must be given the possibility to recognize its own mistake and to make it good. In fact it is impossible to have recourse directly in appeal against a race committee. Only a decision can be appealed, and in order to get a decision in the first instance it is necessary to go through the normal procedure of a protest ending with just such a decision (see point 1 of the comment to rule 77).

What, on the other hand, may alter the procedure mentioned above is the end of the time limit within which the protests must be presented under rule 68.3(e). It may be that the committee has made a mistake during the race (and then it will be possible according to the rule to make the time run from the moment of the yacht's arrival in port); but it may have been made earlier (for example about entries, inspections, etc.) or later (very common, for example, referring to points and classification); and in this case the time limit will begin to run from the moment in which the yacht seeking redress could have known about the mistake (for example from the moment of the publication of the results); and this explains why no protest flag is needed for this particular type of protest.

Before deciding a case of this sort the race committee must first of all put their hand on their hearts and examine their consciences in all humility to see whether they have violated a rule or sailing instruction. If they have, then they must consider whether the mistake "was prejudicial and that the result of the race was altered thereby". It is quite likely that the action or omission of the committee was such that the competitor was in no way affected by it (perhaps because he was irredeemably last). In any case the race committee must look down at what is laid down in rule 70.5. In line with what has been laid down by rule 12 (Yacht materially prejudiced), the remedies allowed to a committee when they have made a mistake and so some competitor has been unfairly handicapped are:

(a) cancellation, if for some justifiable reason there is no longer a possibility of re-sailing the race (see rule 5);
(b) abandonment, if it is possible to re-sail it (see rules 5.3 and 13);
(c) any arrangement deemed equitable, for example a re-sail only for the yachts interested in certain positions; or to keep the classification without a re-sail but give a special prize to the person seeking redress; or to classify yachts misled by a mistake in sailing instructions.

10. Withdrawing a protest

(68.6)

To ensure that protests are not frivolous and to avoid their being used to threaten, or indeed as barter in unorthodox deals, rule 68.6 declares in very explicit terms that "a protest made in writing shall not be withdrawn but shall be decided by the race committee". Once a skipper lodges a protest he has burnt his boats and must stand by it.

The rule speaks of a protest "made in writing" prescribed by rule 68.3(d). But a distinction must be made between protests lodged by a competitor (which can only be in writing), and those initiated by the committee itself in the circumstances foreseen by rules 73.1 and 73.2. It is clear that these procedures initiated officially and not on the impulse of a competitor can (naturally only if there is some valid motive for doing so) be abandoned without having to arrive at a decision. This is not surprising because here the committee does not have to account to anyone while a normal protest concerns two parties involved in a controversy which from that moment on can only be resolved by an arbiter or "judge".

To insist on arguing is an absurd waste of time whenever "full responsibility is acknowledged by one or more yachts". For this reason rule 68.6 allows the protest to be withdrawn if the protested yacht (or the protester, why not?) recognizes that he has made a mistake and decided to retire. And this is so even if the race is over and everyone is in harbour. However, the protest must be withdrawn before the hearing required by rule 70, that is before the race committee begin to examine it.

But you will notice that the acknowledgement of responsibility must be complete, that is such as to leave no possibility of saying that other yachts provoked the incident or of implicating other competitors.

A "race committee is entitled to forfeit retirement points in a case where it considers a yacht has not retired within a reasonable time": IYRU No. 13 (RYA 1963/34 *Fury* v. *Endeavour*). In fact it would be only too easy to admit one's own fault only when the lodging of a protest brings with it the certainty of a disqualification. We think therefore that (even with an admission of guilt and a consequent retirement by the protested boat before the hearing) when the protest committee has doubts about the timing of the retirement, they can nevertheless refuse to allow the protest to be withdrawn and can insist on a hearing to investigate whether their suspicion was founded or not. If in fact it was unfounded they will confirm the withdrawal of the protest; but otherwise they will go on to reach a decision and may penalize or disqualify as they think fit.

Rule 69. 69.1   When the race committee decides that a protest does not conform to the
Refusal of a   requirements of rule 68, (Protests), it shall inform the protesting yacht that
protest   her protest will not be heard and of the reasons for such decision.

            69.2   Such a decision shall not be reached without giving the protesting yacht an
opportunity of bringing evidence that the requirements of rule 68, (Protests),
were complied with.

If the numerous prescriptions of rule 68 are not observed the protest may not
be accepted (that is the protest committee may refuse to examine it at all). In
fact the protest committee must first of all verify (without entering into the
merit of the protest itself) that the various conditions required by rule 68 have
been fulfilled. They must examine the protest to see if:

(a) it has been lodged within the time limit required by rule 68.3 and whether it
is accompanied by the deposit if one is asked for;

(b) it has been lodged by a competitor permitted to do so under rule 68.1;

(c) the protester has displayed a protest flag or whether the omission of this is
justified by a valid reason (rule 68.3(a) and (b));

(d) the protester has tried to inform the protested yacht under rule 68.3(c);

(e) the protest is complete as required by rule 68.3(d) (not forgetting, however,
that rule 68.3(f) permits any defects to be remedied later).

Whenever the protest committee finds that one of the above requirements is
lacking "it shall inform the protesting yacht that her protest will not be heard
and of the reasons for such a decision". This means that in any case the
committee, even if it need not officially start a hearing under rule 70, must at
least hear the protester with the object of "giving the protesting yacht an
opportunity of bringing evidence that the requirements of rule 68 (Protests)
were complied with".

Having heard the relevant argument the committee will decide if the protest
is admissible or not, and whether they should proceed with the hearing or
whether the case should be thrown out under rule 69 without any examination
of the grounds of the protest.

Rule 70. 70.1   When the race committee decides that a protest conforms to all the
Hearings   requirements of rule 68, (Protests), it shall call a hearing as soon as possible.
The protest, or a copy of it, shall be made available to all yachts involved, and
each shall be notified, in writing if practicable, of the time and place set for
the hearing. A reasonable time shall be allowed for the preparation of defence. At the hearing, the race committee shall take the evidence presented
by the parties to the protest and such other evidence as it may consider
necessary. The parties to the protest, or a representative of each, shall have
the right to be present, but all others, except one witness at a time while
testifying, may be excluded. A yacht other than one named in the protest,
which is involved in that protest, shall have all the rights of yachts originally
named in it.

            70.2   A yacht shall not be penalized without a hearing, except as provided in rule
73.1(a), (Race Committee's Action against an Infringing Yacht).

            70.3   Failure on the part of any of the interested parties or a representative to make an effort to attend the hearing of the protest may justify the race committee in deciding the protest as it thinks fit without a full hearing.

70.4   For the purpose of rule 70, the word "protest" shall include, when appropriate, an investigation of redress under rule 12, (Yacht Materially Prejudiced); a request for redress under rule 68.5, (Protests); or a notification of an infringement hearing under rule 73, (Race Committee's Action against an Infringing Yacht).

70.5   When *abandonment* or *cancellation* of a completed race is under consideration by the race committee, the race committee shall not act before satisfying itself by taking appropriate evidence that its action is as equitable as possible to all yachts concerned, for that particular race and the series, if any, as a whole.

1. The preparatory phase

Once the preliminaries in rule 68 are over and the protest has been accepted the protest committee must call a hearing as soon as possible. At this point they will have already met to examine whether the necessary conditions have been fulfilled and it will naturally be easiest for them to notify immediately all the yachts involved of the time and place chosen for the hearing.

It is better still if the sailing instructions and the notice board have beforehand published pre-arranged places for hearings so that misunderstandings, delays and complications are avoided. Note the difference between the pre-existing obligation which the protester has to try to inform the yacht protested against that a protest is being lodged (rule 68.3(c)) and that falling to the protest committee once the protest has been lodged. These are two quite different requirements for the first gives warning of a protest and is the duty of the protesting yacht while the second gives notice of the hearing and is the duty of the protest committee.

"The protest, or a copy of it, shall be made available to all yachts involved" and "a reasonable time should be allowed for the preparation of a defence" at the discretion of the protest committee as may be necessary for the case in question. Logical provisions these, and understandable, as well as mandatory, thus failure to observe them can, when serious, annul the entire proceedings (as happened for example in NAYRU 82 when the written protest was not put at the disposition of the poor protested yacht even at the hearing). Remember that here "protest" includes seeking redress under rule 12, or a hearing arising under rule 73.2.

2. The hearing proper

Finally the time fixed for the hearing arrives. And let us say here at once looking at rule 70.3 that "failure on the part of the interested parties or a representative to make an effort to attend the hearing of the protest may justify the race committee in deciding the protest as it thinks fit without a full hearing". In other words the committee must first of all make sure that both parties have been advised; after which if there do not seem to be reasonable grounds why they cannot appear the protest committee can go ahead without them. Even without the normal testimony the committee may use other available evidence such as photographs, the rounding order at the mark etc. when they can lay their hands on it without difficulty. But the protest committee need not worry too much about something that evidently does not worry the parties overmuch;

remember that the drive to set the procedure going comes, as the spirit of the rule intends, from the initiative of the parties themselves (it is different in the case of rule 73 – Race committee's action against an infringing yacht).

Rule 70.2 also says that a yacht "shall not be penalized without a hearing, except as provided in rule 73.1(a)". Thus it is not legal to inflict any penalty, light or heavy as may be, without going through the formalities listed below, aimed at ensuring that each party to the cause can state his case and bring his evidence before the "judges". This does not mean that a protest committee may dispense with a hearing if they want to dismiss a protest without penalizing either side, but that only decisions of a preliminary character already mentioned in rule 69 can be taken without a hearing. The Italian Appeals Committee (FIV 1965/5, *Aldebaran V* v. *Samanna*) laid down that "a race committee cannot – save in the exceptional case provided for by rule 73.1(a) – penalize or absolve a yacht without a hearing where parties or witnesses are to be heard or other evidence examined about the facts which have given rise to the protest".

3. Presence of the parties'

"The interested parties or a representative" have the right to be present for the entire hearing (except of course when the protest committee wish to discuss the case and make up their minds), in addition a yacht not named in the protest but involved in it has the same right as a yacht that has been named; and this right cannot be denied to the parties without nullifying the entire procedure. This has been laid down by the U.S. Appeals Committee (NAYRU 54) in an appeal alleging that certain protests had been heard without the parties being admitted and without hearing the witnesses.

"The Race Committee did not deny the allegations but responded that its failure to comply with the provisions of rules 70 and 71 was in consequence of the protests having originated in a race held on the last day of a three-race series at which the race committee 'had to deal with a large number of protests which arose out of the racing on that day' and that 'the wind was light that day and the races were not completed until fairly late in the afternoon, and the committee just did not have time to comply with all the formalities usually required.'

"A race committee may be justified, in exceptional circumstances, declining to hear an indefinite number of witnesses called by a party to a protest all of whom are prepared to testify to the same state of facts. However, the provisions of rule 70, that the parties to a protest shall have the right to be present at the hearing represents an important right of which they would not be deprived.

"The difficulties under which the race committee laboured at the time of the hearings are not unusual and are understandable. Nevertheless its failure to comply with the mandatory provisions of rules 70 and 71 determine that the hearing was invalid."

4. The Procedure

From the text it is clear that the hearing may be public (it is always useful and instructive for the audience) but in no case may witnesses be present (so as not to be influenced by hearing others' statements) "except one witness at a time while testifying". Other than the above instructions and the statement that "at the hearing the race committee will take the evidence presented by the

parties to the protest and such other evidence as it may consider necessary",
the rule does not lay down any particular procedure to be followed; but it is
advisable to adopt the following order of work:

1. Read the protest in the presence of both parties;
2. Check that rule 68.3(a) (Flying a protest flag) has been observed;
3. Check whether the protester has tried to inform the protested yacht that a
   protest is being lodged (rule 68.3(c));
4. Invite the protester to explain his protest and then allow the protested yacht
   to ask him questions on facts (avoiding comment and discussion at this
   point);
5. Invite the protested yacht in her turn to furnish her version of the facts and
   then permit the protester first and the race committee afterwards to ask
   questions for clarification;
6. Consider the evidence of the protesting and then the protested yacht; this
   can be provided by witnesses in which case the parties can ask the witness
   questions, or it may be an examination of photographs, films or other
   documentation, and it is not excluded that inspections or experiments may
   be carried out; if some member of the committee has been present at the
   incident he must tell his story and be questioned like any other witness (even
   though this will not stop him taking part in the decision); witnesses who
   have been examined and are no longer necessary can be allowed to go;
7. When all the evidence has been heard each party can make a brief
   reassumption of his arguments; after which both parties will be invited to
   leave the room while the committee discusses and makes their decision.

In conclusion as has been hinted at in the two decisions quoted above, the
dispositions expressly laid down in rule 70 (that is the availability of a copy of
the protest, the notification of the hearing, the concession of a reasonable time
for defence, the right of being present at the hearing, the hearing of evidence)
must be respected integrally otherwise the procedure is null and void.

When organizing the hearing, the parties cannot be deprived of their right to
be heard (even if within the limits of possibility and moderation) and to bring
relevant (though not excessive) evidence otherwise here too the hearing and the
consequent decision may be annulled.

To sum up, a protest committee must try, without worrying too much about
excessive formality (never wrong but unnecessary), to conduct a serious and
scrupulous investigation which is directed towards finding out the truth,
because truth signifies justice; and this holds good even in sport.

Rule 71.
Decisions

The race committee shall make its decision promptly after the hearing. Each
decision shall be communicated to the parties involved, and shall state fully
the facts and grounds on which it is based and shall specify the rules, if any,
infringed. When requested by any of the parties, such decision shall be given
in writing and shall include the race committee's diagram.
The findings of the race committee as to the facts involved shall be final.

1. Composition of committee and voting

Since it is not in anyway excluded that protests be heard by one person, let us see how a protest committee can be composed so as to be regularly constituted and so that its deliberations are valid. On this point the Rules give no directive (consider rule 1) and therefore any particular organization must be based on the sailing instructions or on the internal rules of the organizing club.

If nothing is laid down it makes good practice to consider as valid a decision which has been taken by a majority of those named as members of the protest committee or jury (information which should be published in the programme or posted up before the beginning of the race); thus if a protest committee is composed, for example, of six people at least half plus one must be present for a quorum which in our case is four (including of course the chairman or vice-chairman).

It is a good idea to have an uneven number so that there is always a majority on voting with no worry about being faced with a deadlock. However when the voting *is* equally divided the chairman, as the person most experienced and expert, may be considered to have the casting vote (and for the same reason at the moment of a decision if a vote is taken it should be voiced in an opposite order of seniority, that is beginning with the least senior member and so on to the chairman who should vote last so as not to influence the others).

Sometimes the chairman cannot be present and so the committee decides without him; one appeal (FIV 1970/4) was based, among other things, on the fact that the protest committee had altered its chairman. The Italian Appeals Committee refused to accept that this circumstance voided the decisions taken by the committee and specified "the president of the committee could in case of necessity delegate his functions to another member of the committee itself or be substituted by another person in his place nominated by the organisers."

It can however, happen (and has happened, see FIV 1961/4) that a committee is reduced to only two members and that they do not agree; in this case the Italian National Authority decided as follows:

"even if it is unusual, when a jury is composed of an even number and the voting is equal, the president will have the deciding vote but this cannot apply in the extreme case of a jury reduced to two people only who disagree with each other". This means that in such cases the proposition put to the vote must be considered as dismissed otherwise the decision of the jury would be identified with one person only. And this confirms yet again that such situations must be prevented and that a disparate number of voters is desirable.

While still on the subject of voting, not everyone knows that to arrive at a final decision on a complex problem (as a protest may well be) it is necessary to resolve, little by little, a series of minor questions, leading on one from another; thus a result is arrived at by putting various problems to the vote as one goes along. For example a start might be made by asking the protest committee to vote on the first question:

"Is the fact that the protester did not hoist a protest flag considered justifiable under rule 68.3(b)?"

In the case of a positive vote a second question, on the facts can be put:

"From the evidence which has emerged in the hearing do you consider that yacht A failed to keep clear of yacht B?" If this is also positive the next question may be:

"Was there an obligation for A to keep clear of B?" (this is really asking:

"did the action of A which we decided above comprise an infringement of any rule?") If the answer is "yes" it may be followed with:

"Has there been an infringement of rule X or of rule Y?". And so on until the various problems are cleared out of the way and a final decision can be reached in an orderly fashion.

2. Finding facts   An interesting point was put to the RYA by the chairman of the race committee in *Sinnes* v. *Lord Osis* (IYRU No. 77, RYA 1967/7): "Is the race committee obliged under rule 71 always to find fact, (a) if two boats collide, and (b) if there is no collision? If there is conflicting evidence, and the rules do not stipulate that the onus of proving his case lies with either party, may the race committee dismiss a protest because of lack of evidence, without finding facts?"

And here is the RYA's answer: "If two yachts collide, there must have been an infringement of a rule and the race committee must, under rule 71, on a protest arising from the incident, find the relvant facts and give a decision on them. If there is a protest arising from an incident which did not involve a collision, it is open to the race committee in the face of lack of evidence or of conflicting evidence, to dismiss the protest on the grounds that it is not satisfied that there has been an infringement of any rule."

Although rule 71 requires a decision to be given immediately after a hearing it may occasionally happen that at the end of the hearing the protest committee is compelled for some perfectly reasonable motives to adjourn to a later time; and it may also happen that in the later meeting one of the members of the committee has to be substituted by someone else. The Italian National Authority dealt with such a case as follows (FIV 1967/5): "except in very rare cases when there are unsurmountable reasons the final decision in a protest should be taken by the people who were at the hearing and heard the evidence and it is clear that a jury which has to decide the facts will without any doubt be enormously influenced by the immediate and vivid impressions of hearing the parties and all the particulars of the evidence and will weigh in their minds those shades of meaning which it is virtually impossible to convey in writing".

"The findings of the race committee as to the facts involved shall be final" (and it follows that "a protest which has been decided by the race committee shall be referred to the national authority solely on a question of interpretation of rules" –rule 77.2).To clarify the distinction between fact and law it is enough to say that a question of fact deals with finding out what actually happened while a question of law looks at the rule to be applied to the fact already found.

The facts once found cannot be modified or altered by any appeals committee which is why protest committees must use skill and patience in collecting and writing down the evidence and must avoid hurried and superficial hearings. This does not mean that they should waste time on unnecessary details; indeed a good chairman of a protest committee must stifle long-winded stories about irrelevant circumstances which do not throw any light on the facts and concentrate his investigation on those particulars of the incident which alone can have any influence on the applicability of one rule or another.

When the race committee has failed to hold a hearing, has organized it badly or omitted to document it properly (thus removing every possibility of control from the judges of second instance), the appeals committee may send the case back to the protest committee (the only body competent to find the facts) so that it may re-open and complete the hearing. The parties still have the right to put forward another appeal against the protest committee's new decisions.

Great attention must be paid therefore to reconstructing the incident on the basis of the evidence heard and the appeals committee must reach a conclusion that leaves them with clear consciences in the sense that the findings are firmly based on sound reasons and not chosen more or less by guesswork from among various vague possibilities. We have already seen in fact (RYA 1967/7) that if there has been no collision and if the evidence is insufficient to illustrate clearly what actually happened, it would be better to say so frankly and dismiss the protest for insufficiency of proof; and certainly a protest committee will come out of such a decision with fewer broken bones than with a disqualification based on insufficient or doubtful evidence.

On the subject of proof it is not impossible for one party to succeed in getting' hold of some significant new evidence only after the race committee has already announced its decision; this, it must be understood, must be *new* evidence and not only irrefutable (as a photograph or film may be) but also of a kind to upset the findings already decided and published by the protest committee. In this case can the protest committee revoke its own sentence and re-open the proceedings to examine the new evidence? Finding the truth must be undeniably the first object of any protest procedure and we therefore think that every effort must be made to attain this aim so that when the new evidence effectively appears so convincing and relevant that it may invalidate a previous decision it must be taken into consideration.

We do not believe, however, that a case can be re-opened (whether dealing with a single race or with a series) after the prizegiving when the whole meeting is over, because then no result would ever be final. At a certain point it must be decided that what is done is done and the door closed firmly on any further hearing or evidence.

3. Publication of the decision

Rule 71 does not enlarge on this subject and limits itself to a few mandatory dispositions. The first of these is that the protest committee "shall make its decision promptly after the hearing"; this confirms the desirability mentioned above of the results being final, for the parties to the protest (and all the other competitors who are waiting for the results) should know the outcome as soon as possible so that they may sleep on it quietly.

The decision (that is the decision in the strict sense as to whether the protest has been accepted or dismissed specifying any penalty inflicted) is given orally immediately after the meeting in the presence of the parties and is then pinned up on the noticeboard and appears in the results. Later, and not very much later, the decision must be available in writing and by now in addition to the already published decision it must fully state the facts and grounds on which it is based and specify the rules infringed, if any, and at this point the reasons for the decision have to be divided into facts and law.

Note the term "fully" prescribed by rule 71; this does not mean that volumes have to be written but requires that the facts are clearly and adequately described (indicating the evidence which has led to it being accepted) and an explanation given as to why these facts caused an infringement, stating correctly the exact rule infringed (the protesting yacht may even make a mistake in this – see rules 68.3(d)(ii) and rule 72.1(b) – but not the protest committee).

Away with those lazy decisions that profit from the small space on the printed forms and omit to give even a summary of the facts saying only that "the yacht XYZ is disqualified for infringement of rule 36" – they are useless. Facts found are final and essential for any reconsideration of the case under rule 77 (Appeals), indeed it is just because the matter may go to appeal that rule 71 allows the parties the right to have, at their request, copies of the entire protest decision.

Rule 72. Disqualification after protest and liability for damages

When the race committee, after hearing a protest or acting under rule 73, (Race Committee's Action against an Infringing Yacht), or any appeal authority, is satisfied: –

(a) that a yacht has infringed any of these rules or the sailing instructions, or

(b) that in consequence of her neglect of any of these rules or the sailing instructions she has compelled other yachts to infringe any of these rules or the sailing instructions,

she shall be disqualified unless the sailing instructions applicable to that race provide some other penalty. Such disqualification or other penalty shall be imposed, irrespective of whether the rule or sailing instruction which led to the disqualification or penalty was mentioned in the protest, or the yacht which was at fault was mentioned or protested against, e.g., the protesting yacht or a third yacht might be disqualified and the protested yacht absolved.

72.2　For the purpose of awarding points in a series, a retirement after an infringement of any of these rules or the sailing instructions shall not rank as a disqualification. This penalty can be imposed only in accordance with rules 72, (Disqualification after Protest and Liability for Damages), and 73, (Race Committee's Action against an Infringing Yacht).

72.3　When a yacht either is disqualified or has retired, the next in order shall be awarded her place.

72.4　Alternative Penalties. When so prescribed in the sailing instructions, the procedure and penalty for infringing a rule of Part IV shall be as provided in Appendix 3, Alternative Penalties for Infringement of a Rule of Part IV.

72.5　The question of damages arising from an infringement of any of these rules or the sailing instructions shall be governed by the prescriptions, if any, of the national authority.

Rule 72 contains no surprises. We know that a protest (lodged by a competitor accepted under rules 68 and 69 or begun under rule 73.2) has to be heard by a protest committee in the way described by rule 70. If the collected evidence is adequate to prove that a rule has been infringed during the incident (or one of the prescriptions of the sailing instructions – see rule 3.1) it is logical that the culprit must be disqualified (see rule 31) or at any rate penalized in some other way as indicated in the sailing instructions (see for example alternative penalties in Appendix 3).

All this complies with elementary principles of justice and it makes no difference whether a yacht has been guilty directly – rule 72.1(a) or indirectly – rule 72.1(b) (e.g. if she wrongly forces another onto a mark) the two cases are considered alike. As in rule 68.3(d)ii), rule 72 permits a penalty to be imposed "irrespective of whether the rule or sailing instruction which led to the disqualification or penalty was mentioned in the protest"; in fact it would be absurd to pretend that the poor protesting yacht always knew how to describe in exact legal terms the infringement she was denouncing. This is the protest committee's job and they, at least in theory, should be familiar with the laws that govern racing.

One particular point in rule 72 is the fact that not only a protested yacht but also the protesting yacht and indeed a third yacht may be disqualified if they have been mixed up in the same incident (and this may happen even if the fact that she was involved and had infringed a rule emerges only for the first time in the hearing). Indeed rule 72.1 provides an idea of the very wide coverage of this principle by giving us an example that upsets every expectation, "the protesting yacht or a third yacht may be disqualified and the protested yacht absolved".

All this mounts up to the fact that a protest committee examining a protest has wide powers to investigate every aspect and authority to deal with anyone turning out to have been mixed up in the incident and held to be in the wrong.

The only formality to be respected here too is that of letting the "accused" know that he has been named and which rule he is considered to have infringed (rule 73.2), summoning him to the hearing and if necessary allowing him "a reasonable time for the preparation of his defence" (rule 70.1).

1. A yacht that retires (72.2)

The second paragraph of this rule refers to the case of a yacht which infringes a rule and then retires; specifying that in this case retirement "shall not rank as a disqualification" (in a race in a series this may be important for points).

It does not mean that a culprit can postpone the moment for retiring until it suits her, leaving a way open for herself until the very last moment. It is true that rule 33 only imposes an obligation to retire "promptly" (not immediately) on a yacht that "realizes she has infringed a racing rule or sailing instruction". This means she must retire within a reasonable period after the incident (or, accepting the good faith of the culprit, when he realizes it, usually because someone else points out his mistake to him). Remember on this point that "the race committee is entitled to forfeit retirement points in a case where it considers a yacht has not retired within a reasonable time", as the RYA has laid down in IYRU No. 13 (RYA 1963/34, *Fury* v. *Endeavour*). This was a case where the incident happened at the start and *Fury* retired only after finishing.

2. Placing (72.4)

After all there would be no need to specify (as rule 72.2 does) that a penalty can only be imposed by means of a proper "trial" which has been begun either by a competitor under rule 72 or by one of the methods indicated in rule 73.2. The specification that "when a yacht is either disqualified or has retired the next in order shall be awarded her place", (rule 72.3) is also obvious and needs no explanation.

3. Damages (72.5)

The jurisdiction of the rules and sailing instructions is limited to governing the organization and the running of the race and nothing more. The question of damages arising from the carelessness or negligence of a competitor does not come within their scope and the assessment of damages is well beyond the limits and capabilities of competitive sport, it falls to the complicated and diverse legislation of each particular nation.

One thing is certain that if a court of law is to allot blame or assess damage it must find out (bearing in mind the inevitably and foreseeable increased risks in sport) whether either party contravened any special rules that were relevant. It follows that the findings and opinions expressed by a protest committee when deciding a protest although powerless to award damages, may certainly form the basis on which a civil judge can in his turn decide whether the conduct of a competitor has been what it should; in a court of law the opinion expressed by a protest committee would be considered as technical advice.

Rule 72.5 suggests that national authorities may wish to prescribe specifically. Without going into detail we can say that such arrangements can, if accepted by competitors, have the effect of those agreements to resort to arbitration rather than the civil courts in case of dispute.

Rule 73. Race committee's action against an infringing yacht

WITHOUT A HEARING

(a) A yacht which fails either to *start* or to *finish* may be disqualified without a protest or hearing, after the conclusion of the race, except that she shall be entitled to a hearing when she satisfies the race committee that an error may have been made.

(b) A yacht so penalized shall be informed of the action taken, either by letter or by notification in the racing results.

73.2   WITH A HEARING

When the race committee: —

(a) sees an apparent infringement by a yacht of any of these rules or the sailing instructions (except as provided in rule 73.1), or

(b) learns directly from a written or oral statement by a yacht that she may have infringed a rule or sailing instruction, or

(c) has reasonable grounds for believing that an infringement resulted in serious damage, or

(d) receives a report not later than the same day from a witness who was neither competing in the race, nor otherwise an interested party, alleging an infringement, or

(e) has reasonable grounds for supposing from the evidence at the hearing of a valid protest, or a hearing called in accordance with rule 73.2, that any yacht involved in the incident may have committed an infringement,

the race committee may notify such yacht thereof orally, or when that is not possible, in writing, delivered or mailed not later than 18.00 hours on the day after:

     (i) the finish of the race, or

     (ii) the receipt of the report, or

     (iii) the hearing of the protest.

Such notice shall contain a statement of the pertinent facts and of the particular rule or rules or sailing instructions alleged to have been infringed, and the race committee shall act thereon in the same manner as if it had been a protest made by a competitor.

We have seen that a protest by a competitor is normally required (rule 68) to arrive at a hearing (rule 70) and a decision (rule 71) about an incident during a race. Indeed, except perhaps in small lakes, the area covered by any sailing competition is so large that it is not possible to appoint referees to interfere as soon as they see an infringement. This principle of intervention by a judge on the instigation of an interested party only has however two notable exceptions which are governed by rule 73.

1. Disqualification without protest or hearing

The race committee may act on its own initiative when one of its members sees himself that a yacht fails either to *start* or *finish*; these are mistakes in the execution of either of the two phases of the race which inevitably take part in front of the race committee.

It must be underlined that in order to act under rule 73.1 only an infringement of the definitions of *starting* or *finishing* in the strict sense (or with some sailing instruction connected with them) is involved and not an infringement of any other rule (or sailing instruction) which happens under the eyes of the race committee. For example a yacht can be penalized without protest and without a hearing under rule 73.1 when she crosses the line in the wrong direction, that is to say not in the direction of the first mark at the start, and not from the direction of the last mark at the finish (on this subject see, in addition to the respective definitions, rules 3.2(a)(vi), (vii) – Sailing instructions, 6 – Starting and finishing lines, 51 – Sailing the course and the respective comments), or fails to pass the limit marks on the prescribed side. Only these or similar irregularities come under rule 73.1 (or to some particular prescription which specifies the way to cross the line).* Seeing these infringements directly with their own eyes the race committee has the authority (not the obligation) to disqualify not only without waiting for a protest from a competitor or a report from a third person but without even having to communicate the facts immediately to the yacht in question and without having to summon her to a hearing. However, in order to mitigate mistakes by the race committee (which being composed of men and not of gods is anything but infallible) the rule hastens to add that a yacht thus penalized "shall be entitled to a hearing when she satisfies the race committee that an error may have been made".

Look at the difference between this situation and that foreseen by rule 68.5(a). Here with rule 73.1(a) the penalized competitor must "be informed of the action taken either by letter or by notification in the racing results" (rule 73.1(b)). (It is from this moment that he may try to convince the race committee that there may have been an error. Note that in this preliminary phase it is enough to show only that there is the possibility of a mistake). If, after a first summary examination, the protest committee is persuaded that the yacht may be right they will allow her a hearing (rule 70) that is to say they will

---

* For a yacht which starts or finishes incorrectly rule 73.1 speaks of disqualification. It has been remarked that if she does not start or finish a yacht can only be declared a non-starter (rather than starter under rule 50 – Ranking as a starter) or not finished. In reality one can commit a penalizable infringement with regards to the definition of starting, for example a premature starter that does not obey a recall. On the other hand as far as finishing is concerned we believe that one can either finish or not – there is no way of infringing the definition that would invoke a disqualification; because if we speak strictly only of the definition and of what can be done under rule 73.1, we must not consider touching a finishing line mark (rule 52.1) or seriously hindering a competitor on the line who is still racing (rule 31.2) for those are infringements which can only be pursued by the race committee under rule 73.2, not rule 73.1.

start regular proceedings exactly as if there had been a protest, and will end with a decision revoking or confirming the action of the race committee.

In the other case, rule 68.5(a) no penalty has been inflicted by the race committee but redress is sought against any actions or omissions prejudicing a yacht's finishing position. However the distinction between the two cases is very tenuous in substance and can create confusion; so much so that if we were to receive such a penalty, as provided for by rule 73.1, rather than stand there and try to convince the protest committee that there might have been an error, our idea would be to lodge a formal request for redress under rule 68. What in fact can a yacht do if she does not succeed in "satisfying the race committee etc."; is she still in time to protest or does she at this moment find herself faced with a decision of the race committee which can only be upset on appeal (rule 77.1)? We believe that because the rule does not answer this question it would be prudent to plunge in at the deep end and seek redress from the race committee.

2. A hearing initiated by the race committee (73.2)

Five distinct cases are dealt with here and in each the "accused" must be notified orally or, when that is not possible, in writing of the pertinent facts and of the particular rules or sailing instructions alleged to have been infringed and is summoned to a hearing where the race committee "will act thereon in the same manner as if it had been a protest made by a competitor". The five cases in which the race committee can proceed without a protest from a competitor are as follows:

(a) Where the race committee itself sees an apparent infringement (remembering that if it is a breach of the definition of starting or finishing in the strict sense it will fall within rule 73.1). If, however, the infringment is not seen by the race committee altogether but by only one of its members rule 73.2(d) (below) applies.

(b) Here the yacht herself announces that she has or may have infringed a rule or sailing instruction and refers mainly to races where there are penalties instead of disqualifications (either with Appendix III or in some forms of offshore racing where penalties are awarded for infringement of rules other than those in Part IV).

Having infringed a rule a yacht does not retire but after finishing describes the infringement on her declaration and goes before the race committee unless the sailing instructions specify that the race committee may penalize for breaches acknowledged by the yacht herself without a hearing. It has been noted that there are places where rule 52.2 (re-rounding a mark) are not applicable, such as the Solent in Cowes Week, and a competitor, used to re-rounding, does not quite know what to do when he fouls a mark but need not retire. However, if he declares it the race committee will then hear him and penalize him as the sailing instructions require.

(c) Where there are reasonable grounds for believing that an infringement has given rise to serious damage, these circumstances in themselves authorize an intervention even when the case does not otherwise fall within this rule.

(d) Here the race committee receives (in writing or orally) a report of an alleged infringement. To be acceptable this report must satisfy all the following conditions: it can only be accepted from someone who 1. has witnessed the incident (which excludes the race committee collecting rumours and gossip from the bar); 2. is not a competitor (a competitor should protest) and 3. is not interested in any other way (excluding therefore competitors' relations and other members of the team, managers, hangers-on, etc.).

In addition the report to be valid must be received by the race committee "not later than the same day". It has been held, however, (RYA 1968/13, Tamesis Club) that "as it is laid down that the period of time (within which a competitor must lodge a protest) can be prolonged by a protest committee whenever it is justified by the circumstances, so the committee can similarly extend the time limit to receive a report under rule 73.2(d)". It is worth noting from the same decision that the presumed culprit, once accused under rule 73.2, can always admit his responsibility and retire before the hearing as is explained in rule 68.6 (but with the same possible exceptions which we have mentioned in the comment to it).

Many years ago the RYA was asked (in 1964/6, River Towy Yacht Club, now IYRU No. 18) the following question. "During a conversation within half an hour of coming ashore at the end of a race, a winning helmsman admitted to two members of the race committee and others that he had touched a limit mark on the starting line and had neither retired (nor made a penalty rounding of the mark). Can the race committee disqualify the yacht under rule 73.1 or should rule 73.2 apply?"

And the answer was "even though the race committee had decided that no declaration would be necessary, rule 14.1 would enable it to take action in this case because it affected the winning yacht. Action under rule 73.2(b) could have been taken against any yacht admitting an infringement to the race committee."

(e) Here new information at a hearing gives good grounds for believing that some other yacht has infringed a rule, this is perfectly clear and needs no explanation.

Having noted the five permitted cases we must underline that in each the race committee has the faculty (and not the obligation) to proceed against the presumed offender; if they decide to do so they must inform him before 1800 hours on the day after the end of the race or receiving the information or hearing the protest. This communication may be made by word of mouth or written, and if the latter it must be delivered or mailed.

As to the race committee's power to initiate proceedings it is worth noting FIV 1971/5 (*La Pacioccona* v. *Gabi*) in which a competitor lodged a protest without having displayed the correct protest flag under rule 68.3. The race committee having seen the incident themselves ignored the failure to fly a flag and disqualified the protested yacht. She appealed, maintaining that the race committee could not rely on rule 73.2(a) because the authority to act on their own could not be grounded on an inadmissible protest.

The national authority dismissed the appeal and observed that "the race committee ignoring the fact that no protest flag had been displayed (which would effectively have made any protest inadmissible) correctly availed itself of 73.2(a) which empowers them to proceed when they have directly seen an infringement themselves; this faculty is not in any way restricted by the existence of a protest which is held to be inadmissible because there is no reason why an offender should escape the punishment due to him when he has committed an infringement right under the eyes of those whose duty it is to punish him".

Another FIV case (1972/1, *Bentu* v. Race Committee) came to a different answer in an apparently similar case for here the race committee was not present at the incident. Here too the protest committee held that the protest was inadmissible because no protest flag was displayed and acted on their own initiative and disqualified the protested yacht. She appealed, setting out various arguments to show that she had not infringed any rules and here the decision of the appeals committee was different. "The charge – they held – cannot even be investigated since it arose from a decision which was null and void. A race committee may act on its own initiative under rule 73.2 only in five clear, well-specified cases but none of these arose in the case under examination. Not the first because the race committee saw nothing directly; not the second because the protested yacht did not admit her responsibility; not the third because there was no damage; not the fourth because the information came from a competitor and the protest was inadmissible and not the fifth because no evidence was given at the hearing of any valid protest. We must thus conclude that the race committee could not assume the initiative however praiseworthy their intent, and as a consequence their decision has to be declared null and void without investigating the appeal".

In any case, as we said at the beginning, the presumed culprit must be told the facts of which he is accused and the rules he is supposed to have infringed because only after so doing can the race committee act.

Appendix 11 discusses this problem.

Rule 74.
Penalties for gross infringement of rules or misconduct

74.1   When a gross infringement of any of these rules, the sailing instructions or class rules is proved against the owner, the owner's representative, the helmsman or crew of a yacht, such persons may be disqualified by the national authority, for any period it may think fit, from either steering or sailing in a yacht in any race held under its jurisdiction.
Notice of any penalty adjudged under this rule may be communicated by the national authority to the I.Y.R.U. which shall inform all national authorities.

74.2   After a gross breach of good manners or sportsmanship the race committee may exclude a competitor either from further participation in a series or from the whole series or take other disciplinary action.

It is difficult to describe a grave infringement in general terms to cover each single case.

Normally it is presumed that rule infringements arise from mere ignorance, errors of judgement, inexperience, and unexpected events, whereas rule 74 deals particularly with those infringements caused not only by incorrect behaviour due simply to mistakes but also marked with real intent (possibly preconceived) to act in a way known to be prohibited and to do so with full knowledge that others' rights are being damaged.

These distinctions while they may be fairly useful as an indication are not exhaustive and confirm our opinion that it is not possible to lay down an all-embracing definition when a violation or infringement should be dealt with under rule 74; for example think of that very common case when a competitor knows he should keep clear but does not do so, because of the tolerance of others. In this case he is wrong and acted with some intent, but it does not fall under the heavy sanctions of rule 74.

Note that a helmsman as well as an owner, his representative and crew (who may or may not of course be professional) can all be brought to justice under rule 74. The penalty consists of disqualification for a certain period during which the person concerned may neither steer nor crew a yacht in any race under the jurisdiction of the national authority.

Given the gravity of the sanction only a national authority may inflict it (after being notified by the jury, race committee or even by individuals) "for as long as it sees fit" that is practically limitless. The seriousness of the proceedings is such that the fact must be communicated to all the other national authorities by the IYRU so that they know what to do when faced with the individual in question.

While on the subject of a "gross breach of good manners or sportsmanship" it is best to send the culprit away from the regatta immediately without having to wait for the decision of the national authority (this underlines how rare these particular cases are) since the rule gives the race committee itself the power to exclude a competitor from further participation in a series or from the whole series. IYRU No. 78 gives a good illustration of this. Rule 74.2 allows the committee the alternative of taking "other disciplinary action" although it is difficult to understand what this can mean; in our opinion to stay within the rules and without being arbitrary this can only consist of previously scheduled sanctions written into the sailing instructions, which very rarely exist.

Rule 75. 75.1 No member of either a race committee or of any appeals authority shall take
Interested part in the discussion or decision upon any disputed question in which he is
persons not to an interested party, but this does not preclude him from giving evidence in
take part in such a case.
decision 75.2 The term "interested party" includes anyone who stands to gain or lose as a
result of the decision.

It is easy to understand that the first quality that a good judge must have is that of impartiality and no one can be truly impartial if he desires one outcome rather than another. It is, however, extremely difficult to say where this interest begins and ends. It is not uncommon for a jury member to be genuinely above such problems and to be able to judge equitably even if his own boat is involved. But it is equally common, unfortunately, to find a member of the jury who obviously takes sides because maybe he is dealing with a co-national, co-citizen, or co-member of a club.

In conclusion, rather than try to allow for a judge's interest when he is already sitting on a protest, it is better to be prepared and choose the protest committee from among people of proved impartiality.

However, it is sometimes necessary for the most reputable of judges (less to avoid temptation than not to be embarrassed or subjected to criticism even if unjust and unfounded) to abstain from the hearing and decision in a case where it might be thought that he was showing favouritism, however unconsciously, to a relation, friend or colleague.

We consider it inopportune and unnecessary for a member of the race

committee to abstain when he finds that by chance he is judging a fellow
member of his club or a fellow national (if dealing with international races). A
good judge must already be above this sort of suspicion and he can easily show
himself to be so without refusing to do his duty (maybe hiding a tendency to
avoid his responsibilities under a cover of sensibility). It is worth noting here
that IYRU Appendix 8, *Terms of reference of an international jury under rule
77.6*, para. 3 states: "for the purpose of racing rule 75 members shall not be
regarded as 'interested parties' by reason of their nationality. Their
appointment shall be made regardless of geographical considerations".

Rule 75 lays down that where a judge is an interested party "this does not
preclude him from giving evidence". It is presumed in fact that in giving his
evidence he will rigorously respect the truth as is the duty of every witness. Yet
this does not mean that, just because of his position, the rest of the protest
committee must consider his evidence as carrying more, or less, weight. IYRU
No. 79 (USYRU 181) points out that any procedural objection must be made
at the hearing and cannot be brought up later as might be convenient.

Rule 76.
Expenses
incurred by
protest

Unless otherwise prescribed by the race committee, the fees and expenses
entailed by a protest on measurement or classification shall be paid by the
unsuccessful party.

In deciding a protest where a yacht may have infringed a measurement
scantling or flotation rule or a rating certificate may be invalid, rule 68.4
requires any technical investigation on the subject to be given to an authority
qualified to decide such questions.

To refer questions in such a way often requires a good deal of time on the
part of the competent authorities who have to be paid or, even if they are
generous enough to give their time, need their expenses paying.

We therefore come up against a question of costs and, as in a court of law,
these fall on the losing side (that is they fall on the protesting yacht if the protest
is dismissed, but on the protested yacht if she is considered to have infringed
the rule).

Moreover, as rule 76 suggests, the race committee may decide differently if
there has been right (or wrong) on both sides. They can thus divide costs fairly
between the two parties (half each or proportionately to the blame); or they can
put the cost on to the race organizers and not charge either party.

Rule 77.   77.1
Appeals

Unless otherwise prescribed by the national authority which has recognised
the organising authority concerned, an appeal against the decision of a race
committee shall be governed by rules 77, (Appeals), and 78, (Particulars to
be Supplied in Appeals).

77.2

Unless otherwise prescribed by the national authority or in the sailing instructions (subject to rule 2(j), (Notice of Race), or 3.2(b)(xvii), (Waiver of
Appeal), a protest which has been decided by the race committee shall be
referred to the national authority solely on a question of interpretation of
rules, within such period after the receipt of the race committee's decision as
the national authority may decide: —

(a) when the race committee, at its own instance, thinks proper to do so, or

(b) when any of the parties involved in the protest makes application for such reference.

This reference shall be accompanied by such deposit as the national authority may prescribe, payable by the appellant, to be forfeited to the funds of the national authority in the event of the appeal being dismissed.

77.3   The national authority shall have power to uphold or reverse the decision of the race committee, and when it is of opinion, from the facts found by the race committee, that a yacht involved in a protest has infringed an applicable rule, it shall disqualify her, irrespective of whether the rule or sailing instruction which led to such disqualification was mentioned in the protest.

77.4   For the purpose of rule 77, the word "protest" shall include, when appropriate, an investigation of redress under rule 12, (Yacht Materially Prejudiced); a request for redress under rule 68.5, (Protests); or a notification of an infringement hearing under rule 73, (Race Committee's Action against an Infringing Yacht).

77.5   The decision of the national authority, which shall be final, shall be communicated in writing to all interested parties.

77.6   Decisions of an international jury shall be final, provided that the Terms of Reference of an International Jury and the Conditions for the Decision of an International Jury or Protest Committee to be Final, as set forth in Appendices 8 and 9, are observed:

(a) In the Olympic Regatta and similar regattas open to yachts from different nations and in such other international regattas as may be under the jurisdiction of the I.Y.R.U. or a national authority, or

(b) In other international regattas under the jurisdiction of an international class association, with the approval of the national authority when required.

77.7   An appeal once lodged with the national authority shall not be withdrawn.

1. Presentation of the appeal, method and time limit

Unless the notice of race or the sailing instructions state that there will be a jury and that its decisions are not open to appeal any party to a case (that is the protested and protesting yachts in rules 72 and 73) who thinks that the protest committee made a mistake in applying or interpreting the rule when making a decision has the faculty of having the case re-examined by a second superior "court" which is a separate organization (normally called an appeals committee) of the competent national authority. In the U.K. there is no permanent appeals committee so called. It is in fact the RYA (national authority) Council which is named; in the U.S.A. there are at least two levels of appeal "courts" first district appeals committees and then above them the USYRU (ex-NAYRU) Appeals Committee.

Moreover, remember that an appeal can only be made by a yacht involved in the protest 77.2(b). For example look at IYRU No. 70 (RYA 1974/7, *Rebel* and *Ubibug* v. The Race Committee) in which *Rebel* started prematurely but did not realize it because there was no sound signal and obtained an abandonment and later re-sail of the race. At the end of the day's races *Ubibug* protested the race committee's earlier decision but the protest committee dismissed this protest. *Ubibug* then appealed maintaining, erroneously, that in this case rule 4.8 should have applied. But the RYA declared that *Ubibug* had no right of appeal because under rule 77.2(b) she had not been a party in *Rebel*'s protest.

What is strange is that not only can competitors go to appeal but even the race committee can do so on its own initiative, that is even if the two parties accept its decision and do not appeal. The race committee may refer a case when it thinks proper to do so, generally because the meaning of some rule is not perfectly clear or the committee is uncertain as to whether its own decision has been correct, and thus it prefers a superior court to look at it and give a definitive judgement (which will not only shed light on the case in question but also give a general ruling to future committees in similar cases).

An appeal can only be made against a decision. Therefore if no decision exists in the first instance, there is no hope of going to second instance. As an illustration of cases of this sort (which are fairly frequent) let us look, choosing from among many, a decision of FIV 1970/10 on an appeal from a competitor who was lamenting the fact that the race committee had treated as valid a race that had been sailed at a mean speed of less than the 2·5 knots required by the sailing instructions.

"The appellant has come directly to this appeals committee without first submitting his complaint to the race committee by a regular protest presented according to rule 68.3 with the objects of rule 68.5(a). This "court", which is an appeals committee, can adjudicate (rule 77) only on a protest which has been already decided by a protest committee; it must therefore conclude that the submission with which we are dealing is inadmissiable and cannot be examined."

To invoke the intervention of the appeals committee, the parties or the race committee must lodge their submission (on the forms detailed in rule 78) within a well-determined time limit established by each national authority that begins to run from when the party has received the communication of the decision against which it wishes to appeal.

When the appeal is by the race committee (rule 77.2(a)) this limit runs from the moment in which it has taken its decision.

There is no need to explain that any decision in first instance if appealed against, is suspended until the court of second instance has pronounced sentence. This happens even in the case of a referal put forward by the race committee itself (unless it is limited to a question and answer, asking the appeals committee for advice without actually referring to its own decision). However, as soon as the limit has run its time without anyone appealing the decision of first instance becomes definitive and nothing more can be done about it.

Similarly to what is laid down in rule 68.6 for protests, rule 77 specifies that an appeal once presented cannot be withdrawn.

2. Powers of an appeals committee, questions of fact and law

The power of an appeals committee is limited for it can only examine a case on a question of interpretation of the rules (and of the sailing instructions which are put on an equal standing with the rules by rule 3.1). This limitation is merely the consequence of what has already been prescribed by rule 71 on the finality of the findings of fact by the protest committee.

In other words an appeal court can neither control the investigation carried out in the first instance as to the facts on which the protest is founded nor can it alter the conclusions drawn from the evidence – the facts arrived at by the protest committee. While the findings establish once and for all what happened in an incident an appeals committee can investigate whether the first committee has applied the correct prescriptions of the rule to the facts. That is to say they may examine the protest, strictly on a point of law only, to ensure that the right rule has been employed rightly to judge each specific "fact".

Among many let us look for example at FIV 1961/2. Here the situation in fig. 150 was found as a fact and the protest committee disqualified yacht C for infringing rule 37.1 and also disqualified yacht A for infringing rule 32. The appeals committee whilst accepting the facts interpreted the law in a different

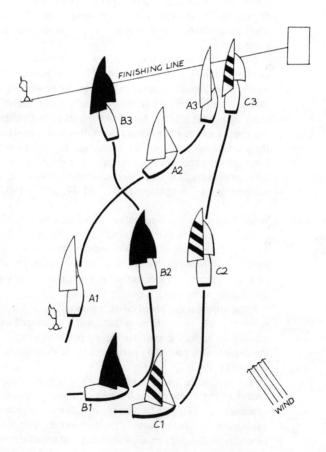

Fig. 150

way and held that the same facts had only caused an infringement of rule 38.1 on the part of yacht C (whose disqualification was confirmed while A was absolved).

To go more deeply into the refinements which may be reached in an appeal look at NAYRU 69. The appellant contested the correctness of the protest committee's finding of fact and in order to uphold his proposal that an appeals committee had the power to investigate and correct certain findings in first instance quoted as a precedent NAYRU Appeal 32 (which the reader will find in the comment to rule 36) where, dealing with an encounter between two yachts on different tacks, the protest committee had expressed the opinion that nothing would have happened even if one of the two yachts instead of changing course to avoid a collision, had continued on her initial course (because "she would have passed about five foot or less astern"), and where in second instance the appeals committee had taken a contrary opinion on this point.

However, replying to the appellant in appeal 69 and having recalled the limits imposed by rule 77.2 the appeals committee laid down: "In Appeal 32 all facts found by the race committee were accepted, except for a hypothetical conclusion, involving a matter of inches arrived at as the result of a computation."

None of this means, however, that when finding facts a protest committee can do what it likes and that faced with a finding plainly incomplete invalidated by errors an appeals committee is altogether powerless. In reality the latter can always check whether a protest committee has remembered to bear in mind some important point or has drawn mistaken or contradictory conclusions or has overlooked any mandatory procedure which guarantees the seriousness of the proceedings (see rule 70 – Hearings). In such cases an appeals committee can send the papers back to the protest committee for them to complete their findings of fact and to take any decision which they had not taken or which was incomplete (see for example IYRU No. 44, or FIV 1965/5).

3. Decisions of an appeals committee

While limited to the application and intepretation of the rules an appeals committee can confirm, or change completely or in part, the questioned decision. It can also send the proceedings back to the original committee (as we have already seen) so that the latter may complete the hearing or correct some procedural error, and then make a new decision which was lacking or appeared insufficient because of the quoted omission.

If the appeal is not based on questions of interpretation or application of the rules but solely on questions of fact it will be dismissed without being examined, because an appeals committee has no powers (except in the exceptional cases mentioned in the preceding paragraph) to re-examine the facts found in the first court (FIV 1963/2).

It must also be borne in mind that the appeals committee's powers do not extend to the whole decision appealed but only to those sections which the appellant considers to be wrong; it is therefore necessary to pinpoint and adequately explain the parts of the decision objected to. In fact those parts not expressly challenged remain as decided and therefore definitive.

In applying what has already been laid down by rule 72.1 (which refers expressly to appeal authorities), rule 77.3 confirms that a court of second instance, "when it is of opinion from the facts found by the race committee that a yacht involved in a protest has infringed an applicable rule, it shall disqualify her, irrespective of whether the rule or sailing instructions which led to such disqualification was mentioned in the protest". As an example look at IYRU No. 37 (RYA 1968/6, *Howdee Doodee* v. *Sooky*) quoted in para. 1 in the comment to rule 42.

The decision of the appeals committee according to rule 77.5 must be communicated to the interested parties in writing and not orally as is permitted for a protest committee (rule 71); and this is easily explicable because the parties are not present when an appeals authority meets.

We have already seen that the notice of race (rule 2(j)) and the sailing instructions (rule 3.2(b)xvii) can prescribe that decisions will be without appeal and this is used "when it is essential to determine the result of a race or a series of races which will qualify a yacht to compete in a later stage of the event". In these cases says the rule "a national authority may prescribe that its approval be required for such a procedure"; and it is just as well that it should do so if only to be able to control the composition of the jury and make sure that it is reliable.

In our opinion, if there is no previous declaration that there will be no appeal, the decisions of any protest committee, will be liable to reversal on appeal to the competent national authority; rule 77 is quite clear and permits no variation.

Rule 78.
Particulars to
be supplied with
appeals

78.1   The reference to the national authority shall be in writing and shall contain the following particulars, in order, so far as they are applicable: —

(a) A copy of the notice of the race and the sailing instructions supplied to the yachts.

(b) A copy of the protest, or protests or request for redress under rule 12, (Yacht Materially Prejudiced) or rule 68.5(a), (Protests), if any, prepared in accordance with rule 68.3(d), and all other written statements which may have been submitted by the parties.

(c) The observations of the race committee thereon, a full statement of the facts found, its decision and the grounds thereof.

(d) An official diagram prepared by the race committee in accordance with the facts found by it, showing: —

(i) The course to the next *mark*, or, when close by, the *mark* itself with the required side;

(ii) the direction and force of the wind;

(iii) the set and rate of the tidal stream or current, if any;

(iv) the depth of water, if relevant; and

(v) the positions and tracks of all the yachts involved.

(vi) It is preferable to show yachts sailing from the bottom of the diagram towards the top.

(e) The grounds of the appeal, to be supplied by either: —

(i) the race committee under rule 77.2(a) (Appeals); or

(ii) the appellant under rule 77.2(b).

(f) Observations, if any, upon the appeal by the race committee or any of the parties.

78.2   The race committee shall notify all parties that an appeal will be lodged and shall invite them to make any observations upon it. Any such observations shall be forwarded with the appeal.

The appeal must be in writing and must furnish all the data (excluding obviously what is not pertinent) listed in rule 78.1. That is all those details which serve to inform an appeals committee first of all of the particular prescriptions which governed the competition (notice of race and sailing instructions – rule 78.1(a)) and then the proceedings at the hearing (copies of the protest and the other declarations made by parties and witnesses – rule 78.1(b) and finally the protest committee's findings of fact and law (that is the decision which has been appealed – 78.1(c)) accompanied by an official sketch prepared by the protest committee (do not forget that its finding of facts are definitive see rule 71) containing all the necessary technical clarifications requested in detail by rule 78.1(d).

Except for the appeal itself, all these documents are to be found with the protest committee or to be more precise with the organizing club which will have them in its files; and it is the organizing club that must make them available to the appellant at his request. Sometimes however the poor appellant may not get copies of these essential documents in time (because he only thinks about them when the time limit for the appeal is almost up and the protest committee has gone home and the organizers, exhausted by the fatigues of the race, are getting their breath back).

The documentation required by rule 78.1 is obligatory and the absence of anything listed as necessary (and any deposit laid down by rule 77.2) can make the appeal unacceptable (FIV 1967/1). Again under threat of inadmissibility the reasons on which the appeal is founded must be stated (rule 78.1(e)), briefly perhaps, but intelligibly; in fact only those parts of the decision which are specifically the object of appeal can be considered, the rest must remain definitive and unalterable.

The observations of all the other parties in the case may be attached to the appeal and because of this the committee is obliged to give notice of the presentation of an appeal in good time (rule 70.2). Similarly the protest committee which gave the decision may also put forward its own point of view. This is another application of that original criterion that in sailing disputes the race committee often has the same facilities as the parties in the case.

LIST OF IYRU APPENDICES TO RACING RULES

1 Amateur
2 "Pumping", "Ooching" and "Rocking"
3 Alternative Penalties for infringement of a Rule of Part IV
4 Team Racing Rules
5 Olympic Scoring System
6 Protest Committee Procedure
7 Protest Form
8 Terms of Reference of an International Jury under Racing Rule 77.6 (Appeals)
9 Conditions for Decisions of an International Jury or Protest Committee to be Final. Racing Rule 77.6 (Appeals)
10 Weighing of Wet Clothing (Racing Rule 22.3)
11 Authority and Responsibility of Race Committee and Jury for Rule Enforcement
12 Organization of Principal Events

Index